Adolescent Coping

Young people need to cope in a variety of settings, including school, home, peer groups and the workplace, and with a range of life problems such as divorce and examinations. This thoroughly revised and updated new edition of *Adolescent Coping* presents the latest research and applications in the field of coping. It highlights the ways in which coping can be measured and, in particular, details a widely used adolescent coping instrument.

Topics include the different ways in which girls and boys cope, coping in the family, how culture and context determine how young people cope, decisional coping, problem solving and social coping, with a particular emphasis on practice. Each topic is considered in light of past and recent research findings and each chapter includes quotations from young people. While topics such as depression, eating disorders, self-harm and grief and loss are addressed, there is a substantial focus on the positive aspects of coping, including an emphasis on resilience and the achievement of happiness. In addition to the wide-ranging research findings that are reported, many of the chapters consider implications and applications of the relevant findings with suggestions for the development of coping skills and coping skills training.

Adolescent Coping will be of interest to students of psychology, social work, sociology, education and youth and community work as well as to an audience of parents, educators and adolescents.

Erica Frydenberg is a clinical, organizational, counselling and educational psychologist who has practised extensively in the Australian educational setting before joining the staff of the University of Melbourne where she is an Associate Professor in psychology in the Melbourne Graduate School of Education.

Adolescence and Society
Series editor: John C. Coleman
Department of Education, University of Oxford

This series has now been running for over 20 years, and during this time has published some of the key texts in the field of adolescent studies. The series has covered a very wide range of subjects, almost all of them being of central concern to students, researchers and practitioners. A mark of the success of the series is that a number of books have gone to second and third editions, illustrating the popularity and reputation of the series.

The primary aim of the series is to make accessible to the widest possible readership important and topical evidence relating to adolescent development. Much of this material is published in relatively inaccessible professional journals, and the objective of the books in this series has been to summarize, review and place in context current work in the field, so as to interest and engage both an undergraduate and a professional audience.

The intention of the authors has always been to raise the profile of adolescent studies among professionals and in institutions of higher education. By publishing relatively short, readable books on topics of current interest to do with youth and society, the series makes people more aware of the relevance of the subject of adolescence to a wide range of social concerns.

The books do not put forward any one theoretical viewpoint. The authors outline the most prominent theories in the field and include a balanced and critical assessment of each of these. Whilst some of the books may have a clinical or applied slant, the majority concentrate on normal development.

The readership rests primarily in two major areas: the undergraduate market, particularly in the fields of psychology, sociology and education; and the professional training market, with particular emphasis on social work, clinical and educational psychology, counselling, youth work, nursing and teacher training.

Also available in this series:

Adolescent Health
Patrick C.L. Heaven
The Adolescent in the Family
Patricia Noller and Victor Callan
Young People's Understanding of Society
Adrian Furnham and Barrie Stacey
Growing up with Unemployment
Anthony H. Winefield, Marika Tiggermann, Helen R. Winefield and Robert D. Goldney
Young People's Leisure and Lifestyles
Leo B. Hendry, Janey Shucksmith, John G. Love and Anthony Glendinning
Adolescent Gambling
Mark Griffiths
Youth, AIDS and Sexually Transmitted Diseases
Susan Moore, Doreen Rosenthal and Anne Mitchell

Fathers and Adolescents
Shmuel Shulman and Inge Seiffge Krenke
Young People's Involvement in Sport
Edited by John Kremer, Karen Trew and Shaun Ogle
The Nature of Adolescence (3rd edition)
John C. Coleman and Leo B. Hendry
Identity in Adolescence (3rd edition)
Jane Kroger
Sexuality in Adolescence
Susan Moore and Doreen Rosenthal
Social Networks in Youth and Adolescence (2nd edition)
John Cotterell
Adolescent Coping
Erica Frydenberg

Adolescent Coping
Advances in Theory, Research and Practice

Erica Frydenberg

Routledge
Taylor & Francis Group

LONDON AND NEW YORK

First published 2008 by Routledge
27 Church Road, Hove, East Sussex BN3 2FA

Simultaneously published in the USA and Canada
by Routledge
270 Madison Avenue, New York, NY, 10016

*Routledge is an imprint of the Taylor & Francis Group, an Informa
business*

Typeset in Times by Garfield Morgan, Swansea, West Glamorgan
Printed and bound in Great Britain by TJ International Ltd, Padstow,
Cornwall
Paperback cover design by Hybert Design

British Library Cataloguing in Publication Data
A catalogue record for this book is available from the British Library

Library of Congress Cataloging in Publication Data
Frydenberg, Erica, 1943–
    Adolescent coping : advances in theory, research, and practice /
Erica Frydenberg.
        p. cm.
    Includes bibliographical references (p.   ) and index.
    ISBN 978-0-415-40571-3 – ISBN 978-0-415-40572-0 1. Adjustment
(Psychology) in adolescence. I. Title.
    BF724.3.A32F78 2008
    155.5'1824–dc22

                                                        2007044291

ISBN: 978-0-415-40571-3 (hbk)
ISBN: 978-0-415-40572-0 (pbk)

To Oscar and Claudia
May they grow to be wonderful adolescents in the world that will be theirs and to all the young people who have contributed their stories

Contents

Figures

Tables

Preface

Coping is the way we can describe the best features of human adaptation – and the worst. Adolescence is an important transition point which enables us to reflect on what has been learned and what is yet to be learned about developing the skills to cope. It is a significant and extensive stage of development within which there are opportunities for us to understand and foster young people's coping skills. Some modes of adaptation are linked to one's temperament or personality disposition; others are learned throughout the course of one's life.

Today information about almost everything is readily available. When it comes to coping, one of the most highly published areas in psychology, there is a mine of information. I recently performed a Google search on adolescent coping and got 55 frames. All results were teaching about coping, such as how to cope with a disaster, a transition, a death, the loss of a pet, examinations, talking in front of a crowd or performing music. All full of good sense, some of it common sense and some of it just good reminders. So why develop programmes, why do research for 15 years on the topic and keep doing it? There is still a great deal for us to learn about young people and their worlds. And when it comes to measurement and interventions we want to rely on sound, empirical data on what works and what does not.

In the international no. 1 best seller *The tipping point: How little things can make a big difference*, Malcolm Gladwell explains the 'tipping point', that magic moment when ideas, trends and social behaviours cross the threshold, tip, and spread like wildfire. Taking a look behind the surface of many familiar occurrences in our everyday world, he explains the fascinating social dynamics that cause rapid change. He espouses principles such as the contagion effect: we can have the contagion of depression and despair or the contagion of optimism, resilience, well-being or happiness – and why not coping?

Gladwell also points out that small beginnings can have big effects and that change happens not gradually but at *one dramatic moment*. He provides substantial evidence to support his case. While it is difficult, if not impossible, to predict the tipping point for recovery from the despair and depression that hits many young people, it is good to aim for it. That is why we need the 'tipping point' and it is my hope that in some way this book will contribute towards that point so that when we talk about coping the positive aspects of human adaptation will outweigh the focus on pathology. More specifically, we can talk about the positive aspects of coping and how we can all learn to do it a little better.

Stress and coping have arguably been the most vigorously researched areas in the field of psychology in the past two decades. In the psychology literature (PsycINFO) alone there have been 46,605 references to stress and coping between 1982 and 1992, 102,221 in the following decade and 136,437 in the most recent five-year period. This has been matched by increasingly frequent references in the education literature (ERIC) (11,401 between 1982 and 1992, 7969 between 1992 and 2002 and 3748 between 2002 and 2007).

When there is so much written about coping, the question has to be asked: why another book? More importantly, what has changed since 1997 in the field of adolescent coping? While the 1997 book drew heavily on the seminal work of Folkman and Lazarus and our own work on coping, this volume seeks to integrate a broader sweep of concepts that not only relate to reactive coping but also bring together the latest research in the proactive coping field; there are also the concepts of communal coping and conservation of resources. Since the 18 conceptual areas of coping identified in the 1990s by Frydenberg and Lewis remain useful for both research and practice, they provide a source of data for a vast body of research that has taken place since the earlier edition.

Additionally, topics like happiness, both the pursuit and the maintenance of it, now receive a great deal of attention, so a chapter is dedicated to happiness and resilience. Factors that often account for lack of happiness, such as boredom and loneliness, are also addressed. While youth suicide has reached a plateau or diminished in some quarters, depression has not, so a section has been devoted to depression and related conditions such as eating disorders and substance abuse. Since 1997 there has been a great deal of progress in the area of social and emotional learning, and this is reflected in the chapter on learning to cope. There has been an explosion of pro-grammes attempting to teach a range of coping-related skills, but few have been well evaluated. Some of these are tabulated but our emphasis remains on the programme the Best of Coping, which we developed and which has been well thought of for several years.

Adolescent coping: Advances in theory, measurement and practice has been written to complement the 1997 edition. It sets out to cover a broad field that orients the reader in relation to theory, research and practice. The book provides a conceptual and developmental framework for understanding coping and attempts to cover the vast field that has been researched and reported on since 1997. In addition to the research reported in the international literature we report on research carried out at the University of Melbourne in the coping skills laboratory by me and my numerous colleagues and students. In particular, I would like to acknowledge my colleague Ramon Lewis, who was my collaborator in the development of the Adolescent Coping Scale and the numerous research publications that have followed. He, more than anyone else, has contributed to the theoretical insights and understandings that have advanced this field.

While the book has a sequence of chapters, we have also attempted to make each chapter a useful resource in its own right, so inevitably there is some overlap between chapters. For example, the chapter on emotions and coping contains information that relates to family and education. Family-related issues feature in many of the studies cited in different chapters. Risk-taking and resilience are as relevant when one talks about cultural difference in coping as they are in their own right. Gender differences in coping are addressed particularly in chapter 5, but throughout the volume there are many references to gender differences as deemed appropriate. Teaching coping skills is addressed particularly in chapters 11 and 12. However, where there are ready implications for practice in other chapters, this is addressed.

Finally, the purpose of this book is to share the plethora of research that relates to coping and well-being and provide a template for how we can manage our lives to do better than just cope. We can all do what we do better. Each of us can enhance our coping and maximize the outcomes in terms of health, well-being and success. It's a matter of having a language or conceptual framework within which we can talk about coping and benefit from the latest research in the field. We need the language to describe the thoughts, feelings and actions in order to be able to learn about what helps us to cope better and what stops us from doing that.

Foreword

An integrated understanding of adolescent coping in their new world

Psychology is often presented in fractured pieces that divide cognitive psychology, the study of emotion, brain and behavior, environmental approaches, and applied psychology. This is of course necessary, as the pieces are each complex and deserve in-depth study. Yet, this fracturing leaves so many key issues to fall between the slats, and it can even feel alienating as different perspectives become codified into opposing positions and camps. It is paramount that integration is accomplished, as it is the final arbiter of the value of research from the perspective of these different research and clinical streams. For adolescent coping, no book integrates these facets better than Erica Frydenberg's, *Adolescent Coping: Advances in Theory, Research, and Practice*. Through reports of her own creative research, integration of complex, disparate literatures, and a special sense for turning these to applications that can be easily accessed, this book has no peer. It is at once, complex, deep, heartfelt, and made simple for the reader at professional-practitioner, academic-research, or student levels.

Dr. Frydenberg approaches adolescents in a way that we sometimes do in humor, as we refer to teenagers, especially our own, as coming from "their own world," "another planet," "a different culture or species." That is, she involves her research and her presentation on how adolescents cope as one would approach the issue of another culture. We have long studied and considered adolescents as "not quite adults," or "older children." But, they do live in and create their own culture. They have their own music, their own way of talking, their own issues that are important to them, and most certain opposition to authority and being over-directed. They also assume a power that children do not have and an independence that adults must lose in order to fit in to work and family life. They must be taken seriously, as the problems they create for themselves are potentially life-threatening to them and those around them. Drugs, violence, suicide, self-harm, eating disorders are all serious concerns with clinical and social implications that reverberate through society. Their development is the final stage setting for the adult self, so styles of coping and dealing with stress will have lifetime impact on their depression, happiness, family life, and the roles they play in society.

In her recent work, Dr. Frydenberg and her research group have approached adolescents from this rather anthropological perspective. She has created instruments and interventions in their own words and from their personal prisms on how they view the world and the challenges they face. This is the product of careful, creative quali-tative research that accompanies her hard-nosed empiricism. In this manner, her group's qualitative research has informed their quanti-tative research in a see-saw approach that has built to a greater, more meaningful gestalt. This approach also makes the volume much more international than most work coming out of the great U.S. research engine. Beginning in Oz (what they call Australia), she has applied her approaches across cultures as diverse as Germany, the U.S., Columbia, Hong Kong, and Palestine. She has studied the coping of youth who must cope with merely growing up in the world of a developed economy, to those who are dealing with daily violence and the painful likely birth of a new nation amidst war and civil unrest. At the same time she bridges all aspects of adolescents' lives from sleep, to social life, to their spirituality. Even her studies within Australia have a cultural context, as she examines how ethnic minority adolescents use more collectivist coping strategies than Anglo-Australian teens. Ado-lescents immigrate with their parents, face wars created and perpetu-ated by adults, and exist in schools and institutions run with a chronic shortage of funds by a world that hollowly declares that "children are our future and our most important asset." Dr. Frydenberg follows them through their journey and so adds greatly to our understanding that adolescents are not only coping with issues of popularity and recreational drug use, but with the major challenges that a world that is economically, politically, socially, and militarily complex entails. The book will help readers appreciate age, gender, and cultural differences in creative ways that the volume does an excellent job in answering with assessment, prevention and intervention approaches.

An important companion to this volume are the questionnaires and skill building approaches that Dr. Frydenberg has developed, tested and refined. I hope you also consider her DVDs that can be used interactively with adolescents to help them develop healthy coping strategies. In this regard, the volume takes the issue of coping as a skill set seriously. It is not merely a series of suggestions about how to behave, but a complex skill set that requires modeling, cognitive processing, practice, feedback and gaining mastery. These allow the volume to be a handbook for practice as well as a guide through key research in the field. Practitioners will know the solid research foundation behind the prevention and intervention approaches that are covered in the volume and researchers will gain insights into how to conduct sound research that can aid practitioners.

Finally, the volume masterfully bridges from more pathological models of adolescent coping to prevent or recover from depression, anxiety, relationship problems, drugs, and other common adolescent disorders and newer work on positive psychology. In this vein, the volume addresses the importance of coping to facilitate positive adjustment, happiness, and quality of life. Again, as in other areas of the book, the focus is on integration of multiple perspectives to create a greater, more meaningful whole. Keep this book handy, have all those post-it notes in multiple colors ready to demark places that you will want to go back to repeatedly, get out the color highlighter to underline quotes for seminars that make key points that you want to emphasize for research or intervention work. And don't lend it to any graduate students – you won't get it back.

Stevan E. Hobfoll
Distinguished Professor
Kent State University and Summa Health System

Acknowledgements

Adolescent coping: Advances in theory, research and practice is based on the research and contribution of numerous people over the past 15 years. First, the many young people who have contributed to our understanding of their worlds, their hopes, aspirations and practices. I owe thanks to my colleague and co-researcher, Ramon Lewis, whose scholarship and positive outlook have contributed throughout all these years to the development of theory in the field of coping. To the many postgraduate students at the University of Melbourne who have contributed through their own research and who are acknowledged for their contributions throughout this book, I am truly appreciative. They have undertaken their investigations with enthusiasm and rigour and in turn have inspired me to continue researching this most rewarding field. Cathy Brandon who made the Best of Coping what it is today and the numerous researchers who have evaluated it in various settings. The invaluable assistance of Clare Ivens who assisted with research and helped bring Coping for Success to completion together with the team from the multimedia unit at the University of Melbourne. Chelsea Eacott provided research and compilation assistance in the final stages. The skilful editing of Venetia Somerset has helped to make this book look and read as it should. My appreciation to Professors Susan Moore, Sandra Christenson, Luc Goosens, and to the series editor John Coleman, for their helpful comments. The editors at Routledge, particularly Tara Stebnicky and Dawn Harris have been a pleasure to work with. The University of Melbourne has provided me with the fertile academic environment where research and writing are made possible. Above all, to my husband, Harry and our two children, Joshua and Lexi, whose wisdom and good humour, along with their inspiration and support, make me truly fortunate, I am most grateful.

1   Adolescent stresses, concerns and resources

> Life is what worries me the most. As you grow up and get older you worry about what is going to happen next and you worry about what you are going to achieve and that and what your future is going to be like.
>
> (Girl, 13)

With over 1.2 billion adolescents in the world today (United Nations Population Fund, n.d.), more than ever there is good reason to focus on their needs, concerns and endeavour to create climates that can foster their healthy development and functioning. Along with the increasing population of adolescents there has been a growing interest in the field of coping. A search of two online databases for 2000–07, PsycINFO and Educational Resources Information Centre (ERIC), reveals at least 24,500 related publications. Thus there is fertile ground for research and a wealth of information that should inform our practice.

Adolescence is that period between childhood and adulthood which can itself be divided into developmental stages. Regardless of developmental stage, adolescents are set to face changes of both a physiological and psychological nature, often with movement towards independence and explorations of identity. Early adolescence is marked by a number of changes, including rapid cognitive, social, emotional and physical changes involving maturation. There are transitions in school life, peer and family relationships and a likely increase in conflicts within the family, characteristically with parents. These conflicts mark the early and middle adolescent years and are generally superseded in late adolescence when parent–child relationships become more settled. The later adolescent years are generally marked by a greater interest in peer relationships and the striving to achieve goals and milestones that determine the directions for an adult future.

Although extensions of adolescent social networks and growing sexual maturation bring opportunities for growth, they also heighten the likelihood of risk. While there is extensive debate in the literature as to whether adolescence is a period of storm and stress or a period of relatively smooth transition into adulthood, there is general agreement that adolescents have a number of adjustment hurdles. These are reflected in the range of issues that are of concern to young people.

Adolescents have many concerns that in extreme circumstances are perceived as both overwhelming and disabling, leading in a minority of cases to severe depression and suicide. Youth who choose death do so because they cannot cope at a time when they are vulnerable to increasing pressures and uncertainties.

Young people today report more psychological problems than ever before. It is estimated that between 2 and 5 per cent of young people experience an anxiety or depressive disorder. A significantly greater number of young people will experience depression by the time they reach adulthood, with estimates approaching 20 per cent (AIHW, 2003). Depression in adolescence leads to such difficulties as impaired school performance and compromised social relationships with peers, siblings and teachers (Birmaher *et al.*, 1996).

Stress research has for a long time focused on incapacity rather than ability. While it is important to determine what stresses young people, how they cope is about looking at capacity and the potential to enhance growth.

Adolescent stresses

Young people face a multitude of ongoing stressful problems including relationship difficulties, illness or death of family and friends, family pressures and the expectations placed on them for academic success. These life stressors have been shown to contribute to an increased risk of emotional, cognitive and behavioural difficulties in adolescents such as depression, behavioural problems in and outside school, various anxiety disorders and academic failure.

In this chapter we consider the concerns and stresses of young people as well as the resources they have with which to cope. In subsequent chapters particular circumstances such as family stresses, schooling and relationship difficulties will be considered in the light of research on coping.

We know from earlier work (Frydenberg and Lewis, 1996) that essentially there are three categories of concerns for young people: those things that relate to achievement, that is, success at school or opportunities for future success; peer and family relationships; and social issues such as the environment, poverty and unemployment, and concern for those who are worse off than themselves. Others have reported similar findings with variations according to age and the cultural setting. In their study of Australian and Finnish adolescents, Nurmi, Poole and Kalakoski (1994) found that older adolescents were more oriented to the future than younger ones, and that Australians adolescents were more interested than their Finnish counterparts in leisure and more concerned about their health and global issues. Overall, these 13–17-year-olds most often mentioned hopes and goals concerning future occupation (77 per cent), education (65 per cent), family/marriage (58 per cent), leisure activities (42 per cent), and property-related topics (39 per cent). These findings are summarized by the authors as representing the fact that adolescents' concerns reflected the developmental tasks of their own age and of early adulthood. These findings are also endorsed by a study in the United States of 333 tenth and eleventh graders in Los Angeles where the stresses in highest frequency reflected future goals (de Anda, Baroni, Boskin, Buchwald, Morgan, Ow, Gold and Weiss, 2000).

These stresses and strains vary according to the context in which the questioning or data-gathering takes place and according to cultural considerations. For example, when considering what prompts a young person to call a teen-helpline for assistance, a signal of a high degree of concern, an American study found that the issues of greatest concern were peer relationships (40 per cent), sexuality (26.6 per cent), family problems (18.8 per cent), the need just to talk (14.0 per cent), self-esteem (11.3 per cent), and drugs and alcohol (9.9 per cent) (Boehm, Schondel *et al.*, 1998).

A complex set of external and internal stresses is part of the adolescent experience. Fortunately, very few adolescent worries are so overwhelming that they lead to suicide. Nevertheless, all adolescent concerns are worthy of consideration. When youth are unable to cope effectively with worries, their behaviour can have an adverse effect not only on their own lives but also on those of their families and on the functioning of the broader community. The community, therefore, has cause to concern itself with what worries the young, and to facilitate the development of sound coping strategies that they can use to deal with their worries.

What is stress?

There are multiple views of what stress is, mainly drawn from the adult arena. In 1932 Cannon was the first to apply the concept of stress to humans. The term is generally borrowed from physics, which compares humans to metals that can resist moderate outside forces but get weighed down or bent under extreme pressure. However, this model does not entirely fit since we know that humans respond to their environment according to their personality, perceptions, or the context in which the stress occurs.

Stresses can be viewed according to the nature of the stimulus, such as an acute, time-limited stress, for example sitting for a final exam or dealing with a difficult relationship; stressor sequences such as parent divorce, bereavement or loss of a relative or a pet; chronic intermittent stress such as completing assignments for school; and a chronic stressor such as an ongoing illness. They can also be viewed according to the situation in which they occur, such as the home or school or in community settings (for a comprehensive treatment of school-related stressors see Burnett and Fanshawe, 1996). Another way of considering stresses is to see whether they represent daily hassles, such as a quarrel with a friend, normative stresses such as dealing with bodily changes during puberty, chronic stresses such as dealing with a permanent physical disability, or traumatic stresses such as a divorce in the family.

Regardless of how one categorizes stress, the homeostatic-transactional view of stress generally credited to Richard Lazarus (1991) regards it as occurring when there is an imbalance between the demands of the environment and the perceived resources of the individual. The imbalance may be underload as much as overload. Underload means circumstances that can be construed as leading to boredom, which is a major stress for adolescents when they do not have something to do or there are too few demands made on them. Resources remain useful if they are seen as having value and as having provided previous benefits. Resources such as optimism or social support, if seen as beneficial or helpful, will be retained. Some people are so rich in coping resources or considered to be hardy that they do not notice the environmental demands. There are no units of comparison to equate the coping demands with the available resources. The closest we come to it is the Holmes and Rahe (1967) stress index which identifies stresses and their relative impact.

Resource theories of stress

A more recent model of stress is the Conservation of Resources model (COR: Hobfoll, 1998). This model posits that people seek to retain and protect what they value and to accumulate resources. What is perceived as threatening is the actual loss of the valued resources. The fact that people actively strive to create pleasure and success is well known in psychology; for example, Sigmund Freud and Abraham Maslow were early proponents of these theories. Thus, according to COR theory, the psychological definition of stress is that it occurs when there is a threat to the net loss of resources, or there is a lack of resource gain following investment of resources. COR theory is based on a single motivational tenet, that individuals actively strive to obtain, retain and protect what they value, that is, gain social and personal resources as tools to achieve goals in order to maximize coping capacity and limit psychological distress.

Thus stress will occur when resources are threatened or lost and when there is no adequate resupply of resources after resources have been used up (the lost resources might have been concrete or intangible such as an investment of effort). Chronic stressful situations chip away at our resources.

Furthermore, according to COR theory resources are defined as objects, for example possessions which are valued for their physical nature but can be associated with socioeconomic status or status in general; personal characteristics, such as the capacity to see things as predictable and happening in one's best interest, being optimistic or mastery-oriented; conditions such as having a friend or receiving an award; or what is described as energy resources such as networks, power, money, time, knowledge and so on, that allow you to obtain other resources. People strive to develop a resource surplus to offset the possibility of future loss. Resource surpluses are likely to be associated with *eu*stress (positive well-being) rather than *dis*tress. Self-protection is about trying to protect against resource loss. We invest time and energy and love and affection in the expectation of the return of the same. Power and money are important resources that allow us to accumulate other resources.

The concept of loss

Gain is important but is secondary to loss – most severe stress events are loss events. Hobfoll's theory provides a challenge to Lazarus' definition that stress occurs when the demands tax or exceed a person's resources. He says that stress only occurs when there is resource loss. Loss is central to any concept of stress. For example, when a relative or just a friendship has been lost, the loss can be of support, status in the peer group, or economic stability. Items in the Holmes Rahe stress index which are about loss have the highest weighting. The most severe events are loss events, such as loss of health, friendship, freedom, money or personal possessions. Loss events are most commonly associated with depression. Transitions are also seen as stressful but that could be because of a perceived loss rather than the perception of gain. There may be a perception that the demands of a new situation can exceed the resources. To offset resource loss there may be resource replacement, for example making new friendships. The stress of doing badly in school or missing out on being selected for a team can be interpreted as threats.

Employing resources for coping is also stressful. When the effort put into a situation outstrips the benefits, it is felt as stressful. For example, when giving others support or helping a parent makes a student late for school, or working hard doesn't allow one to achieve one's goals, it can be stressful. Coping is itself stressful, for example having to put in time or effort or having to test beliefs about oneself just to cope. If coping is unsuccessful, positive beliefs about self are likely to be diminished.

Shifting the focus of attention

One can conserve resources by reinterpreting threat as a challenge. Athletes or performers often do this when they evaluate a difficult situation as an opportunity to demonstrate capacity. There can also be a re-evaluation of resources. Hobfoll considers that one can lower the value placed on something. For example, after failure to do well in an examination it is possible to rationalize or re-evaluate the event as not being important in the first place. Values and developmental history relating to those events that have shaped one's thinking affect how one re-evaluates the situation. That is, previous successes in school can build up confidence while previous failures may have led to a defeatist attitude.

Expectation to gain resources

When people are not under threat they are motivated to gain resources and to build up the resource pool. Marriages or important relationships in the adolescent arena can be seen as an investment in one's future or strengthening the assets (resources) in terms of getting love, affection, security and so on. It can also be described as building up credits or assets. Where the relationship with friends has been nurtured and remains a good one, it can be said that there is less of a consequence if one makes an omission or mistake, such as forgetting to acknowledge a birthday. Resources have both an objective and a subjective component.

Loss and gain spirals

When resources are used to offset resource loss then the resource pool may be further diminished, making the individual more vulnerable to stress. What might have been able to be tolerated becomes unmanageable for a weakened individual, so there is a resource loss spiral and such spirals tend to increase in velocity. For example, if one is feeling down because of bereavement, it may be that one's energies or attention to work are suffering, so there might be a loss of temper, leading to a loss of esteem or confidence.

In contrast, 'gains often beget gains'. That is, a win in a sporting event might result in new team opportunities and further recognition, leading to a boost in esteem and confidence. When esteem is high there might be a greater risk-taking in school or relationships that results in better outcomes or a good return for one's investment.

Resource loss is disproportionately weighted to resource gain. Thus to prevent loss or to build resources there needs to be an investment of resources. Having resources such as money, friends or esteem contributes to further resource gain, and lack of such resources contributes to resource loss. Individuals who have resources in the form of groups as a support are in a better position to resist the negative effects of meeting everyday challenges. Those who are less empowered may be more vulnerable to resource loss. For example, to follow the success at school example, if there had been good results on many occasions there is likely to be a capacity to accept a lesser performance on a single occasion.

Other stress theories are reactive, but according to COR theory people assert themselves proactively. People do not wait for disaster to strike; they invest in resources, take out insurance, thereby purchasing future protection. Gain is important to the extent that it prevents future loss and it provides comfort, which can be a buffer against stress. For example, the purchase of a better computer or surfboard might help one to do better in an assignment or a surfing competition.

Principles of COR theory

1   Resource loss is more powerful than resource gain and the gradient for loss is steeper than that for gain.

2   In order to gain resources and prevent loss one must invest in other resources; those with greater resources are less vulnerable to resource loss and more capable of resource gain.
3   Those who lack resources are not only more vulnerable to resource loss, but that initial loss begets further loss.
4   Those who possess resources are not only more capable of gain, but that gain begets gain.
5   Those who lack resources are likely to apply a defensive position to guard their resources.
6   Those with weak resources use their resources best when challenged by everyday events but are least successful under high stress conditions.
7   Those with a weak resource pool are in contrast to those with rich resource reserves.

Some key resources which are malleable and have broad application:

- high self-esteem
- optimism
- higher socioeconomic status
- good problem-solving skills.

Hobfoll (1998) describes a collection of resources as being 'a caravan of resources' which represents the interconnection between resources as well as the additive qualities of the resource pool. There is considerable support for this conceptualization. For example, in a recent cross-sectional study of United States adolescents, those young people whose parents were more educated, who had a more optimistic outlook on life and who used more engaging or positive coping experienced less stress (Finkelstein, Kubzansky, Capitman and Goodman, 2007). In an extension of Hobfoll's work to the world of adolescents, McKenzie, Frydenberg and Poole (2004) have identified a range of resources that are relevant to adolescents.

A sample of 172 students consisting of 97 females and 75 males, aged from 11 to 18 years, attending three schools in metropolitan Melbourne, Australia, completed a modified version of the Conservation of Resources Evaluation (Hobfoll, 1988). The modified instrument evaluated the importance adolescents placed on a range of resources, and the degree to which they believed they were provided with these resources. The scale measuring students' evaluation of the importance of the resource was scored on a 3-point scale, from 3 'always', 2 'sometimes' to 1 'never'. The item means ranged from 2.14 to 2.88 with an overall mean of 2.53.

The highest-scoring items were: Having friends (mean 2.88, 90 per cent always), Being close with at least one friend (2.78, 82 per cent always), Parent support (2.77, 78 per cent always), Adequate home (2.77, 82 per cent always), Adequate food (2.69, 76 per cent always), Being able to speak up for yourself (2.68, 71 per cent always), and Stable family (2.67, 70 per cent always). The lowest mean was for Belonging to organized groups (2.14, 34 per cent always).

The resources which are of value to young people included, in order of importance:

- having friends
- being close with at least one friend
- having an adequate home
- having support from parents
- having adequate food
- being able to speak up for myself
- having a stable family life
- feeling independent
- having money for one's needs
- having a sense of humour.

On the whole, students indicated that the resources in the inventory were at least of some importance to them, and in particular they valued friends, family, and adequacy in the basics (home, food), and their own skill in being able to present their needs.

What concerns adolescents

The worst thing I have had to deal with was when my mum had a stroke. She has had a couple of strokes and the last time, I was the only one home. I didn't deal with it well. I was a mess. It took me a long time to recover. I had to be there for her and so I just tried to be strong because if I wasn't then she would break down. . . . I learned that life is short. Make the most of it. Take every opportunity that you get and don't waste your time on things that are just trivial matters. You may think at the time that they are of some importance to you, but look at them in the bigger scheme and you realise that they are just not that important to you. Take life seriously but also have fun – that's my theory! . . . Out of something bad, something good can happen because you can learn from your past experiences. It makes you stronger and a better person.

(Girl, 16)

The many attempts to determine what concerns adolescents indicate that young people are interested in a range of issues relating to appearance, school grades, employment, relationships, fear of nuclear war, the environment and so on. Concern about vocational and educational plans appear the most dominant in some investigations while matters of personal health also appear to be important to many young people. But, as with the 16-year-old girl above, circumstances may arise which are totally unpredictable.

The methods of assessing the concerns of adolescents, or modes of questioning, range from eliciting unprompted, spontaneously given descriptions of whatever comes to mind as a concern to the more common approach where a respondent's reaction is sought to each of a limited number of concerns. In most studies of young people's concerns, a single mode of investigation has been used. Investigations have generally shown that adolescent concerns vary according to the context of the questioning (school, home, etc.), mode of questioning, and the different groups of respondents involved.

Classificatory schemas have been developed to identify concerns. These aim to condense a large range of concerns into a smaller number of relatively homogeneous categories. Some have found that social relationships, personal development and career skills are central to any typology of adolescent concerns, while others have developed a four-factor model of adolescent concerns which consist of future and career, health and drugs, the personal self and the social self (Violato and Holden, 1988). We have found that a classificatory system which groups adolescent concerns into three major categories, namely achievement, relationships and social issues, has stood the test of time. Succeeding in school, finding employment or just looking to the future are reflected in the achievement category.

To be happy. To build a happy family.

(Girl, 15)

To have a career that you like and enjoy.

(Girl, 15)

To be the best musician I can be. To make as much money as possible.

(Boy, 16)

Relationships, both peer and family, follow as the next two most prominent concerns, followed by social concerns such as those relating to the environment, poverty and world peace .

> Girls of my age have to deal with boys . . . probably relationships. A lot of girls our age start to really like boys, and they get into relationships, have fights. . . . Some even lose friends over it because they like the guy so much that they choose the guy over their friends and then having fights with their friends. It's not usually good.
>
> (Girl, 15)

> The whole process of puberty. We worry about pimples and stuff. We worry about sports and stuff – that's boys. And about impressing girls!
>
> (Boy, 15)

> I am worried about global warming and the future of our planet.
>
> (Girl, 17)

Another way of conceptualizing concerns is to consider them in different contexts, such as the home, school and the community as well as the overarching context of the self. Therefore there are concerns about school (doing well in an English class, teasing by classmates). In the home situation it can be about who watches what on television (rights and opportunities compared to siblings). In the community it can be about difficulties in getting about or being mobile, dealing with bullying in the wider community context, such as cyber-bullying, or about the self (appearance, career choices). These stresses are often referred to as daily hassles.

For example, in an Australian study of 1083 young people, Moulds (2003) found that the daily hassles could be categorized according to the locations in which they occurred. Seventeen per cent of young people had concerns in relation to issues about the self, such as stammering or the shape of their nose, 73 per cent in relation to school, including peers, teasing by others and canteen queues, and 11 per cent in relation to the family such as bedtime arguments and teasing by siblings. The most frequently reported hassles for young people emanated from their school experience.

Cultural contrasts are prominent. In one cross-cultural study by Verhulst, Achebach and colleagues (2003) of 7137 11–18-year-olds from seven countries (Australia, China, Israel, Jamaica, the Netherlands, Turkey and the United States), youths from China and Jamaica had the highest and Israeli and Turkish adolescents had the lowest mean total problem scores. In a survey of 2103 Hong Kong adolescents, Hui (2000) also found that, while concerns are multidimensional, academic concerns are the most pressing.

In a cross-cultural study of college students in China and the United States (Li, Lin, Bray and Kehle, 2005) it was affirmed that the main areas of stress were primarily related to academic, personal and negative life events. While the majority of Chinese students (74 per cent) exhibited low stress, for 8 per cent of these students there was a high degree of stress related to attending university. These levels of stress are similar for the American students, but the rank ordering is different in that the top academic stressors for Chinese university students were low learning efficiency and competition among students, whereas the top academic stressors for American students were to do with examinations. When it came to personal hassles, what concerned the Chinese students was that they were not being taught or educated properly and were not taught adequate social skills, whereas the main personal stressor for the American students was that associated with intimate relationships and parental conflicts. Some of these cultural differences remain over generations. This has been demonstrated by a study of second-generation Chinese American and European American adolescents, where the former reported higher levels of everyday life events stress and more depression than did the latter group of American young people.

A study of Canadian and Indian students by Sinha, Willson and Watson (2000) reported a reverse finding in that the Indian students reported less stress than the Canadians. A more detailed cross-national study of Russian and American students (Jose, D'Anna, Cafasso, Bryant, Chicker, Gein and Zhezmer, 1998) found, for example, that American adolescents between 10 and 15 years saw the following problems as being of greater concern than did the Russian adolescents:

- having misplaced something
- being bored and not having enough fun things to do
- arguing with brother or sister
- being rushed or not being able to take it easy
- schoolwork being boring
- going to bed too early or too late
- not being able to see grandparents or relatives because they live too far away
- weighing too much or too little

- gangs in the school or in the neighbourhood
- being picked on for nationality or skin colour.

In contrast, the Russian students were more concerned than the American young people about the following:

- when someone in the family was sick
- when they did something foolish or embarrassing in front of others
- not being with mother or father as much as they wanted
- mothers or fathers telling them about their problems
- going to the doctor or dentist or taking medicine
- someone in the family being very angry or crying a lot
- thinking about war
- too many people living in one's house or apartment
- having to translate for family members
- not having enough food to eat.

Overall, the Russian students reported higher levels of everyday life event stress than did the American students. The authors argue that these differences are most likely because the Russian experience for young people was affected by a weak economy, a chaotic political situation at the time and a changing social structure. Nevertheless, the list highlights the qualitatively different concerns that young people in different communities experience.

Stressors rarely occur in isolation, but there is generally a pile-up or accumulation of stressors. Girls generally report more traumatic life events as well as more stress due to these events across all ages (Plunkett, Radmacher and Moll-Phanara, 2000).

Thus, while there are differences in where the questioning is taking place (for example in a school setting there are more likely to be school-related concerns reported), there is a range of hassles which for some may be just a concern and for others a major hassle. The spontaneous eliciting of concerns from young people has not resulted in a reporting of issues relating to body image or evaluation by one's peers, but these issues are included here since there is evidence that these are of major concern, at least for girls.

Body image and weight concerns

Dissatisfaction with one's body has been recognized as a pervasive social problem, more so for girls than for boys. Appearance plays an important part in self-esteem and body weight is one important contributor to a sense of satisfaction with appearance. Current body ideals in most Western communities promote slimness for females and muscularity for males (Grogan, 1999). Dissatisfaction is so pervasive that it is considered by some to be a part of normal behaviour. Its genesis precedes the adolescent years and is considered to become prevalent in the pre-adolescent years, and as early as 6 or 7 years of age. Peer and media influences are considered to be the vehicles by which social ideals are determined (Dohnt and Tiggemann, 2006). The development of body image is culturally bound: for boys it is about being active and functional while for girls it is about being aesthetic and decorative.

Social evaluative concerns

Generally females place a greater emphasis on the maintenance of harmonious relationships and demonstrate more concern about social evaluation (Cross and Madson, 1997). That is, relationships appear to be more central to females than they are to males. Thus the psychological investment in relationships as a way of defining oneself has a cost associated with it and is often reflected in heightened levels of depression among females compared to those reported by males. Females are more likely to worry and distress themselves about significant others. Thus there is a psychological cost to caring. Females also worry about the judgements of peers.

While there are clear costs to caring, there are also benefits in that it is these very concerns that lead to investment in relationships, and generally there is a return for effort. There is effort in fostering harmonious relationships and rewards for refraining from actions that may jeopardize relationships. There are benefits in the form of support satisfaction that can be achieved through healthy relationships. Girls display higher levels of social evaluative concerns and depression than do boys (Rudolph and Conley, 2005). Additionally, those who had good interpersonal competence were less likely to be depressed.

Both gender and age make a difference to adolescent concerns. In a Scottish study that surveyed two cohorts of 15-year-olds in 1987 and 1999 on personal and performance worries, most worries increased for both sexes, with girls worrying more about school performance. West and Sweeting (2003) suggest that girls may have higher levels of stress regarding school performance due to their attempts at meeting expectations, along with the traditional concern for the age group relating to issues of identity, which include questions like 'who am I?' and 'where am I going?' Ethnicity also makes a difference. For example, in another study of Australian adolescents, Collins and Harvey (2001) found that female adolescents from non-Anglo cultures reported more concerns about their identity than their Anglo-Australian peers. In particular, the former expressed more concern about finding a job, working out their attitudes towards religion and fitting into Australian society.

Not only are adolescent girls more concerned about most things than boys, but girls also report experiencing more stressful events and they are more affected by stressful events than are boys (Compas, Phares and Ledoux, 1989). These authors cite a study where young people's concerns were considered across a number of problem modalities: family stresses, peer stresses, academic stresses, intimacy stresses and network stresses. The most consistent finding was that network stresses (stresses that affect others in one's social network without directly influencing the individual, for example friends having emotional problems) were experienced more by girls than boys and that these stresses were associated with psychological symptoms. Not only is there a general trend for female adolescents to report a greater number of stressful events than males but they may also be struggling with different types of stresses.

While rural adolescents were found to employ much the same coping strategies as adolescents in other settings, the things that remained challenging for one group of Australian rural adolescents interviewed by Bourke (2002) was their dealing with authority and interpersonal relationships.

Adolescence is a period of development and change. There are intrapersonal changes such as cognitive development, maturation and emotional development and interpersonal changes such as negotiating relationships with peers and family and adapting to school changes. There is a growing importance of peer relationships as adolescence is traversed. Adolescent stressors fall into three categories: achievement-related concerns, relationship concerns and social issues. Whilst relationship-related concerns are important for adolescents, they are also concerned about getting on in the world and about issues relating to the world in general. There is a clear relationship between long-term stress and negative health outcomes.

As noted earlier there are cultural differences in adolescent concerns. For example: Chinese adolescents report the highest problem score, with academic concerns the most pressing. Daily hassles of Australian adolescents were predominantly school related with a focus on peer problems and teasing. There were differences across collectivist vs individualistic cultures on types of adolescent concerns.

Girls tend to report more traumatic life events and stress than boys; they also deal with different types of stresses. Issues of major concern for girls are body image and related self-esteem, and social-evaluation concerns.

Regardless of how we classify or categorize concerns, they do exist in some measure at some time for all young people. Providing a focus on resource-building and maintenance is likely to help enable management of stresses. Given that individuals actively strive to gain resources in order to achieve their goals and to limit their distress. This is likely to protect against stress.

As detailed on page 5, resources consist of tangible objects, personal characteristics, energy which enables the acquisition of other resources, and conditions in which individuals find themselves or places him or herself in.

Social support, which is a key element in coping, is not only a resource but is seen as facilitating the protection of other resources (such as helping one feel confident that one can cope) or conversely detracting from resources by making an individual reliant on others and thus diminishing confidence in their own capacities to cope. Those who are mastery-oriented (see themselves as having personal control) use social support effectively and they also develop more effective support systems. An important part of building the resource pool is the investment in building up a sound repertoire of coping.

A basic human motivation is to obtain, retain and protect resources. Individuals strive to limit resource loss and maximize resource gain. Because resource loss is more potent than resource gain, loss prevention strategies are particularly important in the coping process. Coping and adaptation require investment of resources, so those who lack resources are vulnerable to initial loss and subsequent loss. In contrast, those with a strong resource pool are likely to achieve more gains. We need to build individuals' resource reserves by creating environments that validate the individual.

Summary

When it comes to managing stress the transactional model of stress proposed by Richard Lazarus is generally accepted. It identifies stress as occurring when there are demands on an individual which exceed his or her perceived resources. According to the Conservation of Resources theory of stress proposed by Stevan Hobfoll, chronic stress depletes the resource pool. Stress occurs as a result of resource loss or the threat of loss. The principles of COR theory are outlined. While

COR theory has generally been applied to adult populations, there have been developments and modifications of this theory that apply to the world of adolescents, whose most important resources have been identified as having friends, being close with at least one friend, parent support, adequate home, adequate food, being able to speak up for oneself, having a stable family, feeling independent, having money for one's needs, and having a sense of humour. Ultimately these are the commodities valued by young people, as both meeting their basic needs and enabling them to go beyond survival.

2 What is coping?

When I am stressed or worried I take a minute to cool down. Prioritise things. Figure out what really needs to be done first and what doesn't really need to be done.

(Boy, 17)

Calm down. Look on the brighter side of life.

(Boy, 18)

Take some time to clear your mind. Just got to keep your head up no matter what.

(Boy, 17)

Sleep is probably the most relaxing. Lying on the couch and watching TV or listening to music.

(Boy, 14)

I relax myself through music. I play music to myself. It can be any song on Video Hits and I will be able to play it without any notes. And I have lots of support from my family and friends and everyone around me.

(Girl, 18)

Watching TV and talking to your friends on the Internet.

(Boy, 15)

In my spare time I like to play basketball with my mates or to play bass guitar for a band at my local church.

(Boy, 15)

When I get home from school I like to play a bit of guitar. Weekly, I used to do karate for eight years. But now I have moved on to judo to get a bit of a change happening.

(Boy, 15)

Sport. I play a lot of netball and it gives me time to relax and to do something that relaxes me. I also like to spend time with family and friends.

(Girl, 17)

I enjoy going out with my friends, and I enjoy playing tennis as well.

(Girl, 18)

Music, television, sport and friends reflect the range of coping strategies that young people spontaneously nominate and when asked specifically, *Who do you turn to for support?* they say things such as:

Depending on where you are. If you are at school and you have a problem then the first thing you do is go to your schoolmates because people just want to get things out, . . . Us kids just need to get it out. So depending on where you are, the first people you see that you trust, you will go up to and start talking about it. So if you are at school, you will go up to a good mate and start talking about it. Or if you are at home it would be a parent. Other guys, it is hard to talk to. You know, guys talking to other guys . . . well they don't like revealing things and that, . . . So you wouldn't go and talk to another guy about your problem. So you might go to a girl or a parent. Unless you have a good mate who understands you then you would go to him.

(Boy, 15)

Most likely I would turn to my friends, my really close ones. And my parents as well.

(Boy, 16)

Friends and parents. Relatives, like cousins.

(Boy, 16)

I kind of find my parents a little embarrassing at times, they go over the top sometimes. So usually I head to some of my closest friends.

(Boy, 16)

My friends and family. My friends help me out a lot.

(Girl, 18)

Probably family members, teachers you have known for a long time or you just think are kind people and you can trust them. Definitely friends are a very important aspect of being at school. They will help you a lot. I have had a lot of help from my friends in different situations.

(Girl, 14)

Teachers, friends and family.

(Girl, 17)

Coping research evolved from stress research and so moved from a deficit model of adaptation to exploring people's capacity to deal with life's circumstances. The relationship to health, well-being and productive coping has recently become of interest. The next phase in coping research is an exploration of how people attain goals, achieve success and meet challenges. Diverse but compatible theories of coping, along with theories of temperament, optimism and emotions, contribute to our appreciation of how individuals deal with circumstances and thrive in their efforts to achieve success.

There is a close relationship between general adaptation and coping. While there are those who emphasize positive affect as the other side of coping (e.g. Folkman and Moskowitz, 2000), it is helpful to construe coping as a continuum that extends from the management of stress and adaptation to achieving success and flourishing in the pursuit of goals. Accomplishment and thriving typically means seeing circumstances as opportunities rather than as burdens or problems.

A review of coping research to date reveals that while the transactional model of stress and coping has been widely adopted there are important developments such as proactive and communal coping. In general, coping can be construed as a multidimensional process, a multi-system series of events that continue throughout the lifespan and to which the interplay of many determinants contributes. It is essentially a dynamic interaction between persons and their environments. A number of heuristic devices and empirically supported models have been developed which describe the process. Recently, concepts such as resource theory of coping and proactive coping have entered the adult literature. The way in which these models can be applied to adolescents, and the way in which there can be a synthesis of theories, promises to move us forward in understanding human endeavour.

Coping as a response to stress

Stress and coping are arguably the most widely researched area in psychology. Some people would claim that this vast body of research has been disappointing in its outcomes in that it has failed to deliver clear definitions of what works and what does not work in terms of human adaptation. Nevertheless, we know a great deal about coping and the gains in the stress and coping field have enabled us to move beyond understanding human adaptation to examining how people succeed in meeting their goals and challenges.

Early interest in the adaptational process dates back to the nineteenth century with the work of Sigmund Freud (1894/1964) and the work he did on psychological defences in an attempt to understand how people manage anxiety. Whenever these unconscious defence processes have proved difficult to assess, psychologists have turned to objective laboratory studies of stress (Selye, 1950) or used checklists of life events (Holmes and Rahe, 1967).

Historically, the human stress response has been characterized metaphorically as fight-or-flight in the face of threat (Cannon, 1932). Recently there has been a major challenge to this theorizing by the work of Shelley Taylor and her colleagues (2000), who point out that the evidence for fight-or-flight has largely been derived from work with male subjects, both human and animal, and has not adequately taken into account the typical responses of females. According to Taylor and colleagues, the biobehavioural female stress response can be more accurately construed as tend-and-befriend (Taylor *et al.*, 2000). This response is directed at maximizing the survival of the self and the offspring by nurturing, protecting the offspring from harm, and affiliating with others to reduce risk. This work throws into question much of our understanding about the gender-neutrality of responses in the stress and coping area. Tend-and-befriend is not likely to replace the fight-or-flight metaphor, since both males and females respond in the same way to situations of extreme stress, but it adds another dimension to our understanding of how people respond to environmental demands.

Selye (1976) described stress as 'the non-specific response of the body to any demands' (p. 472). He makes the distinction between stress that mobilizes the individual to effective performance ('eustress'), such as when there is heightened performance during a competition, and stress that is more negative and has been labelled 'distress'. As indicated in the earlier discussion on stress in chapter 1, Richard Lazarus (1991) describes stress as the mismatch between the perceived demands of a situation and the individual's assessment of his or her resources to deal with these demands. Stresses can be physical, such as those pertaining to the environment like extreme heat or cold; psychosocial stresses such those experienced when relationships are not working; and daily hassles, such as having a quarrel with a friend. It is eustress that energizes and maximizes the achievement of potential. Furthermore, it is both the presence of resources and the positive appraisal of events that are required to maximize success.

Definitions of coping

To date much of the coping research in the child and adolescent area has been predicated on the theorizing (albeit conducted with adults) of Folkman and Lazarus, which emphasizes the context in which the coping actions occur, the attempt rather than the outcome, and the fact that coping is a process that changes over time, as the person and the environment are continuously in a dynamic, mutually influential relationship (Lazarus and Folkman, 1984; Folkman and Lazarus, 1988a). This is generally known as the transactional model of coping. Lazarus (1993) defined coping as the response to the 'ongoing cognitive and behavioural demands that are taxing or exceeding the resources of the person' (p. 237).

Folkman (1997) made modifications to the original theoretical model of stress and coping proposed by Lazarus and Folkman (1984), so as to accommodate positive psychological states. Transactions with the environment are appraised as threatening, harmful or challenging and, according to the model, stress is regulated by emotion-focused strategies designed to reduce the distress or manage the problem. These may lead to a favourable resolution, non-resolution, or an unfavourable resolution. According to this model, emotion is generated at three phases: the appraisal phase, the coping phase, and the outcome phase. There are three pathways. The first is directed by positive psychological states that give meaning to the situation and lead to 'revising goals and planning goal-directed problem-focused coping' (Folkman, 1997, p. 1216). The second pathway is the response to the distress rather than the condition that created it. This accounts for the co-occurrence of both negative and positive states where the negative states, while they may be a result of enduring distress, may lead to the individual striving to find (consciously or unconsciously) positive meaning in the event. Such interpretations may then lead to the use of resources such as hope, social support and self-esteem. The third pathway derives from the positive psychological states that result from the coping processes *per se* and can help the person re-motivate, re-energize and re-engage in goal-directed activities. This formulation of stress and emotion is yet to be tested on young people but it would appear that, at least for adolescents, the search for meaning in relation to some situations like school-related activities and the subsequent impact on mood state is likely to hold true.

Coping is 'action regulation under stress', which refers to 'how people mobilize, guide, manage, energize, and direct behaviour, emotion, and orientation, or how they fail to do so under stressful conditions' (Skinner and Zimmer-Gembeck, 2007, pp. 5–6). Stressful conditions experienced by adolescents have been grouped in several ways (see also chapter 1), one of which is that of the four categories: traumatic events, such as parental death; major chronic stressors, such as economic hardship; normative events, such as puberty; and daily hassles, such as an argument with a parent (Compas, 1995; Coleman and Hendry, 1999; Skinner and Zimmer-Gembeck, 2007). Although daily hassles may seem minor, their ongoing and proximal nature can make them stronger predictors of current psychological symptoms, such as anger and anxious states, than retrospective major life stressors (Moulds, 2003). Despite many situations fitting neatly into one of these four groupings, it is commonly acknowledged that two people who experience the same situation are not necessarily affected in similar ways.

Thus coping refers to the behavioural and cognitive efforts used by individuals to manage the demands of a person–environment relationship. An individual's access to available resources, styles and strategies subsequently influences the coping process. Strategies may vary across time and context depending on the stressor (Compas, 1987), and include aspects of the self, such as problem-solving skills and self-esteem, as well as the social environment (i.e. a supportive social network).

Coping styles are methods of coping that characterize individuals' reactions to stress either over time or across different situations. They may partly reflect the ways of coping preferred by individuals because they are consistent with personal values, beliefs and goals. One of the most widely used models of coping, the transactional model, proposes that coping can be defined in terms of two global coping styles: problem-focused (or behavioural) coping and emotion-focused (or cognitive) coping (Folkman, 1982; Lazarus and Folkman, 1984). Other researchers have found that the strategies can best be grouped to characterize three coping styles that represent two functional and one dysfunctional aspect of coping (Seiffge-Krenke and Shulman, 1990; Frydenberg and Lewis, 1991b).

Functional coping styles represent direct attempts to deal with the problem, with or without reference to others. Dysfunctional coping styles relate to the use of what we call Non-Productive strategies, such as *worry* and *self-blame*, while Productive coping has generally been associated with positive adaptation (Ebata and Moos, 1991). The terms functional and dysfunctional styles do not refer to 'good' or 'bad' styles, since styles of coping are largely dependent on context. In fact, whether one is deemed to be a good or bad coper depends on the skills that one brings to a particular environmental situation. Furthermore, individuals can both change themselves and modify their environments (Aldwin, 2007).

Studies examining the link between coping and well-being have identified characteristics associated with more effective coping in adolescence. These characteristics include temperament, optimism, perceived personal control, familial factors (such as family cohesion, shared values, loving parents and a relationship with at least one parent figure), flexibility and the availability of social support.

Research has found that coping strategies that focus on problem-solving and positive cognitions are related to less emotional, behavioural and substance-use problems (Compas, Malcarne and Fonda-caro, 1988; Ebata and Moos, 1991). In contrast, avoidant or Non-Productive coping is generally associated with poor adaptation and more mental health problems in adolescents (Ebata and Moos, 1991; Sandler, Wolchik, MacKinnon, Ayers and Roosa, 1997; Frydenberg and Lewis, 1999b).

The role of appraisal

The concept of appraisal is one of the basic tenets of Lazarus' theory. It is an important part of the coping process and has explicatory power. Cognitive appraisal is what a person does to evaluate whether a particular encounter is relevant to his or her well-being. In each encounter two forms of appraisal are said to take place: *primary appraisal*, where the question 'What is at stake in terms of potential harm or benefit?' is asked, and *secondary appraisal*, where the question is 'What can be done about the situation or what are the options or resources available?' (Folkman, Lazarus, Gruen and DeLongis, 1986). The appraisals may initiate a chain of activity and coping actions to manage a situation.

Researchers such as Stone and Neale (1984) have developed their own measures of coping and found that appraisal is associated with type and amount of coping. Manzi (1986) found that students assessed what is stressful in a work situation according to whether they regarded the situation as one of loss, threat or challenge. In relation to stressful academic and social events in a school environment, appraisal played a part, in that the severity of the stress was assessed according to whether individuals felt they could do something constructive to deal with the problem (Fahs, 1986). This holds true even for pre-adolescents. According to Muldoon (1996), who examined the interview responses of 9–10-year-olds, events that are harmful or loss-inducing are perceived by children as most stressful, and when asked to describe an event that is stressful children spontaneously described a harmful event.

Resource theories of coping

Two areas of research that have emerged from the field of coping stand out: COR (Conservation of Resources) theory with its extension to communal coping, and proactive coping with its emphasis on goal management.

In his recent work Hobfoll points out that COR theory considers both environmental and internal processes in fairly equal measure (2001). It perhaps best exemplifies that both aspects account for successful outcomes as the individual interacts with his or her environment. He goes on to point out that the self derives from the attachments to intimate biological or social groups and at the same time the individual is nested within a tribe or community which determines the cultural scripts that are brought into an encounter. The study of individual processes without reference to the cultural context is bound to fall short. Additionally, what helps us to move beyond the appraisal models of stress is that the individual is able to be seen as proactive rather than reactive, that is, proactive coping is future-oriented rather than merely compensating for loss or alleviating harm.

The key argument of COR theory is the primacy of loss, that is, loss outweighs the benefit of gain. However, gain becomes important in the context of loss. To safeguard against loss there is an investment of resources which includes 'acquisition, maintenance and fostering'. These in turn are motivational goals consistent with proactive coping. The way in which proactive coping is defined by Greenglass (2002), and Schwarzer and Taubert (2002) would imply that 'acquisition, maintenance and fostering' are important strategies for success. Boekaerts (2002b) presents an educationalist's view of anticipatory and proactive coping in the context of goal attainment. Boekaerts makes the point that the unique way in which students give meaning to learning activities determines how much effort they are prepared to invest to achieve a school-related goal. That is, if the learning goal or task is in accordance with their need and value systems they are likely to succeed. It could be said that all the high achievers (see chapter 11) pursue goals that are congruent with their needs. Whether they were constructing a collection of buildings, playing the piano, or undertaking a long-distance swim, the endeavour was consistent with their personal goals and values. According to Boekaerts, self-regulated learning is about having the metacognitive skills to orient, plan, execute, monitor and repair. It requires forthright volitional control and self-reflection. While proactive coping is linked to anticipatory and preventive coping, it is distinguished from them in that they are generally attempts to avert or minimize the impact of impending threats that are likely to occur in the future. Thus, when it comes to adolescent research, proactive goal-oriented coping with an inherent emphasis on self-improvement is the more useful concept.

But to return to COR theory: with its emphasis on conservation of resources, investment and building up a stockpile of personal, social and economic resources, it points to the proactive aspects of coping. The emphasis on the 'individual – nested in family – nested in tribe' highlights the communal and collectivist aspect of coping. That is, the individual is part of a group that is generally identified as a family, which is in turn located within the community.

COR theory emphasizes that the individual's approach to coping is complemented by the concept of communal coping with its focus on interdependence. Hobfoll (2002) argues for a culturally sensitive approach to coping that may be individualistic or more collectivist. Personal agency is linked to acting more assertively, being more independent from others, and worrying less about social relationships. Communal mastery, in contrast, is linked closely to social means of coping, looking to social support, and greater interdependence. Johnson and Johnson (2002), who emphasize 'group work' in school settings, identify the important elements of working together rather than alone. Hobfoll has found in his team's research that those high in communal mastery were significantly lower in psychological distress than those low in communal mastery. Thus while self-efficacy or a belief in one's own capacity to cope is important, communal coping strategies play an important part in minimizing stress. Nevertheless, it remains culturally and contextually dependent as to what is appropriate, available and valued in a particular setting.

Some theoretical issues

While various authors have defined coping strategies, coping resources, and coping outcomes, it is important to note that the overlap in conceptualizations of certain aspects of adolescent experience has resulted in some measurement anomalies. For example, according to the Folkman and Lazarus conceptualization, if students 'ring up a close friend' this behaviour is an indicator of a coping strategy identified as social support. Such a strategy is assumed to be a characteristic response to issues of concern. Hobfoll's model, however, indicates that having friends is a component of an adolescent's personal resources, which are protected and then used in times of need. It is interesting to note that being with and sharing with friends has also been conceptualized as an outcome of coping. For example, Ebata and Moos (1991) define 'having friends' as an aspect of efficacy, and Reynolds (2001) uses the frequency with which an adolescent is having fun with friends as an indicator of well-being.

Clearly there is some overlap between the concepts underlying coping strategies, resources and outcomes. For example, imagine an adolescent who is unable or unwilling to share his or her concerns, or even to communicate effectively. As a consequence of this characteristic response pattern (i.e. this coping strategy), such an adolescent would have few friends, and could be described in Hobfoll's terms as having limited personal resources on which to draw. One could argue in such a case that a coping pattern has affected resources. Alternatively, it could be argued that a child who has been raised in circumstances that provided limited access to other children, that is, a child who has limited resources, would be unlikely customarily to adopt social support as a preferred coping response. In such a situation, resources determine the coping strategy to be used.

Of all the outcomes that have been associated with coping and resources, most appear to be related to dysfunction. Most studies therefore have sought to examine a direct link with indicators of dysfunction such as depression (Ebata and Moos, 1994; Frydenberg and Lewis, 2002), low self-esteem (Brodzinsky, Elias, Steiger, Simon, Gill and Hitt, 1992), poor academic performance (Band and Weisz, 1988), suicidal ideation (Asarnow, Carlson and Guthrie, 1987; Spirito, Francis, Overholser and Frank, 1996) and substance abuse (Wills, 1986). Others have stated that they are focusing on adolescent well-being but provide as their indicator an absence of dysfunction, for example a lack of mental disorder (Sawyer *et al.*, 2000) or less inability to cope (Frydenberg and Lewis, 1997). Such studies appear to be predicated on the assumption that less dysfunction is equivalent to greater well-being.

Some studies have investigated the relationship between coping and indicators of well-being and, as noted above, have reported the impact of coping on positive outcomes such as achievement (Parsons, Frydenberg and Poole, 1996; Skinner and Wellborn, 1997). Very few have reported the relationship between coping and indicators of both dysfunction and well-being (see for example, Ebata and Moos, 1991).

Proactive coping

Proactive coping is another important development in the coping literature which emphasizes the individual's role in planning so as to maximize an optimum outcome for future events.

Along with Greenglass (2002), Schwarzer and Taubert (2002) make a distinction between anticipatory coping, where one anticipates that critical events are to occur and there is investment in risk management, and preventive coping, where there is an investment of effort to build up 'resistance resources' to minimize the severity of impact. Proactive coping, in contrast, is about building up resources to promote challenging goals and personal growth, that is, it is about 'goal striving'. In that sense it is both consistent with Hobfoll's COR theory and an extension of it. Proactive copers have vision, and coping for them is about goal management. It is not self-defeating but self-initiating and about having a vision that gets transformed into action. This is just what the high achievers do (see chapter 12).

Those with personal goals and resources are less vulnerable to stress. Among the personal resources of affluence, health, optimism, self-efficacy and hope are included coping skills. Greenglass (2002) makes four important points in relation to coping. Coping can have several functions, only one of which may be to minimize stress. Functions that relate to maintaining relationships, keeping to a task or beating a competitor can all be coping. Second, coping is multidimensional rather than bipolar as frequently represented by the dimensions of control/escape, active/passive and problem-focused/emotion-focused. Third, it does not occur in a social vacuum. Fourth, the function of coping is not only to alleviate distress but also increase potential for growth, satisfaction and quality of life. In the adult arena Greenglass illustrates how the use of proactive coping can lead to less emotional exhaustion and anger, and to positive outcomes such as professional efficacy. Similarly, in the adolescent arena it could be expected that those who are proactive are likely to feel better about themselves and less likely to suffer from despair or an incapacity to cope. While proactive coping at different stages of development implies different forms of coping – in the early adolescent years, for example, there is less likelihood of planning, organising and anticipating demands and situations – these emerge as useful strategies that are more likely to be used in middle to later adolescence.

The field has now moved beyond a reactive theory of coping to one where concepts such as mastery, optimization and resources gain are consistent with proactive coping. Concepts such as benefit-finding, sense-making, the search for meaning all broaden the coping concept. There is a negative relationship between proactive coping and depression. Proactive teachers report less exhaustion, less cynicism, more personal accomplishments than their reactive counterparts (Schwarzer and Taubert, 2002). Highly proactive teachers regard their stressors as more challenging and less threatening or loss-based than their reactive counterparts. Proactive teachers have less burnout, more challenges and less threat and loss. Proactive coping is about growth and taking responsibility for making things happen. Qualities of leadership are closely linked to proactive coping. It seems highly beneficial to develop skills of proactive coping.

Thus coping research has been broadened to include a positive purposeful element that focuses on what people do before potentially stressful events, to prevent them or modify them before they occur. Proactive coping differs from traditional coping because it involves anticipating future needs, accumulating resources and acquiring skills to prepare in a general way for stressors. Proactive coping is active rather than reactive, it is about goal management rather than risk management, and it is more positive than negative in that possible stressors are seen as challenging (Aspinwall and Taylor, 1997; Greenglass, 2002). In summary, proactive coping is about skill development, resource accumulation and long-term planning which demands internal control and self-determination. People who engage in proactive coping believe in the potential to change and improve oneself and the environment rather than taking a fatalistic approach to the inevitability of stressful events (Greenglass, 2002; Schwarzer and Taubert, 2002). They set and pursue goals and strive for personal growth.

Since proactive coping has been assessed and conceptualized with adults in mind, little is known about its development or how much it is used by adolescents. While proactive coping with young people is at the early stages of research, it certainly holds promise for theory and practice with adolescents.

Coping and emotions

The relationship between coping and emotions is important in that emotions have been generally seen as interfering with cognitions and coping. Often emotions appear to dominate and the individual can be described as floundering in a sea of emotions. Historically, coping has been viewed as a response to emotion. In more recent years, there has been a shift where the two are understood to be in a reciprocal dynamic relationship. Just as emotion determines how an encounter is appraised, so the outcome in turn determines the individual's emotional state both in the ongoing interaction and in future interactions. Folkman and Lazarus (1988a) distinguish this from the Darwinian approach, where emotions like fear and anger are thought to come to the aid of the organism in the face of threat, and also from the ego psychological approach which includes reference to cognitive processes like denial, repression, suppression, intellectualization and problem-solving in an effort to reduce stress and anxiety. Although there is no readily agreed definition of emotion, there is general agreement that emotions comprise an experiential (affect, appraisal), physiological and behavioural (action for readiness) component (Frijda, 1993; Izard, 1993), and these are expressed through separate systems such as the verbal report of feelings, overt behaviour and expressive physiology (Lang, 1984). The metaphors of negative emotions generally portray them as an irresistible force. Thus in the coping literature much of the emotion-focused conceptualization of coping is concerned with the maladaptive. A more recent perspective on emotions has focused on the adaptive nature of emotion and how individuals can organize social communication, goal achievement and cognitive processes from an early age (Izard, 1993; Pekrun, Goetz, Titz and Perry, 2002). Thus emotions are a major organizing force with intrapersonal and interpersonal regulatory effects. Three theoretical constructs exemplify a functionalist view of emotion in personality research: emotional competence (Saarni, 1990), emotional intelligence (Salovey and Mayer, 1990) and emotional creativity (Averill and Thomas-Knowles, 1991). All contribute to healthy intra- and interpersonal functioning. Emotional competence is essentially self-efficacy in the context of 'emotion-eliciting social transactions' (Saarni, 1997, p. 38). The concept of emotional intelligence has integrated the literature from multiple intelligences (Gardner, 1983) and can be construed as a subset of social intelligence. Emotional creativity is about the creation of emotions that are novel.

Individuals differ in how they perceive, express, understand and manage emotional phenomena. Essentially, emotional intelligence is the ability to monitor one's own and others' feelings and emotions, as well as having the ability to regulate and use emotion-based information to guide thinking and action. Traditional intelligence is considered to be about reasoning and analytic abilities. Emotions are adaptive and functional and they serve to organize cognitive activities (Leeper, 1948; Mowrer, 1960). It was first argued by Charles Darwin in 1872 in *The expressions of emotions in man and animal* (Salovey and Mayer, 1990) that emotions are a higher order of activity. Darwin claimed that emotions energize and signal in a way that helps other members of the species.

A tripartite model of cognitive activity has been proposed as a way of conceptualizing emotions (Folkman and Lazarus, 1988a). The first part is cognitive activity which influences deployment of attention and includes vigilant strategies that neutralize the distress, such as jogging or taking a holiday: what Folkman and Lazarus label 'escape-avoidance', characterized by strategies such as wishful thinking; and tension reduction activities, such as eating, drinking or sleeping too much. These strategies can be either adaptive or maladaptive depending on the circumstance. Next, there are the cognitive activities that alter the subjective meaning of an encounter, such as the use of humour and denial. Similarly, in some circumstances these strategies can be helpful in the release of tension or in preventing the catastrophizing of events, while in other circumstances they can deny the severity of a problem and avoid engaging in appropriate action. These strategies can also be used to remain on task and enhance performance. Included lastly are those actions that alter the person–environment interaction, such as standing one's ground, getting someone to change their mind, or getting more information.

Changes in the emotional response depend on whether the desired outcome is achieved, on how an individual evaluates his or her own response, and what the implications of the present encounter are for future events. Gender is considered to be a moderator of emotional coping and adaptive outcomes. One explanation may be that girls are exposed by caretakers from an early age to a wider range of emotions. Physical and mental health comes from neither emotional inhibition nor exhibition *per se*, but from flexibility (Averill, 1994, p. 102). There needs to be a capacity to deal with demands flexibly as well as a capacity to use those strategies to forge ahead.

Coping actions are determined in part by one's belief that certain consequences are possible (Hock, 1999). This belief in control over one's thoughts, feelings and behaviours, together with a positive attributional style, is associated with the use of more positive coping responses. There is also emerging evidence that what makes the difference is coping efficacy, that is, the belief that one has the strategies to cope. These findings, along with the clear-cut evidence that Non-Productive coping is associated with depression and other forms of emotional and social malfunctioning (Chan, 1998; Lewis, 1999), has informed what to teach and when to teach coping skills to young people (see also chapter 12).

The model in Figure 2.1 posits that coping is a function of the situational determinants and the individual's characteristics, perception of the situation and coping intentions. The individual brings a host of biological dispositional, personal and family history, and family climate characteristics. It is how these impact on the perception of the situation that is of interest. Following an appraisal of the situation, the individual assesses the likely impact of the stress, that is, whether the consequences are likely to lead to 'loss', 'harm', 'threat' or 'challenge', and what resources (personal or interpersonal) are available to deal with the situation. The intent of the action, along with the action itself, determines the outcome. Following a response, the outcome is reviewed or reappraised (*tertiary appraisal* or *reappraisal*) and another response may follow. There may be a subsequent development in an individual's coping repertoire. Thus the circular nature of the process illustrates the fact that strategies are likely to be tried again or rejected from future use, and is consequent on the coping experience of the individual.

If the encounter is amenable to change, problem-focused strategies are frequently used. Where the situation is assessed as unchangeable, emotion-focused strategies are more likely to be used (Folkman and Lazarus, 1980). For example, males tend to appraise 'hassles' as a challenge and employ problem-focused strategies, while females are more inclined to appraise situations as threatening or harmful and are more inclined to use emotion-focused coping (Griffith, Dubow and Ippolito, 2000).

As stated above, whether or not a stressor is controllable is an important factor in how one copes. A study by Hampel and Petermann (2005) found that academic stressors were assessed as more controllable than interpersonal stressors; and generally more problem-focused strategies than emotion-focused strategies were used to deal with the academic than the interpersonal stressors. It was also found that in general when there was low perceived control of the stressor, there was greater use of emotion-focused coping, whereas when there was high perceived control, there was greater use of problem-focused coping. Another interesting finding was that in those cases where the self-reports and maternal reports indicated that emotional or

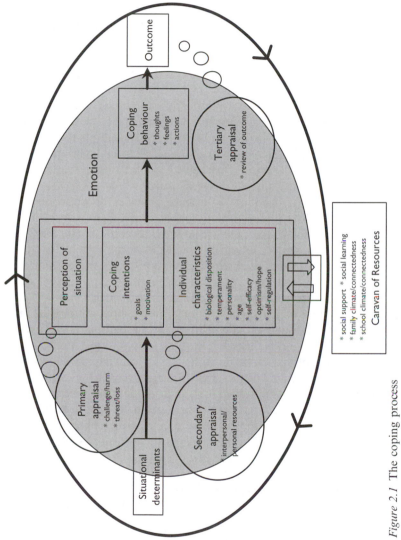

Figure 2.1 The coping process

Outcome

Coping behaviour
* thoughts
* feelings
* actions

Emotion

Tertiary appraisal
* review of outcome

Perception of situation

Coping intentions
* goals
* motivation

Individual characteristics
* biological disposition
* temperament
* personality
* age
* self-efficacy
* optimism/hope
* self-regulation

Situational determinants

Primary appraisal
* challenge/harm
* threat/loss

Secondary appraisal
* interpersonal/personal resources

* social support * social learning
* family climate/connectedness
* school climate/connectedness
Caravan of Resources

behavioural problems existed, there was greater use of emotion-focused coping, and where there were no emotional or behavioural problems, there was greater use of problem-focused coping. Lazarus emphasizes the central role of cognitions in emotional outcomes, asserting that when people experience situations as a 'hassle', it is the meaning that they give to a transaction, and whether they appraise the situation as threatening, harmful or challenging, that may have an impact on the emotion generated and the coping reaction (Folkman, Lazarus, Pimley and Novacek, 1987). That is what is meant by the 'perception of the situation'.

Psychological stress resides neither in the person nor in the situation, but depends on the transaction between the two, that is, how the person appraises the event and how he or she adapts to it. Thus to some young people, each exam, public occasion or interview may be stressful, while to others it is perceived as part of the excitement of living and an opportunity to move forward.

The learning or schooling experience provides an opportunity to develop the skills to cope for life. What is clear from the work of Dweck (Smiley and Dweck, 1994; and see Boekaerts, 2002b; De Corte, Verschaffel and Op't Eynde 2000) is that it is possible to change students' perceptions of themselves in relationship to the learning task. Various cognitive and motivational self-regulatory processes can be promoted to help students become their own teacher. Cues that elicit positive emotions (e.g. joy, contentment, satisfaction, anticipated pride or interest) temporarily broaden the scope of attention, cognition and action. In contrast, cues that elicit negative emotions (e.g. anxiety, fear, frustration, irritation, shame or guilt) temporarily narrow the scope of attention, cognition and action. The consequences for the learning task are evident. Not all children choose challenging tasks when given the opportunity; rather, 37 per cent choose to do the familiar and easy puzzle. However, the response they receive at the completion of the task determines whether they persevere (Smiley and Dweck, 1994).

Students profit from an increased capacity to judge whether a particular action will lead to goal attainment, that is, whether increased effort and persistence will pay off. However, effort investment is related to the perceived value of tasks and the perceived competence of execution. In a diverse and changing school climate students are increasingly being called on to be self-regulated learners. A distinction is also made between self-regulation and self-control in that the latter activates the punishment system while the former is associated with positive emotions. Educators need to foster skills for self-regulation.

The concept of proactive coping needs to be integrated into the world of young people. The link between self-regulated learning and proactive coping can be made. Goals that are in harmony with students' goal structures have a better chance of being adopted and achieved. As Resnick and colleagues (1997) demonstrated in their study of 12,118 adolescents from 80 high schools in the United States, school and parent connectedness are key factors in resiliency. It can generally be assumed that where goals in education are congruent with both the students' and their parents' objectives, the goals are more likely to be achieved, resulting in a situation where there is a strong sense of connectedness with both the school and parents.

Positive affect is helpful in fulfilling the activities that are important in the classroom. The 'broader mindset' with which positive mood state is associated encourages exploration, extension of oneself and the sharing of information. The Resnick survey interviewed young people for emotional distress, suicidal thoughts and behaviours, violence, use of substances (cigarettes, alcohol, marijuana) and two aspects of sexual behaviours (age of sexual debut and pregnancy history). They found that 18.4 per cent of 9th through to 12th graders experienced significant distress. Thus it can be expected that, while most young people go through their school years with a healthy positive affect, there are many for whom addressing their emotional well-being is an imperative. Furthermore, the idea of working in groups in an educational community can contribute here.

Pekrun, Goetz, Titz and Perry (2002) considered the frequency of emotions reported in a number of learning-related areas. They found that although anxiety (the negative emotion associated with stress) was often experienced, positive emotions were experienced as frequently as the negative ones. These researchers established a measure of positive emotions in relation to students' learning, achievement, personality and social environments to determine whether positive emotions are helpful or not. They considered the relative benefit of positive emotions, in contrast to the often considered negative effect of emotions, including unrealistic appraisals and superficial processing of information. They showed that positive mood can facilitate divergent and flexible thinking to enhance problem-solving. They formulated a cognitive motivational model that involves positive activating emotions such as hope and pride and positive deactivating emotions such as relief and relaxation. They go on to borrow terms from motivation research, which relates to outcomes such as where intrinsic emotions are related to enjoyment of the task – a concept somewhat like Csikszentmihalyi's (1990) concept of flow (see p. 191) –

and extrinsic emotions are related to success or failure. Generally the assumption is made that students' pursuit of their goals in an academic setting is more likely to be associated with gaining mastery and avoiding failure than with maintaining mood.

They sum up their findings as showing that emotions like enjoyment, hope and pride relate to students' academic goal pursuits and outcomes in positive ways. Since emotions can make a difference, a case can be made for attending to emotions in the classroom. There is a reciprocal relationship between students' environments and positive emotions. That is, social environments affect positive emotions and positive emotions in turn affect academic learning and achievement. There are implications for classroom practice such as attributional training and designing classroom environments that include co-operative learning. Change is a certainty with which we all need to cope. Coping with change is about feeling that one has personal control, tolerance of ambiguity, and ability to share worries.

Summary

Coping represents thoughts, feelings and actions that an individual uses to deal with problematic situations encountered in everyday life and in particular circumstances. The notion of 'coping' as developed by psychologists has acquired a variety of meanings which are often used interchangeably with such concepts as mastery, defence and adaptation.

Coping is a multidimensional phenomenon in which the appraisal of an event is important. Primary appraisal first determines whether a situation is one of threat or challenge; secondary appraisal establishes whether an individual feels that they have the resources to cope. The extent to which one uses functional and dysfunctional styles of coping generally determines the outcome. The paradigm from which one considers coping will influence the context in which one evaluates a particular coping style or strategy.

The proactive view of coping can lead to less emotional exhaustion and greater positive outcomes. It differs from the traditional view because it has an anticipatory focus where one accumulates resources and prepares for potential stressors. It remains to be seen whether adolescents have the capacity for such forward thinking. Proactive coping goes beyond preparing to deal with stress and loss or merely reacting to it. There has also been a change in focus from individual coping to communal coping and the role of social support and interdependence has been highlighted. This way of coping provides markers for adolescents from both individualistic and collectivist cultural backgrounds, that is, for what may be the strengths and weaknesses in these settings.

While to date much of the literature dealing with emotions and coping has centred on the maladaptive, recently there has been a shift towards the adaptive nature of emotions, emotional competence, emotional intelligence and emotional creativity. Emotion-focused coping can be adaptive or maladaptive depending on the outcome. Use of this style is also largely influenced by gender as girls are socialized to be more emotionally expressive.

Appraisal of how controllable a stressor is, is essential to coping responses. Emotion-focused coping is more likely if a situation is viewed as unchangeable. For example, academic stressors are typically viewed as more controllable than interpersonal stressors.

The school experience provides an ideal arena for developing skills to cope with life. Adolescents need to be taught to be their own self-regulators and to increase their capacity to judge whether a particular response will lead to goal attainment.

Communal and proactive coping, along with positive emotions and self-regulation, contribute to our understanding of well-being and thriving. While it is possible to change individual behaviour and thinking, it is also helpful to change organizational settings in ways that assist individuals to achieve well-being and contribute to their thriving and success.

3   The measurement of coping

I tend to blame myself a lot for things that are not exactly my fault. Just recently a friend died and I just felt like I deserted him when he was sick and blamed things on myself. And then I talked to my friend and she was like 'why do you blame yourself when it was not your fault that he was sick and you were there for him as much as you could be?'

No, it isn't really good to blame oneself. You are already stressed about it and just the fact that when you constantly put things on yourself, it really does bring you down. You really feel small.

(Girl, 17)

There are different ways of determining how people cope. One way is to observe their behaviour and then report on that observation. In the child and adolescent arena reporting is often sought from parents or teachers. However, the most reliable source of information is generally the individual themselves. The most direct approach is to ask the individual to describe how they coped in a particular situation or how they would cope with a hypothetical situation. Sometimes these hypothetical situations are presented in the form of scenarios. Generally these direct modes of questioning yield only one, two or three descriptions of coping. But in order to get a range of descriptions of coping so as to systematically assess, record and analyse individual differences and changes in coping over time, we need consistent and valid ways of measuring the construct. Over the years this has led to the development of a range of coping instruments.

This chapter reports on the traditional and most common approach to assessing the ways in which individuals cope with their concerns, that is through a coping questionnaire or inventory. A number of frequently used and recorded inventories are available. One such inventory, the Adolescent Coping Scale (Frydenberg and Lewis, 1993a), is described in greater detail as an exemplar of questionnaire development. The conceptual groupings identified by that instrument are used in many places throughout this book to report on research findings, and, for example, as an evaluation tool for coping skills intervention programmes (see chapter 12). This chapter also outlines the more recent developments in the adolescent area that have followed from the adult research domains such as Hobfoll's (2002) resource theory of coping and the proactive coping championed by Greenglass (2002) and Schwarzer and Taubert (2002). These theories have led to recent efforts to develop instruments to measure the constructs in the adolescent domains.

Many coping inventories have been developed over the years. The earliest developments assessed adult ways of coping, with interest in the assessment of how younger people cope arising in the late 1980s when the coping literature turned its attention to coping in childhood (Compas, 1987). In her comprehensive review of coping scales Carolyn Aldwin identified 200 references to different coping scales, 51 of which were in the child and adolescent arena.

The measurement of coping

Descriptions of how people cope are generally provided by individuals or derived from the literature. The descriptions of actions are subsequently grouped according to similarity of concept or ideation. The most common categorization or grouping of approaches to coping is the dichotomous grouping of strategies by Lazarus and Folkman (1984; Lazarus, 1993), which identifies problem- and emotion-focused coping. Alternative categorizations range from groupings of 8–10 strategies or scales (e.g. Stark, Spirito, Williams and Guevremont, 1989) to the specificity of 18 strategies that make up the Adolescent Coping Scale (Frydenberg and Lewis, 1993a). Strategies have often been grouped to characterize coping styles that represent functional and dysfunctional aspects of coping (Cox, Gotts, Boot and Kerr, 1985; Seiffge-Krenke and Shulman, 1990; Frydenberg and Lewis, 1996a). The functional styles represent direct attempts to deal with the problem, with or without reference to others, whereas the dysfunctional styles relate to the use of Non-Productive strategies, such as *self-blame* and *worry*.

Since the burgeoning interest in young people's coping over the past two decades, various coping inventories for children and adolescents have been developed. In their important paper, Compas, Connor-Smith, Saltzman, Thomsen and Wadsworth (2001) provided an overview of coping inventories developed since 1988 which have been frequently used to investigate coping in children and adolescents. The overview comprised a summary of 20 coping inventories, which focused on the original forms of the inventories, although the authors did acknowledge that shortened or modified versions may have since been created.

More than a dozen of these inventories have been selected on the basis that they measured adolescent coping only, rather than coping across the lifespan or combined adolescent and child coping. Included in the table are the coping inventories that were reported in the 1997 edition of this book since most of these coping scales are still commonly being used in published studies. Some had also been translated into other languages from their original form, such as the Adolescent Coping Scale (Frydenberg and Lewis, 1993a [Spanish (1996) and Slovenian (2001) editions]) and the Adolescent Coping Orientation for Problem Experiences translated from German into Swedish (Halvarsson, Lunner and Sjödén, 2001). While there appear to be several new measures of stress and related constructs, such as worry, pain and self-efficacy, there have been few recent developments in coping scales for adolescents. One recent important development was the Cross-Cultural Coping Scale by Kuo, Roysircar and Newby-Clark (2006), developed specifically to address young people's coping with stressful situations in various parts of the world. Such a measure is critical to a better understanding of the ways in which young people living away from their country of birth cope, as well as the influence of their family and host country's culture in coping.

Researchers and practitioners in the medical domain have become greatly interested in how adolescents cope with pain, and several coping inventories have been developed that specifically deal with illness-related problems. Three such measures have been included, even though the inventories are not exclusively for adolescents but are for the exploration of coping with pain in both children and adolescents.

In Table 3.1 we have provided summary information of the inventories' key features, namely scale description, scale development, the type of stressor referred to, and the age sample reported. In the earlier edition of this book the inventories or scales were differentiated into three dimensions of coping that we have found to be useful: Productive coping, Reference to Others, and Non-Productive coping. This breakdown is maintained in the current table. An analysis of the

Table 3.1 Adolescent coping inventories

Author(s)	Scale	Scale description	Scale development	Stressor	Age sample reported	Productive coping	Reference to Others	Non-Productive coping
Fanshawe & Burnett (1991)	Coping Inventory for Adolescents (CIA)	54 items (from A-COPE) 5-point scale Self-report 4 factors	Developed from two existing questionnaires: A-COPE & the Academic Stress Scale	General	12–18 years	• Positive avoidance (e.g., think of good things in my life)	• Family communication (e.g., reason with my parents)	• Negative avoidance (e.g., use drugs) • Anger
Patterson & McCubbin (1987)	Adolescent Coping Orientation for Problem Experiences (A-COPE)	54 items (from A-COPE) 5-point scale Self-report 12 factors	Items generated & validated with adolescents	General	11–18 years	• Developing self-reliance • Seeking spiritual support • Engaging in demanding activity	• Developing social support • Solving family problems • Investing in close friends • Seeking professional support	• Avoiding problems • Seeking diversions • Relaxing • Ventilating feelings • Being humorous
Seiffge-Krenke (1995)	Coping Across Situations-Questionnaire (CASQ)	20 items Either 'yes' or 'no' Self-report 3 factors 20 strategies	Items generated & validated with adolescents	Everyday stressors from 8 domains: self, parents, peers, opposite sex, school, leisure time, vocational goals & future	12–19 years	*Internal coping* • I accept my limits • I compromise • I think about the problem and try to find different solutions • I tell myself that there will always be problems • I only think about the problem when it appears	*Active coping* • I look for information in magazines, encyclopedias or books • I try to get help from institutions • I talk straight away about the problem with the person concerned	*Withdrawal coping* • I behave as if everything is all right • I try not to think about the problem • I withdraw because I cannot change anything anyway • I try to forget the problem with alcohol and drugs

continues overleaf

Table 3.1 (continued)

Author(s)	Scale	Scale description	Scale development	Stressor	Age sample reported	Productive coping	Reference to Others	Non-Productive coping
						Withdrawal coping • I try to let my aggression out (with loud music, riding my motorbike, wild dancing, sport, etc.)	• I try to solve the problem with the help of my friends • I discuss the problem with my parents/other adults • I try to get help and comfort from people who are in similar situations	• I let out my anger by shouting, crying, slamming doors, etc.)
Spirito, Stark & Williams (1988)	Kidcope (adolescent version)	10 items Efficacy (5-point scale) Frequency (4-point scale) Self-report	Coping strategies derived from theory. Specifically developed to assess adolescents coping with a serious or chronic illness	A self-identified personal problem within a specific situation	12–18 years	• Problem-solving	• Social support	• Resignation • Cognitive restructuring • Social withdrawal • Wishful thinking • Distraction • Emotional regulation • Blaming others • Self-criticism
Halstead, Johnson & Cunningham (1993)	Modified Ways of Coping Checklist (WCCL)	68 items 4-point scale Self-report 4 factors	Developed from the adult Ways of Coping Checklist from Folkman & Lazarus (1985)	The self-identified most stressful event of past month	12–17 years	• Problem-focused	• Seek social support	• Wishful thinking • Avoidance

Authors	Measure	Description	Development	Stressor	Age			
Phelps & Jarvis (1994)	COPE	60 items 4-point scale Self-report 4 factors	Items taken from the adult COPE	A self-identified stressor from last two months	14–18 years	• Active coping • Planning	• Seeking instrumental social support • Seeking emotional social support	• Denial • Behavioral disengagement • Alcohol/drug disengagement
Causey & Dubow (1992)	Self Report Coping Scale (SRCS)	34 items 5-point scale Self-report 5 factors	Developed from theory & validated with an adolescent sample	Self-identified stressors selected from the academic & social domains (one stressor from each domain)	4th to 6th graders	• Self-reliance/problem-solving	• Seeking social support	• Distancing • Externalizing • Internalizing
Brodzinsky, Elias, Steiger, Simon, Gill & Hitt (1992)	Coping Scale for Children & Youth	29 items 4-point scale Self-report 4 factors	44 items were culled from previous research & reduced to the final 22	Self-identified stressor	10–15 years	• Cognitive behavioural problem-solving	• Assistance seeking	• Cognitive avoidance • Behavioural avoidance
Connor-Smith, Compas, Wadsworth, Thomsen & Saltzman (2000)	Response to Stress Questionnaire (RSQ)	57 items 4-point scale measures coping & involuntary responses to stress. There are 19 subscales which fall within a three-tiered model: volitional/ involuntary; engagement/ disengagement; primary/ secondary control	Initially derived from theory	Self-identified interpersonal stressors	11–17 years	• Volitional primary control coping (e.g., problem-solving) • Volitional secondary control coping (e.g., positive thinking)		• Volitional effortful disengagement (e.g., avoidance, denial) • Involuntary disengagement (e.g., inaction, escape) • Involuntary engagement (e.g., intrusive thoughts, emotional arousal)

continues overleaf

Table 3.1 (continued)

Author(s)	Scale	Scale description	Scale development	Stressor	Age sample reported	Productive coping	Reference to Others	Non-Productive coping
Dise-Lewis (1988)	Life Events & Coping Inventory (LECI)	42 items 9-point scale Self-report 5 factors	Items generated & validated with adolescents	Provided with 125 life stressors	11–14 years	• Stress reduction • Endurance		• Aggression • Stress recognition • Distractions
Ebata & Moos (1991)	Coping Response Inventory – Youth Form (CRI-Y)	48 items 4-point scale Self-report 8 factors	Derived from theory & interviews with adolescents	The self-identified most important problems in previous year	12–18 years	• Logical analysis • Taking problem-solving action • Positive reappraisal	• Seeking guidance & support	• Resignation acceptance • Cognitive avoidance • Seeking alternative rewards • Emotional discharge
Frydenberg & Lewis (1993a)	Adolescent Coping Scale (ACS)	80 items 5-point scale Self-report 3 factors: Productive coping, Reference to Others, Non-Productive coping 18 strategies	Items generated & validated with adolescents	General form – concerns in general. Specific form – specific concern identified by informant	12–17 years	• Focus on solving the problem • Focus on the positive • Work hard & achieve • Seek relaxing diversions • Physical recreation	• Seek social support • Invest in close friends • Seek to belong • Social action • Seek professional help • Seek spiritual support	• Ignore the problem • Keep to self • Wishful thinking • Tension reduction • Self-blame • Worry • Not cope
Kuo, Roysicar & Newby-Clark (2006)	Cross-Cultural Coping Scale (CCCS)	Scenario-based assessment of coping. Respondents are asked how they would cope with two specific stress-evoking scenarios. 20 items	Derived from theory and focus groups with adolescents. Specifically developed to measure international	Two specific acculturative stress situations	15 years to young adulthood	*Engagement coping* • Relaxation • Optimism • Action	*Collective coping* • Parent • Friendship • Family • Authority	*Avoidance coping* • Unobtrusive • Forget • Distraction

					Approach coping	*Emotion-focused avoidance*	*Problem-focused avoidance*
		6-point scale 3 factors: avoidance coping, collective coping and engagement coping 10 strategies	students' coping with stressful situations				
Reid, Gilbert & McGrath (1998)	Pain Coping Questionnaire (PCQ)	39 items 5-point scale 8 subscales that fell into 3 factors	Painful events	8–18 years	• Information seeking • Problem-solving • Seeking social support • Positive self-statements	• Externalizing • Internalizing/ catastrophising	• Positive self-statements • Behavioral distraction • Cognitive distraction
Varni, Katz, Colegrove *et al.* (1996)	Paediatric Pain Coping Inventory	41 items 3-point scale 5 factors	Illness-related problems	5–17 years	• Strive to rest and be alone • Problem-solving– self-efficacy • Cognitive self-instruction • Cognitive refocusing	• Seeking social support	

similarities and differences of the coping inventories' key features indicates the complexities of coping measurement.

Scale description

A coping inventory typically comprises a number of items that refer to different ways of dealing with concerns, and respondents indicate their frequency of use of each coping action. Most of the coping inventories reviewed comprise items that fall into broader groupings. Only one inventory, Kidcope, has no broad grouping of items. The inventories range in number of items from 10 (Kidcope: Spirito, Stark and Williams, 1988) to 80 (Adolescent Coping Scale, ACS: Frydenberg and Lewis, 1993a), which indicates that the completion time also varies. Inventories for young respondents must take into account the two competing aims, namely depth of analysis and minimization of response fatigue. This led to the creation of the 18-item short form of the ACS. This allows for the same 18 coping strategies to be assessed as the long form, but it has only one item per strategy. However, the shorter version of the ACS limits the range of coping actions that can be identified and so the initial long form is still commonly used.

All inventories are self-report and use an item response scale comprising four, five or six points for frequency of use. Only one scale, Kidcope, investigated how effective respondents perceived the behaviours or cognitions and how much they used the items.

Scale development

The inventories were developed primarily from one of three different approaches. The first approach was deductive and involved authors developing items from the coping and stress literature. The second approach was inductive and involved adolescent interviews to identify the ways in which young people coped with their concerns. The third approach involved the redevelopment of an adult coping inventory into a version suitable for adolescents. Regardless of the approach used, all inventories were then tested, refined and validated with adolescent samples.

Stressors

Stressors can be sorted into numerous categories (see chapter 1) that include daily hassles such as a quarrel with a friend; normative stresses such as dealing with bodily changes during puberty; chronic stresses such as dealing with a permanent physical disability; and traumatic stresses such as a divorce in the family. There are various ways in which people cope across these categories and with different stressors within each category. Thus there is interest in not only understanding how adolescents cope in general, but also with particular stressors. Some inventories therefore ask respondents about the ways they cope in general; others ask respondents to pick their major recent stressor and refer to that when completing the scale; and others again provide specific stressful situations to guide respondents. Inventories that refer to self-identified recent stressful events provide information about how adolescents cope with severe stressors, which has been the traditional interest in the coping literature. The Coping Across Situations Questionnaire (Seiffge-Krenke, 1995) measures coping with everyday stressors. Finding out how adolescents cope in general is also important for identifying the helpful and unhelpful ways of coping they commonly employ. Moreover, comparing how adolescents cope across different situations is necessary given the complexity and variety of coping responses.

The ACS, for example, is available in two forms: the General Form investigates coping in general, whereas the Specific Form investigates coping with a particular stressor (see later in this chapter). Adolescents completing the Specific Form can be provided with the stressor, or are asked to think of one themselves. When the ACS is used for clinical purposes, it can be useful to compare coping in general with coping with a particular concern.

Adolescents may experience pain through illness or accident, and the level and duration of pain can range from severe to mild and short-term to long-term. How adolescents cope with pain is of particular importance with respect to illnesses such as cancer and diabetes and their treatment. Research suggests that how young people cope with pain may influence pain levels, emotional distress and functional disability. For example, Non-Productive emotion-focused coping strategies such as arguing, yelling and catastrophizing have been associated with greater pain intensity and emotional distress (Reid, Gilbert and McGrath, 1998). Therefore knowing how adolescents cope with pain and helping them to cope more effectively may be a useful component of treatment. Given the adverse effect Non-Productive coping can have on one's experience of pain, it seems that the Paediatric Pain Coping Inventory is less helpful than the Kidcope and the Pain Coping Questionnaire because it does not provide an adequate measure of Non-Productive coping.

Age sample

Adolescents sampled in the development of the inventories ranged in age from 10 years to young adulthood. Age differences in coping exist within the adolescent period, which is to be expected given the significant cognitive growth and experiences that occur over these years. Thus it may be important for future developments or redevelopments of coping inventories to recruit adolescents from a wide age grouping to generate and validate the items.

Dimensions of coping

Not only are there variations in the number of items across coping inventories, but there are also variations in the grouping of items. Factor analysis is the statistical technique used to condense a larger number of items into a smaller number of groupings, or underlying dimensions. Factor analysis has been used both to identify and confirm the dimensions of coping measured by each coping inventory. Different numbers of factors have emerged, ranging from three to 18. In parallel, coping theory has also identified dimensions of coping. The combined coping theory and research has thus generated a number of different ways of categorizing coping, with dichotomous distinctions including those between problem-focused and emotion-focused coping and between functional and dysfunctional and direct and indirect coping.

As discussed in other parts of this book, some researchers have advocated a three-factor model of coping that represents its functional and dysfunctional aspects. The functional styles represent direct attempts to deal with the problem, with or without reference to others, while the dysfunctional styles relate to the use of what we have called Non-Productive strategies. Although the categorizations vary across inventories, Table 3.1 indicates that all but three inventories yield factors that could be placed in the dimensions of Productive coping, Reference to Others and Non-Productive coping. Two inventories that did not fit this model (the Response to Stress Questionnaire and the Life Events and Coping Inventory) lacked one or more factors of coping which involved turning to others for support. As mentioned earlier, the Paediatric Pain Coping Inventory lacked one or more factors which involved Non-Productive coping strategies. It is noteworthy that the development of the Cross-Cultural Coping Scale also revealed a similar three-factor structure of coping.

In sum, numerous coping inventories have been developed over the years, and this review has focused on 14 prominent ones. The many differences among the inventories have been highlighted, namely those related to scale description and development, and the types of stressors assessed. Given this variation, it is interesting that almost all of the inventories reviewed gave measures of the three dimensions of coping that refer to functional coping with and without the assistance of others and to dysfunctional coping. Because many of these inventories were empirically developed with young people, we know that adolescents use a host of coping strategies, of which some are indeed dysfunctional and yet are in frequent use.

The development of the Adolescent Coping Scale

The Adolescent Coping Scale (ACS: Frydenberg and Lewis, 1993a) is an example of this evolution of coping scales. It was developed to address some of the problems relating to coping measurement. The starting point was the generation of items from the language and vocabulary of adolescents, with the objective of developing a comprehensive age-appropriate instrument with due consideration of matters of reliability and validity. Since there is an advantage in knowing how people cope with particular concerns as well as with their concerns in general (Frydenberg and Lewis, 1994) and since much of an individual's coping behaviour is situation-specific, there is a Specific Form of the ACS which allows for the measurement of responses to a particular self-nominated (or administrator-nominated) concern, such as a worry about school. But it has also been demonstrated that an individual's choice of coping strategies is to a large extent consistent, regardless of the nature of the concern. Thus there is a General Form of the ACS which addresses how an individual copes with concerns in general.

Both the General and the Specific Forms of the instrument appear in a Long Form (80 items) and a Short Form (18 items). Thus there are four forms of the instrument. The 18-item format is made up of one generic item from each of the 18 subscales that make up the 18 conceptual areas or strategies of coping (see Table 3.2). The Short Form is recommended as a quick screening device and for use in circumstances where it is not practicable to use an 80-item instrument. The 18 items of the Short Form empirically group into three areas that relate to Problem-Focused coping, Reference to Others and Non-Productive coping.

In order to determine young people's coping an open-ended question was used. Thus the ACS' development commenced with the gathering of 'open data' and continued with a series of studies, the results of which

Table 3.2 The conceptual areas of coping identified by the ACS

1 SEEKING SOCIAL SUPPORT is represented by items that indicate an inclination to share the problem with others and enlist support in its management (e.g. Talk to other people to help me sort it out).

2 FOCUS ON SOLVING THE PROBLEM is a problem-focused strategy which tackles the problem systematically by learning about it and takes into account different points of view or options (e.g. Work at solving the problem to the best of my ability).

3 WORK HARD AND ACHIEVE is a factor describing commitment, ambition and industry (e.g. Work hard).

4 WORRY is characterized by items that indicate a concern about the future in general terms or more specifically concern with happiness in the future (e.g. Worry about what is happening).

5 INVESTING IN CLOSE FRIENDS is about engaging in a particular intimate relationship (e.g. Spend more time with boy/girl friend).

6 SEEK TO BELONG indicates a caring and concern for one's relationship with others in general and more specifically concern with what others think (e.g. Improve my relationship with others).

7 WISHFUL THINKING is characterized by items which are based on hope and anticipation of a positive outcome (e.g. Hope for the best).

8 SOCIAL ACTION is about letting others know what is of concern and enlisting support by writing petitions or organizing an activity such as a meeting or a rally (e.g. Join with people who have the same concern).

9 TENSION REDUCTION is characterized by items which reflect an attempt to make oneself feel better by releasing tension (e.g. Make myself feel better by taking alcohol, cigarettes or other drugs).

10 NOT COPING consists of items which reflect the individual's inability to deal with the problem and the development of psychosomatic symptoms (e.g. I have no way of dealing with the situation).

11 IGNORE THE PROBLEM is characterized by items that reflect a conscious blocking out of the problem (e.g. Ignore the problem).

12 SELF-BLAME indicates that an individual sees themselves as responsible for the concern or worry (e.g. Accept that I am responsible for the problem).

13 KEEP TO SELF is characterized by items which reflect the individual's withdrawal from others and wish to keep others from knowing about concerns (e.g. Keep my feelings to myself).

14 SEEK SPIRITUAL SUPPORT is characterized by items that reflect prayer and belief in the assistance of a spiritual leader or Lord (e.g. Pray for help and guidance so that everything will be all right).

15 FOCUS ON THE POSITIVE is represented by items that indicate a positive and cheerful outlook on the current situation. This includes seeing the 'bright side' of circumstances and seeing oneself as fortunate (e.g. Look on the bright side of things and think of all that is good).

16 SEEK PROFESSIONAL HELP denotes the use of a professional adviser, such as a teacher or counsellor (e.g. Discuss the problem with qualified people).

17 SEEK RELAXING DIVERSIONS is about relaxation in general rather than about sport. It is characterized by items that describe leisure activities such as reading and painting (e.g. Find a way to relax, for example, listen to music, read a book, play a musical instrument, watch TV).

18 PHYSICAL RECREATION is characterized by items that relate to playing sport and keeping fit (e.g. Keep fit and healthy).

shaped the form of the questionnaire. Initially 643 respondents aged 15–18 generated 2041 descriptions of how they coped with their major concern. Over a five-year period with many applications in numerous settings, these statements were reduced to the 80 items on the ACS, which comprises 18 scales, each reflecting a different coping strategy and each containing between three and five items. Apart from the last item, which asks students to write down any things they do to cope, other than those things described in the preceding 79 items, each item describes a specific coping action. Respondents indicate the extent to which the coping activity described was used (1 'doesn't apply or don't do it', 2 'used very little', 3 'used sometimes', 4 'used often' and 5 'used a great deal'). The statistical properties of these scales and the details of the five investigations supporting their development are reported in greater detail elsewhere (Frydenberg and Lewis, 1993a, 1996).

The statistical procedure of oblique factor analysis (principal components with Oblimin rotation) was used to establish the 18 related but distinct strategies (subscales) of coping (see Table 3.2). An oblique procedure was used since it was assumed that the subscales would not be entirely orthogonal or independent. That is, it was expected that, while coping could be conceptualized in terms of a number of areas or strategies, each comprising specific actions, these strategies were unlikely to be totally unrelated.

Internal consistency coefficients (Do the items measure the same construct?), also known as alpha coefficients, can, according to Moos and Billings (1982), be as low as 0.44 for coping measures. The ACS has such coefficients (also referred to as alphas) ranging from 0.62 to 0.87 (mean = 0.73) on the Specific Form of the instrument and from 0.54 to 0.84 (mean = 0.71) on the General Form. These alphas compare favourably with those reported elsewhere.

Overall, the test–retest reliability correlations (Do the subscales measure the same construct on repeated occasions?) are moderate rather than high. However, stability of response is not an entirely appropriate way to assess the reliability of students' coping responses, since coping is perceived as a dynamic phenomenon. Test–retest reliabilities for the same subscales range from 0.49 to 0.82 (mean = 0.68) on the Specific Form, and from 0.44 to 0.84 (mean = 0.69) on the General Form.

Predictive validity

Studies to date using these subscales have shown that they have predictive validity, that is, there is an association between constructs of the ACS and related constructs measured by another instrument, in a range of situations. Included in this chapter are a number of studies that have used the ACS. Collectively these studies demonstrate construct validity and each study also provides interesting insights into young people's coping.

The study by McKenzie, Frydenberg and Poole (2004) mentioned in chapter 1, which identified what were the important resources for adolescents, also considered the relationship between resources and coping. A relationship was found between the degree to which students held the resources and the coping styles they used. The young people high in resources tended to use Productive coping strategies, while those low in resources tended to use the Non-Productive strategies. Key variables that separated those high in resources from those with moderate or low resources were the items *work hard to achieve, seek social support*, and *keep to self*. The study draws attention to the plight of those young people with fewer resources who also report using fewer coping strategies. Interventions may be reconsidered in the light of resources development. The resources approach offers a shift in perspective on stress and coping in adolescence, which has implications for treatment, educational development, and future research. That is, the resources that are valued by young people need to be considered along with efforts to teach coping skills. Young people who are low on resources not only need the benefit of Productive coping strategies and need to be taught to limit the use of Non-Productive strategies, but their resource needs may also require attention.

Two early studies (see Table 3.3 on pp. 55–57), the first by Fallon, Frydenberg and Boldero (1993) and the second by Boldero, Frydenberg and Fallon (1993), supported the construct validity of the instrument. The first, using the ACS and the Family Environment Scale (FES: Moos and Moos, 1986), found that there were higher scores on *work hard* and *solve the problem* in families identified as emphasizing the personal growth dimension of Moos and Moos (1986) (see chapter 6). In addition, these families also report greater use of *seek social support* and lower use of *not cope, tension reduction* and *ignore the problem*. Furthermore, in families that are high on religious functioning young people score higher on the *seek spiritual support* scale, and where families are high on conflict there is higher use of *tension reduction*. In the second study, using the ACS and a multidimensional measure of self-concept (SDQ 11: Marsh, 1989) (see chapter 4), it was found that poor self-concept in the area of parent and same-sex relationships was predictive of Non-Productive coping behaviour represented by subscales such as *worry* and *self-blame*. Similarly, higher self-concept in the area of physical abilities was related to the use of *physical recreation*, and *recourse to social action*, while lower self-concept in the area of physical appearance was related to the use of *self-blame* and *not cope*. Finally, academic self-concept was positively related to the use of focus on *solving the problem* and *work hard to achieve* and negatively related to *not cope*. Additional studies relating to construct validity are reported later in this chapter.

While the description of the coping strategies is consistent with their face validity and findings relating to the constructs are presented later in this chapter and throughout the book, two strategies are flagged for special mention. First, the use of *spiritual support*, though not often reported as being used in some contexts, is often identified as differentiating particular groups of young people, for example in an Australian study European-Australian adolescents were found to use more of that strategy than did the Anglo-Australian or Asian-Australian young people (Frydenberg and Lewis, 1993b). Also in our cross-national studies there was a greater use of that strategy by Colombian and Irish adolescents (Frydenberg, Lewis, Kennedy, Ardila, Frindte and Hannoun, 2003). In another study of Anglo-Australian and non-Anglo-Australian students who were labelled a 'minority group' (D'Anastasi and Frydenberg, 2005) spiritual support was used to a greater extent by the minority group of students than the Anglo-Australian students (see also chapter 4).

Spirituality as an indicator of health outcomes was reviewed in light of what Cotton, Zebracki, Rosenthal, Tsevat and Drotar (2006) termed proximal domains such as seeking spiritual support or finding meaning. For example, they found that a higher level of spiritual connectedness, a strong relationship with God and the use of spiritual coping were inversely related to substance use and voluntary sexual activity. These findings appear to be consistent across Hispanic, Caucasian and African-American ethnic groups. Adolescents with potentially life-threatening physical conditions such as cancer or chronic conditions requiring strict adherence to medical regimes such as diabetes and asthma may use spiritual coping in ways that are similar to adults by creating meaning and using social support during the crisis of the illness. In other words, this is similar to adults when they use meaning-making in the face of uncontrollable health-related stressors.

In their review of religion, spirituality and adolescent health out-comes, Cotton and colleagues (2006) comment that, while proximal domains of religion and spirituality, which include spiritual coping and religious decision-making, are considered important as a pro-tection against negative health outcomes, they caution against the potential negative influences of religion and spirituality, exemplified by anger towards God and perceived punishment from God. They cite examples such as the possible conflict between peer influences regarding sexuality and that expected by a religious community.

The second strategy to take particular note of is *self-blame*. We have known for a long time that blaming oneself when things don't go right is not a Productive coping strategy. In a study designed to examine the relationship between general coping responses and states of well-being, two questionnaires were administered to a sample of 1264 12–16-year-old secondary school students (Lewis and Frydenberg, 2005). Generally an increased use of the strategy is associated positively with dysfunction and negatively with well-being. That is, to have a high sense of well-being there needs to be very little self-blaming.

Finally, it should be pointed out that since the items of the ACS were generated by young people in response to questioning about the strategies that they used to cope, some strategies were not spontaneously mentioned. No questionnaire can capture the full range of young people's coping. For example, humour is a strategy that is used, sometimes for release of tension or for engagement with others, sometimes for distraction. Our sense of humour parallels human development itself. In humans there is a steady progression that begins with tickling, peekaboo and tossing baby in the air, and ends with humour. The first type of humour children enjoy is visual puns, while adolescents use trickster humour where someone is the butt of the joke, and older people use humour to cope with the indignities of age. Therefore questioning about the use of humour or teaching young people to use humour as a coping strategy can be useful in many situations.

Studies using the ACS[1]

A series of studies are presented which report the association between coping responses and measures of either self-perception, achievement or dysfunctional behaviour both to support the construct validity of the instrument and to indicate the sort of things we learn about how young people cope (Frydenberg and Lewis, 1999a). The findings from these studies are summarized in Table 3.3.

Self-perception

A study of self-perception and coping (Neill, 1996) involved 63 Australian and 63 South-East Asian secondary students (62 males and

Table 3.3 Summary of validity studies using the ACS

Study	Test(s)	N	Group(s)	Key findings
Self-Perception				
Boldero, J., Frydenberg, E. & Fallon, B. (1993)	ACS SDQ II	208	Adolescents' view of themselves – high and low self-concept	• Poor self-concept in the area of parent and same-sex relationships predicted Non-Productive coping behaviour, namely *worry* and *self-blame* • High self-concept in the area of physical abilities was related to use of *physical recreation and social action* • High academic self-concept was related to use of focus on *solving the problem, work hard and achieve*, low academic self-concept was related to *not cope*
Jenkin, C. (1997)	ACS	134	Year 8 – Outward Bound programme	• High general self-efficacy more *work hard, solving the problem, focus on the positive*
Neill, L. (1996)	ACS Self-Esteem Scale	126	South-East Asian Yr 11 students studying in Australia compared to Australian students	• Students with low self-esteem use more Non-Productive coping, namely *not cope, worry, self-blame, keep to self* • South-East Asian students more *Reference to Others*
Stevenson, R. (1996)	ACS (Short Specific) SDQ III PSS	162	High and low perceived stress and academic self-concept	• Negative academic self-concept, more Non-Productive coping • Lower perceived stress, more *solving the problem*

continues overleaf

Table 3.3 (continued)

Study	Test(s)	N	Group(s)	Key findings
Achievement Noto, S. (1995)	ACS	90 girls & 374 boys	High achievers (regardless of gender & IQ)	• High achievers more *work hard, solve the problem, social support, focus on the positive* Less *not cope, tension reduction, ignore the problem* • Achievement negatively related to *invest in close friends*
Parsons, A., Frydenberg, E. & Poole, C. (1996)	ACS	374 boys	Overachieving vs other boys	• Overachieving boys used more *social support*, less *not cope*
Dysfunction Chesire, G. (1996)	ACS	60	Learning disabled vs non-learning disabled	• Learning disabled less likely to *relax, work hard, focus on the positive* • Less *solve problem* • More *wishful thinking* and more *not cope*
Cunningham, E. (1997)	ACS (Short General) CDI Teacher depression rating	94 students 47 teachers	High- vs low-risk depression	• Non-Productive coping style predictive of depression • Active problem-focused coping style (inversely) predictive of depression

Reference	Instruments	N	Sample	Findings
Davies, S. (1995)	ACS II	25	12–14 yr gifted accelerated programme	• Rigid beliefs about self, more Non-Productive coping • More *worry, seek to belong, wishful thinking, self-blame and keep to self*
McTaggart, H. (1996)	ACS	32	Mainstream and Teaching Unit (Problem Behaviour)	• Teaching Unit more *worry, ignore, keep to self, tension reduction*
Poot, A.C. (1997)	ACS YSR BDI Self-Esteem	50	Intervention programme for young with problems	• Non-Productive coping associated with more problems, lower self-concept, greater depression
Szczepanski, H. (1995)	ACS DRL Home-sickness	77	High and low homesickness for boarding-school girls	• Less adaptive more *tension reduction, keep to self, less focus on the positive* • Less homesickness more *solve problem, focus on the positive, relax, physical recreation* • Less homesick more Productive coping
Fallon, B., Frydenberg, E. & Boldero, J. (1993)	ACS FES	108	Perceived family functioning and coping	• Adolescents from families who make frequent use of personal growth dimensions (achievement, intellectual/cultural orientation, moral/religious emphasis) use more *work hard, social support and solve the problem* strategies. • Adolescents who report frequent family conflict and control report high use of *tension reduction* strategies.

64 females, aged 15–21) who competed the General Long Form of the ACS and the Rosenberg Self-Esteem Scale (Rosenberg, 1989).

Low self-esteem was significantly associated with Non-Productive coping, with 17 per cent of the variance in Non-Productive coping related to self-esteem. *Not cope, worry, self-blame*, and *keep to self* were each significantly associated with nationality, which predicted at least 10 per cent of the variance of each of these respective strategies. In all cases low self-esteem predicted greater use of these Non-Productive strategies. No significant interactions or gender effects were reported.

In another study, 162 final-year high school students (116 females and 46 males) completed the Specific Short Form of the Adolescent Coping Scale, the Self Description Questionnaire (SDQ 111: Marsh, 1994), and the Perceived Stress Scale (PSS: Australian Catholic University, 1996). Administration was one week prior to the submission of a required Common Assessment Task which in part contributes to the final tertiary entrance score. The investigation focused on the relationship between academic self-concept, perceived stress, and coping styles used by high school students in their final year of schooling (Stevenson, 1996). It was found that higher use of *solving the problem* coping (also referred to as the Productive coping style) was associated with lower perceived stress. Higher Non-Productive coping was associated with both higher perceived stress and lower academic self-concept. Females used more Reference to Others and more Non-Productive coping than males, but the use of *solving the problem* was not different for boys and girls.

Finally, one study examined the relationship between coping and self-efficacy. Jenkin (1997) surveyed 135 13–14-year-old students (81 male and 54 female) who were participants in a school-initiated Outward Bound (rugged outdoor camping) programme. The instruments used were the Specific Long Form of the ACS, a Self-Efficacy scale (Shever *et al.*, 1982), and a Physical Self-Efficacy measure (Ryckman, Robins, Thornton and Cantrell, 1982). A discriminant function analysis[2] found that the best predictors for distinguishing between high and low self-efficacy were the coping strategies *focus on the positive, focus on solving the problem* and *work hard to achieve*. A combination of these strategies accurately predicted low or high self-efficacy (top and bottom quartiles) for 70 per cent of the sample. Whereas 77 per cent of those in the bottom quartile of efficacy could be correctly identified by their lesser use of these strategies, prediction of those in the high efficacy group was less successful (65 per cent). Therefore, although a relative absence of these productive strategies is predictive of self-perceived inability to cope, students scoring higher on self-efficacy are not necessarily those who employ more of these strategies.

Although a number of Outward Bound instructors predicted that, as a result of their programme, there would be a possible increase in seven student coping strategies (*physical recreation, social action, social support and fitting in with friends, work hard to achieve, focus on the positive* and *solving the problem*), only three of these showed an increase. Nevertheless, the fact that the instructors identified these strategies provides a measure of construct validity for each.

Achievement

Two studies looked at the relationship between achievement and coping. In the first (Parsons, Frydenberg and Poole, 1996), 'capable' boys were compared with the regular student body of males using 374 boys in Grades 9, 10 and 11 at an independent boys' school in Melbourne. Capable students were less likely than those less capable to declare that they did not have the strategies to cope. It was also found that boys who achieved better than would be expected on the basis of ability alone ('over-achievement'), used more *social support* as a strategy for coping than did their peers.

Second, in a study by Noto (1995), a sample of 90 female adolescent students (Years 9, 10 and 11) completed the Adolescent Coping Scale and the data were compared to the 374 boys included in the Parsons, Frydenberg and Poole (1996) study. IQ was measured by a widely used Australian paper-and-pencil group test of intelligence. Academic achievement scores were based on an average of all final-year results from the previous year. When measuring the relationship between coping and achievement, Noto controlled for gender and IQ by using partial correlations. When the relationship between coping and academic achievement was investigated, significant positive correlations were reported for the problem-focused strategies *work hard and achieve, focus on solving the problem, seek social support* and *focus on the positive*. Significant negative correlations were reported for three Non-Productive strategies: *not cope, tension reduction* and *ignoring the problem*. It was also found that high use of the strategy *invest in close friends* was negatively associated with achievement.

Dysfunction

In addition to studies of self-perception, achievement and coping, there is a growing body of evidence that supports the construct validity of the ACS by highlighting the finding that various forms of behaviour which could be characterized as dysfunctional are associated with a greater use of Non-Productive coping responses, or a lesser use of Productive ones.

First, 30 learning-disabled students (aged 13 to 15 years, $M = 13.5$ years, $SD = 0.63$) completed the Long Form of the ACS. Their coping responses were compared to a group of average or high-achieving non-learning-disabled students, matched in age, gender and ethnicity (Cheshire and Campbell, 1996). The matched design of the study effectively controlled for differences in coping strategies for gender, ethnicity and age. A MANOVA analysis found that the learning-disabled group used more *wishful thinking* and believing that they were not coping than the average achieving adolescents. Further, Productive strategies such as *focusing on the positive*, *relaxing* and *working to solve the problem* were used less by the learning-disabled group. Overall, learning-disabled students used significantly less of a coping style that focused on the problem than did their average-achieving peers. The remaining styles, which reflected Reference to Others and Non-Productive coping, showed no significant differences between the two groups.

Second, the coping strategies of eight students (6 male and 2 female) attending a special setting for behaviourally disordered post-primary students were compared to those used by 24 peers (8 male and 16 female) drawn from Year 8 classes in two mainstream settings. To assess their coping the General Long Form of the ACS was employed (McTaggart, 1996). The students in the specific setting were attending a Teaching Unit and were considered to be at risk of exclusion from high school since they had been suspended for more than 10 days within the previous six months or the current school year.

Students in the two settings differed significantly in their use of the strategies *work hard*, *solve the problem*, *keep to self*, *social support*, *seek professional help* and *relax*. The main effect for work by school group membership is most evident. Analyses for coping styles by school indicated that effective coping (*solve the problem*) is significantly associated with school type, whereas there were no significant differences on the main effects in mean scores for Reference to Others and Non-Productive coping.

Membership of the mainstream groups is associated with greater use of *solve the problem*, which in conjunction with greater use of *work hard*, represents a powerful combination of approach (solution-focused) coping. Strategies more closely associated with membership of the Teaching Unit Group were *keep to self*, *seek professional help* and *social action*. These data indicate that membership of the mainstream is clearly associated with the use of effective, problem-focused coping strategies. However, differences between groups in Non-Productive coping were not as apparent as expected, and the small sample size limits the confidence that can be placed in the results.

In a third study which examined the relationship between adolescent self-reported coping, teacher evaluations, and depression, 94 Year 9 students (40 males and 54 females with an average age of 14.5 years) at a secondary school in outer metropolitan Melbourne (Cunningham, 1997) were administered the General Short Form of the ACS and the Children's Depression Inventory (Kovacs, 1992). Each of the 47 participating teachers completed a 10-item teacher depression rating scale, derived from the Children's Depression Scale (Lang and Tisher, 2004), on the participating students.

A hierarchical regression analysis was used to determine to what extent teachers' perceptions of depression and self-reported coping strategies predict self-reported depression. It was found that the Non-Productive coping style of the ACS was capable of predicting an additional 38 per cent of the variance in depression scores above teacher ratings alone. The inclusion of an active coping style comprising the strategies *solve the problem*, *seek social support*, *physical recreation*, *relaxation* and *focus on the positive* contributed a further 12 per cent. While the three predictor variables accounted for 60 per cent of the variance in depression scores, only Non-Productive and active coping styles remained significant predictors when all three variables were included.

Discriminant function analysis was used to predict two levels of depression, using the dichotomy high-risk/low-risk. A variate associated with more Non-Productive coping and less active coping, combined with teacher ratings, accurately categorized 89 per cent of adolescents as either high-risk or low-risk. The results were cross-validated on an independent sample and support a strong positive relationship between self-reported depression and Non-Productive or avoidance coping style, and a negative association with an active or problem-focused coping style. Thus, the less one was actively and positively engaged in activities (a measure of depression being the absence of positive affect), the more one used Non-Productive or avoidance coping strategies, and the less one used adaptive coping strategies. Furthermore, Non-Productive coping was associated more strongly with the depressive measure than was active coping, while the converse held for the positive depression measure.

The fourth study of 50 adolescents (35 males and 15 female with an average age of 14 years) reports an investigation of participants in a brief intervention programme for young people with emotional, behavioural, social and/or psychotic difficulties (Poot, 1997). Measures used were the Youth Self-Report Scale (Achenbach, 1988), the ACS (Frydenberg and Lewis, 1993a), the Beck Depression Inventory (Beck, 1987) and a Self-Esteem scale (Coopersmith, 1967). The analysis produced a two-factor orthogonal factor solution on 24 young people who provided complete data on the four measures. The factor analysis accounted for 80.2 per cent of the variance. Poot identified a factor she termed Dysfunction which accounted for 50 per cent of the variance of the four measures. Dysfunction was characterized by more reported problems, lower self-concept, greater depression and the ACS coping style labelled Non-Productive coping. The loadings of the other ACS styles, Reference to Others and *solving the problem*, on this factor were .04 and .06. The second factor, which Poot called Productive Coping, had only two significant loadings, the two ACS coping styles Reference to Others and *solving the problem*. None of the other aforementioned measures loaded significantly on this factor.

Finally, two studies focused on less severe forms of dysfunction. The first investigated homesickness (Szczepanski, 1995) and the second sampled 25 gifted young people selected for an accelerated high school programme (Davies, 1995). In the first study (Szczepanski, 1995) 77 female boarding-school students aged 12–18 years (in Grades 7–12) completed three instruments. Twenty-four of the students were in their first year of boarding and 53 were in their second, third and fourth years. The students were attending a middle-sized independent girls' secondary school located in metropolitan Melbourne. The instruments completed were first, the Specific Form of the ACS, second, a self-evaluation questionnaire about homesickness, with questions relating to duration of boarding, previous boarding experiences, sister at school, and frequency of homesickness; and third, the Dundee Relocation Inventory (DRI: Fisher, 1989).

Szczepanski (1995), using the DRI, identified two factors which significantly predicted self-reported level of homesickness. She then investigated the association between scores on these two factors, general adaptation to environment and missing home, and the strategies and styles assessed by the ACS. Coping strategies that significantly correlated with homesickness were *worry*, *not cope*, *self-blame* and *keep to self*. Thus the more homesick students are more likely to use Non-Productive strategies. Less successful adaptation to the new environment was associated statistically with greater use of *tension reduction* and *keep to self*, and a lesser use of *focus on the positive*. Further, less homesickness was associated with greater use of *solve the problem, focus on the positive, relaxation* and *physical recreation*. In terms of the three styles assessed by the ACS, more use of the effective coping style is associated with better integration into the new environment and less homesickness.

In the second study, Davies (1995) investigated the relationship between rigid beliefs about oneself and coping. Twenty-five Year 8 students (17 males and 8 females) aged 12–14 years, who attended an accelerated learning programme in a government secondary school in metropolitan Melbourne, completed the General and Specific Forms of the ACS, and the Idea Inventory (II: Kassinove, Crisci and Teigerman, 1977). The II is a 33-item instrument that assesses the degree of endorsement of a number of irrational ideas about the self and others. The II scores ranged from 33 to 99, with lower scores indicating rigid beliefs and higher scores indicating more flexible beliefs. A cut-off score of 66 was used to determine group allocation. Students with scores below 66 (n = 13) were considered as characterized by rigid beliefs and students with scores above 66 (n = 11) were allocated to a group containing students with more flexible beliefs. Students in Group 1 (Rigid Beliefs) used Non-Productive coping strategies to a significantly greater extent than students in Group 2. Group 1 students used *worry, seek to belong, wishful thinking, self-blame* and *keep to self* more than those in Group 2 for coping with General Concerns, and *worry, wishful thinking, ignore the problem* and *self-blame* to a greater extent for Coping with Specific Concerns.

Implications of these studies

In summary, the above studies illustrate that significant relationships exist between a range of socially significant variables and the nature of coping. Generally, greater use of Non-Productive strategies such as *keep to self, tension reduction, worry* and *self-blame* are associated with greater dysfunction. Conversely, lesser use of these strategies is associated with greater academic performance and academic self-concept. In addition, greater use of some Productive strategies such as *work hard, solve the problem* and *seek social support* are also associated with greater academic performance. Additionally, these studies provide strong support for the construct validity of the ACS.

Research decisions on whether to use individual strategies or styles depend on the type of analysis, the sample size, the research question of interest, and the power of the test. The ACS, comprising the 18 strategies and three styles, has the potential for both fine-grained analyses and those using a broader grouping of strategies.

When the studies reported above are considered, it can be seen that some studies reported results for strategies and styles whereas others reported on either strategies or styles but not on both. One study adopts a methodology whereby the only strategies investigated are those that comprise a style that is a statistically significant predictor (Neill, 1996).

The data for strategies are of most interest because they show a need to retain this fine-grained level of measurement or run the risk of 'washing out' potentially significant results. For example, in her comparison of achievement and coping, Noto (1995) observes that when the effects of IQ and sex are controlled, achievement is significantly negatively associated with the strategy *invest in close friends* but positively associated with *social support*. Consequently, although these strategies may naturally occur in conjunction, to add their effects confounds the analysis. Similarly, McTaggart (1996) reports that 'students at risk' are more likely to attempt to *solve the problem* but less likely to *seek professional help*. Consequently, adding these two conceptually associated strategies also introduces Type 11 errors by covering up real effects. That is, there is a difference and we have missed it.

Finally, Chesire and Campbell (1997) report that the learning-disabled are significantly less likely to *focus on the positive* yet more likely to engage in *wishful thinking*. Therefore, any emotion-focused coping style that combines these strategies would probably have no significant associations with learning disability.

In sum, the ACS has been shown to be useful in a range of settings and to have adequate reliability and strong evidence of validity. The use of the Long Form should be encouraged for investigations of coping patterns of adolescents since combining strategies to form styles may lead to Type 11 errors, whereas genuine differences between sub-samples remain undetected. This is the case even when such strategies are naturally associated.

This last point is particularly important because the establishment of styles is generally based on an investigation of empirical relationships using procedures such as factor analysis. Such statistical analyses use a natural association between strategies as their criterion for the formation of styles, and do not consider associations between each of these respective strategies and outcome measures. Consequently the findings reported in this section provide support for the argument put forward by Ebata and Moos (1994) and Stanton, Danoff-Burg, Cameron and Ellis (1994) to retain consideration of fine-grained measures (such as the 18 strategies provided by the ACS) in addition to any styles that may be used by combining strategies.

Features of the ACS

Utility of function compensates for any lack in validity and reliability data available for what is generally termed a transactional process. Like the adult measures such as the WOCQ (Folkman and Lazarus, 1988b), the ACS uses a combination of conceptual groupings and factor-analytic approaches, and the broad groupings can be divided according to finer categorizations.

The issue of dispositional and episodic coping and the distinction between inter- and intra-individual differences has been addressed by referring respectively to the General and Specific elements of the construct. It has been found that the Specific Form of the ACS that asks a young person to focus on a particular problem can be used to minimize the situational determinants, while the General Form provides a convenient way of determining how an individual copes over a range of circumstances. The importance of 'shifting flexibility' in coping styles, as pointed out by Seiffge-Krenke and Shulman (1990), was also anticipated in the conceptualization and measurement of coping by obtaining responses to the specific and general elements of the construct.

The functional value of the ACS is related to the fact that it identifies a greater number of conceptual areas of coping than do most other instruments. When a diverse set of coping strategies has been identified, the information can be used to draw up a profile of coping for individuals or groups. The individual items, or the strategies, collectively act as mental prompts and enable young people to reflect meaningfully on their coping actions. This in turn may lead to behavioural change in self-nominated directions. For example, if a young person had identified that he or she had used *wishful thinking* a great deal when managing relationship issues like being excluded by friends, they might be counselled to approach a friend to discuss what was happening and how best to deal with it (*seeking social support*). In the case of Samantha, a 14-year-old who was feeling shut out by girls in her class, her ability to use the support of others enabled her to make a decision to develop friendships with girls with whom she shared sporting interests (problem-focused coping).

All coping instruments have potential clinical applications in that they provide the data about an individual's coping that can then be used as part of a clinical intervention. However, where the subscale represents too broad a range of actions, the limited range of subscales restricts an instrument's potential for clinical utility.

A feature of the ACS is its ready application in clinical contexts in that it identifies 79 coping actions and a comprehensive range (18) of coping strategies. While no list of coping actions is exhaustive, and indeed interviews with young people reveal that there is great variation in the coping actions they use, the 79 items provide a starting point that enables young people to focus on their coping actions and provide a stimulus for introspection or self-reflection. The 18 coping strategies can be presented as an ideographic profile discussion or reflection. This profile is informative in its own right or it can be used to target strategies whose use may be reduced or extended.

Candy and Amy

Two profiles are presented below as ideographic representations of young people's coping. The circumstances of the two girls presented are somewhat similar but their ways of coping are highly contrasted.

Candy and Amy are two 13-year-old girls whose parents have divorced, Candy's when she was 8 and Amy's when she was 3 years old. Candy, who was experiencing ongoing family conflict, illustrates by her general coping profile that she often uses many Non-Productive coping strategies. She keeps to herself a great deal but tempers this with substantial relaxation. Included in her Non-Productive coping strategies, however, is the frequent use of *worry, wishful thinking, tension reduction, ignoring the problem* and frequent feelings of helplessness and a declared inability to cope. In contrast, at the time of completing the questionnaire Amy's mother was about to remarry but Amy was having difficulties with her stepfather. She frequently resorts to *solving her problems* and *working hard* and is less likely to use Non-Productive coping strategies.

Summary

Since coping is such a widely researched phenomenon there is considerable diversity in the number of identified constructs and styles or strategies. This is reflected in the groupings of items. In the last decade there has been an increase in the range of coping inventories developed and used around the globe. There are three main methods of scale development: a deductive approach with items developed from stress/coping literature; an inductive approach using adolescent reviews; and redevelopment of adult inventories.

One approach to scale development used widely and developed by Frydenberg and Lewis for use with adolescents, namely the Adolescent Coping Scale, was presented as an example of scale development. Numerous studies that use this instrument are reported throughout the

© 1993 Erica Frydenberg, Ramon Lewis

Name _____   Date _____   Form ☐ General ☐ Specific

Scale	Description
1. SocSup	**Seek Social Support** – sharing my problem with others; enlisting their support, encouragement and advice.
2. SolvProb	**Focus on Solving the Problem** – tackling my problem systematically by thinking about it and taking other points of view into account.
3. Work	**Work Hard and Achieve** – being conscientious about my (school) work; working hard, and achieving high standards.
4. Worry	**Worry** – worrying about the future in general and my personal happiness in particular.
5. Friends	**Invest in Close Friends** – spending time being with close friends and making new friendships.
6. Belong	**Seek to Belong** – being concerned with what others think, and doing things to gain their approval.
7. WishThink	**Wishful Thinking** – hoping for the best, that things will sort themselves out, that a miracle will happen.
8. NotCope	**Not Coping** – not doing anything about my problem, giving up, feeling ill.
9. TensRed	**Tension Reduction** – making myself feel better by letting off steam, taking my frustration out on others, crying, screaming, taking alcohol, cigarettes or drugs.
10. SocAc	**Social Action** – enlisting support by organising group action to deal with my concerns, and attending meetings and rallies.
11. Ignore	**Ignore the Problem** – consciously blocking out the problem, pretending it doesn't exist.
12. SelfBl	**Self-Blame** – being hard on myself, seeing myself as being responsible for the problem.
13. KeepSelf	**Keep to Self** – keeping my concerns and feelings to myself, avoiding other people.
14. Spirit	**Seek Spiritual Support** – praying for help and guidance, reading a holy book.
15. FocPos	**Focus on the Positive** – looking on the bright side of things, reminding myself that there are others who are worse off, trying to stay cheerful.
16. ProfHelp	**Seek Professional Help** – discussing my problem with a professionally qualified person.
17. Relax	**Seek Relaxing Diversions** – taking my mind off the problem by finding ways to relax such as reading a book, watching television, going out and having a good time.
18. PhysRec	**Physical Recreation** – playing sport and keeping fit.

Scale axis: Adjusted Score (Gen. / Spec.) — Not used at all — Used very little — Used sometimes — Used frequently — Used a great deal

Scale	Not used at all	Used very little	Used sometimes	Used frequently	Used a great deal
1. SocSup	20 / 30	40 / 50	60 / 70	80 / 90	100
2. SolvProb	20 / 30	40 / 50	60 / 70	80 / 90	100
3. Work	20 / 30	40 / 50	60 / 70	80 / 90	100
4. Worry	20 / 30	40 / 50	60 / 70	80 / 90	100
5. Friends	20 / 30	40 / 50	60 / 70	80 / 90	100
6. Belong	20 / 30	40 / 50	60 / 70	80 / 90	100
7. WishThink	20 / 30	40 / 50	60 / 70	80 / 90	100
8. NotCope	20 / 30	40 / 50	60 / 70	80 / 90	100
9. TensRed	20 / 30	40 / 50	60 / 70	80 / 90	100
10. SocAc	20 / 30	40 / 50	60 / 70	80 / 90	100
11. Ignore	20 / 30	40 / 50	60 / 70	80 / 90	100
12. SelfBl	20 / 30	40 / 50	60 / 70	80 / 90	100
13. KeepSelf	20 / 30	40 / 50	60 / 70	80 / 90	100
14. Spirit	20 / 30	40 / 50	60 / 70	80 / 90	100
15. FocPos	20 / 30	40 / 50	60 / 70	80 / 90	100
16. ProfHelp	20 / 30	40 / 50	60 / 70	80 / 90	100
17. Relax	21 / 31	42 / 52	63 / 73	84 / 94	105
18. PhysRec	21 / 31	42 / 52	63 / 73	84 / 94	105

Candy ———   Amy – – – – –

Figure 3.1 Candy and Amy profile

book. The ACS identifies 18 conceptual areas which are then grouped into three coping styles: Productive, Non-Productive and Reference to Others. Studies that have used the ACS have focused on depression, self-perception, self-efficacy, achievement and dysfunction. Generally use of Non-Productive strategies is associated with greater dysfunction. Analysis of the 18 strategies yields more fine-grained results and a deeper analysis of potential differences between groups of adolescents. Some significant findings are reported. For example, spiritual support differentiates groups of adolescents on a cultural basis and there is greater use of that strategy within chronically ill populations. Conflicts may arise as a result of strict religious beliefs and ideas about sexuality, intimacy, alcohol and drug use. Development of coping with pain inventories measures how coping style influences pain levels and distress experienced. Finally, there is a strong connection between use of self-blame and dysfunction.

Generally, the chapter demonstrates the broad applicability of the ACS across different settings. Information obtained from the ACS is useful for large-scale sampling, group comparisons and/or individual clinical intervention.

4   The correlates of coping: age, personality and ethnicity

When I was in primary school I had fun and didn't get stressed about work

(Girl, 14)

I get really angry at myself or someone else and then I break something . . . I go to my room and just break something.

(Boy, 15)

I was born in Australia. My father came from Italy and my mum from Saudi Arabia. My dad speaks Italian with his friends. My mum was born in Saudi Arabia but she speaks Greek. It's pretty much what you see on TV, the feasts come in for special occasions. Yeah, it's pretty woggish.

(Girl, 16)

There are numerous constructs that can be interpreted as correlates of coping. Age and gender are frequently cited, as are personality characteristics such as hope, resilience, optimism and self-esteem. By their very nature these constructs are culturally embedded. Just as there are both similarities and differences in the way young people from different communities identify their concerns, so there are similarities and differences in the way they cope. Each of the above correlates will be addressed in turn. Gender can also be considered as a correlate of coping but since it is the most frequently identified correlate it is addressed in chapter 5. Each of the correlates may contribute in its own way to the coping actions of the individual. Sometimes it is not possible to account for the impact of one factor to the exclusion of another, but the studies below indicate the influence that each of the factors being considered may have on the coping actions of the individual.

Age and coping

An accumulation of research findings over the years indicates that there are important differences in coping across the lifespan. Skinner and Zimmer-Gembeck (2007) advocate that it is time we applied a developmental framework to coping. In infancy, coping is akin to emotional regulation. Over time, coping develops from being simple reactions to stress responses to highly co-ordinated and specialized cognitive efforts to regulate the stressor, or to control the effects of the stressor on the individual. The adolescent years represent a period of rapid physical, social, emotional and cognitive development. Similarly, there are changes in coping from early to late adolescence, which have been identified in both cross-sectional and longitudinal studies.

There is a body of evidence from both sorts of studies that functional coping decreases with age (Compas, Malcarne and Fondacaro, 1988; Seiffge-Krenke and Shulman, 1990; Frydenberg and Lewis, 2000; see later in this chapter), while emotional coping increases with school grade (Compas *et al.*, 1988). For example, older adolescents generally use more tension-reducing strategies (use of alcohol, cigarettes or other drugs) than do younger adolescents (Compas *et al.*, 1988; Frydenberg and Lewis, 1993b). In one study it was found that those who used more approach (problem-focused) coping were older, more active, appraised the immediate stressor as controllable and as a challenge, and had more ongoing social resources (Ebata and Moos, 1994).

One cross-sectional study compared the coping actions of 829 Australian secondary students using the ACS (Frydenberg and Lewis, 1999b). Students were grouped according to age. The early adolescent group comprised students aged 11–13 years, the middle adolescent group comprised students aged 14–16 years and the late adolescent group comprised students aged 17–19 years. Overall, results indicated that the students most frequently called on the coping strategies of *solve the problem* and *work hard*. They also commonly used the strategies of *physical recreation, seek social support, invest in close friendships, wishful thinking* and *focus on the positive*. In contrast, the students reported very little use of *seek professional help, social action* and *spiritual support*. The strongest age-related findings were that older adolescents were more likely to blame themselves for things gone wrong and use tension reduction strategies, such as *drink alcohol and smoking*, than younger adolescents. Moreover, results indicated that students aged 14 and above reported less use of the strategies of *solve the problem, work hard, seek spiritual support* and *focus on the positive*.

The tendency of older adolescents to use Non-Productive coping strategies was higher in female students than male students. In sum, this study indicated that, although adolescents of all ages reported working hard in order to deal with their concerns, their use of problem-solving decreased and their use of Non-Productive strategies increased, which indicates an increase in adolescent vulnerability with age.

A German cross-sectional study investigated how children and adolescents cope with their concerns and also reported age differences in coping (Hampel and Petermann, 2005). Eleven hundred and twenty-three children and adolescents aged 8 to 14 years (M = 10.76, 526 males, 597 females) were separated into three age groups: late childhood, early adolescence and middle adolescence (Stressverarbeitungs-fragebogen für Kinder und Jugendliche, SVF-KJ), which is a 36-item self-report questionnaire that assesses nine different coping strategies and three domains of coping: emotion-focused coping, problem-focused coping (similar to solving the problem) and maladaptive coping. Findings indicated that both adolescent groups' reported use of the maladaptive strategies of rumination and aggression were significantly higher than the late childhood group's reported use. In contrast, the late childhood group's reported use of the adaptive and emotion-focused strategy of distraction/recreation was significantly higher than both adolescent groups' reported use.

Closer inspection of the results revealed a poorer coping profile for early adolescent girls. Specifically, early adolescent girls reported using significantly more maladaptive coping and less adaptive coping than late childhood and middle adolescent girls and all boys. These findings differ from the Australian study, which showed an increasing vulnerability with age. However, because the German study did not include late adolescents it is difficult to compare findings across the two studies. Nonetheless, the studies do indicate that there are developmental changes in coping and that early adolescence may represent a shift to a more maladaptive pattern of coping, particularly in girls.

Age differences have most commonly been investigated using cross-sectional designs such as in the above studies. Because of the difficulties in accessing participants over a number of years, there are fewer longitudinal studies that assess changes in coping over time. But although few in number, these studies do provide powerful information to verify findings from cross-sectional studies. In a longitudinal study of 168 adolescents, coping was assessed over a period of five years (Frydenberg and Lewis, 2000)[1] using the ACS. Students were assessed at three points in time, when they were in Year 7 (12–13 years), Year 9 (14–15 years) and Year 11 (16–17 years). Overall, the frequency of use of coping strategies reported by adolescents in this study was similar to the Australian cross-sectional study described earlier (Frydenberg and Lewis, 1999b). Students were most likely to employ the strategies of *work hard, solve the problem* and *relax* and were least likely to use the strategies of *social action* and *seek professional help*.

The age and gender differences found in this study suggest a different developmental pattern of coping for boys and girls. While both boys and girls increased their use of Non-Productive strategies and reduced their use of Productive strategies, namely *social action, physical recreation* and *seek professional help*, over the years, the pattern was augmented for girls. By the age of 16 or 17, adolescent girls were more likely to call on Non-Productive strategies such as *self-blame* and *tension reduction* than older adolescent boys. One of the most important changes was in the strategy *not cope*, particularly for girls, who reported a significantly greater inability to cope by age 16. This study further demonstrates the heightened vulnerability to poorer coping that can develop with age, especially for adolescent girls.

The three studies discussed here demonstrate that there are age differences in coping. The relationship between age and coping is made more complex by gender differences and other changes co-occurring within the individual and their social environment during the adolescent years. Overall, it appears that an increase in age does not necessarily equate to an increase in adaptive coping. For example, older adolescent girls use more *self-blame* than younger adolescent girls. Not all changes are negative and coping efforts such as *social support* and *problem-solving* become more differentiated and specialized in accordance with cognitive development (Skinner and Zimmer-Gembeck, 2005). For example, adolescents become increasingly more able to pinpoint the appropriate people to approach for support in accordance with the type of support required. Moreover, their ability to self-reflect on their coping and to make changes in coping highlights a capacity to intervene positively in the detrimental development of some coping strategies. Adolescents can be taught to call upon Productive strategies that are pinned at the appropriate cognitive level. For example, although early adolescents may not have the capacity to master the finer points of problem-solving such as lateral or creative thinking, they can be taught the skills of brainstorming and encouraged to consider multiple options.

In summary, these studies offer some noteworthy insights into age effects in coping in adolescents and in particular draw our attention to the emergence of a more maladaptive pattern of coping in girls during the adolescent years, which indicates the importance of promoting and teaching for positive adaptation.

Impact of childhood experience on later coping

It is not age alone that makes the difference. Often it is what happens in the earlier years. Several studies have examined the coping of students after their schooling experience to determine how childhood experiences, especially in situations of extreme stress and abuse, affect early adult coping. One study by Leitenberg, Gibson and Novy (2004) of 828 undergraduate women from New England State University in the United States, considered these women's coping with recent stressors, according to whether they had had none, one, two or three types of adverse and/or abusive childhood experiences (sexual abuse, physical abuse, witnessing domestic violence, having an alcoholic parent, and parental rejection). It was found that those with cumulative adverse histories used more disengagement methods of coping (such as *wishful thinking, problem avoidance, social withdrawal* and *self-criticism*). What was interesting was that the engagement methods of coping (such as problem-solving, cognitive restructuring, social support, and the capacity to express emotions) did not show a corresponding decrease as a result of increased exposure to the stressful events. Even more concerning in a study of 577 college students, some of whom had been sexually abused, was that the group who had been abused were more likely to use drugs or alcohol to cope, act out sexually, withdraw from people and seek therapy services. Of particular interest in that study was the capacity to predict post-traumatic stress and possible re-victimization through the more frequent use of Non-Productive coping strategies, in particular the use of *self-blame* at the time of the abuse and currently (Filipas and Ullman, 2006). Similarly, in a smaller-scale study of adolescents in foster care, it was also found that those who had been abused used more Non-Productive coping strategies (Browne, 2002). Overall, we know that what happens in childhood, particularly in adverse circumstances, determines how one copes in later years.

Personality

There has been a strong re-emergence of interest in the role that personality traits play in coping and adaptation (Costa, Somerfield and McCrae, 1996; Suls, David and Harvey, 1996; Watson and Hubbard, 1996), although situational measures have dominated coping for 20

years (Lazarus and Folkman, 1984). In line with this interest in per-
sonological factors, several dispositional measures of coping have been
developed (Ayers, Sandler, West and Roosa, 1996; Carver, Scheier and
Weintraub, 1989) which ask if what people typically do in response to
stressful events is substantially stable over time and broadly consistent
in different situations. This is in contrast to situational measures like
the Ways of Coping Checklist (Folkman and Lazarus, 1988b). There
are also measures which take account of the person and the situation by
gauging the General and Specific coping of individuals. There is evidence for cross-situational consistency of coping and temporal changes
(Frydenberg and Lewis, 1994, 2000). Research over the past decade has
shown that coping behaviours are heavily influenced by the characteristics of the individual, especially personality traits (Bolger, 1990;
Costa *et al.*, 1996; Watson, David and Suls, 1999). What people do in
response to stress and in dealing with their lives is largely determined by
who they are and by their enduring dispositions. Personality traits are
not easily changed, so coping and the achievement of success will
always be easier for some than for others.

The role of temperament is often cited as an important determinant
of coping responses (e.g. Rutter, 1981; Kagan, 1983). It is also the
foundation of personality. Temperament generally refers to an individual's stable and consistent dispositions, the usual style of emotional
and behavioural responses of an individual that are predictable.
Temperament has been defined as 'those aspects of behaviour that
reflect the intrinsic non-maturational stylistic qualities that the individual brings to any particular situation' (Rutter and Rutter, 1992, p.
185). Rutter and Rutter argue that these intrinsic qualities have a
biological basis that includes a genetic component, although these
qualities or traits are tempered and influenced by experiences.

In the theory of temperament put forward by Buss and Plomin
(1984), three broad dimensions of personality are considered to be
present in an individual's early years and continue to be relatively
stable throughout later life. These dimensions are emotionality (the
tendency to be easily distressed), activity and sociability. It is suggested that these dimensions may play an important role in moder-
ating the effects of stress during childhood and adolescence. Hauser
and Bowlds (1990), for example, argue that temperament influences
the available range of coping strategies an individual may draw on in
stressful situations, and at the same time temperament affects the type
of events that are recognized as being stressful by an individual. Ebata
and Moos (1994) used a longitudinal and cross-sectional study of 315
adolescents and found that those who reported greater distress were

more likely to use *cognitive avoidance, resigned acceptance* and *emotional discharge* as coping strategies (avoidance methods). In contrast, those who were more active used more *positive reappraisal, guidance/ support, problem-solving* and *alternative rewards* (approach methods). The findings from other studies of adolescents support these results (e.g. Kurdek and Sinclair, 1988).

The Australian Temperament Project, which followed 2000 young people through each developmental stage of their lives (Prior, Sanson, Smart and Oberklaid, 2000), found that easy temperament as rated by teachers, the warmth of the mother–child relationship and the level of stress as perceived by the child were the best predictors of coping.

It is clear that neither nature nor nurture has an exclusive effect on temperament (and hence coping), since most traits rely on the interaction of genes and environment. It has long been accepted, based on studies of twins, that shared family experiences play a role in personality development. For example, in a study of 7144 adult twin pairs drawn from a Finnish cohort, the relative contribution of genetic influences along with common experience were clearly affirmed in relationship to personality (Extroversion and Neuroticism) as measured by the Eysenck Personality Inventory such that increased social contact is associated with increased personality resemblance (Rose, Koskenvuo, Kaprio, Sarna and Langinvainio, 1988). Moos and Holahan (2003) point out the contextual and dispositional perspectives on coping, highlighting the relatively stable coping styles or dispositions that come into play. In addition to longitudinal studies of temperament and twin studies this was illustrated in an analysis of adolescent coping (Frydenberg and Lewis, 1994). The delineation of the relative contribution of nature and nurture to the coping process is awaiting clarification, but this may be an impossible task.

The indices of resilience appear early in life. Prior (1999) gives the example of resilient children in the Werner and Smith (1989, 1992) survey of Hawaiian children. They tried to predict adjustment at the ages of 10, 18 and 30 for children who had experienced risks such as chronic poverty, low maternal education and moderate to severe perinatal stress. It was found that as early as infancy, resilient children had been active, affectionate, good-natured and easy to manage, with fewer eating and sleeping problems. Resilient children were more nurturing, responsible and achievement-oriented. In the second year of their life these children were described as alert, independent, curious and sociable. In later years teachers reported their success with peers and their ability to focus on academic tasks, particularly among the girls, who had good reasoning capacities and good reading skills. These girls had many interests and hobbies and completed high school with a sense of control and positive self-concept.

Analyses of an Australian data set attempted to shed light on the role of biology in the development of coping skills. A study using the 18 strategies identified by the ACS with a sample of 1035 monozygotic and 1229 dizygotic twins, aged 12–24 years (Tat, 1993), found that the biologically identical twins used more *work hard and achieve* strategies than their non-identical counterparts. An argument can be mounted for the role of the environment, as monozygotic twins may need to work harder to distinguish themselves as individuals, thereby avoiding the inevitable comparison of one twin against the other (White, Hill, Hopper and Frydenberg, 1995). In that study personality traits were identified and subjects were grouped as being extroverted, neurotic or psychotic. The strategies used to cope with situations were analysed. As one might expect, extroverted adolescents cope more positively and successfully than do the other two groups. They work hard, remain positive and relaxed, fit in with friends and use social support.

Hope

One approach to considering the positive cognitions is the research in the area of hope. Hope can be construed as a consolation for other troubles in life. It can also be construed as a sense that something desired might happen. Since the late 1950s and through the 1960s psychiatrists (Menninger, 1959; Schachtel, 1959; Frank, 1968; Melges and Bowlby, 1969; Frankl, 1992) and psychologists (Mowrer, 1960; Cantril, 1964; Schmale and Iker, 1966; Farber, 1968; Stotland, 1969) have engaged in systematic studies of hope. It is generally agreed that hope taps the positive expectations for goal attainment. According to Smith (1983) in the mid-1970s there was renewed interest in examining stress, coping and illness and the part that negative and positive thoughts could play. It was found that negative thoughts and emotions could block recovery and positive processes such as hope could promote it (Mason, Clark, Reeves and Wagner, 1969; Frank, 1975; Cousins, 1976; Simonton, Matthews-Simonton and Creighton, 1978). Generally, perceptions of control or mastery are positively related to psychological well-being (Taylor and Brown, 1988; Snyder, 1989; Taylor, 1989; Snyder, 1994; Taylor and Brown, 1994 for reviews). In the 1980s and 1990s specific theoretical viewpoints about coping benefits that flow from positive cognitive and emotional motivational states were being described as a thought process in which people have a sense of agency and pathways for goals (Snyder, 1994, 1998; Snyder *et al.*, 1997). Together, goals, pathways and agency form the motivational concept of hope.

Goal pursuit thoughts drive emotional experiences. In the context of hope theory, successful coping rests on thinking so as to achieve one's desired goals. 'The more adaptive positive emotional response occurs because higher hope people can generate additional, alternative paths when blocked via the original route' (Snyder, 1994, p. 208). Higher hope helps people deal more successfully with the stress in their lives (p. 209). According to Snyder and colleagues (1997, p. 209), basic components of hope should be established by the age of 3. High hope is positively correlated to competency in life areas, that is, a perception of scholastic competence, social competence, athletic ability, physical appearance and an increased feeling of self-worth. In adults this adds up to an increased feeling of self-worth (Snyder *et al.*, 1996; Curry, Snyder, Cook, Ruby and Rehm, 1997), self-esteem (Snyder, Cheavens and Micheal, 1999) and lower depression (Snyder *et al.*, 1997). This may be due to a different attributional style (depressive attributional style is more internal, stable and global for bad events and external, stable and global for good events) (Kaslow, Tanenbaum and Seligman, 1978). This is likely to be true for some adolescents. While high hope is not related to intelligence, Snyder and colleagues (1997) suggest that high-hope college students have increased success in the academic realm (Snyder *et al.*, 1999). High hope is positively related to problem-solving (see Snyder *et al.*, 1991 for a review). Moreover hope is a significant and unique predictor of problem-related coping when controlling for negative affectivity, and optimism. Neither negative affectivity nor optimism added any significant unique predictive value above that of hope. High-hope people focus on success rather than failure when pursuing goals and use adaptive coping strategies (Snyder *et al.*, 1991). Furthermore, there is a positive relationship between hope and increased *perceived* problem-solving ability (Snyder *et al.*, 1999).

Self-esteem

Global self-esteem, the degree to which an individual likes him or herself as a person overall, has been shown to have an effect on how adolescents cope with their concerns. Chapman and Mullis (1999) investigated the relationship between adolescent coping and self-esteem in 361 Australian secondary school students (mean age of 15.5 years), comprising 60 per cent girls and 40 per cent boys. Coping was measured using the A-COPE, which is a 54-item self-report questionnaire that investigates the use of different coping actions. The A-COPE items are grouped together to provide scores on 12 coping subscales. Self-esteem was measured using the Coopersmith Self-Esteem Inventory, Short Form (SEI), which is a 25-item self-report questionnaire that investigates self-esteem in relation to one's peers, parents, school and personal interests. Students were grouped according to whether they scored low or high on the SEI. Results indicated that self-esteem had a significant effect on the students' use of three of the 12 subscales. Students who scored low on self-esteem had higher mean scores for ventilating feelings, relaxation and avoiding problems. Specifically, students with low self-esteem tended to avoid their problems in contrast to students with high self-esteem, who took a more active and direct approach to their problems. This has been a consistent finding in the coping literature. The question that needs to be asked is whether teaching coping skills is a vehicle for raising self-esteem rather than attempting to tackle self-esteem directly, which to date has proved difficult to do.

An Australian study by Byrne (2000) of 224 students from Years 7 (12–13 years), 9 (14–15 years) and 12 (17–18 years) found that girls are likely to report lower self-esteem than boys when in Years 7 and 9 but not by Year 12.

Resilience and protective factors

It is a truism that individuals who experience the same negative life event are not necessarily affected in similar ways. In addition to the host of personal attributes and experiences that a person may bring to a situation, they may also have access to interpersonal supports and resources. Social support, sometimes termed social resources, is the support of others, in both a material and an emotional sense, and has been recognized as an important coping resource, if not one of the most critical. The study of individual differences is also helpful in trying to understand why some children experience adjustment problems in response to stressful life events, while others adapt successfully. The concept of resilience was developed from rated research questionnaires and refers to the individual's capacity to bounce back from adversity. In the search for the risk and protective factors that influence resilience in adolescents, Herman-Stahl and Petersen (1996) examined the role of coping and social resources in buffering young people from depression during early adolescence, a period characterized by rapid psychosocial change. The authors hypothesized that active coping, mastery, optimism and peer and family relationships would be associated with lower levels of depressive symptoms and that these factors would also protect young people against the effects of negative life events. This American study involved 458 sixth-graders (mean age 11.76 years), half of whom were girls and half of whom were boys. Various questionnaires were used to obtain data on the dependent variables of coping, optimism and social resources. Levels of depression were obtained using the 13-item Childhood Depression Inventory. Information on stressful life events and daily hassles was also obtained using the Adolescent Life Event Scale, which lists 47 positive and negative life events and asks the informant to indicate the events they have experienced over the previous six months, such as parental divorce, or failing to make a sports team.

On the basis of symptoms of depression and negative life events, students were placed into four groups. These groups were formed by differentiating students who scored high on depression symptoms from those who scored low, and by differentiating students who had experienced three or more negative life events (high levels of stress) from those who had experienced less than three such events (low levels of stress). Students who were low on both indices were labelled positively adjusted; students who were high on both indices were deemed vulnerable; students who scored low on depression and high on negative life events were identified as resilient; students who scored high on depression and low on negative life events were considered to be negatively adjusted.

Group differences in the dependent variables of coping, optimism and social resources were then explored. Results indicated that positively adjusted students scored higher on approach-oriented coping, optimism and perceived mastery and lower on avoidant coping, and had more positive social relations than did vulnerable and negatively adjusted students. Higher approach-oriented coping, optimism and perceived mastery and lower avoidant coping and positive social relations also differentiated the resilient group from the vulnerable group. This suggests that approach coping, optimism, perceived mastery when coping with problems and positive social relations with family and peers may protect adolescents from symptoms of depression, even if they have recently experienced several negative life events.

Resilience in adolescence was also examined in a French study, in which participants were sorted into three groups based on their scores on a depression inventory and a measure of daily hassles (as opposed to negative life events) (Dumont and Provost, 1999). Students who scored high on both indices were classified as vulnerable; students who scored low on both indices were classified as well adjusted; and students who scored high on daily hassles and low for depression were classified as resilient. Similar to the Herman-Stahl and Petersen (1996) study, group differences in coping and social resources were examined. In addition, the current study investigated group differences in self-esteem and involvement in social activities. Of all dependent variables investigated, self-esteem was found to be the strongest predictor of group differences. Students in the well-adjusted group reported the highest self-esteem, followed by the resilient group and then the vulnerable group. Thus it appears that evaluating oneself positively has important stress-buffering effects. The second-strongest predictor for group differences was involvement in illegal or antisocial activities. A linear trend was identified: students in the vulnerable group engaged in illegal or antisocial activities more than the resilient group, who in turn engaged in such activities more than the well-adjusted group. The third-strongest predictor of group differences was the Productive coping style of problem-solving. Interestingly, students in the resilient group called on problem-solving the most and students in the well-adjusted group used it the least. This finding suggests that adolescents do call on problem-solving to deal with their concerns, and that problem-solving can act as a buffer against depression when adolescents are experiencing an accumulation of daily hassles (also see chapter 11 for problem-solving).

The current study did not find that social support significantly differentiated the three groups. This was an unexpected finding and is in contrast to the Herman-Stahl and Petersen (1996) study. It is possible that the different measures and analyses used in the two studies contributed to the conflicting findings. Moreover, Dumont and Provost (1999) explained that social support may still have its place in protecting adolescents against depression when daily hassles accumulate, and that it should be considered along with other important factors such as self-esteem, how one spends one's leisure time, and approach-oriented coping.

Together, the Herman-Stahl and Petersen (1996) and the Dumont and Provost (1999) studies indicate that there are various protective factors that may contribute to resiliency over vulnerability in adolescents, namely self-esteem, optimism, perceived mastery of challenge, social supports and approach-oriented coping such as problem-solving. This again highlights the importance of providing adolescents with training in coping skills. Adolescents who call on Productive coping strategies to deal with their concerns may show more adaptive outcomes to negative life events and daily hassles, especially when their effective coping is matched by high self-esteem, an optimistic outlook and supportive relationships with significant others. This demonstrates the importance of giving all young people the opportunity to learn more effective ways of dealing with their concerns and to foster a more positive outlook on life and on oneself. Moreover, it suggests that coping interventions for adolescents who are currently experiencing negative life events or multiple daily hassles may reduce negative outcomes such as depression. Like most correlates with coping, the relationship between self-esteem and coping is bi-directional, which makes it important to focus on both constructs when intervening in the lives of adolescents in difficult times. The importance of social support indicates that group coping programmes for adolescents who have experienced negative life events may be beneficial in addition to, or as replacement for, individual intervention such as psychotherapy. The social support provided in a group-based intervention may have a direct positive influence on depression symptoms, and may also have an indirect effect via the role social support plays in increasing self-esteem. Young people who receive social approval, warmth and affiliation from their peers may show improvements in self-esteem because how an adolescent evaluates him or herself is greatly influenced by the degree to which they feel others approve, respect and like them.

While supports may be a coping resource and a protective resource that an individual needs, the question might also be asked: Who do young people get help from and for what? Boldero and Fallon (1995) looked at the help-seeking profile of 1013 adolescents aged 11–18 years. They found that 25.5 per cent of adolescents reported that a problem with their families had caused them considerable distress during the last six months. Interpersonal problems were reported by 19.5 per cent of respondents, health problems concerned 18.1 per cent, and educational problems caused distress for 16.7 per cent. When asked who they sought help from for their specific problems, 438 respondents had not asked for help, while 556 indicated that they had asked for help – from friends (214), from teachers (61) and parents (193). So it seems that while many young people do not seek help, peers loom large as a source of support, as do parents and teachers.

Ethnicity and coping

My parents were born in Samoa on the same island. . . . It's strict in a way. There are a lot of traditions and cultures that we try to follow. We are always busy. I have a lot of Samoan friends and lots of non-Samoan friends. My parents are strict about what we do at home. We have a lot of chores to do, like wash the dishes and clean the house.

(Boy, 16)

My parents were born in Italy. It is fairly strict, there are some rules and curfews. You have to be more aware of what you are doing. Because there are lots of Italians around, so you just have to be careful with what you do. You just can't lie to your parents!

(Girl, 17)

I was born in Australia but my parents were born overseas. So half the time I talk Turkish with my mother and English with my dad.

(Boy, 15)

Cross-cultural investigations to determine how adolescents of different ethnic backgrounds cope with life stressors have indicated the diversity of the coping experience. An exploration of how adolescents from different ethnic backgrounds cope highlights this diversity for individuals in different contexts. There is evidence that adolescents from different cultural backgrounds and nationalities draw on different coping strategies. An appreciation of these differences is useful when developing programmes to meet the unique needs of individual ethnic communities.

Despite the socioculturally embedded nature of coping, few studies have compared young people's coping across communities. The limited range of studies includes those by Schönpflug and Jansen (1995), who compared German and Polish adolescents; by Jose and colleagues (1998), who compared Russian and American adolescents; by Seiffge-Krenke (1992), who compared German, Finnish and Israeli adolescents; by Alsaker and Flammer, (1999) in the Euronet project from 13 samples drawn from Central, Eastern and Western Europe, and the one sample from the United States, and by Gibson-Kline (1996), who compared adolescents from 13 different nations. Taken together, the findings indicate more similarities than differences in young people's coping across different communities.

Gibson-Kline (1996) found that, irrespective of nationality, adolescents frequently called on the will to assist, problem-solving and interpersonal strategies, of which the problem-solving strategy was the most commonly reported. However, participants in that study were asked to nominate how they coped, which is an approach that generally yields only a few coping responses. Therefore, it is unclear whether the similar narrow range of coping responses reported by adolescents across cultures is a real finding, or is, at least in part, a consequence of the method used to obtain the responses. Perhaps more sensitive methods for identifying the range of coping strategies used by young people would produce differences as well as similarities in their responses.

In a study of German, Finnish and Israeli adolescents using a 20-item questionnaire to record adolescents' responses to eight problem areas, Seiffge-Krenke (1992) identified a three-dimensional structure of coping: active coping, internal coping and withdrawal. Within these broad areas a comparison was made between the three urban communities. It was concluded that there was a universal capacity for young people to use the two functional styles of coping, namely active and internal coping, and to a lesser extent the dysfunctional style of withdrawal.

Another study reported differences in young people's coping across cultures. Jerusalem and Schwarzer (1988) compared Turkish and German adolescents and found that when coping was broken down into two broad categories of emotional and instrumental coping, Turkish adolescents reported using more emotional coping strategies than did the German adolescents. A further study by Frydenberg, Lewis, Ardila, Cairns and Kennedy (2000) compared 319 students from three different nations (Colombia, Northern Ireland and Australia) on how they coped with social issues of pollution, discrimination, fear of global war and community violence. Results indicated similarities, but also significant differences, in the coping strategies used across these groups.

Northern Irish students were more likely than Colombian and Australian students to use Non-Productive coping strategies such as *self-blame, tension reduction* and *not coping*. They also rated highest in the *use of friends* and *seeking social support* strategies. In contrast, Colombian students were more likely than Northern Irish and Australian students to use *solve the problem, spiritual support, social action, seek professional help* and *worry* strategies. The only strategy that Australian students used more than the others was that of *relaxation*. Regardless of nationality, students reported using the strategies of *focusing on the positive, fitting in with friends* and *physical recreation* more to cope with community violence than to cope with the other three social issues. Further similarities across groups were that females were more likely than males to use *tension reduction* strategies and less likely than males to use *relaxation, physical recreation, ignore the problem* and *keep to self* strategies.

While young people in different communities have different issues to contend with, it is illuminating to determine how they cope not only with particular issues like social concerns but with concerns in general. In a study with urban high school students in four communities, Australia, Colombia, Germany and Palestine, students completed the ACS to assess whether there were cultural differences in general coping patterns in the four communities (Frydenberg, Lewis, Kennedy, Ardila, Frindte and Hannoun, 2003). A comparison of young people's use of three coping styles and 18 coping strategies within these communities indicated that Palestinian youth report greater use of all but three strategies (*physical recreation, relaxation* and *tension reduction*) and German youth report the least use of two-thirds of the strategies assessed. Both Palestinian and Colombian youth were noted to use more *seek to belong, focus on the positive, social action, solve the problem, seek spiritual support* and *worry* than were German or Australian adolescents.

When the relative use of coping strategies within national settings was considered, some noticeable differences were apparent. For example, it was found that regardless of the national setting young people reported most frequent use of *work hard* and *problem-solving* strategies. When it comes to more culturally determined activities such as *physical recreation*, the Australian and German students ranked this strategy more highly in their coping repertoires than did the Colombians and, more noticeably, the Palestinian students. For example, although *physical recreation* is ranked as the second most commonly used strategy for the German sample, it is ranked sixteenth by the Palestinians. The study demonstrates the importance of identifying coping strategies that reflect each community under investigation. Similarity in coping cannot be assumed across different student populations. Consequently, caution needs to be exercised when importing coping research and programmes from one community to another.

Supporting the above concern is the finding of Alsaker and Flammer (1999), who investigated the coping of adolescents aged between 14 and 16 years across 13 different communities (12 in Europe and one in the United States of America). Their results indicated that certain contextual factors significantly influenced adolescent coping: daily activities, which include time spent in school, eating, sleeping and leisure, and future orientation factors, which refer to values and beliefs characterizing the community in which the adolescents are located. They concluded that all authors investigating adolescent coping across communities must be mindful of the importance of context when interpreting results.

Studies have also reported cultural differences among adolescents residing in the same community. One such study mentioned in chapter 3 in relationship to *seeking spriritual support* was conducted by Frydenberg and Lewis (1993b), who classified 673 Australian students into three broad categories: Anglo-Australian, European Australian and Asian Australian. Results distinguished Anglo-Australian students as a group because they reported using more *tension reduction* strategies and less *work* and *worry* strategies than did students in the other two groups. Asian-Australian students were also distinguished as a group because they reported using more *social action, work* and *seek professional help* strategies than did students in the other two groups. European-Australian students were also distinguished as a group because they reported using more *seek spiritual support* strategies than did students in the other two groups.

In another study of young people in an Australian school setting from diverse backgrounds, also mentioned in chapter 3, 105 students aged 12–15 years in metropolitan Melbourne were divided into an Australian and an Australian minority group (which consisted of students from non-English-speaking backgrounds (D'Anastasi and Frydenberg, 2005). The study found that there were significant differences in the use of the coping strategy *social action*, which the Australian minority-group students used more than the Anglo-Australian group. The significant use of *social action* by the Australian minority group was similar to that reported in our earlier research conducted by Frydenberg and Lewis (1993b), which found that South-East Asian Australians, who are also one of the most recently arrived ethnic groups within Australia, used this coping strategy more than European Australians and Anglo-Australians. A greater use of this strategy by these minority groups may be attributed to the fact that many of these ethnic groups have a greater consciousness of their ethnic group membership because they are more likely to have personal experience and knowledge of others with a refugee status and thus are more likely to have greater political awareness, which may encourage them to use more *social action* coping strategies.

There was also a significant difference in the use of the coping strategy *seek spiritual support* by the Australian minority group, who used it more than the Anglo-Australian group.

Immigrant adolescents

One question that has been considered is whether immigrant children are at higher risk for social disadvantage and therefore experience difficulties in adjustment more than local children. Several North American studies have shown that immigrant children adjust no differently from local children, when all factors are accounted for (Tam and Lam, 2005). However, a particular community like Hong Kong can be considered a special case because the island has been developed through a continuous state of migration since the nineteenth century. Further, the Basic Law in practice since the return of sovereignty to China in 1997 has granted residence to Chinese relatives of the Hong Kong residents, which has resulted in an annual migration of 50,000. A study of 1116 Chinese adolescents in Grades 7 and 9 from 15 schools in Hong Kong that examined how migrants and local-born adolescents coped in Hong Kong (Tam and Lam, 2005) found that compared to their local-born counterparts migrants showed no difference in perceived stress and in fact were less likely to use withdrawal coping, showed higher self-esteem and less delinquent behaviour. Overall, though, the results did relate to the educational level of the father and years of residence in Hong Kong. Of course, it could be argued that these populations were relatively homogeneous in that both groups were Chinese, but the study also highlights the fact that young people can adjust, and if there are difficulties it is likely to be where there are major cultural discrepancies. Those would be the groups to be concerned about.

Summary

While coping varies according to age, adolescents of all ages identify working hard as the most frequently used coping strategy when dealing with their concerns. Older adolescents are more likely to blame themselves when things go wrong and engage more frequently in tension-reducing activities such as drinking alcohol, smoking and eating or sleeping too much. This tendency towards use of Non-Productive strategies is frequently seen in girls. The findings suggest that adolescents reduce their ability to deal with problems as age increases, making themselves more vulnerable to unhelpful coping strategies.

There are strong implications from cross-cultural research that cultural differences are generally present. For example, German girls during the early adolescent years showed the most frequent use of maladaptive coping. However, there are usually more reported similarities than differences in adolescent coping across cultures. Differences that exist are often culturally and contextually determined as a result of the social and cultural norms that prevail in any community.

Nevertheless, all studies demonstrate developmental changes in coping and a tendency towards the use of maladaptive coping strategies in girls. An understanding of age variations in coping within particular cultural contexts allows for targeting of interventions towards particular age groups. Interventions that take account of age and developmental stage are also particularly relevant for adolescents who have experienced traumatic life events; the trajectory typically indicates negative patterns of coping for those young people.

Both personality and temperament play their part in determining an individual's coping responses. Personality dimensions that relate to emotionality, activity and sociability moderate the effects of stress during childhood and adolescence. Since both dispositional and contextual elements play their part, neither nature or nature has an exclusive influence on coping.

Coping is affected by an individual's resilience, hope and self-esteem as well as their access to and use of social support. Those with high hope and high self-esteem are more likely to cope effectively. This idea goes back to the concept of appraisal: how one approaches a problem and perceives it will ultimately determine the type of coping response used. Those who see problems as challenges and believe in their ability to solve them are likely to experience more positive coping outcomes. Similarly, those who identify greater access to the support of others are likely to have the confidence to solve their problems.

5 Gender and coping

Girls and boys do it differently

Girls worry about the boys . . . probably relationships. A lot of girls our age start to really like boys, and they get into relationships, have fights . . . Some even lose friends over it because they like the guy so much that they choose the guy over their friends and then have fights with their friends. It's not usually good.

(Girl, 16)

Boys and girls have different concerns because they are two different kinds of people. But sometimes they are the same, like school and that. . . . Girls have to worry about guys and guys have to worry about girls – that's one different thing. Girls have to worry about what they wear so they look good to their friends and guys like them. Guys . . . I don't know. . . . I don't know how to think like a guy!

(Girl, 13)

We both think differently. Like we worry about how we look and they do too, but the way we exercise is different to how they exercise. And they want all the top fashion and they like shopping, whereas we just wear what we can see looks good.

(Boy, 13)

Girls and boys definitely have different concerns. Guys are more into sports and making themselves look good, whereas girls basically want to look good and get in with the right guys.

(Boy, 16)

> Bullying is different for girls and boys. For girls, it is all back-stabbing and 'she said that someone else did something'. And with guys it's basically beat each other up and they might be friends again the next day.
>
> (Girl, 14)

> It's normal for boys to cry . . . but you just can't do it in front of other boys.
>
> (Boy, 18)

It is no new insight that boys and girls are different. They have different concerns and they deal with their concerns in different ways.

> At the moment my Dad's best friend has cancer. Apparently he may only be able to live for just one month more. I am not sure if I will be able to see him again. I used to see him nearly every single week and then one day he found out he had cancer. And he found out way too late and there was pretty much nothing he could do. My parents see him nearly every night and I can tell that they're upset about it, but they never show any emotion in front of me or my sister. But I can imagine how hard it must be for his family especially – he has three daughters. And just the fact that knowing that someone that has been close to you since you were born, especially towards my parents, is going to go soon – it's a tough thought.
>
> (Boy, 17)

Despite the general consensus that boys and girls see events differently, the young 17-year-old above illustrates that sometimes the scripts that relate to how boys and girls feel are indistinguishable. Both the context and individual differences are all important. Nevertheless, within the context of a culture, gender emerges as a clear concomitant of coping. How maleness and femaleness is perceived varies from one community to another. Prior (1999) makes the point that the literature is dominated by the Western cultural group and it is this group that determines what is male coping and what is female coping. For example, in many Western communities when it comes to sexual transition, boys have socially sanctioned freedom to 'sow their wild oats' while girls romanticize and idealize their sexual encounters, leaving themselves open to emotional hurt and disappointment. Thus there is a gendered approach to coping practice (Moore, 1999). For example, in the Australian context it was found that boys are more likely to play sport while girls are likely to turn to others when coping with their stresses (Frydenberg and Lewis, 1993b). Coping is clearly determined both by gender and culture. The Frydenberg and Lewis (1993b) study found that when country of origin is taken into account there are differences in how young people in different communities cope. Indeed, that study found that Australian European students use more spiritual support than do the Anglo-Australian group or the Asian Australian group.

What we can add to the mix is that not only are there differences in gender but there are age differences in how adolescents cope with their concerns (Fields and Prinz, 1997). Nevertheless, the most frequently reported discriminator of how people cope is gender. However, in this chapter several studies will be considered which take into account not only gender but age and socioeconomic status.

Research since the early 1980s has convincingly demonstrated that adolescent girls use more social supportive strategies than boys (Frydenberg and Lewis, 1991a, 1993b). (See also Donohue and Gullotta, 1983; Patterson and McCubbin, 1987; Spirito *et al.*, 1988; Stark *et al.*, 1989; Seiffge-Krenke and Shulman, 1990). In contrast, boys, at least in the Australian context, use more physical recreation than girls (Frydenberg and Lewis, 1993b).

Self-perception and dysfunction

The Australian study by Byrne (2000), noted in chapter 4, found that self-esteem was assessed more poorly by girls in the early and middle adolescent years than by boys. Byrne also affirmed that internalizing disorders such as depression and anxiety is more prevalent in females than males across the lifespan. The study found that not only are girls more likely than boys to report higher levels of anxiety, but they also report lower self-esteem and greater fear. Two hundred and twenty-four students from Years 7 (12–13 years), 9 (14–15 years) and 12 (17–18 years) (M = 15.05 years, 106 boys, 118 girls) participated in that study to examine the relationship between anxiety, fear, self-esteem and coping. The levels of anxiety across the three age groups were compared for boys and girls. Results revealed that girls in Years 9 and 12 had significantly higher levels of anxiety than boys of the same age. Levels of anxiety increased across the three age groups for girls, whereas boys in Year 12 reported lower levels of anxiety than boys in Years 7 and 9. A similar pattern for fear was also revealed across the three age groups for boys and girls. Girls reported significantly more fear than boys in Years 9 and 12. The level of fear reported by boys decreased over the years, whereas girls reported similar levels of fear across the age groups. Girls had significantly lower levels of self-esteem than boys in Years 7 and 9, but not in Year 12. Moreover, self-esteem remained relatively constant over the years for both boys and girls. Differences in coping strategies were also revealed, which indicated that by Year 12, girls and boys were using different strategies to manage their fear and anxiety. Less reliance on emotion-focused coping may have contributed to the reduction in both fear and anxiety in boys over the year levels.

Overall, the strongest finding of this study was that boys fare better than girls for self-esteem, anxiety and fear. Increases in both anxiety and fear in girls in Years 9 and 12 were paralleled by a shift from problem-focused to emotion-focused coping, which indicates that the early secondary years are a pivotal time for intervention. Moreover, empowering girls to manage their fear and anxiety effectively is likely to augment their self-esteem.

Two additional studies which considered gender and coping in young people, along with the concomitants of age and socioeconomic status, are presented in this chapter. One of the studies is cross-sectional (that is, it compares different groups of young people across the different age groups) and was reported by Frydenberg and Lewis (1999b); the second study is longitudinal (that is, follows the same group of young people and assesses their coping on three occasions during a five-year period) and was reported by Frydenberg and Lewis (2000). Both of these studies incorporate the use of the Adolescent Coping Scale (ACS) to measure adolescent coping.

The cross-sectional study[1] examined the way in which coping varies with age, socioeconomic status (SES) and gender. A total of 1249 students from 11 government and private coeducational schools situated in metropolitan Melbourne were involved. The students ranged from Year 7 (approximate age 11 years) to Year 12 (18 years). Information obtained on socioeconomic status of father (SES) (dichotomized into upper-professional and white-collar employment, and lower, blue-collar and unemployed), ethnicity and gender indicated that the students were comparable to other students in the area.

The main strategies used by adolescents were identified as *relaxing, working hard, engaging in physical recreation, dealing with problems, investing in close friendships, wishful thinking* and *focusing on the positive. Relaxing* and *working hard* were strategies resorted to frequently, whereas strategies such as *physical recreation, dealing with problems, investing in close friendships, wishful thinking* and *focusing on the positive* were used sometimes. Strategies used least were *seeking professional help, social action* and *spiritual support,* which on average were used very little.

Taking into account gender, age and SES results indicates first that girls seek more social support than boys but are less likely to seek professional advice. In addition, girls profess less ability to cope and are more likely to be using strategies such as *tension reduction, self-blame* and *worry.* All of these strategies have been described elsewhere as part of a Non-Productive coping style. Boys, in contrast, are more likely to *seek relaxing diversions* or *physical recreation,* and to *ignore the problem* and to *keep it to themselves.*

A relationship was found between gender, age and coping strategies used. It was demonstrated that younger adolescents, regardless of gender, were more similar in level of use of *tension reduction* and *self-blame* strategies. Girls also used more of both of these, and increased their use with age more than boys did. Consequently, it is contended that not only is there a general increase in the use of *self-blame* and *tension reduction* strategies according to age but the tendency is more noticeable for girls. In terms of social support, findings show that the girls made consistent use of this strategy across all age groups and boys interestingly increased their use by ages 17–19 years. Figures 5.1 and 5.2 illustrate these findings.

The gender differences in coping found in this study are consistent with earlier findings. A major finding from the present study, that girls are more likely to tell us that they feel they don't have the strategies to cope, warrants attention. For example, is there a readiness to resort to helplessness? Reflection on such a finding could emphasize the boys' greater inclination to 'get on' with life (by relaxing and keeping fit). Alternatively, the fact that boys are more likely to ignore problems and keep them to themselves may represent denial and this is likely to be at a cost.

Girls' willingness to turn to others more readily than boys may be indicative, in some circumstances, of a quest for independence, while in other circumstances it is a reflection of dependence on parents, friends and significant others. Whether the use of social support is a reflection of dependence or a matter of independence is a judgement that needs to be tested against the experience of the individual.

The second study was longitudinal[2] and examined the development of coping strategies among adolescents in order to establish how coping styles change developmentally with age and at what stage intervention may be most appropriate. Adolescent concerns and coping were assessed in 1991, 1993 and 1995 in six coeducational post-primary schools, in metropolitan Melbourne. During the five-year

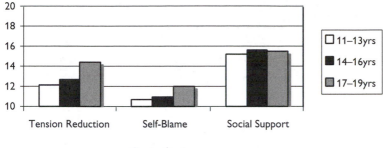

Figure 5.1 Relationship between strategy and age for females

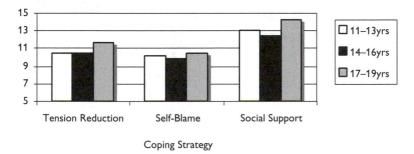

Figure 5.2 Relationship between strategy and age for males

period, 168 students (45 per cent girls and 55 per cent boys) were tracked first to document the patterns of coping behaviour of girls and boys at Years 7 (12–13 years), 9 (14–15 years) and 11 (16–17 years), and second to determine what changes were apparent in their adaptation. The number of students involved at various stages of the study varied. In 1991, 265 students were involved. In 1993, there were 253 students, and finally in 1995, 200 students provided data. Of this group 189 were present on the three testing occasions and of these 168 provided complete data. The reduction in numbers from Year 7 to Year 11 is about 30 per cent. Heaven (1997) reports this as characteristic of Australian schools as well as schools in many developed nations, where 70 per cent of young people are typically retained from Year 7 to Year 11. Inspection of the final sample indicated that 51 per cent were attending government schools in the eastern region of Melbourne, 21 per cent were in government schools in the western region of Melbourne and 38 per cent attended coeducational private schools in Melbourne's eastern suburbs. Sixty-five per cent of the

Table 5.1 Means and standard deviations of coping strategies
across three ages

Scale	12 years		14 years		16 years	
	Mean	SD	Mean	SD	Mean	SD
Social support	2.82	.86	2.80	.85	2.99	.76
Solving problem	3.21	.67	3.28	.73	3.42	.56
Work hard	3.83	.61	3.73	.63	3.67	.58
Worry	2.71	.81	2.74	.78	2.90	.71
Friends	2.88	.94	2.95	.93	3.04	.78
Belong	2.93	.75	2.97	.69	2.97	.59
Wishful thinking	3.13	.77	3.09	.81	3.11	.80
Not coping	2.00	.61	1.99	.59	2.12	.57
Tension reduction	1.91	.58	2.04	.69	2.41	.81
Social action	1.68	.66	1.51	.59	1.55	.51
Ignore the problem	2.31	.75	2.27	.72	2.38	.69
Self-blame	2.57	.88	2.59	.88	2.82	.80
Keep self	2.64	.84	2.65	.76	2.89	.80
Spiritual support	2.01	1.05	1.71	1.00	1.67	.95
Focus on positive	3.13	.76	3.01	.73	2.98	.64
Professional help	1.56	.63	1.39	.53	1.63	.72
Relaxing diversions	3.92	.76	3.96	.76	4.00	.65
Physical recreation	3.44	.77	3.25	.91	3.19	1.02
Non-Productive	20.24	3.68	20.36	3.57	21.61	3.65
Productive	26.58	3.82	26.12	3.99	26.15	3.09
Reference to Others	8.05	2.25	7.43	1.89	7.87	1.72

parents were in white-collar occupations, 34 per cent in blue-collar occupations, and two parents were unemployed. These figures indicate a trend towards higher socioeconomic status due to the relatively large proportion of students attending private schools.

In this investigation, change in both coping styles and strategies was reported. As noted earlier, strategies reflect the 18 narrow-band categories of coping while the styles represent three broad-band groupings made up of the strategies (Productive, Non-Productive and Reference to Others). Ebata and Moos (1994) pointed out the utility in not only employing composite styles but also in retaining the narrow-band coping distinctions. Use of the 18 respective strategies was investigated according to students' age during year of administration and gender. This analysis was then repeated using the three coping styles. Table 5.1 reports the use of the 18 strategies for the adolescents on the three testing occasions (at 12 years, 14 years and 16 years).

In general, young people, regardless of gender, reported that they were coping well, with few declaring an inability to cope. The use of all 18 strategies was fairly constant from Year 7 to Year 11. In looking at the frequency of use of specific coping strategies more closely the following usage was identified:

- Used most frequently: *work hard to achieve* and *relaxation*
- Used sometimes: *engaging in physical recreation, solving the problem, focusing on the positive, wishful thinking, seeking to belong, investing in close friends, seeking social support* and *worry*
- Used occasionally: *keep to self, self-blame, ignore the problem, seek spiritual support* and *tension reduction*
- Rarely used: *seeking professional help* and *social action.*

However, findings showed that there were some significant relationships between students' gender and age and their use of particular strategies and coping styles. Four of these relationships related to coping strategies, namely *self-blame, social support, tension reduction* and *not cope*. The fifth relationship was related to the Non-Productive coping style. As can be seen in Figures 5.3 and 5.4, girls generally increased their use of Non-Productive coping responses at a more consistent rate than boys. It is interesting that for two of these strategies, *self-blame* and *social support*, boys' usage reduced from ages 12 to 14 but by 16 had increased and returned to a level similar to when they were 12.

It is worthwhile highlighting one of the most significant findings of the study which relates to self-professed inability to cope. The relationship between gender and age for the *not cope* scale indicated that, while boys and girls remained relatively stable in their declared inability to cope between 12 to 14 years, and boys reported much the same low level two years later, girls reported a slightly greater inability to cope by the time they were 16 in comparison to boys.

Findings – year level

The findings relating to age are considered regardless of gender in the first instance, since there are clear indicators as to when we should be teaching coping skills both to boys and to girls. In total, 12 strategies displayed significant change according to year level. Five strategies, namely *social support, solve problem, self-blame, keep to self* and *tension reduction*, remained stable in frequency of use between 12 and 14 years but increased significantly by the age of 16. The increase in use

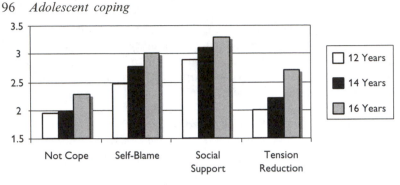

Figure 5.3 Relationship between age and coping for females

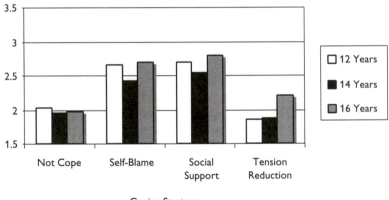

Figure 5.4 Relationship between age and coping for males

of the dysfunctional strategies (*self-blame, keep to self* and *tension reduction*) is of concern.

Three strategies (*social action, spiritual support* and *physical recreation*) showed an opposite pattern in frequency of use to those reported above. Use of these strategies decreased between 12 and 14 years then remained relatively stable. The final strategy, *professional help*, showed a significant reduction in use at the age of 14 in comparison to that at the ages of 12 and 16. *Worry* and *not cope* also showed significant change with year level.

In terms of coping styles, Non-Productive coping and Reference to Others showed significant change over time. Reference to Others coping reduced between the ages of 12 and 14 years then returned to

12-year-old level by the age of 16. In terms of Non-Productive coping, an increase in use was noted between the ages of 14 and 16 years, but this increase is almost entirely attributed to girls.

Findings – gender

In terms of significant gender differences, *social support* and *tension reduction* were used more by girls and *ignore* and *relaxation* more by boys. In terms of coping styles, girls showed greater likelihood overall to Refer to Others and to use a Non-Productive style of coping. It must be recognized that the latter case is primarily due to gender differences, which occur between the ages of 14 and 16.

The gender differences reported in this longitudinal study are supported by the large German study (reported in chapter 4) which comprised 1123 children and adolescents aged 8 to 14 years (M = 10.76, 526 males, 597 females) who were separated into three age groups: late childhood, early adolescence and middle adolescence (Hampel and Petermann, 2005, 2006). This study used the German Coping Questionnaire for Children and Adolescents (Stressverarbeitungsfragebogen für Kinder und Jugendliche, SVF-KJ), which is a 36-item self-report questionnaire that assesses nine different coping strategies and three domains of coping: emotion-focused coping (Productive), problem-focused coping (similar to *solving the problem*) and maladaptive coping (Non-Productive) (Hampel, Petermann and Dickow, 2001). Participants completed the questionnaire twice, once in relation to an interpersonal stressor (such as peer conflict) and once in relation to an academic stress (such as too much homework). Statistical analyses conducted revealed a significant main effect for gender. Specifically, girls used significantly more maladaptive (Non-Productive) coping strategies and significantly less emotion-focused (Productive) strategies than did boys. For problem-focused (*solving the problem*) coping, girls reported using more social support and less positive self-instruction than did boys. These results were consistent with those reported in a previous Australian study which found that adolescent girls report more stressors and greater stress than do adolescent boys, as well as using less productive means of coping (Frydenberg and Lewis, 1991a). Drawing on previous research on gender differences and stress, the authors concluded that girls are more prone than boys to develop psychological malfunctioning.

What the studies collectively show is that the gender differences in coping noted in these investigations are consistent with earlier findings. Generally girls seek more social support than do boys but are less likely to seek professional advice. In addition, girls profess less ability to cope and are more likely to use strategies such as *tension reduction, self-blame* and *worry*. All of these strategies have been described elsewhere as part of a Non-Productive coping style. Boys in contrast are more likely to *seek relaxing diversions* or *physical recreation,* and to *ignore the problem* and *keep it to themselves.*

A major finding from the longitudinal study, that girls are more likely to tell us that they feel they don't have the strategies to cope, warrants further consideration. Reflection on such a finding could emphasize the boys' greater inclination to 'get on' with life (by relaxing and keeping fit). Alternatively, as mentioned earlier, the fact that boys are more likely to ignore problems and keep problems to themselves may represent denial, which may come at a cost.

In general, age-related effects indicate an increase in a selection of Productive and Non-Productive strategies between the ages 14 and 16. At the age of 14 a number of Productive strategies, namely *social action, seek spiritual support, physical recreation* and *seek professional help,* are used with less frequency. Only *seek professional help* recovers between 14 and 16, which may be due largely to the dependence of senior secondary students on their teachers.

It is somewhat distressing to note that the most significant age-related findings indicate that older adolescents are more likely to blame themselves for their stresses and to resort to tension-reducing strategies such as eating or drinking. Older adolescents are also less likely to *work hard, seek professional advice* or use *spiritual support.*

While the findings from this investigation are consistent with earlier cross-sectional findings, what this longitudinal study reveals is that there is a different developmental pattern for boys and girls. The gap between females and males generally increases with age, with the older girls appearing to rely more on dysfunctional strategies than boys. This trend is consistent with the observation that girls more readily declare their inability to cope between the ages of 14 and 16.

The above findings also appear consistent with research which indicates that mid-adolescent girls develop lower self-esteem and lower self-efficacy (see Pipher, 1995). This has been interpreted as girls becoming increasingly sensitive to cultural messages that highlight a female ideal. It can be argued that media emphasis on how girls should be, physically and emotionally, could explain some of the differences found in this study. It would appear from our findings that such differential socialization of males and females may have an impact between the ages of approximately 14 and 16 (Year 9 and Year 11). The increased sensitivity of girls to cultural messages, however, may not only be due to increased media attention. As indicated by some recent research which investigated Year 11 and 12 students' level of concern with a wide range of social, relationship and achievement issues, a 'greater degree of concern is expressed by female students in all concern areas' (Frydenberg and Lewis, 1996b, p. 61). Such heightened concern may be, in part, an explanation for their greater reporting of an increased inability to cope and use of avoidant coping strategies.

Our findings indicate that there appears to be a need to intervene in the coping skills development of adolescents at approximately the age of 14 in order to capture their attention and to capitalize on the particular developmental stage that they are traversing. This is suggested because it can be seen that the greatest shift in coping occurs between the ages of 14 and 16. This shift encompasses both Productive and Non-Productive strategies. However, the finding that, overall, students profess significantly less ability to cope at 16 than they did at 14 should be seen as a matter of concern. Consequently, it is suggested that Year 9 (14 years) would be the optimum time to engage adolescents in reflection on their coping behaviour so that they can consider the utility of particular strategies.

Achievement

Two studies (already mentioned in chapter 3) looked at the relationship between achievement and coping. In the first (Parsons, Frydenberg and Poole, 1996), 'capable' boys were compared with the regular student body of males using 374 boys in Grades 9, 10 and 11 at an independent boys' school in Melbourne. Capable students were less likely than those less capable to declare that they did not have the strategies to cope. It was also found that boys who achieved better than would be expected on the basis of ability alone ('overachievement') used more *social support* as a strategy for coping than did their peers. While we cannot say that the use of social support affects educational achievement, it is an important consideration that boys who do better at school than would be the result of ability alone use *social support*, a strategy generally used more frequently by girls than boys.

The second study, by Noto (1995), examined a sample of 90 female adolescent students (Years 9, 10 and 11) who completed the ACS and the ACER Higher Test (ML/MQ) (see chapter 3). When measuring the relationship between coping and achievement, Noto controlled for gender and IQ by using partial correlations. When the relationship between coping and academic achievement was investigated, significant positive correlations were reported for the problem-focused strategies *work hard and achieve, focus on solving the problem, seek social support* and *focus on the positive*. This means that since Productive coping and academic achievement increased simultaneously so that it could be assumed that, when educational achievement increased, so did the use of Productive coping strategies, it could be argued likewise that when Productive coping increased so did educational achievement. Significant negative correlations were reported for three Non-Productive strategies, *not cope, tension reduction* and *ignoring the problem*. This means that as academic achievement decreased, use of Non-Productive coping strategies increased. Or it could be argued that, as the use of Non-Productive strategies increased, academic achievement decreased. It was also found that high use of the strategy *invest in close friends* (an attempt to fit in with a peer group), which could be construed as Non-Productive, was negatively associated with achievement such that individuals who used this strategy more often achieved less.

Several case studies illustrate the above range of findings. Below are two sets of profiles, one of Lainie and Jason, and one of Wayne and Kim. Lainie is a 16-year-old female who is frequently in fights at school; her family circumstances are difficult in that Lainie's profile shows that she often feels helpless and declares, at least to herself, that she does not have the strategies to cope. Although she often spends time with friends she almost never uses *social support* and very rarely sees herself as a *problem-solver*. Rarely does she *focus on the positive*. In contrast, Jason, a 15-year-old boy who was also considered to be defiant and thought to bully other children, frequently *focuses on the positive*, sees himself as sometimes being able to *solve problems* and never declares his *inability to cope*. The lack of a positive outlook and the self-declared helplessness by Lainie is a sharp contrast to the positive outlook and belief in the self as exemplified by Jason.

Kim is a 15-year-old female with learning disabilities but with a supportive family. Her profile shows how frequently she worries and daydreams. At the same time she is able to *focus on the positive* and generally *ignore the problem*, which for her at least is an intractable one so it may be an adaptive strategy for her to accept the situation.

In contrast, Wayne uses *relaxation* and *physical recreation* but at the same time he does not *blame himself* or *keep to himself* too much. He does *worry* and *ignore problems* to a considerable extent.

While boys and girls often fall within the gendered stereotypes in survey research, when it comes to individual circumstances there are

Adolescent Coping Scale | Individual Profile of Coping Strategies

© 1993 Erica Frydenberg, Ramon Lewis

Name _____ Date _____

Form ☐ General ☐ Specific

Scale	Adjusted Score (Gen. / Spec.)	Not used at all	Used very little	Used sometimes	Used frequently	Used a great deal	Description
1. SocSup		20	30 40 50	60 70 80	90	100	**Seek Social Support** – sharing my problem with others; enlisting their support, encouragement and advice.
2. SolvProb		20	30 40 50	60 70 80	90	100	**Focus on Solving the Problem** – tackling my problem systematically by thinking about it and taking other points of view into account.
3. Work		20	30 40 50	60 70 80	90	100	**Work Hard and Achieve** – being conscientious about my (school) work; working hard, and achieving high standards.
4. Worry		20	30 40 50	60 70 80	90	100	**Worry** – worrying about the future in general and my personal happiness in particular.
5. Friends		20	30 40 50	60 70 80	90	100	**Invest in Close Friends** – spending time being with close friends and making new friendships.
6. Belong		20	30 40 50	60 70 80	90	100	**Seek to Belong** – being concerned with what others think, and doing things to gain their approval.
7. WishThink		20	30 40 50	60 70 80	90	100	**Wishful Thinking** – hoping for the best, that things will sort themselves out, that a miracle will happen.
8. NotCope		20	30 40 50	60 70 80	90	100	**Not Coping** – not doing anything about my problem, giving up, feeling ill.
9. TensRed		20	30 40 50	60 70 80	90	100	**Tension Reduction** – making myself feel better by letting off steam, taking my frustration out on others, crying, screaming, taking alcohol, cigarettes or drugs.
10. SocAc		20	30 40 50	60 70 80	90	100	**Social Action** – enlisting support by organising group action to deal with my concerns, and attending meetings and rallies.
11. Ignore		20	30 40 50	60 70 80	90	100	**Ignore the Problem** – consciously blocking out the problem, pretending it doesn't exist.
12. SelfBl		20	30 40 50	60 70 80	90	100	**Self-Blame** – being hard on myself, seeing myself as being responsible for the problem.
13. KeepSelf		20	30 40 50	60 70 80	90	100	**Keep to Self** – keeping my concerns and feelings to myself, avoiding other people.
14. Spirit		20	30 40 50	60 70 80	90	100	**Seek Spiritual Support** – praying for help and guidance, reading a holy book.
15. FocPos		20	30 40 50	60 70 80	90	100	**Focus on the Positive** – looking on the bright side of things, reminding myself that there are others who are worse off, trying to stay cheerful.
16. ProfHelp		20	30 40 50	60 70 80	90	100	**Seek Professional Help** – discussing my problem with a professionally qualified person.
17. Relax		21	31 42 52	63 73 84	94	105	**Seek Relaxing Diversions** – taking my mind off the problem by finding ways to relax such as reading a book, watching television, going out and having a good time.
18. PhysRec		21	31 42 52	63 73 84	94	105	**Physical Recreation** – playing sport and keeping fit.

Lainie – – – – –   Jason ———

Figure 5.5 Lainie and Jason profile

Adolescent Coping Scale

Name _____

Date _____

Individual Profile of Coping Strategies

Form ☐ General
☐ Specific

Scale		Used very little	Used sometimes	Used frequently	Used a great deal	

1. SocSup — **Seek Social Support** – sharing my problem with others; enlisting their support, encouragement and advice.

2. SolvProb — **Focus on Solving the Problem** – tackling my problem systematically by thinking about it and taking other points of view into account.

3. Work — **Work Hard and Achieve** – being conscientious about my (school) work; working hard, and achieving high standards.

4. Worry — **Worry** – worrying about the future in general and my personal happiness in particular.

5. Friends — **Invest in Close Friends** – spending time being with close friends and making new friendships.

6. Belong — **Seek to Belong** – being concerned with what others think, and doing things to gain their approval.

7. WishThink — **Wishful Thinking** – hoping for the best, that things will sort themselves out, that a miracle will happen.

8. NotCope — **Not Coping** – not doing anything about my problem, giving up, feeling ill.

9. TensRed — **Tension Reduction** – making myself feel better by letting off steam, taking my frustration out on others, crying, screaming, taking alcohol, cigarettes or drugs.

10. SocAc — **Social Action** – enlisting support by organising group action to deal with my concerns, and attending meetings and rallies.

11. Ignore — **Ignore the Problem** – consciously blocking out the problem, pretending it doesn't exist.

12. SelfBl — **Self-Blame** – being hard on myself, seeing myself as being responsible for the problem.

13. KeepSelf — **Keep to Self** – keeping my concerns and feelings to myself, avoiding other people.

14. Spirit — **Seek Spiritual Support** – praying for help and guidance, reading a holy book.

15. FocPos — **Focus on the Positive** – looking on the bright side of things, reminding myself that there are others who are worse off, trying to stay cheerful.

16. ProfHelp — **Seek Professional Help** – discussing my problem with a professionally qualified person.

17. Relax — **Seek Relaxing Diversions** – taking my mind off the problem by finding ways to relax such as reading a book, watching television, going out and having a good time.

18. PhysRec — **Physical Recreation** – playing sport and keeping fit.

Kim ———   Wayne – – – –

Figure 5.6 Kim and Wayne profile

variations. A helpful family background, such as in Kim's case, may make all the difference to her acceptance of her learning difficulties.

Implications for adolescents (see also chapter 12)

One way in which adolescents can be stimulated to learn coping is to have them appreciate their current coping repertoire and then evaluate this by considering the coping behaviour of others. This often means that girls should consider what works for boys and where appropriate learn to use those strategies; and vice versa, boys can learn from girls' coping. The investigations reviewed in both this chapter and the previous one provide insights into the general coping strategies of adolescents. They identify differences related to age, ethnicity and gender and show how these findings may be used to facilitate reflection by adolescents on their coping behaviour.

It could be argued that through the use of instruments such as the ACS the opportunity exists for rapid feedback; these instruments also provide the opportunity for discourse on the use of coping strategies and styles. As a result young people can be challenged to reflect on their current coping repertoire and the relationship that exists between their relative uses of the strategies assessed by the ACS for different types of concerns. Individuals who are high on use of particular styles can discuss how these are operationalized as a way of facilitating coping behaviour patterns of students. The discussions can be extended by getting young people to reflect on the ways in which they deploy these strategies, when they use them, and with what results.

However, one needs to be cautious in assuming that there is a direct relationship between the use of particular coping strategies and adjustment. Using longitudinal data which examined coping and adjustment, Feldman, Fisher, Ransom and Dimiceli (1995) have pointed out that what is good for girls is not necessarily good for boys. Their study demonstrated that boys who sought *social support* and *spiritual support* during adolescence were doing less well in adulthood (according to indicators of adjustment) than boys who were less inclined to use these strategies during their adolescent years. The converse is true for girls.

Although not a universal finding in relation to coping strategies, the issue of the girls' tendency to use strategies such as *tension reduction* and *self-blame* increasingly with age may be of concern. When we are considering this issue, however, it is the circumstances of the individual, along with the outcomes in his or her life, that need to be taken into account as much as the coping actions that are used. Generally, young people can benefit from reflecting on and understanding the actions of others. Discussion of these issues will help them to understand what is going on in their lives and in the lives of their peers and to consider the ways in which they may improve their coping responses.

Summary

The most commonly reported discriminator of coping is gender. Past and current research consistently supports the greater tendency for girls to turn to others for support, while boys turn to sport and relaxing diversions. Girls are more likely to report higher anxiety, lower self-esteem and greater fear than boys and are more likely to employ emotion-focused coping responses. Australian research has shown that, although girls are more likely to turn to others for support, they are also more likely to profess an inability to cope. Boys have a greater tendency to ignore problems or keep them to themselves. This may reflect common conceptualizations of masculinity within Australian males and the value placed on males being self-reliant. Similarly, the greater likelihood of adolescent girls turning to others may be the result of female socialization as nurturers and communicators. The gap between coping patterns of male and female adolescents appears to increase with age.

The main implication of the longitudinal study reported is that if one were to consider intervening in the education of adolescents in order to improve coping behaviour, and more specifically to avert the development of Non-Productive strategies, it would be advisable to consider both the gender of the students for whom the curriculum is being developed as well as their age.

Chapters 4 and 5 have provided adolescents, parents, teachers and other professionals who work with young people important insights on the relationship between age, gender, personality and culture in the form of ethnicity and coping. By identifying when and which adolescents are most vulnerable to ineffective and Non-Productive coping we will be better prepared to intervene, and encourage and educate adolescents to develop Productive coping repertoires. With knowledge that coping strategies differ according to gender and vary significantly between the ages of 12 and 16, adolescents and the adults in their lives can work towards maximizing effective coping right through this developmental period.

6   Coping in context: the family

Family is more important than anything else. Being young, we tend to stress about things that our parents wouldn't. Like, about friends it's something small to them but it's big to us. But then when something tragic happens, you realise that those things are just not that important, that family comes first.

(Girl, 16)

When I need support, first off I would probably go to my family – unless it's a family problem and then I would go to my friends. And if it's a friend's problem I go to my family and vice versa. But most of the time it's my family and some of my close friends. They usually understand me and so I will confide in them my problems.

(Boy, 15)

When adolescent development is viewed broadly from a cultural perspective both the adolescent and his or her family unit are construed as being within a broader social ecological frame. Social structures are constructed by humans and therefore can and do change as circumstances and values change. Often this is done from a historical perspective as to what is valued in any particular community at any particular point in time. Edgar (1999) points out that theories of child development have reflected the dominant paradigms of their times, ranging from viewing children as miniature adults, the religious view of a child as sinful, Rousseau's ideal where children learn from their own consequences, to Froebel's garden where children grow and blossom into adulthood. Each of these values in their own time and setting permeate family life and practices and thus determine how young people learn to cope and how they are expected to cope. Additionally, in contemporary Western society, what constitutes a family continues to be debated. Whether the family comprises a group that is nuclear, extended, dual or single-parent, same-sex, blended or reconstituted, or some other unique culturally determined combination of children and adults living together, is a matter under discussion. Nevertheless, despite the recurring fears that it is dying in Western communities and not socializing young people properly, the family remains the basic institution of human learning.

> It is the key mediating structure of that surrounding culture and its values, the crucible in which is forged the child's developing competence. Our first experience of social others takes place in the family; our first social bonds form here; our first experience of roles as patterns of expected behaviour is here. Our first learning of words and other symbols which allow us to separate ourselves from other objects and interact subjectively as a self with other people happens in the family, as do our early feelings of power and authority (in the shape of parental rights to control us). All these family-based experiences are, in themselves, problems that have to be coped with. They also shape the ways in which we will attempt to cope and bring our environment within our own control.
>
> (Edgar, 1999, pp. 109–110)

Even though the family is admitted to be a powerful force in children's learning, it is important to place the adolescent and his or her family within the wider social ecology that frames their experience. Whatever innate temperament and capacities the individual may have, the circumstances that surround him or her from birth will provide both the opportunities and the constraints in terms of adaptation. Family structure and family climate are also presented in this chapter as indices for optimum development. More particularly, the features of family life that help with the development of coping skills are considered.

The three major contexts that influence development – the family, the school and the community – act at times individually and at other times in concert. As Resnick and colleagues (1997) demonstrated in their study of 12,118 adolescents from 80 US high schools who were interviewed for emotional distress, suicidal thoughts and behaviours, violence, use of substances (cigarettes, alcohol, marijuana) and two types of sexual behaviours (age of sexual debut and pregnancy history), family connectedness and school connectedness were protective factors against each of the risk-behaviours except pregnancy history.

Overall, adolescents with more positive relationships use more active coping with problems at home and at school (Zimmer-Gembeck and Locke, 2007).

While a supportive family and school milieu are helpful, it remains a challenge for the researcher to determine how that connectedness is best achieved. Good communicative practices play an integral part. Where there is connectedness there are likely to be good communicative practices in place, and where there are good communicative practices there is likely to be connectedness. Attachment and bonding, along with family cohesiveness, are important components. But as Edgar (1999) points out, attachment is determined by a host of temperament and environmental factors. Parent–child interactions and social skills development provide insight into effective communicative practices both inside and outside the family.

Edgar, in recognizing the role of the family in the broader cultural context, locates the family as part of a cultural ecological system, within which schools and the community play their part.

Culture

The cultural context in which families are embedded determines how we learn to cope. It determines what is perceived as effective coping and what is not. This is most evident when we are considering how young people make the developmental transition into sexual maturity. The transition itself is guided by social practices and accompanying social pressures as to what is perceived as convention in one community and not in another. There are the pressures of the dominant culture (for example, the majority practice in any community, how peers mature and so on) and the subculture, such as the restrictions that may be placed by parents on children's movements. When it comes to sexuality there are strong norms, which may vary from one community to another. Young people conform according to the norms associated with developmental timetables which include the first date, first kiss, first sexual encounter (see Moore, 1999). Most importantly, context and culture can provide both a resource and a challenge to the individual in the pursuit of social, emotional and developmental maturity. How a young person copes with this transition is determined by peer and familial influences. Each developmental milestone is associated with its own protective factors. For example, how puberty is traversed is aided by a strong family support system and a strong peer system. Moore points out that as yet research programmes which specifically link characteristics of sexual transitions with later coping, or coping style with successful sexual transitions, do not exist and so we must draw conclusions from these broader data about adolescent development in general. While sexual transitions are suitable topics for coping researchers, they are accompanied by stresses relating to timing, social pressure, lack of information, or unpredictable or non-standard development.

An important question within each cultural context is the level of agency afforded to the individual. To what extent do people have the capacity (and opportunity) to assess and shape their own activity? Where there is a belief by parents, mentors, teachers, peers or significant others in the individual's capacity to guide their own development, people generally do better.

The family

The family is the 'key mediating' structure for the surrounding culture and provides the values for the development of young people. It is the most basic institution for human learning. The family is the setting where, for example, collaborative learning can take place and where there is 'scaffolding' or support to help the young person to the next stage of competence. It is a setting where modelling and social learning take place, as well as a setting for competition, conflict and the provision of resources (or the denial of access). From the sociological perspective the family provides resources and feedback to the individual, who then interprets their experience in a unique way. Thus the perception of the individual determines what he or she takes from the family experience. Nevertheless, as Edgar (1999) points out, the family's impact on child development is embedded in the wider culture. It is not just about, for example, maternal attachment but often about overcoming socioeconomic circumstances. There is strong evidence for the link between socioeconomic status, child abuse, infant morbidity and community stress. Similarly, marital happiness, family cohesion, external support for the family, the absence of maternal depression or difficult temperament, the ability to set firm limits, in the context of an authoritative rather than authoritarian parenting style, contribute to determining the outcome in terms of child development (see Edgar, 1999).

While social skills are high currency in a complex society, particularly where the individual is confronted with ever-changing roles and adjustments, many of these skills are specific to a cultural context. Nevertheless, there is evidence of a core set of practices that transcend cultural boundaries, such as the universal nature of facial expressions when an individual is happy, sad or angry (Argyle, 1999; see also chapter 11). However, questions remain as to the transferability of a broader range of skills from one context to another, with each context being culturally determined. The evidence from clinical practice is that characteristics of the individual, such as self-perceptions and self-efficacy in each domain or setting, be it school, home or community, play their part in advancing or inhibiting healthy development. Furthermore, if one does not see oneself as, for example, effective in making oneself heard within the family, it is unlikely that one will feel effective in asserting oneself in another setting. While for many the core social skills are acquired through the course of everyday living, opportunities to learn these skills may need to be provided both within the family and the wider community, including the school setting.

The foundations of genderedness are laid early. Chambers (1999) identifies the different ways mothers talk to daughters, which is generally about relationships; with sons they are more likely to focus on performance in relation to peers. The fact that parents use more positive emotion words as well as more frequent and varied emotion words with daughters (Adams, Kuebli, Boyle and Fivush, 1995) signals the differential relationships that exist between parents and their male and female children.

Bi-directionality

The cognitive-phenomenological theory of coping is based on the person–environment interaction model put forward by Lewin (1936). Essentially, this model posits that the individual and the environment are in a constant state of action and reaction. What a person does impacts on the environment, which in turn impacts on the individual, and so on. For example, when there is a dispute and one individual confronts the other, there is a reaction and, depending on the type of reaction (generally agreement, disagreement or hostility), there is a counter-reaction, and so on. The person–environment interaction is in a constant dynamic state. Lazarus and Launier (1978) point out that 'most social psychologists accept the multifactorial and interactional view of the determinants of human action and reaction' (p. 289). There is an ongoing transaction and relationship encompassing a series of stimuli followed by responses. Subsequent to reappraisal, the stimuli are followed by altered response and so the cycle begins again. Thus it is a dynamic cognitive approach. This holds as true within the family as it does outside it.

Chambers (1999), citing Rothbaum and Weisz (1994), highlights the role of responsivity in parent–child dyadic interactions and the bi-directional nature of conversations as recurring themes within the family. For example, where mothers are highly elaborative (Fivush and Fromhoff, 1988), children recall more information and provide more information to mothers' questioning. The predictive power of mothers' use of elaborative language in early years to children's use of more elaboration and description which continues in later year is evident. Bi-directionality (influence of the child as well as the parent) has been pointed out by Bloom and colleagues (1996). Interaction facilitates cognitive development and subsequent performance. However, given the reciprocity of parent–child behaviour, it is suggested that, where there are difficulties on the part of either the parent or the child (for example lack of communication or lack of responsiveness), direct instruction may be called for.

Risk factors

The issues surrounding adaptation and coping can be conceptualized as a series of risk and protective factors. It is possible to differentiate between them. Risk factors can be defined as challenges for the individual and the community to deal with; in addition to temperament and biological predispositions, they include factors such as poverty, divorce and parent mental health. Protective factors, on the other hand, include temperament, a supportive family and external supports. Some young people overcome the impediments produced by these risk factors through support and a range of educational and communal resource provisions. There is generally a confluence of circumstances that work together to produce risk or protection for the individual.

When considering the individual characteristics that contribute to coping, Prior (1999) draws on longitudinal studies of temperament. The relationship between temperament and coping has been investigated in a variety of risk conditions such as family disadvantage, parental disruption, chronic illness, handicap, war and social disadvantage. When it comes to divorce (a life transition experienced by as many as one in three or one in two young people in many Western communities), some children show resilience (Emery, 1988; Hetherington, 1989), while others show developmental delays. Long-term effects appear to relate more to the child's developmental status, gender and temperament, qualities of the home and parenting environment, and the resources and support systems available to the child rather than to aspects of the divorce or separation *per se* (Farber, Primavera and Felner, 1983; Lee, Burkam, Zimiles and Ladewski, 1994). Nevertheless, there is emerging evidence that once the initial disruption has passed the adaptation depends on how parents relate to each other and what relationships occur subsequent to divorce, such as whether parents remarry (Buchanan, Maccoby and Dornbusch, 1996). Dreman (1999) reports that while parent remarrying is associated with positive adjustment, parent cohabiting is associated with negative adjustment. Post-divorce adjustment is different for boys and girls, with males being more troubled after divorce (Mott *et al.*, 1997). There are indications that a positive parent–child relationship can ameliorate the negative effects of divorce for both parents and children (Hines, 1997).

The importance of how conflict is resolved between parents and children is pertinent in all families and is an issue that has been addressed in relation to families and divorce by Dreman (1999). The role of family support, including the importance of social support from the extended family for parents and children, such as a supportive grandfather and grandmother (the latter especially where the mother is living with the grandmother), contributes to adjustment. Family support and adult support are better than peer support. Often changed routines associated with a more 'chaotic' lifestyle have implications for adjustment in both the home and the school setting. Thus there are suggestions that where school and home supports work in tandem, in particular where there is trauma or major disruption in the family, the collaboration provides the best help for the child.

The deleterious effects of poverty and school dropout are pointed out by Rollin and colleagues (1999) and Christenson and Carroll (1999). High-risk behaviours are associated with relationship concerns which affect sex, peers and parents and involve health-compromising behaviours as a strategy for coping with stress. The implications are that young people need to be taught non-risky ways to deal with stress.

Protective factors

Protective factors such as personality, temperament and intelligence can be intrinsic, and factors such as caring family, mentors and good school experience may be extrinsic (see Christenson and Carroll, 1999) while providing strong attachments. Garmezy (1988) postulates that a trio of protective factors relating to individual differences between children, such as temperament, supportive family relationships and supportive relationships outside the family, act as a buffer or protection against developmental stresses.

Citing her longitudinal study, Prior (1999) points out that the ability to cope (using social competence as an index of coping) is a stable quality that was found to be associated with temperament in three groups of teens: those who are coping well, those who are coping in an average way, and those who are not coping. Coping is associated with co-operation, assertion, self-control, responsibility and empathy. Between the ages of 10 and 14, during which time the groups had experienced the same number and types of adverse circumstances, the poor copers always cope worse and the good copers always cope better. However, the following family characteristics play a part: smaller families, less closely spaced children, absence of separation from the primary caretaker during infancy, and close attachment with at least one caregiver who gives positive attention and provides a positive role model. Thus there are factors additional to the stable trait-like characteristics that militate for and against good coping.

When it comes to overcoming negative peer influences, Dornbusch and colleagues (1999) found that more time with parents, especially on weekends, is associated with less delinquency. Furthermore, proximity to ethnic culture was found to be important. That is, when adolescents have closer ties to their traditional ethnic cultures, they are less likely to be involved in delinquent behaviour.

In the South African context, Straker, Mendelsohn and Tudin (1995) point out that resilience in the context of war was found to be associated with an ability to see others beyond their family and social group as human and to desist from involvement in violence. In this context, therefore, resilience is related to both psychological adjustment and moral development (Muldoon and Cairns, 1999). These researchers also point out that ideology as a strategy may help to buffer the experience of war and this would suggest that, at least in some circumstances where there is a strong belief in a cause or ideal, it is helpful in dealing with major stresses.

While the sociocultural context is important, as are development, temperament and the part that family plays, there are clear indices relating to family functioning and coping.

Family functioning and coping

The study of family functioning, already mentioned in chapter 3 (Fallon, Frydenberg and Boldero, 1993), found that where families are perceived as having an 'achievement orientation' and are focused on 'personal growth' and being 'cohesive', adolescents use Productive strategies to cope. Where families are 'moral and religious' in their orientation, young people resort to *seeking spiritual support.* In contrast, where families are perceived as 'authoritarian or controlling', there is little *hard work* or industriousness and young people resort to using *relaxing diversions.* In families that are high on conflict, young people generally declare that they do not have the strategies to cope and resort to *self-blame.* In such circumstances, they also resort to *tension reduction* strategies and engage in *social action.* In families that are perceived as being high on 'intimacy', young people use *social* and *spiritual support.* In these settings they do not *keep things to themselves* as often and are less likely to *ignore problems.* Finally, in families that are 'democratic rather than authoritarian', young people *work hard to achieve* and resort to *social action.* Generally, where families are perceived as functioning well, adolescents use Productive strategies to cope.

Lohman and Jarvis (2000) examined the congruence between adolescents' self-reports of their stressors and their parents' reports of the adolescents' stressors. Adolescents also reported on their parents. They found that in a sample of 11–18-year-olds, where there was congruence between the adolescents' and parents' perceptions about each others' stressors there was a more cohesive family environment and more adaptive coping strategies were adopted by the adolescents.

Family stress

Concerns in the family impact on the lives of adolescents in different ways. What the major family-related concerns of adolescents are and how they cope with these concerns is of interest to psychologists and related professionals. Indeed, conflict in the family has been found to be the third major stressor for young people after death of a parent and divorce (Elkind, 1988).

From earlier research we know that problems occur more in families than in any other place (Kanner, Feldman, Weinberger and Ford, 1987; Spiritio *et al.*, 1988; Stern and Zevon, 1990) and they occur in most families. Stresses within the family elicit different coping behaviours from other stressors (Stern and Zevon, 1990). For example, adolescents used more emotion-based coping with family problems than they did with school problems, and younger adolescents were more inclined to use *wishful thinking, detachment* and *tension reduction* than deal directly with the problem (Stern and

Zevon, 1990). The major stressor for young people within the family is arguments or quarrels. Where there is the experience of separation or divorce, that is the overwhelming family stressor (see chapter 7 in this volume). Thus the best way to inoculate against these stressors in the context of family life is to make young people build up their armament of coping resources, and in particular teach them how to use the support of others during difficult times.

Young people have concerns both within and outside the family. Studies investigating the concerns of adolescents in general have found that young people worry about a wide range of issues relating to appearance, school grades, employment, relationships and fear of nuclear war. Concern about vocational and educational plans appear the most dominant in some investigations (Collins and Harper, 1974; Offer and Offer, 1975; Rutter, Maughan, Mortimore, Ouston and Smith, 1979; Rutter, 1980; Nicholson and Antill, 1981). Issues relating to personal health and family relationships (Phelps and Jarvis, 1994) also appear to be important to young people. In addition to the stresses placed on the adolescent by school and the peer group, the family also makes demands on the resources of the individual. Overall, young people contend with a range of stresses in the course of family life (Lohman and Jarvis, 2000).

When questioned, one in three young people are concerned about issues relating to the family, whether the family is intact or separated. In a study of 11–14-year-olds in intact and separated families (Frydenberg and Lewis, 1993c), young people were asked what was their greatest concern in relation to their family. Forty-three per cent of the respondents in intact families mentioned general family-related 'happiness', 26 per cent mentioned fights with siblings and parents (in equal numbers), 6 per cent were worried about the family staying together and 24 per cent said they had no worries. When young people in separated households were asked what concerned them about the separation of their parents, 37 per cent said they had no concerns, 30 per cent were concerned about the lack of access to the non-resident parent, 7 per cent were concerned about fighting in the family and 27 per cent described a diverse range of individual concerns.

Emery (1988) points out that,

> In considering how children cope with divorce, the difficulties typically involved in adaptation should not be minimised, while the frequency with which family transition leads to abnormal outcomes must not be overstated . . . divorce has become a very common event. . . . To suggest its impact on children is inevitably

pathological is an injustice to a large number of families. To suggest that divorce is an insignificant transition reveals insensitivity.

(p. 11)

While divorce does not invariably have negative effects (Emery, 1988; Hauser and Bowlds, 1990), generally boys are reported as having more problems as a result of parental divorce (Hetherington, Stanley-Hagan and Anderson, 1989). How young people cope with divorce and separation of parents has implications for their psycho-educational adjustment and well-being.

In intact families, young people cope with family-related issues in a manner similar to the way in which they cope with their general concerns. In contrast, children whose parents have separated not only reported less use of both Productive and Non-Productive styles, but they also modified more noticeably their general coping patterns to deal with the separation of their parents by reducing their use of Reference to Others and problem-solving actions.

While in the previously mentioned study of intact and separated families (Frydenberg and Lewis, 1993c) family status does appear to exacerbate the trend towards maladaptive coping, young people appear to have the requisite strategies within their coping repertoire. It is a matter of helping them to gain access to these when under stress in the family (see chapter 7).

The most interesting results in the above study were associated with gender and relate to the difference between the proportion of boys and girls in both types of families expressing no concern. The finding can be interpreted as indicating that girls are almost twice as distressed as boys in both separated and intact families, or alternatively, boys are more likely than girls to deny their concerns. Of the girls, 17 per cent reported no worries compared to 28 per cent of the boys. In intact families, it appears that fighting with parents was a more common concern for girls (36 per cent) than it was for boys (20 per cent). In separated families, girls professed more concern about their lack of access to the non-residential parent (35 per cent) than did boys (22 per cent).

Boekaerts (1999) gave 626 high school students the task of considering, 'your parents prevent you from doing the things you want to do'. Some of the young people considered the situation as a normal aspect of daily functioning whereas others saw it as a developmental challenge. Students who focused on more long-term conflict resolution reported using more of what Boekaerts termed a 'fighting the stressor' form of coping and they perceived their peers as more supportive than students who framed their goal in terms of maintaining or restoring their well-being. They did show higher levels of stress. There were no differences between the two groups in 'coming to terms with the stressor' form of coping.

The ideal family

The family is one of the most significant influences and settings in which adolescents find themselves. Thus understanding the connection between family life and coping is an important piece in the mosaic of lifespan development. When there are conflicts, who does the adjusting – the adolescent or the family? Since functional family climate is associated with functional styles of coping, the prototype for an ideal family is presented.

The family is the context in which young people spend much of their time. For example, a study of US high school students found that 41 per cent of time is spent at home, 32 per cent of time in school, of which 29 per cent is spent in the classroom, and 27 per cent in public settings. Studying occupies 25 per cent of working time and 40 per cent of young people's time is spent in leisure activities (Csikszentmihalyi and Larson, 1984).

In most Western countries there is a tendency for adolescents to move away from the family and spend more time with peers. An international study on how children and adolescents spend their time has shown that adolescents from Western countries are granted much more spare time than adolescents from Asian nations, and a large amount of this time is spent with peers in leisure activities (Larson and Verma, 1999).

Parental control over the life of adolescents does not diminish until the end of adolescence (Stern and Zevon, 1990). However, relationship patterns change and become more accommodating to the emergent adult. For example, parental involvement in the management of children provides opportunities for social interactions. Parents may supervise and guide these interactions from time to time. Involvement in relationships is the basis on which independence is established, and is not perceived to contradict or interfere with the development of independence.

The 'ideal' family is one where

- communication is positive and effective
- adolescents receive strong support from parents

- adolescents are free to express feelings and opinions
- issues are discussed and conflicts raised
- family plans are negotiated
- co-operation and trust exist between parents and adolescents
- parents can express concerns about likely consequences.

Family patterns of coping

When family patterns of coping are considered, generally there are more differences found than similarities. This is supported by twin studies (see chapter 4, where biologically identical twins used different coping strategies, for example *work hard*, from those used by the non-identical twins) and in our study of mother and daughter patterns of coping. Daughters do not necessarily follow their mother's coping style. In the study of mothers and daughters (Lade, Frydenberg and Poole, 1998) there was found to be both similarity and dissimilarity between coping strategies used by mothers and daughters. In the study of 61 mother–daughter pairs, the rank-order correlations indicate that the overall choice of coping strategies between mothers and daughters reflect some similarities and some differences. What the mother–daughter pairs showed was that within the same families *seek spiritual support* is a strong determinant, but when mothers use *seek social support* or *work hard and achieve* the daughters are likely to do otherwise. That is, where families have a religious orientation, the daughters are likely to follow their mothers in that regard alone, but not in other aspects of coping. The use of *social support* and *work hard* may in fact take the parent away from the home and thus affect their perceived availability to the daughters, causing the daughters to act in the opposite way.

Mother–daughter pairs are unrelated in how they cope except where *religion, hard work* and *social support* are concerned, then this relationship may be either positive or negative. These findings support the likelihood of there being familial patterns of coping, albeit to a limited extent. In general, however, there appears to be an adult and an adolescent pattern of coping.

When the 18 strategies of the ACS were ranked in the above study according to use, mothers gave a higher priority to *focus on the positive* and *seek professional help*. Daughters, on the other hand, gave a higher priority to the use of *tension reduction*. Mothers used significantly more coping strategies of *focus on solving the problem, work hard and achieve, social action, focus on the positive* and *seek professional help* than daughters. These strategies can be described as problem-focused modes of coping. Daughters, on the other hand, were more likely than their mothers to use strategies that reflected an emotional focus or a desire to relax (*wishful thinking, not cope, tension reduction, ignore the problem, keep to self, seek relaxing diversions* and *physical recreation*). This study shows that age is a clear determinant of coping. While the relationship between mothers and daughters in a family may be more alike than those across families, the importance of age as an index of coping cannot be ignored. But when it comes to strategies like *spiritual support*, culture is a strong determinant. It remains for longitudinal studies to determine whether in time daughters will become more like their mothers and the extent to which the impact of life circumstances is a major determinant.

Summary

The family is part of a broader ecological system and as such is duly influenced by the environment in which it is embedded. The family is where early learning takes place and values systems are established. It is the most important single influence in the development of adolescents, and has an impact on subsequent coping. Families in which relationships are positive are likely to deal with conflicts constructively. Additionally, good communications generally go hand in hand within families where secure attachments are present.

Since the family is embedded in the broader social context, familial risk and protective factors do not alone determine outcomes. That is, family risk factors do not guarantee negative outcomes; the same could also be said for protective factors. There are other systems in place such as the school and community system which determine outcomes for the individual.

Nevertheless, adolescents are a product of their families, such that coping strategies modelled by parents and other family members are likely to manifest in the young person. It is possible to teach adolescents new ways to cope but it becomes increasingly difficult if the home environment is not conducive to fostering these changes.

While there is limited research determining the family patterns of coping, there are dissimilarities in coping. Daughters are unlikely to resemble their mothers in most areas of coping except *religion*; *hard work* and *social support* show an opposite pattern. Similarities are largely influenced by adolescents' perceptions of effectiveness of particular strategies and ways of coping displayed by their parents.

7 Coping with separation and adversity

My cousin passed away when he was eight from leukaemia. This was pretty tough on me because we were like brothers. That was one of my hurdles in life. I was ten. . . . I cried a lot. My family was my main support. We all helped each other get through it.

(Boy, 18)

My grandmother passed away when I was 14. This was hard on me. I still have not gotten over it. I still feel that she is still here with me. . . . It still hurts. . . . I cried like a baby.

(Boy, 17)

I have to deal with having a father with cancer and a mother with multiple sclerosis.

(Girl, 14)

Adolescence is a period of tremendous developmental, social and psychological change that young people generally traverse with some ease. But, as with other periods of the lifespan, there are challenges that some young people have to contend with beyond what is normal growth and development. Such circumstances include trauma and disasters of various sorts that often present as post-traumatic stress. According to Conservation of Resources theory (Hobfoll, 2001) individuals protect themselves against possible loss. More importantly, in situations where there is no capacity to be proactive, such as death, divorce, illness or even being victimized at school, there is a primacy of loss which outweighs the benefit of gain. That is, the impact is harsh and challenges the individual to amass and use all their resources. Some of these loss events are dealt with in this chapter. For example, when it comes to dealing with grief and loss, family stresses such as separation and divorce loom large for many young people, and then there are chronic illnesses, peer pressure and bullying that others have to deal with. This chapter evaluates two programmes that relate to dealing with grief and loss. The first is a grief and loss programme and the second is a general coping skills programme provided for young people who had experienced divorce or separation.

The adolescent experience of losing a loved one

The death of a loved one is one of the most traumatic events we experience. Regardless of age, we are never fully prepared for the sadness and pain that accompany the loss. American research has revealed that approximately one in 20 children experience the death of a parent before the age of 18 (Worden, 2001). Although parental death may be the ultimate loss for young people, the death of other relatives (e.g. sibling or grandparent), close friend or romantic partner can also be devastating, which suggests that coping with the loss of a loved one is something that many young people may encounter at one time or another, or even several times over. To estimate the prevalence of the experience of bereavement in the United Kingdom, Harrison and Harrington (2001) conducted a study of 1746 adolescents aged 11–16 years in secondary schools in northern England. Students were asked whether they had ever experienced the death of a 'significant other', defined as a first-degree relative, second-degree relative, close friend or treasured pet. Only 7.6 per cent of students reported not having experienced the death of a first-degree relative. Of the total deaths experienced, the majority were loss of grandparents (66 per cent) followed by loss of treasured pets (47.6 per cent). The authors estimated that the risk of parental death by the age of 16 was about 6 per cent and the risk of death of a sibling (including stillbirths) was about 5 per cent. Overall, this study indicates that the loss of a significant other during childhood and adolescence is common, with adolescents who have not experienced such bereavement being in the minority.

The adolescent experience of bereavement is different from the child or adult experience. Adolescents have a greater understanding of death than children and thus require more accurate and honest information than children. Their reaction to death also differs from that of adults. For example, adolescent thinking is often egocentric in nature and may compel adolescents to believe that their experience is unique, which may heighten the intensity and the privacy of their grief reaction (Worden, 2001; Christ, Siegel and Christ, 2002; Gumbiner, 2003; Noppe and Noppe, 2004). This points to the need to consider how loss affects adolescents separately from adults and children.

There has been a plethora of research into the effects of bereavement, which has revealed the short- and longer-term outcomes for adolescents. When compared to adolescents who have not experienced loss, those who have experienced it have more depressive symptoms (Harrison and Harrington, 2001), reduced academic performance (Abdelnoor and Hollins, 2004) and lowered self-esteem (Amato and Keith, 1991; Amato, 2001). Long-term outcomes include elevated levels of mental illness such as depression (Sandler *et al.*, 2003), poorer emotional well-being (Cherlin, Kiernan and Chase-Lansdale, 1995) and relationship dysfunction (Chase-Lansdale, 1995). For example, in Harrison and Harrington's (2001) investigation into the prevalence of bereavement in young people, current depressive symptoms were found to be higher for those adolescents who had experienced bereavement than for those who had not, with adolescents who had experienced the death of a parent, first-degree relative or close friend scoring the highest for depressive symptoms. Interestingly, the length of time since the death had occurred did not influence the depressive symptoms of adolescents, with those who had experienced the death five years earlier scoring similarly to those who had experienced deaths in more recent times.

Previous research has highlighted the devastating impact that death of a loved one can have on young people's lives. But not all adolescents experience bereavement in the same way and there are various factors that influence the short- and longer-term impacts of loss. These factors include personal characteristics such as gender, temperament, previous experience of loss, and external characteristics such as family dynamics and the support given to adolescents during and after the death. For example, Hutchinson (2005) reported that the impact of death of a loved one on academic performance was influenced by how important the relationship with the deceased was to the adolescent and the amount of emotional support the adolescent received after the death. Other research has highlighted that adolescents with good self-concepts cope better with bereavement than those with poor self-concepts (Noppe and Noppe, 2004). In addition, previous experiences of losing a loved one may influence current experiences because it suggests that losing loved ones through death is fairly common. Multiple losses have been associated with depression, with adolescents who have experienced death of two or more significant others reporting higher levels of depression than adolescents who have had a single experience (Harrison and Harrington, 2001). In sum, how an adolescent copes in the short and longer term with the loss of a loved one is complex, and although it is impossible to protect young people completely from such experiences, there is much we can do to assist them through the grieving process and beyond.

Helping adolescents cope with the death of a loved one

One of the most helpful resources during times of grief is social support. Adolescents' personal networks such as members of their family, school and friendship groups can each provide helpful words, a reassuring presence and the necessary shoulder to cry on. Professional support through community agencies can also provide important psycho-education and assistance during such times. While there are various services to help individuals and families cope with the death of a loved one, such services are not readily used by adolescents. For example, Harrison and Harrington (2001) examined the attitudes towards professional help in their sample of nearly 1500 adolescents who had experienced the death of a significant other. Results indicated that most had not talked to professionals, such as bereavement counsellors or psychologists, about their bereavements but had turned instead to their parents, siblings or friends. This suggests that adolescents may not actively seek or desire the assistance of professionals, especially those with whom they have no prior relationship.

Because it is important that adolescents be given opportunities to work through their grief and to reduce the psychological distress that may accompany bereavement, it is necessary that the appropriate support be available to them. Adolescents are less inclined to seek professional support than adults in times of need, and they may not be open to support if it is forced on them. This indicates that services for adolescents dealing with a bereavement should be promoted in schools and other relevant settings, and these need to be readily accessible and be appealing to young people. In efforts to tailor interventions for adolescents who have experienced bereavement, various elements have been identified as important. Providing support to groups of young people is appealing to individual adolescents because it draws on their natural tendency to rely on each other for social support (Richardson and Rosen, 1999). Moreover, by being among others who have also experienced loss, adolescents realize that they are not unique and their sense of social isolation may diminish (Noppe and Noppe, 2004). By sharing their experiences and related emotions adolescents are able to work through their grief.

While a peer support group provides social support, such a group is most effective when it is formed with a definite aim and purpose. Over recent years there have been a number of programmes developed for children and adolescents who have experienced loss either through parental separation or divorce, or death of a loved one (Richardson and Rosen, 1999). Typically, these programmes are run in schools by trained facilitators and give adolescents the opportunity to understand and cope with their loss through the process of sharing and reflection. Intrapersonal factors such as one's self-concept and use of coping strategies have also been associated with the mental health of bereaved young people and may be positively influenced via therapeutic group interventions (Worden and Silverman, 1996). Seasons for Growth is one such programme that has been designed and implemented in numerous schools and community settings throughout Australia, New Zealand, England, Ireland and Scotland. An overview of the Seasons for Growth programme is presented along with an evaluation in terms of the impact of these programmes on coping. The programme is provided as an exemplar of an intervention for groups of bereaved adolescents.

The Seasons for Growth programme

Developed by the Good Grief organization in 1996, Seasons for Growth gives young people the opportunity to understand and cope with grief and loss. The programme is not restricted to loss only through death, nor is it restricted to human deaths, as young people who have experienced the separation or divorce of their parents or the death of a pet can also participate. There are six versions of the programme which target different age groups: 6–8 years, 9–10, 11–12, 13–15, 16–24 and 25 plus. In this study the focus was on the adolescent versions. Seasons for Growth is grounded in psychological research, in particular the work of Worden (1991), who conceptualized grief as a process comprising a series of tasks that need to be accomplished by people who have experienced loss. Moreover, the programme teaches young people about decision-making, problem-solving and effective communication and encourages new ways of thinking, all of which help to enhance individuals' self-esteem and emotional well-being (Graham, 2004).

Seasons for Growth has 11 sessions, as depicted in Table 7.1. The first eight sessions are approximately 50 minutes long and comprise the formal part of the programme. Each session has specific learning outcomes and involves a comprehensive range of creative learning activities, such as role plays, art, mime, music and journalism, all of which help young people to explore and express their feelings (Graham, 2004). The ninth session is a celebration of the progress

Table 7.1 Outline of the Seasons for Growth programme

Season	Session	Title	Focus
Autumn	1	Significance of Seasons	Acknowledge the reality of change and loss in life
	2	Effects of Change	
Winter	3	Each Loss is Unique	Learn about possible reactions to change and loss and how
	4	So Many Feelings	each participant has experienced these
Spring	5	Signs of Hope	Develop skills to assist in
	6	My Memories are Important	processing grief
Summer	7	Choices I Make	Explore ways of letting go and
	8	Moving On	moving forward
Celebration	9	Celebration	To celebrate participant progress and bring closure to the group
Reconnector	10	Reflecting on Seasons for Growth	Reflect and discuss on what participants have learnt Explore ways of coping with
	11	Preparing for the Holidays	holiday periods and special occasions

made and the relationships formed and denotes the end of the programme. The last two sessions occur after six to eight weeks in order for participants to regroup and reflect on their learning and to explore how to cope with their feelings of loss during special times such as birthdays and Christmas.

Evaluation of Seasons for Growth

Two evaluations of Seasons for Growth have been conducted, one in 1999 (Muller and Saulwick, 1999) and the other in 2006 (Frydenberg, Muller and Ivens, 2006). The first evaluation collected data from over 220 primary and secondary schools in Australia. Information was gleaned from a number of programme participants, their parents, school principals and facilitators. Results indicated that the programme had a strong positive effect on students of all ages. For example, students reported more positive attitudes towards themselves and their circumstances, as well as feeling more confident, happy and able to express their feelings. Information collected from parents, school principals and facilitators also validated the effectiveness of the programme, as all informants believed students benefited from participating.

The second evaluation focused specifically on adolescents aged 12–18 and used both quantitative (questionnaire) and qualitative (interview) methods to determine the programme's effectiveness. The evaluation involved a total of 186 students from eight schools in Australia, of which 81 (26 males, 55 females) completed the Adolescent Coping Scale before and after participating in the Seasons for Growth programme, and 44 were interviewed after the programme. Scores on the ACS were analysed separately for male and female students. Results indicated that the programme had a similar effect on adolescent females and adolescent males, but the impact was somewhat stronger for females than for males. Specifically, the programme made it easier for adolescent females to turn to others for help, which is seen as an important way for them to cope. Generally, adolescent females increased their use of Productive coping strategies and reduced their use of Non-Productive strategies. Generally, males also became more positive in their outlook.

The qualitative data yielded rich accounts of the interviews held with a number of adolescents and also showed positive outcomes for both males and females.

Students commented on the effects of the programme:

> Seasons helped me to deal with my emotions. Talking in a group helped me to feel more at home about it, because other people were talking and were dealing with the same problems.
>
> (Girl, 14)

Trust was important:

> I could trust them because they were trusting me. And we've become heaps closer.
>
> (Girl, 13)

> . . . because they'd been through the same type of things that I'd been through, and I trusted them because most of them are my friends.
>
> (Girl, 14)

It allowed students to open up:

> It's really helped me a lot. When my family problems first occurred, I absolutely hated talking about it. It would always

make me cry. But now I can talk about it freely and I can cope
with it. Seasons really helped me.

(Boy, 14)

What students learned:

It was about learning acceptance. That's what I got out of it
most. And how to go on and keep living without having to worry
about it all the time.

(Girl, 16)

I accepted that anything could change. It made me upset knowing
that nothing would be the same again, but inside myself I began
to understand that things would be different.

(Girl, 16)

Live my life to the max.

(Boy, 14)

Female and male students benefited from being in groups together:

Guys don't really like to talk about their feelings. It was interesting to see how the girls showed their thoughts or pain.

(Boy, 16)

I found girls have a totally different way of thinking about these
things. There was a [female] teacher intern and she put something
into a sentence which completely changed the way I looked at my
situation, although her situation had nothing to do with mine. It
changed my way of thinking.

(Boy, 14)

Finally:

Give it a go. It's a good programme. It teaches you to cope with
sadness. You won't feel alone.

(Boy, Year 8)

The two evaluations of Seasons for Growth suggest that the programme is beneficial for both male and female adolescents who have
experienced loss, through either death of a loved one or divorce.
Results of the second evaluation suggest that female students

benefited more from the programme than did male students. This concurs with previous research which indicates that female adolescents seek peer support more than their male counterparts. Gender differences in the outcomes of group programmes are important to consider when developing or delivering such interventions. At times it may be beneficial to provide small-group programmes to girls and boys in separate groups, especially when sensitive topics are being discussed. It also seems that girls are more likely to ask for support and participate in grief and loss programmes than are boys. This does not mean that girls necessarily need the support more than boys, just that they will seek it more. Thus, future efforts need to consider how support and programmes to assist adolescents in times of need can be made more attractive to boys in particular.

Coping with parental separation or divorce

Children today are more likely to experience the divorce or separation of their parents than any previous generation. Rates of divorce have risen over the decades across the globe. For example, recent data collected from 192 developed countries indicated that the rate of divorce increased in the 1990s from 13 divorces per 100 men and women in the 1970s to 24 divorces per 100 men and 27 per 100 women (United Nations, 2004). Divorces in developing countries have also increased over this time, from 7 to 12 divorces per 100 men and from 5 to 15 divorces per 100 women. The United States has the highest rate of divorce when compared to countries such as Japan, Germany, Australia, Austria, Italy and Spain, with over a million children each year experiencing the divorce of their parents.

It is important not to focus solely on divorce rates, as there are also many parents who separate and do not divorce, or who were never married, making divorce statistics a clear underestimate of the total number of children affected. This was highlighted in an Australian report by de Vaus and Gray (2004). Using data from the 2001 Household, Income and Labour Dynamics in Australia survey, the authors estimated that nearly 25 per cent of children will experience parental separation before the age of 15. This figure suggests that parental divorce and separation, and their effects on children, are major public health issues. For our purposes, parental separation and divorce will be referred to hereafter as parental separation.

Because of the rather common occurrence of family dissolution in modern times, educators, clinicians and social scientists have directed efforts at understanding its effects on all family members and its broader impact on society. At the centre of such efforts have been the children who experience the separation of their parents, a situation that is almost always beyond their control. It is important to view separation as a process, since the actual separation often follows a long period of conflict and is preceded by many changes to which children must adapt (relocation, separation from one parent, living between two homes) (Buchanan, Maccoby and Dornbusch, 1996). The events that precede and follow the separation greatly influence child and adolescent adaptation. Research suggests that interparental conflict before the separation may explain negative outcomes in children and adolescents more than the separation *per se* (Sun, 2001). This also draws our attention to interparental conflict that occurs in intact families, which is a detrimental stressor in such children's lives, particularly when the conflicts are common, unresolved and parents show aggression towards each other. Thus, for some young people, the separation of their parents may bring relief. However, interparental conflict that continues after the separation is distressing for adolescents. Adolescents may feel stuck in the middle; they may be afraid of hurting one parent's feelings, or both, which can lead to self-blame and feelings of sadness or even depression. Typically, parental separation is accompanied by many changes for young people, which may create additional daily hassles in their lives. Interviews with adolescent girls who have experienced parental separation identified four categories of additional stressors: different living arrangements, less time or no time with non-custodial parent, financial difficulties, and being caught in the middle (Ivens, 2006). Clearly, the changes and events related to parental separation in addition to distress caused by family breakdown can have detrimental influences on adolescent adaptation. However, there is also a strong body of research to indicate that parental separation does not lead directly to adolescent psychopathology for all young people. For example, Ruschena, Prior, Sanson and Smart (2005) compared adolescents from separated families with adolescents from intact families on measures of behaviour and academic performance and found no group differences. While this study highlighted the resilience of adolescents affected by parental separation, several meta-analyses conducted over the years have concluded that parental separation is a risk factor for a host of problems, including those from the social (poor quality of peer relations), psychological (depression and poorer well-being) and academic (lower academic performance) domains (Amato, 2001; Amato and Keith, 1991). Individual variables such as age, gender and temperament combine with the external variables described above and with additional risk and protective factors to determine the extent and severity of problems faced by adolescents who experience parental separation.

Coping with parental separation

How adolescents cope with parental separation and the associated stressors can be a risk or a protective factor, depending on whether the coping strategies used are Productive or Non-Productive. The experience of parental separation may have an adverse impact on coping, with adolescents who have experienced parental separation reporting greater use of Non-Productive coping strategies than Productive ones when dealing with their family concerns (Moos, 1990; Causey and Dubow, 1992; Griffith *et al.*, 2000). Girls are more likely than boys to call on maladaptive strategies such as *self-blame* for uncontrollable family stressors (Cummings *et al.*, 1994). Adolescent girls' use of *self-blame* for parental separation is a matter of concern, as it has been found to be the most detrimental strategy for well-being and is commonly related to psychological problems such as depression. It is possible that the early use of maladaptive coping to deal with family concerns may then become part of an individual's coping repertoire and influence how they deal with subsequent concerns (Lazarus and Folkman, 1984; Folkman, Lazarus, Gruen and DeLongis, 1986; Aseltine, 1996; Sun, 2001). This possibility has led some researchers to argue that coping is one of the most important factors influencing adjustment outcomes in children of parental separation (Kot and Shoemaker, 1999). Similarly, adaptive coping has been identified as a protective factor for post-separation outcomes in adolescents (O'Halloran and Carr, 2000). While it may not be possible to give adolescents with separated parents more control over their family structure, it is possible to influence positively how they cope with their family situation, and their lives in general.

As indicated previously, separation is a process that unfolds over time. Applying a systemic framework to this process provides an understanding of how the effects of parental divorce can be widespread and far-reaching. For example, grandparents are often devastated by the separation of their son or daughter and their partner and feel deeply for their grandchildren. Not only can all family members be saddened by the separation, but extended family members can also give support during the period of the separation and beyond. As one 17-year-old girl stated:

> The most difficult thing I have had to deal with so far is my parents being divorced. Around six years ago when I was entering

Table 7.2 Types of support for adolescents who experience parental separation

	Direct	Indirect
Formal	Individual counselling Group programme for adolescents of parental separation Telephone counselling	Parent counselling Parent participation in group programme for parents who have separated Information via family court, books and websites
Informal	Parents Siblings Friends Extended family	Extended family's support for parents Parents' friends Parents' colleagues

high school, my parents got divorced. And I was also worried about having to jump from primary school to high school. The best way that I could deal with it was talking to my family, like my cousins and other family members that were not involved in it. Because I could get an opinion from people that were outside and don't see and hear everything that goes on. So it's good to get a valid opinion, something that is not biased.

Adolescents who have experienced parental separation can be supported both directly and indirectly and through both formal and informal means, as indicated in Table 7.2. The adolescent years are a time when friends become a major source of social support for all sorts of concerns and thus friends represent an important informal support network for young people. Parents are also important for assisting their children to cope with the changed family structure. Children may be affected by how upset their parents are and by how much the separation alters their relationship with both parents. For example, children and adolescents often find being apart from their non-custodial parent difficult, especially in the early months (Ivens, 2006). When parents model effective coping strategies with difficult and painful circumstances there is potential for children also to call on such strategies. The parental relationship after separation also influences adolescent adaptation. Dreman (1999) reported on several studies showing that children fare better when their parents co-operate with each other after the separation and are able to resolve their conflicts effectively. Consequently, it is important for parents to resolve their differences as best they can and show an amicable front to their children.

Other family members, such as older siblings and grandparents, can also help adolescents cope with parental separation by giving them support and a stable, familiar presence. Again, young people can learn how to cope with difficult situations by observing how their siblings are faring and what they do to deal with their family stressors.

It is important that parents receive formal support not only to help them cope with the separation but also for parenting support after separation. Whether the separation be amicable or the sole decision of one parent, it is stressful for both parties. Common feelings include a mixture of loneliness, euphoria, depression, optimism, disbelief and anxiety. Parents are vulnerable to psychological and physical problems in the time immediately following divorce. Mothers in particular may experience emotional disturbances such as depression (Dreman, 1999). Because emotional disturbances and parents' own adjustment difficulties can hamper their parenting, professionals can provide support and information for parents about how to help their children cope. Counselling may also help parents to resolve residual anger and hurt towards their ex-partners, which makes it easier for them to engage in co-operative parenting over important issues such as schooling, discipline and visiting.

Adolescents seek professional support themselves via their school student welfare services or via a telephone counselling service. For example, the most common reason children aged 5–18 called the Australian telephone counselling service Kids Help Line in 2006 was for problems to do with family relationships. Most of these calls were about family conflict and breakdown (48 per cent) (Kids Help Line, 2006). Girls are more likely than boys to seek professional support and support from their family members and friends.

Supporting adolescents of parental separation in the school

School counselling services are one of the possible resources available at the time of family breakdown because in some settings they may be readily accessible by adolescents and are available within their familiar environments. Individual counselling during and after the separation may help adolescents adjust and do their grief work. Alternatively, small-group counselling for adolescents who have experienced parental separation may be advantageous. Similar to group work with bereaved adolescents, small-group counselling may be optimal with adolescents of parental separation for several reasons. First, the small-group context provides a safe space for adolescents to reflect on current and residual family concerns, matters they often find difficult to discuss with their families and friends (Richardson and Rosen, 1999). Second, sharing experiences gives an awareness that one is not alone, bringing comfort to adolescents who do not want to see themselves as different from their peers. Third, the small-group format is particularly attractive to young adolescents, who tend to prefer peer over adult support for their concerns. Fourth, trust between members, which is a prerequisite when discussing sensitive topics, is readily created in small groups (Hawkins *et al.*, 2006).

Small-group counselling for adolescents of parental separation is best provided as a programme that focuses on strategies and approaches known to help young people adapt to their new family structure. One of the most widely used and extensively evaluated programmes for such adolescents is the 10-week Children of Divorce Intervention Program (CODIP), which focuses on adaptive coping, problem-solving, challenging beliefs about the divorce, and enhancing self-esteem (Pedro-Carroll and Cowen, 1985). CODIP was one of nine American programmes reviewed by O'Halloran and Carr (2000) for a report on the effectiveness of school-based interventions for children and adolescents of parental separation. The authors concluded that the programme was effective in helping young people adjust to their parents' separation and had a positive effect on their negative mood states and self-esteem.

As indicated previously, Seasons for Growth is a programme for adolescents who have experienced death of a loved one or parental separation. Evaluations of this programme have indicated that it also helped adolescents of parental separation cope more productively with their concerns (Muller and Saulwick, 1999; Frydenberg *et al.*, 2006). The Best of Coping programme (BOC), described in more detail in chapter 12, has also been used with a small sample of female adolescents, all of whom had separated parents, because the programme had many elements to suggest its usefulness. O'Halloran and Carr (2000) identified several factors that underpin effective programmes for children and adolescents of parental separation, namely supportive psycho-education, problem-solving skills, social skills training and stress management training, which are all elements of the BOC programme.

In one study by Ivens (2006), 27 adolescent girls aged 13 and 14 participated in the BOC programme in small groups of five or six participants. The BOC programme was modified slightly for this study. It included the original 10 modules and an additional module designed by the researcher. This additional module, Coping with Conflict and Taming Anger, was included because research indicates that children of divorced or separated families may have, and continue to have, a substantial amount of conflict in their lives (Sun, 2001). Girls completed the ACS and a measure of general well-being before and after the programme and were also interviewed after it. The most powerful finding of the study was the overall improvement in general well-being. Before the Best of Coping programme, nearly a third of the girls reported high levels of psychological distress, whereas, upon completion, only two girls reported such high levels. Results on the ACS, which measures the three coping styles of Productive coping, Non-Productive coping and Reference to Others, showed significant pre- to post-programme improvements in Productive and Non-Productive coping, but not in Reference to Others coping. It was surprising that Reference to Others coping, which comprises strategies of seeking support from others in their social network and professionals, did not improve over the duration of this study. The author postulated that the girls may have not increased their use of Reference to Others coping because their participation in the BOC programme resulted in their not needing to seek such support for their problems, since they were receiving it within the group. The significant reduction in Non-Productive coping from before the programme to after it is considered to be beneficial for girls who have experienced parental separation, whose habitual ways of coping may have been adversely influenced by the experience of uncontrollable family stressors (Moos, 1990; Causey and Dubow, 1992; Griffith *et al.*, 2000). The reduction in *self-blame* is particularly noteworthy given that *self-blame* has been shown to be salient in girls of parental separation, and is the coping strategy most commonly linked to poorer well-being. Thus, a reduced tendency to *self-blame* is beneficial for global well-being. Moreover, some girls also reported that it helped them to feel better about their parents' separation. This indicates that the focus on *self-blame* in the BOC programme is particularly relevant for girls of parental separation.

Important information about the experience of parental separation and the efficacy of the programme also emerged from the individual interviews with the participants. Of the 21 girls who could remember the time of the separation, 18 recalled that it had been a very difficult time. Moreover, nearly half the girls expressed residual negative feelings about the divorce before the programme. All reported additional daily hassles to those commonly reported by adolescents, namely different living arrangements, less time (or no relationship) with biological father, financial difficulties and being caught in the middle.

> Well, it's kind of like extra stress. Like with school work, if I leave something at one house I have to go around and it's just a waste of more time. Yeah, it makes things harder.

> . . . and just annoying little things like oh, okay it's time to go to Dad's place so bring all your stuff to Dad's. Oops! I forgot something, so I have to go back and get it. That's little but it's annoying.

Many of the extra hassles the girls spoke of, such as financial hardship and different living arrangements, could not be readily altered, yet they could be dealt with more effectively. Taken together, these initial findings supported the notion that adolescent girls of parental separation would probably benefit from training in coping skills to enhance how they deal with their current and future stressors.

All girls reported positive changes to coping in general. Many replaced Non-Productive coping strategies such as *self-blame*, *ignoring problems*, and yelling and crying (*tension reduction*) with more helpful strategies. The most common improvements were more effective communication (assertiveness), anger management, problem-solving and positive thinking. These had led to positive outcomes in several domains, namely friendship, family and academic. Learning how to solve problems had the broadest influence and girls reported that this skill was helping them across all three domains of coping.

For 18 girls (66.6 per cent), the programme also had a positive impact on feelings about the separation. These girls verbally attributed the changes to acceptance of the divorce/separation, less self-blame and sadness, and more positive thinking:

> I now know that it is not my fault they divorced, it's their own. I used to blame myself for their divorce and get upset. I don't think that now.

For the nine girls (33.3 per cent) who reported no change in their feelings about the separation, seven stated this was because they were already 'OK' or 'had accepted it' before the programme. The other two girls spoke of residual anger that had not been resolved through the programme. Nonetheless, the programme had provided a forum for them to talk about their anger. For one girl, 'getting stuff off [my] chest' had been the best part of the programme.

Many girls also reported improvements in their relationships, such as having fewer fights with family members and friends. This was attributed to several factors, namely, learning how to be assertive, problem-solving, considering other people's points of view and thinking before acting:

> With the assertiveness, it makes me feel a lot better once I get what I want to say straight out to them, and they're OK about it and I am OK about it. It makes me feel a lot better, rather than losing my temper and feeling bad about it later.

Also emerging powerfully from the qualitative data was the import-ance of the small-group counselling context. Almost all girls referred to social aspects as being the best thing about the programme, namely becoming closer or meeting new people, trust and sharing, and having similar experiences (parental divorce/separation). Having separated parents was a common bond that provided trust, comfort and a sense of belonging right from the programme's outset:

> It was good 'cos you could trust everyone around you and you could talk about everything – things you could not talk about with other people.

In such a context, they felt safe to share and disclose stories. They were able to personalize the programme's content and learn vicariously through others:

> I learned about what they have done differently and how they have coped, and that can also help me.

Ivens (2006) proposed that the changes in adolescent coping found in this study occurred via a feedback loop depicted in Figure 7.1 below. She suggested that 'trust, sharing and a sense of belonging – all strong at program outset – continued to burgeon over time and provided an optimal context for learning about coping' (p. 38). This draws our attention to the powerful and reciprocal role adolescents play in coping training, particularly when the focus is on coping with a particular type of situation. For these girls, being part of a group of adolescents, each of whom had experienced parental separation, helped them to under-stand their family circumstances and to learn more effective ways of dealing with ongoing family stressors. In summary, it appears that a combination of the programme's content and being part of a sup-portive group both contributed to improved well-being and other programme outcomes such as more effective coping.

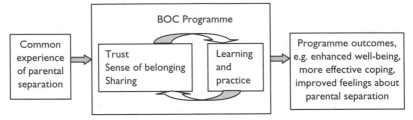

Figure 7.1 The process by which change occurred in the BOC programme (Ivens, 2006)

The above study highlighted the efficacy of group work for adolescents of parental separation. This is promising for school psychologists and other school mental health workers, who often have demanding caseloads. There may also be times when adolescents are seen individually for family-related concerns such as parental conflict, or issues to do with parental separation or blended families. Regardless of the specific issue, training in coping skills is an important part of the intervention. For example, *self-blame* should be thoroughly assessed and explored to alleviate feelings of responsibility and guilt. Decision-making and assertiveness training is also important for adolescents of parental separation, who may feel caught in the middle and experience the burden of wanting to please both parents. In addition, conflict management is particularly useful for adolescents who have experienced a high degree of family conflict as they may not have learned effective ways of resolving disagreements or managing anger.

While group and individual counselling provide important support for adolescents of parental separation, their adaptation and well-being rests greatly on post-separation family factors such as parents' mental health, parental conflict, financial hardship and contact with non-custodial parent. This means that parents must take active steps to ensure their parenting is effective and to resolve differences with their ex-partners, at least to a level that allows them discuss important issues relating to their children and come to mutual decisions.

Moving between two homes may create additional daily hassles for adolescents who find it difficult to plan their time, organize their belongings and balance social engagements with their school commitments. Spending set amounts of time with each parent may lead to additional stress, which, if not dealt with effectively, may lead to feelings of resentment, anger and frustration and cause problems at school and home. Therefore, time management and problem-solving skills are especially important for adolescents of parental separation.

Adults who are concurrently experiencing their own stress may not be in a position to assist a student experiencing parental separation who may exhibit signs of depression, such as tearfulness, irritability, difficulty concentrating, anger or withdrawal. Identifying resources and support personnel who are additional to the family is highly desirable.

In addition to grief and loss and family separation and divorce, adolescents experience numerous other stressors that can be interpreted as a loss of resources in that confidence, esteem, opportunities and commodities can be threatened or diminished. How they deal with these circumstances is coping.

Chronic illness

Chronic illness is one that lasts for a substantial period or that has consequences that are debilitating for a long time. It generally interferes with daily life for longer than three months or requires hospitalization (Boice, 1998). These illnesses include asthma, diabetes, lupus, cystic fibrosis, cardio-vascular diseases, HIV and other sexually transmitted diseases. While in the past many of these diseases would have resulted in shortened life expectancy, today many of these young people survive into and through adolescence. Nevertheless, these conditions tax the family and the individual's resources. There are issues that relate to peer acceptance. Families of ill adolescents often tend to be socially isolated or preoccupied with managing the illness, and siblings are often neglected. Biological issues related to the timing of puberty emerge. For example, those with Crohn's disease, cystic fibrosis and chronic renal disease may have a later than average entry into puberty. Perception of the adolescent's physical appearance and physical capacity may psychologically affect how they feel about themselves. There are uncertainties relating to treatment outcomes and life expectancy which can lead to anxiety. Sexual issues may also add to anxiety. Since achieving autonomy and independence are important milestones in adolescence, restrictions in these can be quite stressful.

While the management of the different illnesses requires different coping strategies on the part of the family and the individual, the common reality is that there is a range of issues that adolescents with a chronic illness have to deal with in addition to those dealt with by adolescents in general. Although there is a breadth of research on coping with chronic illness in adolescence, fewer studies have investigated the specific coping strategies this group of adolescents use to deal with chronic illness (Seiffge-Krenke, 2001). Cognitive and problem-focused coping are largely utilized by this population. However,

Seiffge-Krenke (1998) contends that within the existent literature on defence reactions of adolescents dealing with chronic illness, widespread use of defence mechanisms (such as denial and rationalization) are reported.

Overall, when reviewing the literature on chronic illness, Meijer, Sinnema, Bijstra, Mellenbergh and Wolters (2002) make the point that chronically ill adolescents do not generally cope differently with illness-related stressors from how they deal with their other stressors. It is not so much the diagnosis as the chronicity of the condition. These researchers collected data from 84 adolescents and the coping style they found to be most relevant to adjustment was what they called 'confrontational coping', which was characterized by active and purposeful problem-solving and the adequate use of social skills along with the absence of anxiety in social situations (although to a lesser extent) and the use of assertive behaviour. They point out that this was in line with the results they found in an earlier study with healthy adolescents. Overall, their work has highlighted the utility of an active coping style which includes a healthy use of social support.

Schmidt, Petersen and Bullinger (2003) make the point that coping and development are inextricably linked in that coping varies according to age and stage of development and coping in turn affects development. When reviewing the literature on chronic disease and coping, they found only a small number of articles that took account of the young persons' response to an age-appropriate questionnaire. Coping in chronically ill adolescents remains stable over time (Spirito *et al.*, 1995). There are a number of empirically developed inventories, generally employing a cognitive behavioural framework, used to assess coping with chronic disease. Varni *et al.* (1996) and Reid *et al.* (1998) assess coping with pain with Kidcope (Spirito *et al.*, 1995), which is standardized in chronically ill children and has an adolescent version for 13–16-year-olds. When coping with the disease is compared with general coping inventories, there seems to be much similarity between identified strategies (see chapter 3).

One study compared 47 young people (8–13-year-olds) with asthma, 52 with atopic dermatitis, and 57 with cancer to 58 healthy controls matched by gender and age on self-report of academic and interpersonal stressors (Hampel, Rudolph, Stachow, Lass-Lentzsch and Petermann (2005). Academic stressors included items such as '*when something at school bothers me I am really worried, e.g. taking a difficult exam or dealing with too much homework*', while interpersonal stressors include items '*when other children are bothering me I am really upset, e.g. a conflict with peers or malicious gossip expressed by peers*'. Coping with everyday stressors was improved for early adolescents suffering from one of the chronic diseases compared to their healthy controls. Those adolescents with chronic diseases used less passive avoidance on cross-situational coping and more situation-specific coping with social and school-related stresses. Cross-situational coping was obtained by calculating mean scores across data on coping with both stress situations.

In another study with an older age group (12–15 years), a sample of 521 students suffering inflammatory bowel diseases, chronic liver disease, congenital disease, coeliac disease or food allergy were compared to 245 healthy controls. They used the Coping Inventory for Stressful Situations (CISS-21), which has been used frequently with children experiencing chronic disease. In that study there was no difference between diagnostic groups or between diagnostic groups and the controls (Calsbeek, Rijken, Bekkers, van Berge Henegouwen and Dekker, 2006). There are indications that young people who experience chronic stresses due to illness appear to be able to harness their coping resources in order to manage adequately.

Coping with bullying

> There was a girl . . . They would verbally abuse her by saying things like 'you are fat' or 'you have no friends'. And it got worse when they started throwing books at her and banging her into others, or smashing her into the lockers. Then a few of us started appearing at the scene and saying 'stop'. It got to the point that she had to go to the police. It stopped for a while and the school thought it was over. And then it started up again. Now she is still being bullied.
>
> (Girl, 18)

> Bullying is different for girls and boys. For girls, it's all back-stabbing and 'she said that someone else did something'. And with guys it's basically beat each other up and they might be friends again the next day.
>
> (Girl, 17)

> Peer pressure is when people ask you to do this that you might not want to do. Like doing drugs, smoking, alcohol, bullying. They might come up to you in a big group and say 'Come on, you have to do this because you will be cool if you do.' It's basically bullying.
>
> (Girl, 18)

In 2003 a headline in a British newspaper read, 'Mother says the bullies drove book-loving son, 11, to suicide.' According to Thomas' mother, her son was picked on because he stood out from the crowd, he was extremely clever, loved music that was different from his peers, was well-spoken and loved reading. Not all bullying experiences result in such tragic outcomes but the prevalence of bullying and harassment is widespread. They are pervasive in schools, with prevalence rates ranging from 15 to 25 per cent in countries such as Germany, Australia, England, Norway and the United States (Nansel *et al.*, 2001; Olweus, 1993; Rigby and Slee, 1991; Whitney and Smith, 1993; Wolke, Woods, Stanford and Schulz, 2001). Low self-esteem, proneness to depression and anxiety, maladjustment, low levels of well-being, suicidal ideation, and poor school attendance are among the cumulative negative effects of ongoing victimization from peers (Coggan, Bennett, Hooper and Dickinson, 2003; Craig, 1998; Kokkinos and Panayiotou, 2004; Kumpulainen, Rasanen and Puura, 2001). In Australia, as in other parts of the world, interventions to counter bullying are now regarded as a matter of urgency by educational authorities (Lodge and Frydenberg, 2006).

In addition to the traditional forms of bullying that include aggression, teasing and exclusion, a more recent development has been cyber-bullying, which is growing in prevalence where young people have access to computers and mobile (cell) phones. According to Nelson (2003), 'cyber-bullying is often very serious, including stalking and death threats'. A British survey found that one in four young people aged 11–19 had been cyber-bullied (National Children's Home, 2005). A Canadian survey also showed that one-quarter of young Canadian Internet users reported receiving messages saying hateful things about others (Mnet, 2001). When environments where young people who used computers were examined, text-based name-calling, use of coarse language, profanity and personal attacks were found (Kiesler and Sproull, 1992).

The nature of new technology makes it possible for cyber-bullying to occur more secretly, spread more rapidly, and be easily preserved (e.g. cutting and pasting messages). Text or images may be posted on personal websites or blogs, or material can be transmitted via email, discussion groups, message boards, online personal polling sites, chat, IM, or by using SMS or MMS on mobile phones. While research with these new technologies is recent, some data are starting to emerge.

For example, in a recent study of 551 adolescents (Lodge and Frydenberg, 2007), 66 per cent of boys and 32 per cent of girls reported peer victimization several times during a school term. Overall, the prevalence rate for victimization for both boys and girls ranged from 7 per cent to 44 per cent for the term. Victimization on this scale causes considerable psychological distress. Girls reported experiencing more cyber-bullying than boys and boys reported more general bullying than girls. When it came to coping, the girls exemplified a more resigned Non-Productive style of coping while the boys were apprehensive but were characterized by active coping actions. Furthermore, girls with an apprehensive avoidant coping profile were found to experience more victimization via computers and mobile phones, while boys with an apprehensive but active coping profile were more likely to be victims of cyber-bullying than relaxed active boys (Lodge and Frydenberg, 2007).

To help set in place policies that reduce the likelihood of bullying we need to equip young people to cope with these contemporary tools that have potential to harm them, both emotionally and socially.

Summary

When it comes to the loss of a loved one, the adolescent experience is different from that of a child as the adolescent understands more and consequently requires honest information. There is a connection between this type of loss experience and depressive symptoms, reduced academic performance, motivation and concentration and lowered self-esteem. Death of a loved one can have devastating impacts on an adolescent's life. However, like other life experiences, this is mediated by a range of factors: temperament, past experience, family dynamics and provision of support. Social support provided through personal networks is of greatest benefit to adolescents dealing with grief. Bereaved adolescents are more reluctant to seek specialized help than adults.

One way of assisting adolescents in dealing with grief is through the provision of group programmes. An example of one such programme is Seasons for Growth, an internationally recognised bereavement programme. It targets different age groups and is grounded in Worden's psychological theory that grief comprises a series of tasks that must be accomplished in order to move forward with the loss. Australian-based evaluations have shown that, following the programme, students felt more positive about circumstances and more confident and able to express their feelings. One national evaluation reported similar programme effects for males and females but greater improvements for females in their willingness to turn to others for help. This finding is consistent with research on gender and coping.

Increasing help-seeking in boys may be something to focus on in future developments of bereavement programmes.

Another loss experience for adolescents is parental separation and divorce. The rate of parental separation and divorce is higher than ever before, thus increasing the number of children affected by it. Children of parental separation are required to adapt to a range of changes that often stir a mixture of distress and relief. Prior to separation, and often beyond, inter-parental conflict is frequently the greatest source of stress for adolescents, especially when conflicts remain unresolved and ongoing. Once again, the effects of this stress are mediated by personal and familial factors. Girls who've experienced parental separation are more likely than boys to turn to the Non-Productive coping strategy of self-blame to deal with uncontrollable family stressors. Use of this strategy generally has significant adverse affects. Adaptive coping can act as a protective mechanism for adolescents post parental separation. Support from extended family and amicable relationships between the separated parents can also positively influence the adolescents' adaptation to the situation.

In many settings school-based counselling makes support readily accessible to adolescents who've experienced parental separation. Small-group counselling may be advantageous for these adolescents as it creates a shared understanding and a ready setting for support.

The Best of Coping has also been used successfully with this population. The most powerful finding was the reduction of psychological distress after the programme, reductions in the use of Non-Productive coping and, more specifically, the use of self-blame was reduced. Through the provision of a supportive environment and skills training, adolescents who've experienced parental separation can be taught to cope more effectively, thereby increasing their chances for positive adaptation and well-being.

Another major challenge for some adolescents is chronic illness. The illness often isolates the individual socially and presents them with uncertainties regarding the future. Adolescents generally cope with illness-related stressors in a way similar to other stressors. Confrontational coping has been found to be most related to adjustment. That is, purposeful problem-solving, use of social skills, and use of assertive behaviour, without anxiety. Coping in this population is more stable over time than it is in the general population of adolescents.

A more recent development is an awareness of the prevalence of bullying as a pervasive problem in schools. Girls more frequently report the experience of cyber-bullying. Overall, victims of bullying are more likely to display a resigned Non-Productive coping style.

In sum, there are extreme stresses to which young people are exposed. Many of these stresses are experienced widely within the community. Overall, adolescents have the skills to cope. But while some circumstances stretch their resources excessively, in other situations they have a large reserve of coping resources that they tap into in circumstances of illness and severe stress.

8 Anxiety, depression and other related conditions

> I have hit walls a couple of times. I just get frustrated and say
> 'you should have done it, you shouldn't have done it wrong'. . . .
> I'd go mad at myself in basketball, when I have had a wide open
> shot and I've missed, or if I have lost my player in defence, or
> especially if I get a bad call from the refs.
>
> (Boy, 16)

There is a continuum between feeling down, being bored, lonely and
in the dumps, feeling anxious, being depressed, and in extreme circumstances experiencing despair to the point of resorting to self-harm
or suicide. Anxiety is often a precursor to depression. Since there is
frequently co-morbidity or co-occurrence between depression, anxiety
and related conditions such as eating disorders, this chapter will also
address eating disorders, self-harm, boredom, loneliness and related
conditions.

Anxiety

Anxiety is 'the tense anticipation of a threatening but vague event, a
feeling of uneasy suspense' (Rachman, 1998, p. 2). The relationship
between anxiety and depression is well documented in that anxiety is
often a precursor to depression, which in turn is often the reaction to
severe anxiety. In two-thirds of major depressive disorder cases anxiety
precedes the depression. Highly anxious adolescents engage in more
problem behaviour, are more disliked by peers, and have poorer self-
concept and lower school achievement. There is evidence that anxious
adolescents are more likely to engage in substance abuse (Dacey and
Fiore, 2000). Adolescents who are vulnerable to unpleasant emotional
states are also likely to be involved in dangerous driving and sexual
risk-taking. When the relationship between *worry* (one of the coping

strategies) and negative feelings and substance use was investigated, however, it was suggested that worrying may take the place of substance use as a means of coping with unpleasant feelings in some adolescents (Shoal, Castaneda and Giancola, 2005). This is easy to understand since, according to cognitive theorists, worry has been defined as repeated mental rehearsal of possible dangers or problems without arriving at a satisfactory solution or resolution. Like substance abuse, it can be construed as a proactive avoidant behaviour. Byrne (2000) investigated the relationship between anxiety, fear, self-esteem and coping strategies in post-primary students (13, 15 and 17 years) in Australia. The girls had consistently lower levels of self-esteem. And there was an inverse relationship between self-esteem and anxiety, that is, the more the anxiety, the less the self-esteem and vice versa. Fifteen-year-old girls had significant increase in anxiety and fear from age 13, while the boys, in contrast, had less anxiety and fear by the time they were 17.

There are various forms of anxiety experienced by adolescents, namely generalized anxiety, post-traumatic stress, separation anxiety, social phobia, obsessive-compulsive disorder and panic disorder (American Psychiatric Association, 2000). These disorders are generally characterized by excessive anxiety and worry, which an individual finds difficult to control; typical symptoms experienced may include restlessness, fatigue, difficulty in concentrating, irritability, muscle tension and sleep disturbances (American Psychiatric Association, 2000). The anxiety disorders can coexist: for example, an adolescent may experience both social phobia and separation anxiety. It is also fairly common for anxiety to occur in conjunction with depression as depression is often a reaction to severe anxiety. For example, children who are anxious are more likely to develop depression than children who are not (Dacey and Fiore, 2000), and to experience anxiety disorders as adolescents and adults (Mattison, 1992; Rapee and Barlow, 1993; March, 1995; Spence, 1996). The anxiety disorders are more common in girls than in boys (Anderson, 1994; Verhulst, 2001).

Boyd, Kostanski and colleagues (2000) looked at worldwide prevalence rates, which included figures from Canada, the United States, the United Kingdom, Bulgaria, Poland, Russia and Hong Kong. Because different questionnaires were used across studies, direct comparison is difficult, but the survey does give some interesting broad findings. Overall, there were both differences and similarities in the prevalence of depression and anxiety across countries. The prevalence of depression and anxiety in Western countries such as Australia (~14 per cent and 13 per cent respectively) and Canada (~10 per cent and

25 per cent respectively), was similar to that found in Asian countries, such as Hong Kong (~12 per cent and 13.5 per cent respectively). But the prevalence rates in Western and Asian counties were markedly lower than those reported in the Eastern European countries, Poland, Russia and Bulgaria (~44 per cent for depression). Overall, however, this study showed that a considerable number of young people experience anxiety and depression.

Anxiety sensitivity

More recently, the conceptualization of anxiety has been expanded to include the traditionally recognized trait anxiety and the newer construct, anxiety sensitivity. Trait anxiety refers to an individual's predisposition to respond or react to threatening stimuli in a particular way (Spielberger, 1966). Young people with high trait anxiety typically experience their worlds as more dangerous, exhibit more fears, and experience anxiety in a range of situations in comparison to young people with low trait anxiety. Anxiety sensitivity refers to the fear of anxiety-related bodily sensations. Individuals with high anxiety sensitivity fear anxiety symptoms because they believe such symptoms have both physiological and socially harmful consequences (Reiss and McNally, 1985). For example, young people with high anxiety sensitivity may fear heart palpitations because they believe such symptoms lead to cardiac arrest, or they may fear stuttering when speaking in public because they believe this will lead to ridicule from others. It has been found that a high level of both trait anxiety and anxiety sensitivity results in more anxiety symptoms in children and therefore may act as a predictor of anxiety disorders in childhood and adolescence (Jones and Frydenberg, 2003).

Between 10 and 30 per cent of adolescents have been found to experience anxiety severe enough to impair performance. While low levels of anxiety can enhance performance, such as that experienced by performers or athletes, high levels contribute to a range of psychosocial problems. These include somatic problems such as sleeping disorders or eating disorders, and relational difficulties. While anxiety and fear are related, they are different in that trait anxiety is a predisposition to respond to a threat in a particular way and anxiety sensitivity is the fear of the symptoms of anxiety where there is a belief that the anxiety has negative somatic, social or psychological effects. For example, it could be fear of palpitations, breathlessness or sweatiness. Fear, in contrast, has a special focus and once the fear stimulus is removed from the individual, the fear abates. Fear can be a normal reaction to a threat, while clinical fear or phobia is an excessive reaction which often anticipates a fear situation. Thus fear reactions, including panic attacks and phobias, arise from three fundamental fears: anxiety sensitivity, fear of negative evaluation, and sensitivity to illness and injury (Taylor, 1993). Adolescents do have panic attacks, with females reporting them more frequently than males, and panickers report a higher level of anxiety (King, Gullone, Tonge and Ollendick, 1993).

Fear of evaluation and criticism become important in adolescence and there are gender differences. For example, females have more fears relating to animals, unknown psychic stress, death, danger, and fear of dying, while failure and criticism are more important for males.

Parenting style

There is strong evidence that depressed mothers generally have depressed daughters (Cogan, Riddell and Mayes, 2004), but parenting style has also been linked to anxiety and coping behaviour in adolescents. The psychological pressure from perceived parenting style which was authoritarian was linked to depersonalization and trait anxiety in adolescents. In contrast, a parenting style that was perceived as warm and authoritative was positively associated with active coping and negatively associated with anxiety (Wolfradt, Hempel and Miles, 2003). This parenting style is generally recognized as the one associated with better well-being and adjustment and less school misconduct and substance abuse. These authors deduce that this warm authoritative parental style operates as a form of social support and enhances the psychological resource of self-esteem and consequently helps the individual to cope.

Depression

Depression is a complex yet common mental health disorder, which afflicts more adolescents than any other form of mental health problem. In Australia and other Western countries, at any point in time, between 2 and 5 per cent of young people will experience depression that is severe enough to warrant treatment; and around 20 per cent of young people will have experienced depression by the time they reach adulthood (Australian Institute of Health and Welfare, 2003). The World Health Organisation (WHO, 2001) estimates that by 2020 depression will be the second leading cause of disability worldwide.

There are various types of depressive disorders, the most common being major depressive disorder, dysthymic disorder and bipolar disorder. Major depressive disorder is characterized by sadness, a loss of interest and a lack of pleasure in activities, and lethargy. Other symptoms of depression include altered sleeping patterns, withdrawal from family, friends and social situations, poor concentration and indecision, frustration, tearfulness, headaches, muscle tension, temper outbursts, recurrent thoughts of death and suicide and feelings of failure and worthlessness. Although it is common for adolescents to express several of these symptoms from time to time, it is a combination of these symptoms that *persists over time* that may indicate depression. The Diagnostic and Statistical Manual of Mental Disorders (referred to as DSM-IV-TR), which is the official diagnostic system employed by mental health professionals in America and Australia, specifies that five or more of the symptoms listed above must persist for more than two weeks to meet the criteria for major depressive disorder (American Psychiatric Association, 2000) (see Table 8.1). The ICD-10 Classification of Mental and Behavioural Disorders (WHO, 1992) is an international resource for mental health professionals. It lists similar characteristics in its definition of a Depressive Episode: the individual suffers from lowering of mood, loss of interest and enjoyment, and reduced energy leading to increased fatigue and diminished activity. A duration period of at least two weeks, independent of severity, is also required for a diagnosis. Dysthymic disorder is a mild form of depression characterized by a chronic disturbance of mood of at least two years' duration, whereas major depressive disorder is an episode of a more intense mood disturbance that on average lasts for seven to nine months (Mental Health: A Report of the Surgeon General, 1999). Bipolar disorder is characterized by the two extremes, the poles of depressed mood and mania. When manic, adolescents may be much more energetic, confident, creative and impulsive. Depression during adolescence often co-occurs with other mental health problems such as anxiety, substance abuse disorders, adjustment difficulties, and increased risk of self-harm and suicide (Roberts, 1999).

The number of young people diagnosed with depression increases dramatically with the onset of puberty, but depression is much more pervasive and detrimental than the typical 'puberty blues'. For example, a study conducted by the National Institute of Mental Health in the United States reported that as many as 7 per cent of adolescents diagnosed with major depression may go on to commit suicide in adulthood (Weissmann *et al.*, 1999). This suggests that the ongoing effects of depression can be devastating, and so are the immediate effects on adolescents. Given that depression can last for a few months to a few years, it may have a lasting impact on all aspects of an

Table 8.1 Identifying Depression

	DSM-IV-TR (APA, 2000) *Major Depressive Episode*	*ICD-10 (WHO, 1992)* *Depressive Episode*
Diagnostic features	The essential feature of a Major Depressive Episode is a period of at least two weeks during which there is either (1) depressed mood or (2) loss of interest or pleasure in nearly all activities.	In typical depressive episodes, independent of severity, the individual usually suffers from depressed mood, loss of interest and enjoyment, and reduced energy leading to increased fatiguability and diminished activity. For depressive episodes of all grades of severity, a duration of at least 2 weeks is usually required for diagnosis, but shorter periods may be reasonable if symptoms are unusually severe and of rapid onset.
Symptoms	The individual must also experience at least four of the following additional symptoms: a. significant changes in appetite or weight; consider failure to make expected weight gains in children; b. insomnia or hypersomnia; c. changes in psychomotor activity including agitation or retardation; d. decreased energy. e. feelings of worthlessness or guilt; f. difficulty thinking; concentrating and making decisions; g. recurrent thoughts of death or suicidal ideation.	Other common symptoms are: a. reduced concentration and attention; b. reduced self-esteem and self-confidence; c. ideas of guilt and unworthiness (even in a mild type of episode); d. bleak and pessimistic views of the future; e. ideas or acts of self-harm or suicide; f. disturbed sleep g. diminished appetite. Some of the above symptoms may be marked and develop characteristic features that are widely regarded as having special clinical significance. The most typical examples of these 'somatic' symptoms are: loss of interest or pleasure in activities that are normally enjoyable; lack of emotional reactivity to normally pleasurable surroundings and events; waking in the morning 2 hours or more before the usual time; depression worse in the

continues overleaf

Table 8.1 (continued)

	DSM-IV-TR (APA, 2000) Major Depressive Episode	ICD-10 (WHO, 1992) Depressive Episode
		morning; objective evidence of definite psychomotor retardation or agitation (remarked on or reported by other people); marked loss of appetite; weight loss (often defined as 5% or more of body weight in the past month); marked loss of libido. Usually, this somatic syndrome is not regarded as present unless about four of these symptoms are definitely present.
Adolescent characteristics	In children and adolescents, the mood may be irritable rather than sad.	Atypical presentations are particularly common in adolescence.
Necessary conditions or additional criteria	A symptom must either be newly present or clearly worsened from previous functioning. The symptoms must persist for most of the day, nearly every day for at least 2 consecutive weeks. The symptoms: 1. must be accompanied by clinically significant impairment in social, occupational, educational or other important areas of functioning; 2. are not due to the direct effects of a drug or general medical condition; and 3. are not better accounted for by uncomplicated bereavement.	The lowered mood varies little from day to day, and is often unresponsive to circumstances, yet may show a characteristic diurnal variation as the day goes on. In some cases, anxiety, distress, and motor agitation may be more prominent at times than the depression, and the mood change may also be masked by added features such as irritability, excessive consumption of alcohol, histrionic behaviour, and exacerbation of pre-existing phobic or obsessional symptoms, or by hypochondriacal preoccupations.

Sources: Adapted from DSM-IV (APA, 2000), ICD-10 (WHO, 1992) and Carr (1994).

adolescent's life, including their relationships with family members and friends, their school work and how they view themselves and their place in the world.

The relationship between coping and depression provides an important way of looking at the prevention, early intervention and intervention for depression. This includes the building up of both external and intrapersonal resources such as cognitive appraisal and cognitive approaches to managing the demands of everyday life so that the individual can handle circumstances and deal with depression should the need arise. We know that the ways in which young people cope is related to well-being. It is therefore also reasonable to assume that there is a relationship between those who cope in Non-Productive ways and their reported prevalence of depression. This is indeed supported by the research data.

Coping and depression

There is a clear association between depression and coping, with adolescents who are depressed commonly reporting greater use of the less helpful coping strategies, such as *ignoring the problem* or *keeping problems to oneself*. Although retreating from a problem may be useful in the short term for problems outside an adolescent's control, withdrawal is rarely helpful in the long term. For example, a young person who retreats to her room and listens to music on her headphones whenever her parents argue may not develop the skills needed to cope with conflict in later years. Moreover, when adolescents call on avoidant strategies, they may use more damaging means such as turning to alcohol or drugs to forget about their concerns. Thus, avoidant coping strategies fall into the category of Non-Productive coping, the very type of coping that we wish to minimize. Not only is this type of coping less likely to bring about successful resolution of problems, but it has also been directly related to depression. Although it is difficult to establish a causal relationship between Non-Productive coping and depression, there is no denying the link between the two.

Seiffge-Krenke (2000), who sought to establish the causal links between adolescent symptomatology and stress and coping, followed 94 German adolescents and their mothers for three annual assessments of critical life events, daily stressors and coping styles. Of particular concern was their use of the strategy labelled *withdrawal*, which is an avoidant coping strategy that was clearly associated with overall symptomatology. This supported the findings of another study by Seiffge-Krenke and Klessinger (2000) in which long-lasting effects of avoidant coping were linked with depression. In the latter study it was clear that all forms of avoidant coping were linked with high levels of depressive symptoms two years later. A Norwegian study (Murberg and Bru, 2005) of 327 adolescents aged 13–16 further revealed that participants who used a more aggressive coping style, such as getting angry, venting feelings and letting off steam, were more at risk of developing depression. In contrast, participants who sought parental support were less likely to be depressed. An American study (Galaif, Sussman, Chou and Wills, 2003) of 931 adolescents aged 14–19 reported that anger coping was associated with sustained depression and perceived stress. Thus both avoidant coping and anger are associated with depression.

Australian research on the relationship between adolescent coping and depression has clearly indicated that Non-Productive coping or use of an avoidant coping style is a predictor of depression (Cunningham & Walker, 1999; Poot, 1997), refer to page 61 and 62 for detailed results in Chapter 3 as evidence of construct validity of the Adolescent Coping Scale.

Adolescent girls generally use more emotion-related coping, experience greater depression and are likely to be more ruminative (Li, DiGiuseppe and Froh, 2006). One factor that is likely to contribute to adolescent girls' greater vulnerability to stress is how they cope.

Do changes in coping generate changes in depressive symptoms? This was investigated in a short-term longitudinal study of 903 adolescents in Years 6–11 who were assessed twice with an interval of 12 months (Herman-Stahl, Stemmler and Petersen, 1995). Results indicated that adolescents who used more avoidant coping strategies reported the greatest number of depressive symptoms, whereas adolescents who used more approach-oriented coping strategies reported substantially fewer such symptoms. Importantly, this study found that participants who altered their coping profiles also had alterations in depressive symptoms over a 12-month period. Those who went from using approach-oriented to avoidant coping strategies showed an increase in depressive symptoms, whereas those who went from using avoidant to approach-oriented coping strategies showed a decrease. A vicious cycle may develop in adolescents, in which depressive symptoms increase Non-Productive coping, which in turn has long-term effects on symptomatology, and the cycle continues (Seiffge-Krenke, 2000). More promisingly, it appears that high levels of symptomatology may be reduced by a reorientation to more Productive coping.

In a study of over 1300 students attending a vocational educational school in the Netherlands whose average age was 18 (Kraaij, Garnefski, de Wilde, Dijkstra, Gebhardt, Maes and ter Doest, 2003), it was found that parental bonding and cognitive coping are related to a lower prevalence of depressive symptoms. Adolescents who reported more negative life events, more parental control, more self-blame, more rumination and more catastrophizing, had significantly higher depression scores, while adolescents who reported more positive reappraisal had lower depression scores. Those adolescents who reported a parental bonding style of low care and high control, labelled 'affectionless control', reported more stress and more depressive symptoms.

Suicide

In recent decades suicide and suicide attempts have increased (WHO, 2002). Suicide is now a leading cause of death for young adults and is among the top three causes of death in the 15–34-year age group for both sexes. This represents a massive loss to societies on a global scale. Data on suicide attempts are available from only a few countries; in general they indicate that the number of suicide attempts may be up to 20 times higher than the number of completed suicides (WHO, 2001).

A systematic review of the international literature on the prevalence of suicidal phenomena in adolescents which involved a total of 128 studies and a sample of 513,188 adolescents was conducted by Evans, Hawton, Rodham and Deeks (2005). Studies from the following countries were included: North America, Europe, Australia/New Zealand, Asia, South/Central America, Mexico and Africa. Their review confirmed that suicidal thoughts and behaviours are relatively common in adolescents, with 20–30 per cent of adolescents reporting having had suicidal thoughts. The findings also suggest that approximately 10 per cent of adolescents will have attempted suicide and 13 per cent engaged in deliberate self-harm at some time, and 6 per cent will have attempted suicide within a one-year period. Higher rates of suicidal phenomena were generally found in studies from North America compared with those from European countries, which is in contrast to the depression statistics reported earlier. Rates for suicide attempts in the previous year and lifetime were 12.6 per cent and 7.7 per cent respectively for North American studies, and 6.9 per cent and 2.0 per cent respectively for European studies. Both suicidal thoughts and behaviours were found to be more common in females, with this gender difference reported in almost every study reviewed. Overall, there appeared to be lower rates of suicidal phenomena in Asian adolescents compared to White adolescents. The prevalence of suicidal phenomena for White and Native American adolescents was almost equal, but the prevalence of recent suicidal ideation appeared to be lower in Hispanic than in White adolescents (Evans *et al.*, 2005). Establishing accurate prevalence rates is important so as to ascertain the magnitude of the problem, examine trends, identify risk factors and provide a platform for preventive programmes.

According to WHO (2006), suicidal behaviours among children and adolescents often involve complicated motives including depressive moods, emotional, behavioural and social problems, and substance abuse. Other factors include loss of romantic relationships, inability to cope with academic pressures and other life stressors, and issues associated with poor problem-solving skills, low self-esteem, and confused sexual identity. An additional risk factor for adolescent suicide is the completed suicide of a family member, peer or prominent figure. Among young people the phenomenon of cluster suicides also exists – a phenomenon that has also been labelled the contagion effect. That is, well-publicized attempts or completed suicides can lead to self-injurious behaviour in related peer groups. This emphasizes the importance of implementing preventive measures in schools in the case of a suicide within the school community.

A family history of psychiatric illness, along with high levels of family dysfunction, rejection by family, and childhood abuse and neglect increase the potential for suicide. For example, completed youth suicides have higher rates of family psychiatric disturbance, reduced family support, past suicidal ideation or behaviour, disciplinary or legal problems, and access to loaded firearms in the home. Suicidal ideation and attempted suicide is more common in children and adolescents who have suffered abuse from peers and adults.

Among adolescents 16 years and above, substance abuse significantly increases the risk of suicide during times of distress. Mood and anxiety disorders, running away, and a sense of hopelessness also increase the risk for adolescent suicide attempts. Adolescent suicide attempts are often associated with a humiliating life experience such as school failure, or conflict with a romantic partner. Interestingly, as many as 80 per cent of adolescents who commit suicide could meet the diagnosis for conduct disorder, post-traumatic stress disorder (PTSD), or violent or aggressive symptoms.

Breaking the cycle

The relationship between depression and Non-Productive coping is best perceived as a cycle, in which each is maintained by the effects of the other. For example, an adolescent boy with depression may continue to deal with his peers' taunts by withdrawing from his classmates and spending lunch breaks on his own. In turn, the boy's depressive symptoms may increase, since to avoid the taunts he has chosen to isolate himself from all of his classmates. This in turn causes him to feel isolated and disconnected from school. He may choose to avoid other social situations and activities in order to avoid being teased, which in turn leads to more isolation, hopelessness and depression. In this example, it can be seen that, irrespective of whether poor coping initially caused the depression or the reverse, both coping and depression must be targeted in order to break the cycle.

When an adolescent is presenting with symptoms of depression, it is helpful to explore his or her ways of coping to determine how Non-Productive coping may be contributing to sustained depression. Depression is characterized by pessimistic and negative cognitions. Depressed individuals have a tendency to see the world and their future as bleak and to attribute responsibility for things that go wrong to themselves and for things that go right to external factors (Shapiro, Friedberg and Bardenstein, 2006).

Because depression affects cognition, it can affect how depressed individuals deal with their problems. Attribution theory, which has been used in research with depressed individuals, is the study of how individuals explain and assign cause for events. Significant differences have been found between the attributions made by non-depressed and depressed individuals, which Shapiro and colleagues have captured along three dimensions: unstable versus stable attributions, specific versus global attributions, and internal versus external attributions.

When something goes wrong, non-depressed individuals are more likely to attribute the misfortune to temporary or unstable factors, whereas depressed individuals are more likely to attribute the misfortune to comparatively stable factors. For example, a non-depressed adolescent may attribute failing an unexpected science test to having no time to study (a one-off factor), whereas a depressed adolescent may attribute it to having a terrible science teacher (a relatively stable factor). Non-depressed individuals are also more likely to attribute negative outcomes to specific causes, whereas depressed individuals tend to attribute blame to more global causes. For example, a non-depressed adolescent who does not win a place in a running race may attribute this to the poor running conditions (a specific cause), whereas a depressed adolescent may attribute this to a lack of general fitness (a global cause). When good things occur, non-depressed adolescents are more likely to attribute this to themselves and to be proud of their achievements, whereas depressed adolescents are more likely to attribute success to external factors. For example, scoring the winning goal in basketball may be attributed to one's ability by the non-depressed adolescent and to luck by the depressed adolescent. In addition, depressed adolescents tend to blame themselves for things that go wrong and fail to consider external factors that may have influenced the outcome.

Attribution theory explains why adolescents who are at risk for depression or who are currently experiencing depression are more likely to use the Non-Productive coping strategy of *self-blame*. Depressed adolescents are often their own harshest critics and often see the world and their place in it more negatively than their family members and friends.

In order to turn depressive cognitions into coping cognitions, adolescents can be taught to identify and challenge irrational and negative thoughts. When a negative event is experienced, a depressed adolescent can be asked to explore his or her attributions of the outcomes and encouraged to replace stable, global and internal attributions for unstable, specific and external attributions, with the outcome being a more realistic and optimistic understanding of an undesired event.

Other important suggestions for reducing depression include exercise, positive thinking, activity and remaining socially connected, all of which are Productive coping strategies. In contrast, depression is maintained by sluggishness, negative thinking, inactivity and isolation, which are Non-Productive strategies. Thus, coping with depression is similar to coping with other problems, and if we help depressed adolescents to use more Productive coping strategies and less Non-Productive ones then we are helping them to deal concurrently with their depression and other types of problems.

It is fairly common for adolescents who have experienced some form of trauma or loss to experience a bout of depression. However, the goal is for the depression to improve in time and for general well-being to be restored. The experience of stressors can lead to maladaptive patterns of coping, especially during adolescence when young people experience various and numerous stressors, often for the first time. Because emotional regulation and cognitive abilities are still developing, adolescents may lack the maturity to deal appropriately with extreme stressors or with multiple stressors simultaneously. Passive and avoidant coping may be called upon, which may have some benefit in the short term but are never the best ways of dealing with stressors. Such experiences can trigger a maladaptive pattern of coping in which avoidant coping is selected over approach-oriented coping. It is therefore important to support adolescents who have recently experienced negative events, or are currently experiencing such events, and encourage them to call upon Productive coping strategies such as *social support, problem-solving* and *positive thinking*. For example, a young person grieving over the death of a family member may be encouraged to write a farewell letter, plant a tree, or create a photo collage in memory of the deceased. This active approach to coping with loss allows for the expression of emotions, which facilitates movement through the grief process rather than stagnation.

It is worth exploring adolescents' use of Non-Productive coping, even with adolescents who are not currently experiencing depression, because of the strong association between depression and avoidant coping. Improvements in coping may help to buffer against depression. Thus, adolescents' use of avoidant coping strategies may form part of the screening for students at risk of depression. In turn, school-based programmes for students at risk of depression should incorporate coping skills training as part of the overall intervention.

Adolescents who have experienced or are experiencing high levels of stress, and adolescents who use avoidant coping strategies as their primary ways of coping are at risk for depression. They are likely to benefit from coping skills training that promotes the reduction of Non-Productive coping strategies and facilitates more Productive ways of coping. Such training can be provided formally and informally. Formal coping skills programmes may be run in schools for groups of students who have been identified as at risk for depression. Alternatively, coping skills programmes may be run for all students as universal prevention. Psychologists and school counsellors may also teach adolescents effective coping skills as part of individual therapy.

Adolescents may also learn about coping informally, through observation of how other people in their social sphere deal with their problems. Parents, teachers, older siblings and peers are important role models. In particular, parents and others associated with young people should be cognizant of their own coping and model effective ways of dealing with problems as they arise. In addition, parents can explicitly assist their children to deal with their concerns by high-lighting the ineffectiveness of retreating from problems. An active approach may not always come naturally to young people and may require the encouragement and support of carers. Parents should thus be mindful of their reaction to their children when they come to them with undesirable news. For the adolescent boy who breaks his mother's best china bowl, telling his mother about this may require substantially more courage than concealing the accident. He should be praised for owning up to the accident, rather than told off, and then be encouraged to come up with a workable solution. The boy will be more likely to deal with future difficult situations in a similar way, which facilitates a pattern of effective coping responses. In contrast, had the boy experienced a negative reaction, he might be less likely to take responsibility for problems in the future and turn to more passive ways of dealing with difficulties, which sets up a maladaptive pattern of coping responses.

Prevention of adolescent depression through programmes of instruction

It is important to keep in mind that depression is a complex mental health problem, which is influenced by a variety of factors, namely biological, environmental and psychological. Therefore, preventing depression and treating depressed adolescents is no easy feat and often involves a multimodal approach and the collaboration of various individuals, namely the adolescent, their parents and family, teacher and mental health workers. Programmes that target depressed adolescents have become more common in schools over the years. While there is a substantial research body that attests to the efficacy of such programmes, there are also important research findings that caution us *not* to perceive them as the sole answer to adolescent depression. One Australian study (Sheffield *et al.*, 2006) that involved nearly 2500 students aged 13–15, independent research teams and 34 schools found that depressive symptoms did not change as a result of participation in an eight-week universal and/or selective intervention programme. The Problem Solving for Life programme was designed to be delivered in schools by trained teachers and focuses on cognitive restructuring and problem-solving skills. It sought to teach students the relationship between thoughts, feelings and behaviours, and the cognitive techniques to challenge negative thoughts. In addition, it taught effective problem-solving skills. In comparison to the universal implementation of the programme, the intervention for students at risk for depression consisted of longer sessions and a small-group format. Overall, no differences were found between the three intervention groups and the control group over the duration of the study. This was unexpected, as previous evaluations of the programme had shown its efficacy for reducing depressive symptoms in adolescents who are at risk for depression (Spence, Sheffield and Donovan, 2003). It was particularly surprising in the more recent study by Sheffield and colleagues that adolescents at risk for depression who completed the programme with their classmates and then in a small group did not show a reduction in depression symptomatology.

The authors suggested several possible explanations for their failure to find significant effects, including the important notion that school-based programmes on their own may not reduce symptoms of depression. External environmental factors may also need to be addressed. Moreover, it is worth noting that this study did not investigate coping. Coping was not a focus of the intervention and adolescents' use of coping strategies was not measured. Although problem-solving was a primary focus of the intervention, and is an important coping strategy, there were many other important aspects of coping that were not addressed. Given that a reduction in avoidant coping has been associated with a reduction in depressive symptoms, it might have been useful for the programme to provide training in coping skills (Herman-Stahl *et al.*, 1995).

In contrast to the above study's lack of support for school-based programmes, an American study (Chaplin *et al.*, 2006) found support for their ability to reduce depressive symptoms. Chaplin and colleagues evaluated the Penn Resiliency Program, which is a 12-session programme that targets cognitions and problem-solving skills, similar to the Problem Solving for Life programme used by Sheffield and colleagues in their study. The differences are that the Penn Resiliency Program was delivered every other week for 12 weeks and had only a small-group format. Leaders also received week-long training, whereas leaders of the Problem Solving for Life programme received only six hours of training. Whether these differences contributed to the more positive outcomes in Chaplin and colleagues' study is unclear. It is also possible that there were substantial differences in the topics covered within each session. Another important difference is that the Penn Resiliency Program was not restricted to students at risk for depression and therefore its ability to reduce depression in individuals with higher levels of depressive symptoms is unclear.

Chaplin and colleagues (2006) were interested in determining whether depression-prevention programmes are more effective for girls when run with all-girl groups in comparison to co-ed groups. In total, there were 208 students aged 11–14 (105 boys and 103 girls) who received the Penn Resiliency Program in groups of 9–14. Results indicated that both single-sex and co-ed groups equally reduced depressive symptoms, but there were more benefits for single-sex groups, with participants showing substantially greater reductions in measures of hopelessness and greater attendance. This study indicated that, whether the programme was delivered to all-girls groups or to co-ed groups, it was effective in reducing depressive symptoms.

The Best of Coping programme (Frydenberg and Brandon, 2002a, b, 2007a, b), described and evaluated more extensively in chapter 12, is a 10-week coping skills programme that introduces adolescents to the language of coping, assists them to identify their own coping profiles and then encourages them to reduce their use of Non-Productive coping strategies in favour of more Productive ones. Although not designed solely for depression prevention, the BOC programme has been shown to reduce depressive symptoms in adolescents at risk for depression (Bugalski and Frydenberg, 2000). In this study of 113 adolescents aged 15–17, one-fifth were identified as at risk for depression. Results indicated that students at risk for depression benefited more from the intervention than healthy adolescents. Not only were there reductions in depressive symptoms, but the use of Non-Productive coping strategies also significantly reduced over the duration of the programme. This supports the notion that a reduction in Non-Productive coping leads to a reduction in depressive symptoms. The BOC programme is similar to the Problem Solving for Life and Penn Resiliency programmes in its focus on cognitions and problem-solving, though its focus on coping is more extensive. Best of Coping focuses on both discouraging use of Non-Productive coping, while encouraging Productive coping through targeting both cognitions and behaviours. Participants are taught to think more optimistically and to be assertive and are equipped with the skills of effective problem-solving and decision-making.

The relationship between depression, stress and coping

An American study (Galaif, Sussman, Chou and Wills, 2003) investigated the relationship between depression, stress and coping in a high-risk adolescent sample comprising 931 students aged 14–19. Measures of depression, stress and coping were repeated after 12 months to obtain longitudinal information about the relationship between these variables. The authors investigated two constructs of coping: anger coping, which includes behaviours such as getting mad and getting revenge, and seeking social support. Results indicated that depressed adolescents reported high levels of stress and were more likely than non-depressed adolescents to call upon anger coping. Greater stress was associated with more anger coping and depression. There was also a significant positive correlation between anger coping and depression, perceived stress and drug use. Interestingly, depression at time 1 significantly predicted greater levels of stress at time 2, which suggests that perceived stress is not only a predictor of depression but also a consequence. Similarly, anger coping at time 1 was significantly associated with increases in depression, drug use and stress, and decreases in social support at time 2. Social support at time 1 predicted reductions in anger coping and perceived stress at time 2. Overall, this study yielded some important insights into stress, coping and depression in high-risk youths. It showed that troubled youth do call upon social supports to deal with their concerns, which is an adaptive means of dealing with problems, and they are less likely to react to problems with anger. In addition, this study revealed that depression can increase perceived stress. One of the most important findings was that negative outcomes were predicted from anger coping, with the strongest link between anger coping and depression. Female adolescents in particular used anger coping to deal with their depression. Externalizing behaviours are more commonly used by boys in the general adolescent population, which appears not to be the case in high-risk adolescents. Thus it may be beneficial for interventions with troubled females (and males) to include anger management training and the facilitation of more functional coping strategies. Moreover, adults working with troubled adolescents should encourage them to obtain support in their social networks. Assisting adolescents to ask for help and talk about their concerns is important.

Gender differences

Depression rates in boys and girls are about equal throughout childhood. The onset of puberty at about the age of 11 appears to be a pivotal marker for depression, with many more adolescents than children experiencing depression. Sex differences in rates of depression arise during adolescence and are maintained into adulthood. It is estimated that depression is at least twice as common in adolescent females than it is in adolescent males (Lewinsohn, Petit, Joiner and Seeley, 2003). That American study of 1709 adolescents reported that not only were girls twice as likely to meet the criteria for at least one major depressive episode, but they were also more likely to have recurrences of depression. From the total sample, 564 adolescents met the criteria for at least one depressive episode and were assessed at three points in time: when they were in secondary school (mean age =

16.6 years), 13 months later, and at the age of 24. Results revealed that almost half of all girls, and a quarter of all boys who met the criteria for depression at time 1 experienced at least one more episode of depression by the age of 24. The gap between male and females increased with increasing number of episodes. For example, of those adolescents who experienced three episodes, 79 per cent were female, of those who experienced four episodes, 88 per cent were female, and only females experienced five or more episodes.

In spite of these gender differences in prevalence, depressive symptoms were expressed similarly in adolescent males and adolescent females, except for the symptoms of crying, tearfulness and weight fluctuations, which were reported more frequently by girls than by boys. While this study also found that depressive symptoms did not systematically change with the transition from adolescence to adulthood, symptoms were shown to vary from episode to episode, making it difficult to predict the recurrence of depression.

Because recurrences of depression are estimated for one in every two adolescent girls and one in every four adolescent boys who meet the criteria for major depression, interventions for adolescents with depression should treat the current depressive symptoms as well as prevent future episodes. A number of reasons are given for why more females experience depression than males.

One area closely related to sex differences in depression is to do with the importance individuals place on their relationships with others and how others perceive them, collectively called social-evaluative concerns. It has been consistently shown that females are more concerned about relationships than are males. In their paper on social-evaluative concerns during adolescence, Rudolph and Conley (2005) summarize important research findings which demonstrate that, in comparison to males, females tend to make more psychological investments in relationships, are more worried about those closest to them, and more commonly use relationships as a measure of their self-worth. Traditionally, greater social-evaluative concerns in females have been perceived as a hindrance to well-being, by creating distress and leading to depression. Rudolph and Conley, however, sought to investigate not only the costs of social-evaluative concerns in adolescent girls, but also the benefits. Being concerned about relationships may lead to heightened emotionality and contribute to emotional disturbances such as depression. On the other hand, it may also lead to prosocial behaviours such as greater concern for others, co-operation and empathy and thus more effective interpersonal relations. To test this, Rudolph and Conley conducted a longitudinal study with 474 students of mean age

11 years (50.2 per cent female) to assess the outcomes of heightened social-evaluative concerns.

As expected, girls reported higher levels of social-evaluative concerns, such as '*I worry about what other kids think of me*', and higher levels of depression than did boys. Higher levels of social-evaluative concerns were also associated with higher levels of depression and explained about 70 per cent of the observed sex differences in depression. These findings clearly showed the negative consequences of particular relational styles, which are most common for girls. Results also indicated that girls had significantly higher levels of interpersonal competence than did boys. When the buffering effect of depression was controlled for, it became clear that higher social-evaluative concerns were associated with greater interpersonal competence. In summary, this study demonstrated both the cost and the benefits of social-evaluative concerns. On the one hand, social-emotional concerns are associated with emotional distress and, on the other, with interpersonal competence. Overall, it appears that high levels of social-emotional concerns have more costs than benefits, with depression suppressing the link between concerns and interpersonal competence. Rudolph and Conley extend their study by demonstrating that a moderate level of social-emotional concerns may be optimal because it is not predictive of depression (whereas a high level is) and may still have many of the interpersonal benefits.

A reduction in social-evaluative concerns may assist adolescent girls to cope with their depression and also be an important component of depression prevention. To follow is a list of strategies that may assist adolescent girls (and boys) to moderate their social-evaluative concerns:

- Help the adolescent to notice, value and appreciate her personal strengths, attributes and achievements.
- Help the adolescent explore her own relationship needs and to investigate whether her needs are being met.
- Teach the adolescent that our perceptions of an event may not be what actually happened. For example, an adolescent may perceive a group of students laughing as gossiping about her, whereas the reality may be that they were laughing at a joke. There are an infinite number of ways of viewing the same situation. Rather than interpreting something someone says or does as a reflection of her own negative self-worth, an adolescent could be taught to evaluate the evidence, to provide various accounts of the event and to come up with an interpretation that is realistic and optimistic.

- Teach the adolescent that ultimately we are all responsible for our own happiness. While it is appropriate to be concerned and interested in our family members' and friends' well-being, we cannot make or break someone's happiness.
- Help the adolescent to gain a realistic perspective of human relations. We cannot expect to like and want to be friends with everyone we meet. Nor can we expect everyone to like us and want to be our friend. At the same time, however, no one has the right to harm another person. Everyone has the right to feel safe and respected.
- Help the adolescent to be her own best friend. This means using positive affirmations, a healthy lifestyle, pursuing her own goals and interests, spoiling herself from time to time and patting herself on the back.

Co-rumination in the friendships of girls and boys

It is generally known that self-disclosure and discussing with friends leads to close relationships, and similarly it is known that focusing on negative topics leads to emotional difficulties. A study of 608 third-, fifth-, seventh- and ninth-graders by Rose (2002) examined a new construct, co-rumination, which refers to extensively discussing and revisiting problems, speculating about problems, and focusing on negative feelings. It found that co-rumination was related to high-quality close friendships and aspects of depression and anxiety. Girls reported co-ruminating more than boys and consequently had more positive friendships and also more internalizing symptoms. Given that depression can be contagious, co-ruminating or keeping company with those who are stressed and depressed can be debilitating.

Self-harm

> Teasing – that goes on. It doesn't make you feel good. And some people, well, they may go home and hurt themselves or do something like that to try and get away from it all. A few people you hear about go and do stupid things like that, like cut themselves or try to commit suicide.
>
> (Girl, 16)

Self-harm is a frequently reported occurrence among depressed adolescents. It has been often associated with poor problem-solving skills. The concept of deliberate self-harm is contested in that there are a number of terms that include self-mutilation, self-destructive behaviour, self-wounding, or self-cutting, attempted suicide or para-suicide (Best, 2006). In the United States the term 'suicide attempter' is used, while in Europe 'deliberate self-harm' is the preferred term in relationship to suicide. Some would even include anorexia and bulimia as self-harming practices. Because there is no agreed definition, prevalence data are not readily available. A recently conducted series of interviews with teachers and other related professionals in the United Kingdom found that one school professional reported self-harm in five or six out of the 30 young people they were working with, while a senior teacher in an independent girls' school reported seven or eight girls as self-harming in a population of 380 (Best, 2006). Since there is generally secrecy around these activities, what is reported is thought to be the tip of the iceberg. A survey in the National Statistics Office (Meltzer *et al.*, 2001) found that 5.8 per cent of 11–15-year-olds reported that they had tried to hurt, harm or kill themselves at some time, and interestingly 1.8 per cent of parents believed that this would be the case with their children. What is clear is that these young people are not disclosing or resorting to support or professional help.

When it comes to other forms of coping, in an adult population, self-mutilators saw themselves as having less control over problem-solving options and using more avoidant coping (Haines and Williams, 2003). Similarly, in a large study of 6020 15–16-year-olds who responded to an anonymous self-reported questionnaire conducted in England, young people who had deliberately self-harmed in the past year, interestingly, did not identify themselves as having more serious problems than other adolescents. They were less likely to ask for help from family members or teachers but were more likely to get help from their friends. Generally they employed more avoidant strategies and were less likely to focus on dealing with the problems they were confronted with (Evans, Hawton and Rodham, 2005).

Eating disorders

Anorexia nervosa, along with other eating disorders, is closely associated with depression. There is some evidence to suggest that anorexia may lead to depression, yet how this occurs is not entirely clear.

There are three common types of eating disorders: anorexia nervosa, bulimia nervosa, and binge-eating disorder. The DSM-IV-TR provides the diagnostic criteria for the three types of eating disorder. The diagnoses of these disorders have several common characteristics, such as an extreme fear of being fat, distorted body image and serious disturbances in eating behaviour.

Anorexia nervosa

Anorexia nervosa is characterized by a refusal to maintain a minimally normal body weight, and a refusal to eat enough food to provide sufficient calorie intake because of an intense fear of being fat. To meet the diagnosis of anorexia nervosa:

- The person refuses to maintain a normal weight for their age and height. There is weight loss that leads to the person weighing less than 85 per cent of what is considered to be healthy for their height and age. Typically, refusal of food leads to the weight loss, but excessive exercise and laxative use may also be used to reduce and maintain low body-weight.
- The person has an intense fear of being fat that remains even when they are extremely underweight.
- The person has a distorted body image. They are preoccupied with their body's weight and shape and perceive themselves as much larger than they really are.
- For females who were previously menstruating, amenorrhea occurs, which is the uninterrupted absence of at least three menstrual cycles (American Psychiatric Association, 2000).

The DSM-IV further classifies anorexia into two subtypes, namely the restricting type and the binge-eating purging type, which depends on whether weight loss occurs solely through food restriction or through the combination of food restriction, binge eating and purging (American Psychiatric Association, 2000).

Anorexia nervosa mainly affects adolescent girls and young adult women, with females 10 times more likely than males to develop the disorder. Approximately 1 per cent of adolescent females and women meet the diagnosis of anorexia nervosa. It is estimated that around 70 per cent of people with anorexia will recover, but it often takes some years for maintenance of a healthy weight and normal eating patterns to be established. For those who do not recover, death may result, which is most often through suicide or due to secondary complications such as cardiac arrest. The death rate for anorexia nervosa is alarmingly high (Davison, Neale and Kring, 2004); for females aged 15–24, it is 12 times higher than for the general population (Sullivan, 1995).

Bulimia nervosa

Bulimia nervosa is characterized by repeated episodes of binge eating followed by inappropriate compensatory behaviours such as self-induced vomiting, and sometimes other forms of calorie-reducing behaviour such as laxative use or excessive exercise. The DSM-IV-TR criteria for bulimia nervosa are as follows:

* Recurrent binge eating that comprises episodes of consuming substantially more food than one would normally eat within a two-hour period, which is accompanied by a sense that their eating behaviour is beyond their control;
* Repeated self-induced vomiting or other compensatory behaviours, such as laxatives, to prevent increases in weight;
* On average, both the binging and the purging behaviours occur at least twice a week for three months;
* Self-evaluation is disproportionately influenced by weight and body shape;

> *Note:* If the binge and purging occurs with anorexia nervosa, then the diagnosis of anorexia nervosa binge-purging type is made (American Psychiatric Association, 2000).

The DSM-IV-TR specifies two types of bulimia nervosa: the purging and the non-purging types depending on whether self-induced vomiting or forms of laxatives are used to eliminate the food consumption (purging type) or other forms of compensatory behaviours such as excessive exercise, use of laxatives or fasting (non-purging type) (American Psychiatric Association, 2000).

Like people with anorexia nervosa, individuals with bulimia have a desire to be thin and are severely dissatisfied with their body weight and shape. However, an important difference is that people with bulimia are often not underweight, because the purging is their compensatory behaviour for consuming a great many calories. Nonetheless, the recurrent purging behaviours cause serious physical damage. Extreme emotions are brought on by the binging and purging: at one extreme there is much guilt and disgust for the amount of food eaten and at the other, a great sense of relief after purging.

Bulimia nervosa, like anorexia nervosa, primarily affects adolescent girls and young adult women, with nine out of 10 sufferers being female. Bulimia nervosa is slightly more common than anorexia nervosa, with estimates that between 1 and 2 per cent of people have the disorder. Complete recovery from bulimia nervosa and suicide rates are comparable to those reported for anorexia nervosa, yet the overall mortality rate is lower (Davison, Neale and Kring, 2004).

Binge-eating disorder

Binge-eating disorder is a relatively new and contested type of eating disorder provisionally included in the DSM-IV-TR. It is characterized by recurring binging episodes in the absence of compensatory behaviours, which means that individuals may weigh outside the healthy weight range. Symptoms of binge-eating disorder are:

*   Recurrent binge eating that comprises episodes of consuming substantially more food than one would normally eat within a two-hour period, which is accompanied by a sense that their eating behaviour is beyond their control.
*   On average, binging occurs at least twice a week for six months.
*   Self-evaluation is disproportionately influenced by weight and body shape.
*   Extreme distress follows the binge eating (Davison, Neale and Kring, 2004).

Binge-eating disorder is more common than either anorexia nervosa or bulimia nervosa. It is estimated that in the general population, 3 per cent of college students and 5 per cent of obese people meet the diagnosis for binge-eating disorder.

In general, at any given time, 10 per cent or more of late adolescent and adult women report symptoms of eating disorders. Although these symptoms may not satisfy full diagnostic criteria, they do often cause distress and impairment. Interventions with these individuals may be helpful and may prevent the development of more serious disorders.

Eating disorders are closely associated with other mental heath problems, such as depression, anxiety and obsessive-compulsive disorders. Co-morbidities for eating disorders were investigated in a large study of 2438 female inpatients (Blinder, Cumella and Sanathara, 2006). Results indicated that 97 per cent of the inpatients had a co-morbid diagnosis with at least one other mental health problem. The most common co-morbidity (94 per cent) was with mood disorders, which was mostly major depressive disorder. Anxiety was also relatively common (56 per cent), followed by substance use (22 per cent). Whereas the prevalence of mood disorders and anxiety were equal over the different types of eating disorders, substance use was more common in patients with bulimia nervosa and obsessive-compulsive disorder was more common in patients with anorexia nervosa. The authors concluded that co-morbidity in eating disorders is best represented by a rank-ordering model of mood, anxiety and substance use disorders.

Eating disorders are prevalent in communities where food is abundant. In reviewing the many possible causes of eating disorder, Polivy and Herman (2002) note the sociocultural factors such as the media's promotion of the 'body ideal' and the possible influence of peers; family factors such as the excessive closeness or enmeshment within the family, parents being critical of body shape and size and being excessively controlling of the adolescent, leading to a strong will to establish autonomy; and esteem factors where there is dissatisfaction with the self and particularly with body size and shape. The family factors have been extended to include additional risk factors such as lack of parental caring, sexual and/or physical abuse. There are also problems of identity and control, the co-occurrence with mood disorders and cognitive factors such as obsessive thoughts and rigid thinking patterns. With such a range of complex possible causes and risk factors it is not surprising that there has not been a universally accepted treatment that has been deemed to be effective.

What does this all mean in the context of coping? Regardless of the underlying causes for eating disorders, which may be societal in that a thin body ideal is promoted through media and adult role models, or situational in that it may represent attempts to manage conflict in the family, achieve control over oneself or others, the important thing is to acknowledge that these are Non-Productive forms of coping. Some intervention approaches are directed at assisting the individual to gain insight into their motives and the causes of their eating disorder. Other types of interventions have been evaluated with randomized controlled trials and there is evidence that cognitive behaviour therapy (CBT) is an effective treatment for bulimia nervosa (Hay and Bacaltchuk, 2001) and CBT delivered via the Internet (Heinicke, Paxton, McLean and Wertheim, 2007) also has demonstrated good outcomes. Since coping skills in a general sense are taught through a CBT framework where the individual makes changes in their cognitions and actions, it could be helpful to include structured coping skills training within an intervention programme. Minimally, it should be helpful to decrease Non-Productive coping and increase Productive coping as well as identify alternative forms of support and finding substitutes, within the context of a management programme. Finally, a systematic approach can take account of both of these approaches

and include the expectation that there will be changes in the circumstances and the relationship of those experiencing an eating disorder.

Coping with boredom

A headline in a local newspaper read 'Boredom kills: Boredom in the
suburbs'. It was accompanied by a photograph of young people
lounging around outside a suburban shopping mall in the middle of
the day. Boredom has been linked to a number of problem behaviours
such as alcohol and drug abuse, higher rates of dropping out of
school, and vandalism (Caldwell, Darling, Payne and Dowdey, 1999).
It is often associated with depression – if not a result of it, it may
contribute to it. When young people completed a face-to-face interview and diary over two weeks, it was found that when they were
autonomous and self-determined they were less bored. However, the
role of parents was found to be important. The lack of autonomy in
social control situations, that is, having to go to an event, and perceived parental monitoring, was negatively associated with boredom.
In trying to understand why low levels of parental monitoring were
associated with boredom in 13-year-olds, these authors explained that
young people of this age were in the process of achieving some freedom in decision-making, so they might not have construed parental
control as restrictive. Alternatively, parents who facilitate and monitor activities may play a part in alleviating the boredom of these
young people.

Having a lack of something to do was associated with higher levels
of boredom. Adolescents who are active producers of their own
development are healthier and more productive. The findings of these
authors is consistent with the long-held understanding that intrinsic
motivation and self-determination, as hallmarks of leisure, are anti-
thetical to the experience of boredom.

Loneliness and coping

There is value in having relationships and costs in being without
them. The benefits include the happiness of being in love and being
with friends. Larson (1990) found that when subjects were paged on
random occasions they were in the most positive mood when they
were with friends, followed by being with family and being alone.

The satisfaction from friendships can be explained both by the
pleasurable things that friends do together and the positive verbal and

non-verbal signals exchanged. For example, smiling is a powerful reinforcer (Argyle, 1994).

In a different vein, Bolger and Eckenrode (1991) found that students taking exams became much less anxious if they were closely integrated in friendship networks. Many studies have shown that social relationships can 'buffer' stress. Poor social skills lead to rejection and isolation, which are major forms of stress (Argyle, 1994). Furthermore, those in close relationships enjoy better health and live longer

Berkman and Syme (1979) followed up 6900 individuals in California over nine years and obtained measures of their supportive networks – family, friends and organizations like churches. It was found that the death rate over this period was much greater for those who had weaker social support. Other studies have shown that death from heart attacks is most affected when there is lack of social support, though other medical causes of death are affected too. The reason that social relationships are good for health is partly because those involved look after each other better and engage in better 'health behaviour', that is, they drink and smoke less, have a better diet, do what the doctor orders, but in addition relationships activate the immune system.

Loneliness is a cost of not having relationships and is a major source of unhappiness and depression. There are many reasons why people are lonely, including the fact that they lack friends because they do not have the social skills to initiate and sustain relationships (Peplau and Perlman, 1982). Weiss (1974) suggested that there are two kinds of loneliness, corresponding to two different social needs. 'Emotional loneliness' is when there is a lack of a close attachment, such as marriage, 'social loneliness' when there is lack of a network of friends. This has been strongly supported in later research. Loneliness is deemed to be most prevalent in the adolescent years. While in some respects loneliness during adolescence may be normative in that the period is one of transition and change in terms of roles, relationships and identity, persistent feelings of loneliness are not normative (Heinrich and Gullone, 2006). Thus loneliness can occur if the adolescent has unrealistic expectations of his or her social relationships or the requisite social skills have not been developed.

Loneliness is a risk factor for depression and can contribute to it. A study of high-risk adolescents enrolled in an alternative high school in the United States (43 males and 33 females) explored the correlates of loneliness. Loneliness in that study was defined for high-risk adolescents as 'a distressing emotional condition that arises when one feels rejected by, estranged from, or misunderstood by others, and when one lacks companions for social activities and emotional intimacy' (Rook, 1984). While there are many correlates of loneliness, they examined empathy, self-esteem and coping. A body of research has identified that those who have a capacity to be empathic are less likely to be lonely. Different types of coping have been related to loneliness. For example, when gifted young people were feeling rejected they were more likely to engage in individual pursuits (Woodward and Kalyan-Masih, 1990).

Risk-taking

Adolescents are generally considered to engage in risky behaviours such as substance abuse, unprotected sex or driving hazardously. A recent study that explored adolescents' perception of risk vulnerability to personal behaviours (e.g. binge drinking, unprotected sex) and natural hazards (e.g. tornadoes, hurricanes, lightning) reported that adolescents were *less likely* than young adults to perceive themselves as invulnerable to risks (Millstein and Halpern-Felsher, 2002). This goes against traditional theory that describes adolescence as a period marked by a sense of personal invincibility to threats, harms and challenges. On the contrary, younger adolescents perceived greater risks than did older ones, who in turn perceived greater risks than young adults. To explain such results the authors invoked research on the development of meta-cognitive skills and information-processing and an increase in social knowledge and awareness. Perhaps young adolescents perceive more risk from natural hazards and risky behaviours than do older adolescents and young adults because they have been educated about the adverse outcomes that may arise, but have not yet realized that adverse outcomes are not the norm. Further, egocentric thinking, a characteristic of adolescence, may have young people placing a higher risk judgement on the likelihood that something bad will happen to them as opposed to other people, which in turn buffers the illusion of invulnerability.

The finding that adolescents perceive themselves to be more vulnerable to risks than adults has implications for how best to intervene with young people. While we do not want adolescents engaging in risky behaviours, we also do not want them to be overly fearful of natural hazards and, at the extreme, to view the world as unsafe and dangerous. When it comes to reducing risk-taking behaviours, Millstein and Halpern-Felsher (2002) suggest interventions that accentuate the meaning and the impact of negative outcomes, rather than the probability of their occurrences. For example, having a young adult who is paraplegic as a result of a car accident speak at a school assembly may help adolescents to realize the devastation that can result from speeding.

Summary

Anxious adolescents engage in more problem behaviour and have poorer self-concept. This is concerning as there are about 10 to 30 per cent of adolescents who experience anxiety severe enough to impact performance. There is a trajectory from anxiety to depression in adolescence through to depression in adulthood. There is a connection between anxiety experienced by adolescents and parenting styles that are authoritarian. Anxiety and depression rates, whilst widespread, are lower in Western and Asian countries than in Eastern Europe, a finding that may be attributed to the political climate.

Depression affects more adolescents than any other mental health problem. The incidence is concerning given the relationship between depression and suicidal behaviour. Depressed adolescents are generally predisposed to resort to unhelpful methods of coping: there is a direct relationship between depression and the use of Non-Productive coping strategies. Additionally, long-term avoidance of problems can be detrimental. Sex differences in depression arise in adolescence, with depression twice as common in females. This is likely to be linked to the fact that girls place greater importance on social-evaluative concerns. The good news is that positive changes in coping can lead to a reduction in depressive symptoms.

A large-scale international review reported that thoughts of suicide are relatively common in adolescents, with higher rates of suicidal phenomena in North American studies compared to European. Additionally, a significant number of young people admit to being engaged in self-harm. It is important to ascertain the degree to which adolescents view these behaviours as genuine coping responses. For example, eating disorders can be construed as a form of self-harm and also manifest as Non-Productive coping. While risky behaviour is complex and in general terms is a lack of fear of damage to oneself, it can also be construed as a form of Non-Productive coping.

Intervention should focus on breaking the cycle of depression and negative coping and should include an analysis of cognitions and attribution. Attribution explains the relationship between depression and negative coping. Coping skills training may also serve as a buffer against depression for non-depressed adolescents. The universal delivery of programmes is a promising way of achieving this as it creates a culture of coping in the wider community rather than merely targeting at-risk individuals. The jury is still out on the success of these approaches, with mixed findings for the reduction of depressive symptoms being reported. However, since there is also a strong link between anger coping and depression, there is also support for anger management training as part of coping skills development.

Loneliness is also a risk factor for depression. Therefore, the protective role and importance of social support as both a resource and a mechanism for coping are highlighted.

9   Resilience and happiness

Positive thinking and confidence

> If you are a positive person and you have a lot of confidence and
> you make a mistake, then you can say to yourself 'OK, you have
> made a mistake, get up and try again. If you make another one
> you can always eventually get it right, even if you have to ask for
> help.' But I think if you are very non-confident person, then you
> think 'Oh, I have made a mistake. I can't do it!' And that's one of
> the main things I have heard from friends, that 'I can't do it'. But
> you always have to try!
>
> (Girl, 14)

Since the turn of the twenty-first century, key figures in the field of
psychology such as Martin Seligman and Mihaly Csikszentmihalyi
(2000) have called on us to explore human capacity rather than
focusing on failings or inadequacies. In 2000 the *American Psychologist* devoted much of the sixth issue of volume 55 to papers that made
the argument from many perspectives. Additionally, the *Handbook of
positive psychology* (Snyder and Lopez, 2002) has alerted us to the
benefits of considering psychology from a positive perspective rather
than one of pathology and incapacity. Consistent with that approach
is the ever-growing interest in the areas of health promotion and
prevention and in those of coping and resilience. Resilience and how
to achieve it is part of the well-being factor. Two additional areas, the
achievement of happiness and the development of emotional intelligence assisted by social coping skills, contribute to today's positive
orientation of psychology.

Resilience

Since the prevalence of depression among young people has became of major concern in some communities, researchers have been pre-occupied by the search for factors which are protective and which determine that one person is resilient to stress while another is not. A transactional model of stress where the individual and the environment are in a reciprocal interaction posits that depression, for example in children, results from the interplay of a number of factors that may be enduring, such as strong family supports (protective factor), and transient circumstances such as changing schools (vulnerability factor). These may act as a buffer or they may provide a challenge (see Harrington, 1993). The co-occurrence of the predisposing characteristics of an individual along with circumstances that are externally determined may lead to depression. Vulnerability factors increase the risk of a disorder occurring. It has generally been accepted that resilience is determined, at least in part, by a positive disposition of the personality, a supportive family milieu, and external societal agencies that function as a support system (Garmezy, 1985).

The three major contexts that influence development – family, school and community – exert their impact at times singly and at others in concert. As the large-scale study by Resnick and colleagues (1997, cited in chapters 2 and 8) demonstrated, family connectedness and school connectedness were protective factors against health risk behaviours such as violence, suicidal thoughts, substance abuse (cigarettes, alcohol, marijuana) and early pregnancy. Furthermore, the combination of coping responses that are maximally associated with well-being involves the use of positive reappraisal and problem-solving and resigned acceptance. Adolescents who used less problem-solving, less positive reappraisal, more logical analysis, more cognitive avoidance, and more resigned acceptance, were more depressed and anxious. Thus family and school connectedness can be construed as resources that come to the service of the individual.

The promotion of resilience does not lie in the avoidance of stress but the encountering of stress allows self-confidence to build up and competence to increase through a sense of mastery (Rutter, 1985; Seligman, 1995). These adaptive qualities are not constitutional or unmodifiable: young people can be helped to develop them.

There is a suggestion that a lack of achievement (educational or physical) may lead to anxiety and/or depression (see Goodyer, 1990). Goodyer points out that one implication of these findings is that it is not only environmental or constitutional factors but current outcomes that may play a part in depression. A transactional model of stress can also be used to explain how age and developmental level determine what is perceived as a buffer or a challenge. For example, the buffering effect of a close same-sex or opposite-sex relationship may operate at a particular age and stage during adolescence, and may be dependent on maturational and other factors.

Efficacious outcomes

In addition to issues relating to resilience, and the minimization of dysfunction, there is the question of what makes young people function well. Adolescent happiness is one such index of well-being and has been linked to young people's involvement with prosocial activities. For example, there is emerging evidence that teaching prosocial behaviours has far-reaching benefits (Roker, Player and Coleman, 1999).

Along with many others, Olsson, Bond, Burns, Vella-Brodrick and Sawyer (2003) argue that there is need for clarity around the concept of resilience as it relates to adolescence. They reviewed the literature between 1990 and 2000. Metaphors relating to resilience include being 'elastic' – having a capacity to bounce back in the face of adversity. Resilience is about the interplay of risk factors and protective factors that can buffer the individual against adverse circumstances. It is not an invulnerability to stress but a capacity to recover when confronted with adversity. It is part of 'normal development under difficult conditions' (Fonagy, Steele, Steele, Higgitt and Target, 1994, p. 233).

Olsson and colleagues (2003) point out in their review that, while 'it is tempting to define adolescent resilience solely in terms of maintenance of emotional wellbeing in the face of adversity' (p. 3), it is reasonable to expect that for adolescents, unlike adults, distressing emotions act as an index of adversity. 'Young people functioning well under high stress often show higher levels of emotional stress compared to their low stress peers' (Luthar, 1993, p. 3). Thus resilient people are not necessarily devoid of distressing emotions but can function well or show successful coping despite the presence of such emotions. One way to construe resilience is to regard it as 'overt competence under stress' (p. 3). So measures of well-being alone do not give an adequate picture.

These authors show how resilience may be developed by promoting protective factors. The proposed interventions are about believing in the worth of the individual and providing resources in the home and school setting for the individual, the family and the broader social environment. Werner and Smith (1992) and Prior (1999) also note that a positive temperament increases the likelihood of eliciting a positive response from others from an early age and subsequently these positive experiences contribute to resilience. Regardless of factors determined by heredity, providing the individual with a good range of coping skills and understanding of the self is an important component in developing resilience.

Resilience involves individuals, their families and their societies. Within the individual, protective processes such as resources, competencies, talent and skills play a part. A supportive family that is ideal in the sense of being neither authoritarian nor laissez-faire in parenting style is an important contributor to the individual's capacity to remain resilient. As well, supportive peer groups within which the individual and the peer group exhibit good social skills play their part, as do the community and the school, which also provide an external supportive framework.

Resilience as a multifactorial concept

It is clear that risk and resilience are best thought of as processes rather than a single event or capacity. The Christchurch longitudinal study (Fergusson and Lynskey, 1996) illustrates the linear relationship between the accumulation of a number of risk factors such as poverty, parent conflict, separation and poor parent–child interaction. So if a negative chain of events increases the risk adversely, it could also be inferred that protective factors provide a positive chain leading to favourable developmental outcomes (Werner and Smith, 1992). This is somewhat like Hobfoll's concept of a caravan of resources.

In the experience of parental divorce (see chapter 7) there are elements such as tension in the family, material resource implications and multiple loyalties with which the adolescent has to deal. These present a risk in many circumstance, but not in all.

Resilience and positive emotions

In keeping with the concept of resilience as the capacity to bounce back from stressful experiences, three studies using college students (Tugade and Fredrickson, 2004) provide empirical evidence for this theory. They demonstrate the use of positive emotions to rebound from stress and to find positive meaning in stressful encounters. In the adult literature it has been demonstrated that positive emotions help to buffer against stress and that the use of positive reappraisal, problem-focused coping and the infusion of events with positive meaning are related to the occurrence and maintenance of positive affect (Folkman and Moskowitz, 2000); this predicts increases in psychological health and well-being (Affleck and Tennen, 1996). The broaden-and-build theory of positive emotions articulated by Fredrickson (1998, 2001) demonstrates how positive and negative emotions provide distinct and complementary adaptive functions. The cognitive and physiological effects can be felt in that positive emotions broaden one's coping repertoire while negative emotions tend to focus on the 'attack when angry and escape when afraid'. Linked with this view of emotions is the concept of emotional intelligence, described by Salovey and Mayer (1989–90) as the capacity to identify and regulate one's emotions and use them to guide one's thinking and actions. Positive emotions beget positive emotions and help to achieve an upward spiral of resources that will enhance emotional well-being.

Additionally, in the educational context, for example, a positive mood enhances elaborate processing, even of negative information. There has been convincing evidence that enjoyment of a learning task has had a positive influence on performance. Pekrun, Goetz, Titz and Perry (2002) tested the assumption that intrinsic activating positive emotions enhance motivation, facilitate elaborate information-processing, benefit from creative and flexible ways of thinking, direct attention towards task performance, and help self-regulation, implying that they should contribute to academic achievement. They found that positive emotions do in fact relate in significant ways to learning achievement. Enjoyment, hope and pride related positively to students' metacognitive strategies for learning, and to flexible cognitive strategies of elaboration, organization and critical thinking.

Emotional intelligence

According to Goleman (1998), emotional intelligence includes self-awareness and impulse control, persistence, zeal, self-motivation, empathy and social expressiveness. He points out that IQ accounts for only 20 per cent of factors that determine success in life. Thus, he asserts that academic intelligence has little to do with emotional well-being. A whole host of factors, including what he describes as emotional intelligence, account for the greater part of an individual's successful transition through life. He points out that there are different ways of being smart and emotional intelligence is one of them. The price of what he calls 'emotional illiteracy' is too high and can be seen in the levels of depression and despair experienced by people.

Emotional intelligence is not fixed at birth but can be nurtured and strengthened. While there is no emotional centre of the brain, there are several systems or circuits that disperse regulation of a given emotion.

Emotional competence is made up of two major components: personal competence and social competence (Goleman, 1998). The former includes self-awareness, self-regulation and motivation. Motivation consists of achievement, drive, commitment, initiative and optimism, which involves pursuing goals despite setbacks. Personal competence includes emotional awareness or the recognition of how our emotions are affecting our performance, accurate self-assessment, a sense of our strengths and limits, and self-confidence that provides the courage to move forward based on 'certainty about capabilities, values and goals'. People with this type of competence 'know which emotions they are feeling and why; realise the links between their feelings and what they think, do and say; realise how their feelings affect their performance and have a guiding awareness of their values and goals' (p. 54).

Emotions

While the emphasis in recent years has been on positive emotions, health and well-being and how normal people flourish, Lazarus (2003) cautions us about only emphasizing the positive without due regard to the part that negative emotions play: 'We need the bad, which is part of life, to fully appreciate the good' (p. 94).

While Lazarus' theorizing drew on his work with adults, it is not difficult to extrapolate from it to the world of adolescents. This is quite evident in the research related to resilience and coping with difficult circumstances such as illness and trauma in the world of adolescence (see chapter 7). In the same article Lazarus comments that creating categories of emotions such as positive and negative fails to take account of the context. For example, what may be a joyful experience for one person (spending time with friends) may be an anxiety-provoking one for another. Similarly, the context may determine how one feels – is it when one is on holiday or when one is trying to study for exams? Similarly, what is construed as positive emotions such as 'hope' is a combination of wish and belief that a desired outcome might happen, but there is also anxiety associated with the possibility that the desired outcome will not happen. Additionally, emotions such as joy and happiness are not permanent states; for example, after the joy of doing well in an assignment, the reality may follow of having to continue to strive. Having pointed out the difficulties in valence of emotions and in individual and situational differences, Lazarus goes on to point out the complexities of measuring emotions. He clearly articulates the role of coping in contributing to the variance concerning harmful or favourable consequences.

Happiness

Long before the advent of the positive movement in psychology, researchers were interested in what makes people happy. The concept of health is more than the mere absence of illness: it contains mental and social well-being. Debates around the importance of genetic disposition, material possessions, social relationships, family support have surrounded the concept of happiness. More recently concepts such as well-being, resilience, engagement and flow have been added to the mix.

We could ask, why the flurry of interest in happiness? Classic philosophers like Nietzsche, Kant and Schopenhauer were preoccupied with the meaning of life, the angst that went with the human struggle to exist, and today we are all looking for an illusive perpetual state of happiness. Psychologists often refer to it as a subjective well-being. There is no evidence to say that we were happier 20 or 50 years ago but there is also no evidence to the contrary. However, there has been an increase in suicide, substance abuse, divorce and depression. To turn that around we will need to tip the balance from despair and poor well-being to more positive ways of valuing and enjoying our time on the planet.

Our greater material wealth has not made us happier. For example, Diener and Lucas (1999) and Myers (2000) reported that although personal income has doubled over the previous 50 years in the United States, personal happiness has remained constant. They concluded that we should focus on the human rather than the material.

Ed Diener, from the University of Illinois, who is known as the 'father' of the study of well-being, points out that there is no single factor that makes everyone happy but there is a range of strategies supported by research which can contribute to achieving happiness. Generally, having a purpose gives us meaning and also a sense of personal control. Sonya Lyubomirsky at the University of California reviewed 225 studies of happiness and found that happiness leads to success at work, relationships and health, not the other way round. Happy individuals seek new goals in life. That also means that by teaching goal-setting as an intrinsic activity you can contribute to a probable sense of happiness and well-being. Mihaly Csikszentmihalyi

(1990) has promoted the concept of flow: when the individual is so absorbed in what he or she is doing to the point at which they cease to be conscious/aware of their surroundings and a sense of time, he describes that as a state of happiness. Diener says don't make a big deal of trivial hassles, instead make a habit of noticing good things.

Thus the strategies, both cognitive and action-based that contribute to happiness, include:

1   Having close friends and supportive relationships. Our need to belong, says David Myers from Hope College in Michigan, is instinctual.
2   Making others happy. This is an indirect way of achieving happiness. Rather than the hedonistic pursuit of pleasure for oneself and being self-indulgent, making others happy has payoffs. In a BBC Documentary *Making Slough Happy*, experts gave 50 volunteers the 'seeds of happiness' which they were to drop throughout the town. One was to smile or say hello to people in the town at least once a day. Happy people are active, not reactive or passive. They are purposeful. Happy people are more helpful, according to Myers, but doing good also makes you feel good (see also the study by Magen, in this chapter).
3   Seeking benefits that are intrinsic not instrumental, that is, by doing things for their own sake, not because they will bring rewards or recognition. That is, have passions or things that you enjoy doing. Helping students to find an interest in the things they are learning rather than the external merit points *per se* that are to be gained. It also means learning the art of self-satisfaction or self-feedback rather than counting on external sources of approval and praise. This is what Dweck (1998) means when she talks about instrumental versus achievement goals. This reduces the need for status and social comparisons.
4   Striving for balance in career, family and leisure is good in its own right but a balance between these things is needed.
5   Cultivating optimism. Those who see their setbacks as being a result of bad luck are not likely to be put off the trail of their pursuits.
6   Thinking happy and acting happy. Myers points out that putting on a happy face, smiling at people and going through the motions can trigger the emotions.
7   Counting one's blessings. Martin Seligman, author of *Authentic happiness*, goes to bed every night saying ' I am grateful for all I have, all the people in my life . . .'.

8   Looking downwards and seeing yourself as fortunate rather than looking upwards at those who have more. Myers says that happiness is less about getting what you want but wanting what you have got.

9   Getting back to nature. We only left hunting and gathering 10,000 years ago so there is a mismatch between our bodies and technology; for example, we have improved our food supply but have taken the effort out of gathering our food and hence the obesity epidemic. We need to exercise, and as a bonus we get the endorphin rush.

So what is happiness? Since most of the research on happiness emanates from the adult arena we need to extrapolate to the world of young people. Happiness is generally defined in terms of positive affect or positive emotional states such as joy, pleasure, optimism, a high life satisfaction and low negative affect (Lyubomirsky, Sheldon and Schkade, 2005). The term 'subjective well-being' is often used. They describe what they call the 'architecture of sustainable happiness'.

Since it is not success that leads to happiness but happiness that leads to success, the inner disposition of a person affects the outward circumstances. Success in this sense is measured by those things that are valued in a culture (Lyubomirsky, King and Diener, 2005). Happiness itself is valued in present Western culture and that is reflected in a multitude of ways. For example, the preoccupation with self-help books and the use of substances, while sometimes used to block out pain, are also used to get a good feeling, a social lubricant. There are many tangible benefits for those who are happy, and these come in the form of more successful relations, more support from others, greater pleasure in what they do, hence a better sense of well-being and general health, greater self-control and hence better coping. They flourish more inwardly and more outwardly. They are more prosocial, more co-operative and more other-centred.

Lyubomirsky and colleagues make an important distinction between sustainable and temporary happiness. Sustainable happiness refers to an individual's baseline level of happiness, which captures one's average level over a period of months or a year. In contrast, temporary happiness refers to one's current or short-term level of happiness, which is more influenced by the current state of affairs. Perceiving happiness in this light is similar to how body weight can be measured. Like fluctuations in body weight from day to day depending on what food has been eaten or the level of activity, fluctuations in happiness may occur as the result of positive or negative circumstances. Likewise, it is more useful to obtain an average body weight index and a chronic happiness[1] level, and to attempt to make *sustainable* changes to these baselines. So how can the happiness baseline be altered?

According to Lyubomirsky and colleagues, a person's chronic happiness level is determined by three main factors, what they describe as, first, a genetically determined set point for happiness or at least a point that can be considered a stable trait. Second, there need to be happiness-relevant circumstantial factors, such as living in the right setting, going to a good school or having happy family circumstances. And third, intentional practices, that is, what people do, is the one that holds the most promise because inherent in this is the capacity for the individual to have control and to be able to make gains.

These three factors do not contribute to happiness equally. Genetics contributes 50 per cent, circumstances 10 per cent and intentional practices and activities 40 per cent. This means that, while some of our ability to achieve sustainable happiness is not amenable to change because it is predetermined, a great deal can be done to improve happiness and we must direct our attention towards the circumstantial factors and the intentional practices that can be altered.

Circumstantial factors encompass a broad array of relatively stable variables that can be broken down into three groups: demographics, life events and life-status variables. Demographics includes characteristics of the population one is a part of, such as culture, political position and climate, and individual characteristics such as gender and age. Life events encompass previous significant experiences such as the death of a parent, abuse or migration. Life-status variables are one's positions or standings in society and are more important in adulthood than childhood and adolescence as they include marital status and earnings. It is easy to see that only some circumstantial factors are amenable to change and, for those that are, some change is inevitable. For example, although gender is pretty much set at birth, age increases over time.

The hedonic treadmill

As already mentioned, Lyubomirsky and colleagues believe that circumstantial factors explain about a fifth of alterable chronic happiness, yet they caution that changes in circumstances have only a limited potential. Beyond a comfortable level of safety and financial security, changes in circumstances do little to improve one's overall happiness level. This finding goes against what we commonly believe in today's society, where often we measure happiness in terms of material possessions and financial gain. Indeed, new possessions, promotions at work and the like do provide increases in happiness, but these are merely boosters; they do not equate to sustainable happiness.

For adolescents, the pressure they may feel to own the latest technology or the coolest clothes or to have what their friends have can be intense. This is because adolescence is characteristically a period when peer acceptance is all-important and when young people may be judged harshly in terms of their possessions. Moreover, adolescents have less control over circumstantial factors than do adults. Yet the ability for circumstantial factors to influence happiness is limited, as it is for adults. Adolescents quickly tire of the latest gadget or fad and it is not long before something new appears on their radar, which, when it becomes theirs and the novelty wears off, leads to a desire for the next commodity.

It is easy to see that a cycle is created that traps both adults and children. This has been referred to as the 'hedonic treadmill' (Brickman and Campbell, 1971), which captures the ongoing human concern for pleasure that is restricted by our adaptability. Because humans are designed to be highly adaptive, any situation or circumstance that brought us pleasure or pain at one point in time may not at another. An easy example is when you immerse your hand in very cold water. At first, the feeling is almost unbearable but over several seconds you have adapted and the coldness is bearable. It is the same with a pungent odour or the most beautiful perfume – a scent fails to have the same effect the longer you sense it. Another more relevant example is when a new outfit is purchased. The first time you may feel confident, dressed to impress, chic and savvy. But wear that outfit several times and the confidence and positive feelings decline – it's the same outfit but it's no longer new.

Because adults and adolescents can be caught on the hedonic treadmill, it is difficult to get off. Parents understand their children's desire for material possessions and may believe that buying such items will indeed make their children happier. But materialistic possessions are merely boosters. While they may increase happiness in the short term, acquiring new items will not sustain young people's happiness.

Intent

If there is not much that can be done to alter our genetic predisposition to happiness, and changes in circumstances have only a limited ability to increase chronic happiness, then it is pertinent that attention be directed at what can be influenced. The term 'intentional activities' is used broadly to refer to both behaviours and thoughts, as it is not only what we do but what we think that is important. Lyubomirsky and colleagues used the word 'intentional' to point out that only activities which are intended by the person, which involve effort and cannot simply happen of their own accord, fall into this category. Of central importance is the volitional activity of setting meaningful goals and pursuing them. These authors call on their research to show that hedonic adaptation occurs less for activities than it does for circumstances. Thus, if one sets a goal, pursues and achieves it, the positive effect this success has on well-being can be maintained. However, if the positive effect is to last it is important that the individual continues to do well in that area even after the goal has been accomplished. For example, a student who sets herself the goal of improving her average science grade by 20 per cent may experience a long-term improvement in happiness only if her science grade is maintained.

Several factors contribute to the influence intentional activities can have on sustainable happiness. All of them amount to intentional activities being less prone to adaptation and thus more able to sustain any improvements in happiness. Activities are designed for temporary engagement; rarely do we spend all our time engaged in one pursuit. It is the number of different activities and the time between sessions of any one particular activity that minimizes adaptation and boredom. For example, an adolescent boy may love playing football and gain a great deal of happiness from playing in the local league. But if that boy were to do nothing but play football every day of the season, the activity would lose its happiness-inducing potential. The variability of an activity also helps to sustain its happiness-inducing potential. In the example of the adolescent boy and football, not only does this activity involve the actual football match, it also involves a variety of other forms of activity such as training through running, ball skills and weights, observations of other players, games to improve skills and knowledge, and team meetings.

Flow

In a study of the life trajectories of successful adults in many walks of life such as sports, the arts or business, respondents were asked about their childhood and the sustaining of interest to achieve the successes that they had. Each commented on their passion for their pursuits. The tennis player described the pleasure in the game, the long-distance swimmer the pleasure of swimming and the challenges it posed, the musician the joy of music; the creative businesswoman described the pleasure in her art and in being different (Frydenberg, 2002). Sometimes students report being so involved in a learning activity that they lose all sense of time. They become totally engrossed; the activity is all-important. This state has been described as 'flow', an optimal state of intrinsic motivation (Csikszentmihalyi, 1990). It has been proposed that flow begins when a person takes on a task that offers a challenge just outside a person's effective range of skills. By virtue of engaging with the activity, skills are enhanced and a state of well-being follows.

For activities to raise and maintain happiness, an individual must be able to find newness in them. This may be accomplished by taking a new perspective, asking different questions, or doing the activity under different conditions. For example, a person may continue to gain happiness from hiking by altering the distance and the location of their treks. In summary, the factors that minimize adaptation to intentional activities and therefore provide for changes in happiness to be maintained are their temporal nature, the interval between repetitions of an activity, and the variability within and between activities.

Promoting happiness

So far, the discussion has been about activities that generate happiness, that individuals engage in because they add something to their lives, that break up the day or the week, and that have a sense of purpose. Because activities can become monotonous, which may consequently reduce their happiness-inducing potential, it is important that the monotony be broken. Taking a longer break between sessions of the activity may help. Or an expert may continue to gain enjoyment in their area of expertise by taking a novice under their wing and teaching him or her the ropes. In the school setting this is often organized as part of a peer support programme.

Another way in which activities can provide sustainable happiness is to minimize our adaptation to our normal and everyday practices. The practices of mindfulness and meditation are both important in sustainable happiness. Mindfulness is about being completely aware and fully engaged in whatever you are doing in present time. For example, if you are walking, then it is about using all your senses to experience the walk, such as paying attention to the sounds around you, the different smells, the feeling of your feet as you step on the surface or of the breeze tousling your hair, the colours of the trees, the sky and the grass, the texture of the leaf you pick up. Meditation is the emptying of the mind of thoughts. Time stands still as you take a respite from your everyday activities and concentrate on your breathing or on just one thing such as reciting a mantra or a chant. Directly after a meditation there is often a sense of calmness and peace and the person may be more relaxed than they were before. Both mindfulness and meditation help people to feel gratitude for the simple things in life, draw attention to aspects of our environment and life we take for granted, and thus reduce adaptation to their constant circumstances.

Over the years, research has investigated the ability of meditation and mindfulness activities to improve symptoms of depression and anxiety. We know that both are important components of interventions for adults, and more recently the same has been reported for adolescents and even children. For meditation to be beneficial, it must be taught, practised and become a part of one's intentional daily activities. It is common now for psychologists to teach adolescents some form of meditation in therapy when they present with symptoms of depression or anxiety. However, meditation and mindfulness activities are not only for individuals with deflated mood – all people can benefit from such practices that generate gratitude for the simple things in life and counteract the effects of hedonic adaptation.

The act of giving has also been shown to improve well-being and it seems that doing good leads to feeling good. Numerous studies over the years have shown that from the act of giving, whether it be kindness, time, skills, labour or money, the giver may in turn experience improvements in well-being. When we are giving, we are stepping off the hedonic treadmill and thus it is easy to see how this can contribute to increased happiness (see also Magen study below).

Seligman (1992) drew our attention to this when he noted that nuns have a positive disposition and related this in part to their living a life of purpose and giving to others. Seligman not only draws our attention to the importance of charity, but also the importance of gratitude. In his own teaching, Seligman asked his university-aged students to think about an individual they were grateful to, who had helped them in some important and special way. They were asked to invite this individual to a special night which would be their opportunity to thank this person, explicitly and publicly. In his book *Learning optimism*, Seligman (1992) writes about the effect this might have on his students, the invited guests and himself. Each person was touched by the occasion and, clearly, the importance of taking the time to appreciate those who have helped along the way was demonstrated. On the night, there were tears not of sadness but of connection and thanks, and all involved continued to reflect positively on the experience.

While Seligman's example highlighted the positive effect that gratitude can have and how students can be taught the importance of giving thanks, Lyubomirsky, King and Diener (2005) have shown more broadly how acts of kindness can improve happiness. Students were required to perform five acts of kindness a week for six weeks. These acts could be performed on the one day or spread out over the week. The acts they were to perform were of their own choice and were not meant to take up an exhausting amount of time, which ensured that students maintained their commitment. Examples were helping a friend with an assignment or writing and sending a letter of gratitude. Happiness was measured before and after the six-week period. Students formed one of three groups: acts of kindness on one day, acts of kindness spread out, and the control group. Results indicated that the control group's level of happiness decreased over time, whereas the group who performed their acts of kindness in one day showed a significant increase in happiness. Interestingly, students who performed their acts of kindness over the week did not report a significant change in happiness. This suggests that, even with being kind, we can adapt to it and thus that small acts of kindness may individually fail to increase sustainable happiness, but larger acts spread over time can.

Adolescent happiness

Magen (1998) set out to answer the questions, what makes adolescents happy, what makes them feel good about themselves and the world, and what invests their experience with meaning? She was intrigued by the young people who were engaged in activities benefiting social causes and/or individuals in need, and tried to ascertain what typified them, and whether they would experience life events as more inspiring and joyous.

The Positive Experience Questionnaire (PEQ) was one of the research instruments used by Magen (1998) and her fellow researchers. It is an open-ended questionnaire designed to elicit an adolescent's most joyful remembered experiences. It was used to evaluate depth or intensity of the life experience on a four-point scale of intensity, ranging from shallow to peak intensity. The content area of the experience was assessed in relation to three major content categories: self-experiences, characterized by self-confidence and self-knowledge; external world experiences, characterized by love of the environment and the physical world, objects and belongings; and interpersonal experiences, characterized by liking and compassion for others, and being prepared to take action on their behalf.

The Life Aspirations Questionnaire (1998), Magen's second research instrument, is a single open-ended question used to determine whether adolescents in fact had the desire to give of themselves. The responses were scored on the basis of the expression of commitment to others, also on a four-point scale, from hedonistic and self-involved to fully expressing a desire for transpersonal or socially oriented commitment. Adolescents who had experienced a full year of helping those less fortunate than themselves showed a higher level of verbally expressed transpersonal commitment and a stronger capacity to experience happy moments in life fully and intensely, as well as a greater sense of happiness.

In an earlier study examining adolescents' involvement in prosocial activities and their relationship to happiness, Magen and Aharoni (1991) found that adolescents who were involved in giving to others described joyous moments of a peak intensity, and none of them reported an experience that was barely positive in nature. Magen's research demonstrates that even adolescents who have little or no access to positive and life-affirming experiences can be helped to achieve self-actualizing, transpersonal commitment and even happiness.

Being kind to oneself is an important determinant of sustained happiness and requires both kind thoughts about oneself and kind actions. Focusing on the positive, using affirmations and seeing the bright side of negative events and circumstances helps one to maintain a positive disposition. Similarly, so do behaviours such as keeping fit, getting enough sleep, taking breaks from difficult or cumbersome work and rewarding oneself for achievements and the fulfilment of goals. Adolescents can be taught to be their own best friend, to override negative cognitions with positive ones. Happiness is an active pursuit that is the result of intentional thoughts, behaviours and experiences. Circumstances may change, sometimes negatively, and when they do it is important to remember how skilled we are at adapting to changed circumstances. It is also important to remember the hedonic treadmill we all run and to help adolescents constantly to be mindful of this and to seek happiness not through material possessions or glory but through goal pursuits, kindness and the knowledge that variety in activities can be fulfilling.

In addition to achieving happiness throughout the lifespan outlined earlier, Lyubomirsky and colleagues gave some advice about how intentional activities can be used to induce sustainable happiness. For example, *the adolescent should choose an activity that he or she enjoys.*

Individuals have different interests and strengths and these should be used to select the activity. Parents and teachers should not force an activity on an adolescent and expect him or her to enjoy it. If an activity is required for a group of adolescents, such as a class of students, youth club or for group counselling, then an activity that provides all involved with a sense of belonging, autonomy and self-efficacy should be selected.

Teachers can help students to find happiness in the classroom and their education by matching students' learning with their interests. Almost all subjects taught in classrooms today have the potential to cater for the interests of individual students. For example, in information technology classes, students can be asked to prepare an information brochure on a topic of their choice, or on their favourite animal, country or native plant. When a student is able to work within an area of interest to them they are more motivated, more interested and happier, which can lead to enhanced learning.

These can be achieved by doing the following:

- In times of disappointment or when adolescents have a pessimistic outlook on life, help them to count their blessings and to notice all the things that are easily taken for granted.
- Encourage adolescents to exercise and support their sporting passions and pursuits. Ensure they have an active lifestyle.
- Do not give adolescents everything they ask for. Teach them the importance of saving money, budgeting and to appreciate and value what they have.
- Educate adolescents about the hedonic treadmill in a way that makes sense to them. Allow them to see that they do *not* need the latest gadget to be happy.
- Adults should model a balanced attitude towards materialistic goods. They should show respect for the items they own, moderate their desire for new commodities and aim to step off the hedonic treadmill.
- Help adolescents to find out what their passions are and encourage them to explore those passions fully.
- Encourage adolescents to conduct acts of kindness and to reflect on how helping others can help them to feel good.
- Encourage adolescents to set meaningful and realistic goals and help them to maintain any improvements made through goal fulfilment.
- Provide adolescents with training in positive self-talk, meditation and mindfulness.

- Maintain a healthy and balanced lifestyle and an optimistic outlook yourself so that you are a positive role model for young people.

However, the following caveat should be noted, that it is important that adolescents first have all of their basic needs met before they can begin to increase happiness.

The research on adolescent happiness is less diverse and clear-cut than that conducted on adults. This is not surprising because happiness in childhood and adulthood are somewhat different. In the adult world they are more of a theoretical phenomenon fuelled by adult values. Adolescence is the period between childhood and adulthood and therefore shares some of the elements experienced in both those parts of the lifespan.

We do know that adolescents of divorced families, compared to those from intact families, have a greater tendency to associate happiness with material possessions (Roberts, Tanner and Manolis, 2005). Not surprisingly, those who experience great stress express less happiness. But school context also has a major influence on students' subjective well-being (Konu, Lintonen and Rimpela, 2002). Others have found that it was not feeling efficacious in school but social support from teachers that increased happiness (Natvig, Albreksten and Qvarnstrom, 2003). Others have also found that social support generally increased happiness (Mahon and Yarcheski, 2002). It's all a bit of a vicious cycle in that in a study of 14–19-year-olds loneliness was associated with anxiety and with feeling less attractive, less likeable and less willing to take social risks (Moore and Shultz, 1983).

Well-being and coping

Along with considerations of adolescent resilience and happiness, it is helpful to identify other efficacious coping outcomes. Although some studies examine the relationship between coping and emotional or physical well-being, most studies that consider coping as a predictor of some outcome focus on negative outcomes such as depression, sickness or some other form of dysfunction. Furthermore, well-being is generally seen as the absence of negative indicators of coping. For example, the adolescent component of a national survey of mental health and well-being, the largest study of child and adolescent mental health conducted in Australia, and one of the few national studies conducted in the world, appears to characterize well-being as the absence of 'mental disorders' (Sawyer, Kosky, Graetz, Arney and Zubrick, 2000).

Where the emphasis is not on the absence of a disorder, the interest is often on the avoidance of negative outcomes. There is a demonstrated relationship between negative affectivity (anxiety, depression and hostility) and adverse health outcomes such as alcoholism, depression and suicidal behaviour (Patterson and McCubbin, 1987; Dise-Lewis, 1988).

While in the adult arena it is generally the individual who assesses the effectiveness of his or her own coping, with children and young people objective outcome assessment can more readily be made through observer reports and gradings. A distinction has been made in the adolescent arena between a coping response that is intentional and goal-directed, and a stress response that represents a spontaneous emotional or behavioural reaction. This is because the former emphasizes the outcome of the response in relation to adjustment. Consequently, the transactional models have been replaced with those that emphasize the moderators (characteristics of child and the environment such as gender and development) and mediators (mechanisms linking stress and coping and adjustment such as appraisal and attentional deployment) and the relation to outcome. For example, such a model has been applied to studies that focus on young people who are dealing with illness and pain (Rudolph, Dennig and Weisz, 1995) (see chapter 7).

In their study of well-being, Ebata and Moos (1991) compared 190 12–18-year-olds with behavioural, psychological and physical problems with a control group of healthy adolescents. They used a 48-item instrument which they considered according to the broad dimensions that reflected active or approach (towards the threat) coping and passive or active avoidant (away from the threat) coping. Well-being was measured as an index of perceived happiness and self-worth. Greater use of approach coping (positive reappraisal, guidance/support, problem-solving and alternative rewards) and less use of resigned acceptance was related to higher levels of well-being. Avoidance responses were generally associated with more distress. In general they showed that adolescents who are able to engage in active problem-solving behaviour while being able to 'look on the bright side' and not get caught up in rumination and resignation are likely to be better adjusted.

Three studies which investigated facets of well-being used the Adolescent Coping Scale. In examining empirical relationships between the measures of coping provided by the ACS and theoretically related characteristics associated with adolescent well-being, a positivist view was adopted which examined correlations and other statistical indicators of association between a number of indicators of general well-being (such as self-concept, self-efficacy and achievement). Various measures of dysfunction, and coping scale scores, were reported in chapter 3.

To examine the relationship between general coping responses and states of well-being, two questionnaires were administered to a sample of 1264 12–16-year-old secondary school students in metropolitan Melbourne (Frydenberg and Lewis, 2002). The first questionnaire was a slightly modified version of the Short Form of the ACS (see chapter 3). The other was a 'State of Being' scale (Reynolds, 2001), which comprises 12 items. The study found that young people who use more *self-blame* are in a significantly more dysfunctional state of being than those who use less, and those who use less are experiencing more well-being. This finding is supported by a Norwegian study of ninth-graders (Thuen and Bru, 2004) which found that emotional problems like feeling blue, worrying or stewing about things, nervousness or shakiness inside, feeling fearful, feeling hopeless about the future, feeling no interest in things, and suddenly scared for no reason, were associated with self-blaming and aggressive coping.

Trauma PTSD and resilience

In reviewing the literature on coping with a range of extreme stresses, such as trauma after exposure to life-threatening stresses, Agaibi and Wilson (2005) defined post-traumatic resilience as the behavioural adaptation to situational stress associated with recovery. They see recovery as being, first, reliant on the unique characteristics of the individual; second, they identify the processes by which resilience is attained through development and life experience or skill-building; and third, they identify the cognitive mechanisms that govern resilient adaptations. Wilson and Agaibi (2005) suggest that it is conceptually advantageous to define resilience as a 'complex repertoire of behavioural tendencies' (p. 197). They point out that, in the most basic sense, resilience has been defined as the ability to adapt and cope successfully despite threatening or challenging situations. Resilience is a good outcome despite high demands, costs, stress or risk. Resilience is sustained competence in response to demands that tax coping resources. Resilience is healthy recovery from extreme stress and trauma (p. 198).

In a now famous study of Hawaiian children, Werner and Smith (1982, 1992, cited in chapter 6) tried to predict adjustment at a later stage (ages 10, 18 and 30) for children who had experienced risks such as poverty, low maternal education and moderate to severe perinatal stress. One-third of the Hawaiian sample tested was considered resilient as they did not develop problems and were psychologically healthy at the test points. Resilient children received more attention as infants, presented as more active and socially responsive. In summarizing her work, Werner (2004) stated that the resilient children 'were consistently characterised by their mothers as active, affectionate, cuddly, good-natured, and easy to deal with' (p. 61) – a finding that has consistently been reported by temperament researchers.

Recovery

Recovery from setbacks can be construed as a form of resilience, the capacity to bounce back. Stallard, Velleman, Langford and Baldwin (2001) describe post-traumatic stress after being involved in a traffic accident. Here the respondents used more avoidant, emotion-focused strategies of social withdrawal, distraction and emotional regulation and blaming others. Therefore recovery in that context is about overcoming or compensating for a deficit state such as fatigue or a decrease in performance.

Much of the research on recovery has been done in the sporting world (see Kellman 2003). Athletes have injuries and setbacks. While these are often not life-threatening, they can come at a time that is an important interruption to the pursuit of goals. Recovery is the opposite of fatigue; it is about coping. Generally it includes the following:

- *Compensation of a deficit state*: for example, if a friend is lost then a new interest is developed where other friends are made.
- *A re-establishment of the initial state – homeostatic balance – restored efficiency*: There is a return to an original sense of well-being either through finding an alternative form of satisfaction or returning to previous levels of successful activity.

Elements of recovery include:

- Psychological recovery
- Mood-related recovery
- Emotional recovery
- Behavioural recovery
- Social recovery
- Physiological recovery (regeneration).

Generally these elements depend on:

- break from stress
- being specific to the individual
- involving various organismic processes, e.g. passive, active or proactive
- being usually self-initiated or maintained
- using the 18 coping strategies
- reducing Non-Productive coping
- increasing Productive coping
- avoiding problems outsizing – tackle them early
- going for change when feeling trapped
- avoiding stress carriers (that is, others who are highly stressed).

Summary

Resiliency is a positive attribute that is known to have a buffering effect against stress and to minimize dysfunction. We know from studies that have followed the lives of young people from birth through to adulthood that nature plays an important part in the development of resilience. Nevertheless, it is possible to foster resilience through maximizing system resources, namely those of the individual, the family, and within the school and community.

Emotional intelligence has acquired widespread currency in recent years. That is, those who can understand and regulate their own emotions and deal with those of others appropriately are likely to do well. Likewise, the use of positive emotions is known to be associated with success in diverse spheres in life. The good news is that both emotional intelligence and positive emotions can be nurtured and strengthened to assist an individual's transition through life.

In recent years there has also been an interest in happiness. Although happiness is not a new concept, a re-focus on this state of being reinforces the success and gains one can achieve by being happy. Like other emotional states, happiness can be viewed as sustained, temporary or chronic. Lyubomirsky and colleagues (Lyubomirsky, King and Diener, 2005) introduce this view of happiness. Circumstantial factors contribute only a small percentage towards altering happiness levels. Happiness levels are influenced mainly by genetic predisposition, circumstance and then intent. Sustainable happiness introduces the concept of mindfulness and caring for others. Adolescents who engage in altruistic acts experience greater happiness. Being kind to oneself also produces a similar positive disposition. The challenge is to change adolescent thinking about happiness from obtaining material possessions to successful goal pursuits, kindness and fulfilment. Additionally, our perception of well-being needs to be more than the absence of dysfunction, and rather one of perceived worth and happiness.

Well-being is more than the absence of disease, it is associated with approach rather than avoidant coping, problem-solving and the use of supports. There is evidence that a reduced use of self-blame is associated with well-being.

Similarly, when it comes to trauma, resilience is not absence of trauma, but ability to bounce back in a healthy way. The term traditionally used in sport psychology is that of 'recovery'. Within the context of coping, recovery is a capacity to overcome a deficit that need not be physical but emotional or psychological.

10 Coping and achievement

> Never give up. I know a lot of people say that. But in my opinion,
> I have always tried and have never given up on anything. Not
> even in games, chasey, footy, cricket . . . I have never given up.
> Not in sports or in school work. I am glad I have never given up
> on anything. Because once you give up, you will think about it
> later on and think 'I could have probably got somewhere'. Once
> you start thinking that, it can make you even more upset than
> before. So, just keep trying at everything and you will get there
> eventually. Even if you don't, you will know you have tried.
>
> (Boy, 17)

In the section on coping and emotions in chapter 9, there is evidence
that goal-setting, motivation and positive emotions all lead to good
learning and achievement. This is affirmed in the work on coping with
examinations. Much of the early research in the field of stress and
coping and young people was done in relation to anxiety and performance, particularly with examinations. Examination anxiety, as
with other forms of performance-related anxiety, is often associated
with meeting the expectations of the self, peers, parents and/or
teachers. Thus it is often a problem associated with high achievers and
young people who strive for the perfect performance or the perfect
grade at school.

Coping and success expectations

Youth with high personal standards in comparison to their peers use
particular coping resources (Nounopoulos, Ashby and Gilman, 2006).
Perfectionism is a quality exhibited by individuals who set themselves
standards that exceed what is considered to be realistically attainable.
There are those who are adaptive perfectionists who are not unduly

discouraged when their performance does not reach their own expectations, and there are the maladaptive perfectionists who are stressed and discouraged by the same thing. It is the adaptive perfectionists who do better academically. These authors assessed five specific coping resources: social confidence (degree of relating to peers, being able to freely disclose opinions and feelings); behavioural control (how well the young person co-operates with others); academic confidence (confidence in the ability to do well in school and to do quality work); family support (degree of family support and acceptance); and peer acceptance (how well the individual is accepted by others). It was found that young people with adaptive perfectionistic tendencies maintain greater confidence in their academic skills. Their perceived positive relations with family members and peers helps them to alleviate academic stressors as they arise. In contrast, adolescents with maladaptive perfectionistic characteristics may view their academic skills and family less favourably when stressful situations arise, and they are likely to report less satisfaction with their school experience. The educational implications of these findings are that in addition to enhancing Productive coping strategies and reducing the use of general Non-Productive strategies such as *worry* and *self-blame*, in the educational context the perfectionistic adolescent should be helped to develop specific skills that will enhance their confidence in their academic ability.

Coping and exam anxiety

Within educational settings, students are primarily evaluated academically on the basis of test results. Therefore the importance of research on test anxiety cannot be understated. Two studies are reported from the diverse literature on the topic. In an Australian sample of adolescents Warner and Moore (2004) investigated self-handicapping tendencies (creating obstacles to reduce chances of success) in relation to academic evaluations. Jones and Berglas (1978) define self-handicapping as the creation of obstacles to reduce success. Self-handicapping serves to protect one's self-esteem through the creation of an obstacle, such as partying before an exam instead of studying, so that the individual can attribute poor performance to an external source e.g. tiredness instead of ability. The researchers found that self-handicapping took the form of procrastination, reduced effort, emotional distress and mild illness. High use of self-handicapping strategies for girls was associated with less efficient study and lower study hours for boys. Interestingly, poor study habits have also been related to test anxiety for students with learning disabilities and behaviour disorders (Swanson and Howell, 1996), suggesting a clear relationship between study habits and test anxiety regardless of academic competence. Girls and boys also differed in terms of coping and attribution; rumination and luck attribution were associated with self-handicapping in boys and ability attributions with behavioural disengagement and instrumental support in girls. Poor use of active coping strategies was related to self-handicapping regardless of gender. Interestingly, the researchers found that coping strategies and attributions were more important predictors of self-handicapping than self-esteem. This highlights the importance of teaching adolescents productive ways of coping before they reach their final years of schooling to assist them in dealing with academic pressures and maximize their performance in examinations and other academic evaluations.

An examination of the relationship between emotions and coping with examination anxiety in a university student population (Spangler, Pekrun, Kramer and Hofmann, 2002) showed that emotional and adrenocortical responses depend on the situation and are co-regulated by stable psychological characteristics and emotional disposition as well as coping abilities. The first study assessed five different trait emotions (anxiety, hopelessness, anger, joy and hope) as well as coping styles (problem-focused, emotion-focused and avoidant coping), and the respective trait emotions were also assessed before and after the exams. In the second study the state emotions were assessed according to events and by using a video-supported semi-structured interview. Whereas the negative emotions were highest before or at the beginning of the exam, positive emotions increased during the exam and reached the highest values afterwards.

Coping and educational achievement

The concept of giftedness is a pluralistic one, with variations of the Marland (1972), Renzulli (1986) or Tannenbaum (1991) definitions commonly adopted in educational policy and practice. These definitions cast a wide net that takes account of achievers and potential achievers in the many areas of talent including and apart from the intellectual: the creative thinkers, dancers, musicians and painters, mechanics and engineers and so on. Tannenbaum expanded his definition into a model which elaborates on the qualities underpinning talent potential. He stated that for potential to be actualized a combination of five factors needs to be present. Although these factors interact, the threshold for each is different according to the specific talent area being considered. The five factors are: superior general intelligence; distinctive special abilities or aptitudes; non-intellective factors that contribute to success, such as energy, effort, motivation, willingness to take risks, task-commitment, health, immersion in an interest, self-concept and 'meta-earning' (sensing the 'name of the game'); a nurturing environment through which the family, school, peer group and community enable the talent to flourish; and chance factors which also play their part in the form of luck (e.g. being in the right place at the right time) and being able to recognize opportunity when it arrives. The biggest of these chance factors is related to the family and circumstances into which an individual is born.

Csikszentmihalyi, Rathunde and Whalen's (1993) research extends the five factors identified by Tannenbaum. The additional factors identified by these researchers in their study of gifted and talented young people are: skills considered useful in the culture; personality traits conducive to concentration (e.g. achievement and endurance); openness to experience (e.g. awareness or sentience); and understanding and learned habits conducive to cultivating talent (e.g. less time socializing and hanging out with friends). These young people choose more active or challenging pursuits; they seek more solitude, accounting for more sombre moods than average teenagers. Their families are psychologically supportive; they have more one-to-one relationships with parents, and spend more time with families; they have more conservative sexual attitudes and exhibit an awareness of the conflict between productive work and peer relations. They have better relationships with their teachers, who are supportive and who model enthusiasm for their field.

Gifted adolescents are generally good problem-solvers. In a comparison between intellectually gifted fifth- and sixth-graders, and a control group of typical children on coping responses to school and peer stressors Preuss and Dubow (2004) reported that when it came to school stressors such as getting a lower grade, and peer stressors such as having a fight with a friend, gifted students endorsed problem-solving strategies to a greater degree than typical students. Nevertheless, gifted adolescents are known to have more peer-related social difficulties.

In a study of older gifted adolescents in grades 9–12, Swiatek (2001) reported that females are more likely than males to deny their giftedness and maintain high activity levels, whereas males are more likely than females to use humour. And generally problem-focused social coping strategies are more adaptive than are emotion-focused denial-based strategies.

Students who say that their giftedness has little or no negative impact on their social experience are likely to have lower self-concept scores in the domain of social acceptance. The social coping strategies that show the greatest number of positive relationships with self-concept are problem-focused strategies that aim at cultivating relationships with peers. Helping others is positively related to self-concept in the domain of scholastic competence, romantic appeal and behavioural conduct. Generally giftedness can be socially stigmatizing for adolescents, so a way of coping for these young people often involves denying their high ability, camouflaging, and 'dis-identifying' by actively separating from the highly gifted group.

Coping and talent

One way to explain why some people avail themselves of resources and others do not is the theory of coping. Coping is an index of how young people use available resources to enable their talents to flourish. Since the 1960s there has been a wealth of literature in the area of adult coping. The research on coping in young people is a more recent phenomenon and research relating to coping and talented young people is in its infancy.

Adolescents in the regular school community, including those who have been identified by their teachers as gifted, have a coping repertoire which indicates they are productive and adaptive in managing their everyday concerns. However, gifted young people use somewhat different strategies from the regular students, in prioritizing their coping strategies, in their inclination to work hard, and in their less frequent use of intimate relationships. Gifted young people focus on dealing directly with problems. They do not declare that they lack the strategies to cope. They are less inclined to just hope for the best or to resort to strategies to release tension. This may be an indication of their superior capacity to cope or, in fact, it may signal that they are less resourceful than young people in the general community. Likewise, the fact that they do not declare their inability to cope may be an indication of capacity, but it may also signal a denial of some of their difficulties. The fact that gifted young people are more likely to work hard and declare that they are able to manage their concerns more than a regular group of students may, in a general sense, reflect their inclination towards hard work and industry (Frydenberg, 1993). But the hard work may be at a personal cost. An issue to examine closely is whether gifted young people 'go it alone' because they are more resourceful than other young people, or because they are less skilled in dealing with their peers. There is likely to be considerable individual variation in the use of coping strategies among gifted and talented youngsters (see Cohen and Frydenberg, 1996).

Several studies on achievement and related issues were reported in chapter 3. In a study of self-perception and coping in 126 Australian and South-East Asian secondary students, Neill (1996) found that students with lower self-esteem used more Non-Productive coping strategies such as *keeping to themselves, worrying* and *self-blaming*. In another study of the relationship between academic self-concept, perceived stress and coping styles used by high school students in their final year of schooling, Stevenson (1996) found that students with a negative academic self-concept used more of a Non-Productive coping style than did students with a positive academic self-concept. Final-year students with lower levels of perceived stress were also more inclined to use more Productive coping styles and students experiencing higher levels of perceived stress tended to have more of a Non-Productive style. In general, young people who view their academic abilities favourably, that is, have high academic self-concept, tend to use more adaptive coping strategies. So it is not so much the ability that one has but the self-perception of that ability that makes a difference.

A study conducted in the American context and using the ACS to establish the relationship between the ACS coping strategies and the self-concept of academically gifted young people found that these young people took action-focused approaches and resorted to the use of *social support*, at the same time as trying to *fit in with friends* and *keeping problems to themselves* (Menaker Tomchin, Callahan, Sowa and May, 1996).

When a group of young people and adults were asked to describe their life events and to explain what had led to their current success in adulthood (Frydenberg, 2002), individual differences emerged from their stories. When the high achievers were interviewed, each of them was found to have a family as both a support and a resource. Each had a well-developed sense of selfhood, and each used the available support effectively. That is, in addition to individual personality characteristics, the interaction of each person with particular facets of their environment contributed to developmental outcomes.

Tara is a champion marathon swimmer, holding both national and international titles, who began swimming at the age of 11, and then only because her parents suggested it as a way to lose weight and improve her fitness. 'My dad is a backstop which is like the Rock of Gibraltar. Both my mum and dad are always there for me. I guess that is what has made me this way.' She attended a local state (public) school and became the state 100- and 200-metre junior champion before she was 13. But after she tired of pool training her father introduced her to competitive sports related to surfing and life-saving when she was 15, and four years later she began swimming international marathons. This requires dedication as well as personal and financial support by her family, who are Dutch immigrants, run a family printing business, and are motivated by their desire to give their three children opportunities they didn't have when they were young. Tara's brother coaches ironmen[1] and triathletes and personally trains with her.

Another interviewee, Jasmin, whose father had died when she was 7, attended an independent girls' secondary school, but was expelled when she was 12 because of 'unacceptable conduct'. She sees the events surrounding her expulsion as crucial to her development because of her mother's response to the situation, recalling her saying, 'You haven't done anything I think is terrible; you just stood up for yourself and I am proud of you.' According to Jasmin, her mother's support made her stronger and more committed and confident in her ideas. She feels that if she does not believe in something she has a right and an obligation to question it. Her confidence and conviction are critical elements in Jasmin's business achievements and she attributes them to her mother's belief in her ability and support for her to follow her own path.

Peer relationships

James, a 16-year-old in Year 11, the penultimate year of high school, talked about school, coping and his ambitions for the future. For James, his friendships, his music and drama were important.

> . . . the best thing I like about schools is the bench, just outside the tuckshop,[2] that faces the sun, and at lunchtime, all the boys sit on that bench and muck around and talk and I have fond memories of that bench and all the laughs and jokes that were made there.

He went on to say:

> Music is something very important to me. It's important to all my friends. It's unbelievable how important music is to us if it's looked at closely because it gives us a feeling like nothing else.

Everyone relates to it. A lot of our talk at school is about what music people are listening to, or concerts they are going to.

James accepts challenges with self-assurance:

> I'm playing Jack (in the school play), who is a middle-aged man in 1930s New York. It's Neil Simon's *Brighton Beach Memoirs*. I know that how a 16-year-old plays a middle-aged man is something that worries my Mum and other people but it just doesn't worry me. I honestly haven't thought about what's an appropriate way for a kid to play an adult's part. Obviously I don't know what it is like to be middle-aged, especially in his sort of situation, so it's hard and I'll just have to do what I can.

The relationship between sense of self and adaptation is evident in many of the young people's lives. That sense of self can be a combination of both interpersonal and intrapersonal factors. James is a boy who values relationships. He also has passions and interests. But with his mates he is more likely to talk about events and objects than about relationships.

School–family coherence

For all these young people there was a congruence between the values, expectations and the culture of the schools they attended and that of their families. Their nurturing came in their schools' general encouragement of excellence and opportunities to pursue individual talent areas. In these cases the school and home environments complemented each other. Although this was not the case initially for Jasmin, eventually she found support after her expulsion when she moved on to an independent coeducational secondary school which respected her differentness, allowed her space to follow her interests, and provided a more compatible peer group so that her social interactions were no longer problematic. It was from this school setting that she sprang into business with no further formal education, so while school was apparently irrelevant to developing her particular talent for business, it did provide an emotionally nurturing environment.

Personality characteristics

There are personal qualities which underscore an individual's relationship with his or her particular environment. Many young people have innate qualities that help them to overcome obstacles like failure to achieve a desired goal, or circumstances such as the death of a parent, or parent's separation. Jasmin, the young businesswoman, demonstrated her characteristic perseverance in overcoming obstacles when she commented:

> The problems I have in my life have a lot to do with approval. I think that is because I've lacked any type of approval from a father so I think I am constantly striving for some type of approval. My coping is that I drop my bundle and come up tougher, better, stronger and more impressive than ever. I almost feel happy when I am at rock bottom because that means that good things are ahead.

Jasmin has always felt different from her peers, and that was a key factor in the behaviour that caused her expulsion from school. But she also thinks there was some pressure from her mother in that direction as well, in respect of wanting Jasmin to be her own person: 'I knew what would make my mother proud of me more than anything else was if I was special, if I was different.' She uses positive self-talk to overcome adversity in order to establish her identity and reputation in the competitive business world. This perseverance underpins the coping strategies she has used for success.

Tara sees losses as a challenge:

> You can't always win. Nobody goes through life with a perfect scenario, where everything you do you are successful in. I believe what you make out of your losses is the strength that makes you a person.

Tara's positive outlook and confidence have developed out of her productive response to the problems she has faced. When young she was teased about her appearance, and also about her relationship with a Vietnamese family her own family had adopted when their father died shortly after immigrating. She learned through this to have empathy with others and feels she became stronger as a result of seeing the situations she cannot change as challenges to overcome rather than stumbling-blocks. She has lost school friends because they did not understand the commitment required to succeed, but she realizes that '*you have to be there to understand why it is so important*'. This philosophical outlook and perseverance has helped her remain focused on achieving her swimming goals in the face of loneliness and the physical and mental stress of training and competing far from home.

Self-knowledge, in the form of a realistic understanding of their abilities and considered interpretation of their personal situations, has helped these young people nurture their own talent development. Through it they have acquired a kind of metacognitive self-management which is evident in Jasmin's and Tara's reflections, as it is in Greg's, who observed:

> Early on I realized that if I couldn't change a bad situation I could change the way I thought about it, so I tended to withdraw and reinterpret things in either a favourable light or at least in a way I could accept. . . . I also realized my mind was very active and I found that focusing on my art helped me to override that excess stimulation from the environment.

Tara regards her brain as a powerful tool which she can control to help her achieve her goals. She says she is

> able not to give in to pain or doubt. I tell myself just five more minutes without giving in will usually see me through the very tough times and my body can work well again.

Sometimes appreciating one's tendency for negativity can help in managing a situation. Jasmin finds that

> success is something that doesn't guarantee happiness; in fact, sometimes it's another reason to hate myself because I feel I don't deserve it. Success can only be utilized if you have a healthy self-opinion.

These young people have found that ultimately it is their own ability to understand and manage themselves that will foster their success, and they have developed effective coping strategies to do so.

But for talent to be actualized, there needs to be appropriate interaction between students and their personal, family and school environments. Reflections by James, Greg, Tara and Jasmin illustrate the importance of a capacity both to use inner resources and to call on external supports in order to develop potential. These young people have been able to capitalize on their emotional intelligence and to exploit a dynamic interaction with their environment. Their experiences demonstrate, first, that the needs of gifted young people are met through a range of resources within different sectors of the community and second, that effective use of those resources is predicated on effective interaction between an individual and his or her environment. Coping provides a lens for examining how young people access these resources and develop their talents.

Students and achievement

From the comprehensive study by Resnick and colleagues (1997), we know that if the school and parents are connected young people do better. Therefore the level of engagement with the school can throw light on adjustment and achievement. In a recent study conducted by Lodge, Frydenberg, Care, Tobin and Begg (2007), with 845 students drawn from middle years classrooms in Melbourne Catholic schools, school engagement profiles were compared on styles of coping with concerns and emotional well-being. Low emotional well-being exemplified students with lower emotional, cognitive and behavioural engagement. These students used fewer problem-solving styles of coping with concerns and tended to rely more on Non-Productive styles of coping when compared to both boys and girls who were high in school engagement. Additionally, when results of a spelling test as an indicator of achievement were included, it was found that those who were engaged with school had better performance.

Check & Connect model

A model for enhancing student engagement, referred to as Check & Connect, is described by Christenson and Carroll (1999). Inherent in the model are assumptions, theoretical underpinnings, and strategies for teaching coping skills and strengthening the family–school partnership, especially for at-risk families and schools. Youth who drop out are more likely to experience higher rates of unemployment and incarceration, receive lower earnings, and require social services during their lifetimes than high school graduates.

This monitoring and student engagement procedure was originally designed to encourage middle school youth with emotional disturbances and learning disabilities to remain engaged in school and on track to graduate. The original longitudinal study was funded in 1990 by the US Department of Education, Office of Special Education Programs (#H023A40019). Subsequent intervention research is being conducted with elementary and high school students in suburban and urban school districts respectively, and with support from multiple sources (such as federal and county funds, and foundations).

Intervention components

Check & Connect focuses on the person–environment fit by using a systematic monitoring and student engagement procedure to address the needs of individual students and build capacity within families to assist their children's educational performance. It has two components: Check is designed to monitor youth behaviour systematically for signs of school withdrawal, and Connect is designed to respond accordingly to students' needs. Because building connections between students and school personnel and families and schools is an essential component of school completion (see Christenson, Sinclair, Thurlow and Evelo, 1999), a monitor is responsible for helping the student stay connected to school. Best conceptualized as building social capital or what Coleman (1987) referred to as adult–child interaction about academic and personal matters, the role of the monitor is to create a person–environment fit in school and home contexts that enhances student engagement with school. Recognizing that human development is a result of interactions across multiple events, monitors work to create positive relationships between youth, family and school, always with the focus on this shared goal: the student's school completion of academic and social skills

Check

The Check part of the procedure was designed to facilitate the continuous assessment of student levels of engagement with school. Levels of engagement are monitored daily or weekly through the use of a monitoring sheet according to alterable risk factors: incidents of tardiness, absenteeism, behavioural referrals, suspensions or course failures. Risk, defined by the number of incidents per month for each risk category, were originally set by a school task force of administrators, teachers and project staff. The specific criteria could be different for different schools, depending on how frequently and for what reasons a policy is used in a school. Risk indicators and criterion levels determined to be problematic are used to identify students who are demonstrating behaviours characteristic of potential dropouts.

Connect

The Connect part of the procedure consists of two levels: basic and intensive. The foundation is four basic interventions, which are administered to all potential dropouts regardless of their level of student engagement and which use minimal resources once a working relationship has been established between the monitor, student, family and educators: (1) sharing general information with the student about the monitoring system; (2) providing regular feedback to the student; (3) regularly discussing the importance of staying in school; and (4) problem-solving with the student regarding alterable risk factors. General information is initially shared with the student about the monitor's role and the purpose of the monitoring sheets. Students are regularly given feedback on their progress in school in general and in relation to risk factors.

The final and most significant aspect is problem-solving with students regarding personal risk factors and staying in school. Students are guided through real and/or hypothetical problems using a five-step cognitive-behavioural problem-solving strategy. For example, attendance is reviewed by dialoguing about the consequences of skipping school or generating lists of strategies students use to get to school every day. The conversation is structured around the Five Step Plan developed by Braswell and Bloomquist (1991): Step 1: 'Stop. Think about the problem.' Step 2: 'What are some choices?' Step 3: 'Choose one.' Step 4: 'Do it.' Step 5: 'How did it work?' Problem-solving provides a structure to enhance students' social decision-making and anger control (Elias and Tobias, 1996).

The second level of support goes beyond those four basic interventions. Three broad types of support are used, namely problem-solving, academic support, and recreational and community service exploration.

The final years of school

Adjusting to the demands of the final years of school is stressful for most adolescents. A challenging set of academic hurdles, course content, the pressure of expectations placed on students by themselves and others, and the balancing of school, work, family and social life add considerably to the normal developmental tasks required of young people. Some adapt smoothly to such pressures while others do not, placing some young people at an increased risk of mental health problems, delinquent behaviour, substance abuse, and dropping out of high school (Janosz, LeBlanc, Boulerice and Tremblay, 1997; Murberg and Bru, 2005).

Research from both Australia and overseas suggests a range of damaging outcomes for early school leavers such as limiting students' future social, financial and psychological well-being (Rumberger, 1987; Dryfoos, 1990; Kaplan, Damphouse and Kaplan, 1994). In the educational system in the state of Victoria, a fairly recent programme, the Victorian Certificate of Applied Learning (VCAL), was developed in an attempt to cater for students who were not expecting to go to university after completing high school. The programme sits alongside the Victorian Certificate of Education (VCE) and offers broader options for Year 11 and 12 students interested in vocational studies as well as those moving straight into employment after school. Studies are taken in four compulsory strands: literacy and numeracy, work-related skills, industry-specific skills, and personal development (VCAA, 2005), and are taught using an applied learning approach which involves practical, hands-on, on-the-job learning activities (Henry, Dalton, Wilde, Walsh and Wilde, 2002).

Since VCAL's introduction, school retention rates in Victoria have increased from 78.7 per cent (1999) to 83 per cent (2004) (ABS, 2005). The majority of students currently enrolled in the programme were previously disengaged from the education system and were at risk of dropping out of school (Henry *et al.*, 2002; Kelly, 2002).

School-related stress

A body of research points to a meaningful association between students' attitudes to school and their overall adaptation. The phrase 'attitudes to school' encompasses students' cognitions, affect and behaviours in relation to school and refers to the extent to which students find school rewarding and enjoyable, their sense of attachment to school, beliefs in the value of schooling, such as relevance to personal development and future career options, the amount of effort students invest in their school work, and their participation in activities both inside and outside the classroom (Cheng and Chan, 2003).

A positive attitude towards school has been found to be a robust protective factor against a number of major adjustment problems for adolescents including substance use, delinquency and school dropout (Janoz *et al.*, 1997; Jenkins, 1997; Resnick *et al.*, 1997), and is therefore the best screening variable for identifying potential school dropouts (Janoz *et al.*, 1997).

Adolescent stress is negatively related to school performance (Johnson, 1979) and positively related to school dropout (Wassef, Ingham, Collins, and Mason, 1995). However, research has shown that not all adolescents who experience stressful life events report physiological or psychosocial health issues because health is more influenced by the way people cope with stress than by the stress itself (Dumont and Provost, 1999).

A recent study in the state of Victoria that specifically examined adolescents in their final year of school reported that the highest source of stress for these students was school-related (Kouzma and Kennedy, 2004). School-related stress refers to the numerous stressors that operate on young people in schools such as academic concerns, future career paths, and relationship issues with school peers and teachers (Murberg and Bru, 2005).

The link between coping, stress at school and well-being

Research has indicated that coping acts as a moderator between young people's well-being and their stress levels (Frydenberg and Lewis, 1999b; Matheny *et al.*, 2002). Studies have found that Non-Productive coping strategies that tend to ignore or avoid the problem are associated with increased perceived stress and decreased levels of well-being (Ebata and Moos, 1991). On the other hand, coping strategies that focus on working to solve the issue and seeking social support are associated with decreased stress (Galaif, Sussman, Chou and Wills, 2003) and increased well-being (Frydenberg and Lewis, 2002).

The type of stressor and developmental level of the individual plays an important part in shaping coping strategies (Skinner, Edge, Altman and Sherwood, 2003). Compared with other areas, very little research has been conducted on stress and coping in relation to school. Nevertheless, it has been established that school-related stress is associated with low levels of well-being (Stevenson, 1996), psychosomatic symptoms (Murberg and Bru, 2004), depression (Murberg and Bru, 2005), poor school performance (Johnson, 1979) and school dropout (Wassef *et al.*, 1995).

Several studies have indicated gender differences in the perception of stress, with adolescent females reporting more frequent and intense stressful events than males (Copeland and Hess, 1995; Smith and Sinclair, 1998; Seiffge-Krenke, 2000). Studies show that adolescent girls generally report lower levels of well-being than boys (Ebata and Moos, 1991), and are twice as likely as boys to develop depression during adolescence (Nolen-Hoeksema and Girgus, 1994).

Ganim and Frydenberg (2006) sought to examine whether there were differences in levels of well-being, school-related stress, and coping strategies used by those with a positive or negative attitude to school. It was predicted that students with a positive attitude to school would use more Productive and Reference to Others coping strategies, and have less school-related stress than those with a negative attitude to school. Gender differences were also investigated.

Findings showed that, in general, school is a rewarding, supportive and enjoyable place for VCAL students. VCAL students' tendency to report positive attitudes towards school indicated that these students believe in the relevance and worthiness of school in terms of personal and social development and future career options, and feel a sense of connectedness to the school (Cheng and Chan, 2003). VCAL students reported using a wide range of coping strategies to deal with their school-related concerns. The students' most favoured strategies reflected a Productive coping style providing a balance between taking steps to solve the problem in an active way, staying socially connected and engaging in leisure activities and physical exercise to relax. These findings are congruent with Victorian research on VCE students of a similar age group (17–19 years) (Frydenberg and Lewis, 1999a).

Attitudes to school

VCAL students with a positive attitude to school reported higher levels of well-being than those with negative attitudes to school, a result consistent with earlier research (Bourke and Smith, 1989). In terms of coping, those with a positive attitude to school reported using strategies which actively work at *solving their problems* and remaining positive while *seeking support* from friends, family and professionals. Alternatively, VCAL students with a negative attitude were more likely to engage in Non-Productive coping strategies such as *ignoring the problem, tension reduction* and *keeping to themselves*, and reported significantly more school-related stress. These findings support previous research indicating that students who experience significant amounts of stress have more difficulties at school (Hess and Copeland, 2001).

The findings for negative school attitudes are cause for concern as empirical research has found that the predominant use of Non-Productive strategies, higher levels of stress, and low well-being are associated with an inability to cope, a greater likelihood of both physiological (Murberg and Bru, 2005) and psychological illness such as depression and anxiety (Seiffge-Krenke and Stemmler, 2002) and an increase in the use of maladaptive behaviours (Kaplan *et al.*, 1994), all of which are associated with high school dropout (Janoz *et al.*, 1997).

For both male and female VCAL students, working hard was predictive of attitudes to school. This suggests that those students who reported being conscientious about school work and aiming to achieve high standards held a more positive attitude to school. Further exploration revealed two predictive variables for females (*work hard, perceived school-related stress*) and four for males (*work hard, tension reduction, well-being,* and *focus on the positive*).

The results of the above study indicate that the degree to which stressful events result in distress and negative attitudes to school may be greater (or more predictive) for females than males. Female VCAL students with high levels of perceived school-related stress may have a more negative attitude towards school, while male VCAL students who hold a negative attitude to school are more likely to report venting their feelings and engaging in risk-taking behaviour such as smoking, drinking and taking drugs.

The frequent use of *focus on the positive* was predictive of attitudes to school and well-being for male VCAL students, suggesting that males who cope with their school-related concerns by looking on the bright side of things and by trying to stay cheerful will have a more positive attitude towards school. The person–environment interactionist model does acknowledge that it is not just a matter of changing attitudes to school but perhaps giving young people the skills to cope productively that is likely to enhance attitudes to school and subsequently increase well-being.

Summary

There is no doubt that school-related issues are of concern to many young people and that positive attitudes to school are linked with well-being and use of Productive coping strategies. Students carry expectations of success within themselves and they also try to meet the expectations of others. In that context exam anxiety has been frequently investigated by stress and coping researchers as both a self-imposed stress and one that is a result of meeting the expectations of others, namely, parents, teachers or peers. Test anxiety can manifest as self-handicapping behaviours that serve as an avoidance of academic evaluations. Adolescents who engage in this type of behaviour could be described as having an external locus of control as they are actively creating an excuse outside themselves for poor academic performance. It is not surprising that academic self-handicappers of both genders utilize less active strategies, that is coping strategies such as problem solving, possibly related to low confidence levels in their ability to perform academically and/or solve problems effectively. Study habits are deemed to play a part in how students cope with exam anxiety.

Gifted and talented young people have a range of coping strategies that help them to cope with their unique qualities. These include focusing on problems effectively but often doing things on their own. The work of Tannenbaum (1991) on gifted adolescents identified a range of factors that need to interact for potential to be realized. It is proposed that a supportive family and the fortunate circumstances into which an individual is born are facilitative factors, further demonstrating the influence of environment on positive outcomes. This is highlighted by the stories of adult high achievers where the support of parents and mentors helped them to persevere and remain motivated to achieve success. This environmental support may become particularly important for gifted adolescents who often have social difficulties in integrating with peers. Generally gifted adolescents utilize more intrapersonal resources to cope such as working hard as opposed to interpersonal resources such as seeking social support or investing in friendships.

On the other end of the spectrum, two programmes that were designed to help students stay engaged and remain at school were described. The first, Check & Connect (Christenson, Sinclair, Thurlow and Evelo, 1999), capitalizes on the potential of the school–parent connection and the role of mentors to provide a secure and supportive environment for the adolescent. This systems approach goes beyond the individual to demonstrate that adaptive functioning is achievable through relationship-building that incorporates active problem-solving skills. The second is an adapted school curriculum that shows that cultivating positive attitudes towards school through providing alternative education options provides benefits. Positive changes to attitude towards school result in less school-related stress and greater use of active coping. Undoubtedly, these alternative education options create empowerment in adolescents who may otherwise be disenfranchised.

Apart from the particular programmes designed to help young people stay on at school, there is a range of programmes that either contribute to coping skills or form part of direct coping skills training. The former are dealt with in chapter 11 and the latter in chapter 12.

11   Learning to cope

Keeping a balance between home and school usually requires checking when work's due and how much time you have got. When I get home from school, I always make a timetable in my head for when I should be doing things. I take half-hour breaks instead of doing everything all at once like I used to. You can't do that in VCE [Year 12] otherwise you hammer yourself. Social time is really important. And it is especially important to take breaks. That's one of the thing I have noticed in VCE. You need to give time to yourself. Otherwise the more you keep going all at once, then the more you are just going to tire yourself out.

(Boy, 17)

There are numerous ways adolescents learn to cope, including what we learn through maturation or experience, sometimes called the school of hard knocks, how we learn by emulating others, a form of social learning through direct instruction and teaching of coping skills and also through the teaching of social and emotional competence in a number of ways. Some of these will be dealt with in this chapter. Chapter 12 deals with programmes that focus on coping skills instruction in a targeted way and in particular the Best of Coping programme is evaluated.

From the plethora of research on adolescent coping we know there are important elements to take into account when teaching young people to cope. For example, numerous research studies have identified key strategies that represent our coping efforts, both the Productive and the Non-Productive ones. We also know that while it is important to expand our coping repertoires to include an ever-growing number of productive strategies to meet diverse challenges, we need to decrease our reliance on the use of Non-Productive strategies. As well, there are important elements of coping that warrant attention. These include social coping, problem-solving and decision-making skills. While much of this knowledge has been taken into account when developing a coping skills programme such as the Best of Coping (Frydenberg and Brandon, 2002a, b, 2007a, b), which is reported and substantially evaluated in chapter 12, skills that relate to social coping, decision-making and problem-solving are presented in this chapter.

Problem-solving and coping

Research over the past 20 years has highlighted the critical role of coping and problem-solving abilities in managing chronic problems, stressful life events and daily hassles (Heppner, Wei, Lee, Wang and Pretorius, 2002). Problem-solving abilities are the cognitive and affective-emotional processes by which individuals identify strategies to deal efficaciously with difficult situations (D'Zurilla and Nezu, 1990). Problem-solving is a process that helps people move from where they are, the 'problem state', to where they want to be, the 'goal state'. Problems are encountered every day, some big and some not so big, and consequently the behavioural, cognitive and emotional expenditures required to resolve problems vary. Rarely is ignoring a problem, or doing nothing, the most effective way of dealing with it. In the minority of cases that warrant doing nothing, this should be a calculated decision that is made at the end of the problem-solving process, *not* at the beginning. For example, an adolescent who is being teased by some of his classmates may deal with this problem by doing nothing because he had decided after comparing several options (e.g. tease back, tell a teacher) that this is the best solution for now. His rationale is that the boys may tire of teasing him if he shows indifference. Had the boy not considered other possibilities for dealing with the teasing, this would have been an avoidance technique. Ignoring problems by avoidance, distraction, escape or denial are largely Non-Productive coping strategies (Frydenberg and Lewis, 1993b; Seiffge-Krenke, 1995). They are non-productive because no attempts are made to resolve the problem or minimize stress; there is also nothing to learn from the experience and generally not much to gain. Adolescents do sometimes call upon such strategies although they are largely ineffective. For example, one study (Lewis and Frydenberg, 2004a) which investigated 1229 Australian adolescents' self-evaluations of the effectiveness of their coping strategies found that between 100 and 200 students in the sample reported using Non-Productive strategies at least sometimes, even though they identified them as never being helpful. Non-Productive coping has been linked to incessantly thinking about one's problems, self-blame, a pessimistic outlook, insecurity and poor feelings of control (Lyubomirsky, Tucker, Caldwell and Berg, 1999; Frye and Goodman, 2000). Within this frame, an individual may feel that nothing can be done and perceive that attempts to deal with the problem will be unsuccessful.

Problem-solving efficacy, that is, the adolescent's belief in his or her ability to deal with problems effectively and get control over the problem's resolution, is closely related to problem-solving abilities (Largo-Wright, Peterson and Chen, 2005). When adolescents have confidence in their ability to solve problems they are likely to view the problems as challenges to be tackled rather than as stressors to be avoided. In contrast, an accumulation of research reported by Ferrari, Nota, Soresi and Frydenberg (2007) indicates that individuals who perceive themselves as inefficient problem-solvers tend to show:

- a greater degree of depression (Heppner, Baumgardner and Jackson, 1985; Nezu and Ronan, 1988);
- higher levels of state and trait anxiety (Larson, Piersel, Imao and Allen, 1990; Chang, 2002);
- more personal problems and greater difficulties in interacting with others (Heppner and Petersen, 1982; Larson and Heppner, 1985; D'Zurilla and Nezu, 1990; D'Zurilla and Sheedy, 1991, 1992);
- more somatic symptoms (Heppner, Kampa and Bruining, 1987);
- a greater number of irrational beliefs and dysfunctional ideas (Heppner, Reeder and Larson, 1983; Nolen-Hoeksema and Girgus, 1994; Grant and Compas, 1995);
- poor self-concept and external locus of control (Heppner and Petersen, 1982; Larson *et al.*, 1990);
- a tendency to procrastination and passiveness (Logan, 1988, 1989; Epstein, 1990, 1994; Larson *et al.*, 1990);
- poor self-efficacy beliefs and poor social abilities (Nota and Soresi, 1998);
- maladaptive coping strategies and higher levels of worry (Belzer, D'Zurilla and Maydeu-Olivares, 2002; Chang, 2002).

In contrast to the above, as pointed out in chapter 4, those who are high on hope, or resilient, are more likely to be good problem-solvers.

Although problem-solving and coping are linked processes, they do not completely overlap. Problem-solving has various domains, of which social problem-solving is the one most related to the concept of coping. D'Zurilla and Nezu (1982) identified three aspects of social problem-solving: problem-solving, solution implementation and behavioural competence. The problem-solving component involves processes of discovering the best solution. The solution implementation component involves actions aimed at implementing the solution. The behavioural competence component involves the coping behaviours and skills used to deal with problems. It is this last aspect of social problem-solving that is most related to coping.

The literature attests to the independent contributions of poor problem-solving abilities and poor self-efficacy on psychosocial problems. In addition, the two factors can combine and have been found to characterize adolescents at greater risk for maladjustment (Nolen-Hoeksema and Girgus, 1994; Grant and Compas, 1995; Frye and Goodman, 2000; Soresi and Nota, 2003). For example, key factors associated with school dropout are how adolescents cope with school-related challenges and their beliefs in their scholastic and social abilities.

A recent Australian study (Lewis and Frydenberg, 2007) examined differences in the coping strategies of adolescents who differentially assessed the efficacy of their own problem-solving strategies. The aim was to determine whether adolescents who perceived themselves as poorer problem-solvers made greater use of Non-Productive coping strategies. Gender differences in coping are well established in the literature, so gender was taken into account. A total of 801 adolescents aged 12–16 years from 12 secondary schools in metropolitan Melbourne were administered a slightly modified version of the ACS Short Form (Frydenberg and Lewis, 1993a). Efficacy of problem-solving was measured by asking adolescents to rate how helpful each coping response was when it was implemented. Use of Non-Productive coping strategies (*keeping to oneself, self-blame* and *acting out*) were more strongly related to poorer problem-solving efficacy in girls. Girls who reported less efficacy in problem-solving ability were more likely to *give up, acknowledge defeat, keep the issue to themselves* and use *self-blame*. For both boys and girls who reported high self-efficacy in problem-solving ability the following Productive coping strategies were employed: *accepting one's best efforts, focusing on the positive* and *engaging in social action*. Boys specifically used more humour and spent time with friends, and girls relied more on *social support, physical recreation* and *worked hard*. Alternative interpretations of these results could include the following. The lack of association between boys' problem-solving efficacy and Non-Productive strategies may suggest that use of strategies such as *self-blame* may not inhibit problem-solving effectiveness, whereas girls who have a tendency towards use of Non-Productive strategies may perceive their problem-solving ability as less effective, or indeed actually be less effective at problem-solving. The implication of this research is that it would be presumptuous to assume that all adolescents use negative emotion-focused coping because they have low perceptions of their problem-solving ability. In fact, adolescent self-evaluations of problem-solving efficacy may be inaccurate.

A recent Italian study reported by Ferrari and colleagues (2007) sought to investigate the relationship between problem-solving abilities and self-efficacy beliefs in adolescents who were at greater risk for maladjustment. Specifically, the study investigated whether such adolescents would be likely to benefit from participation in a coping skills programme. The intervention was an Italian translation of the Best of Coping programme (described in chapter 12). Both problem-solving training and positive self-appraisal form important components of the programme.

Adolescents who participated in this study were from a business high school in an Italian province, which had previously been identified as having a youth population at greater risk for psychosocial problems than other provinces. Initially 209 students aged 15 and 16 completed two self-report instruments in order to distinguish those who were at highest risk of maladjustment. The 20-item questionnaire, *How much confidence do I have in myself?*, measured self-efficacy, and the 23-item questionnaire, *How do I deal with difficult situations?*, measured problem-solving abilities. The 26 students with the highest scores on the combined questionnaires were selected to form the experimental group and the control group. There were 11 girls and two boys in each group. Students also completed an Italian version of the ACS before the test. After the intervention, all three questionnaires were readministered to the intervention and control groups.

The main analysis for the intervention effects focused on the variables self-efficacy and problem-solving abilities, the three coping styles of Productive coping, Non-Productive coping and Reference to Others. In this study, Productive coping was referred to as problem-focused coping. Before the main analysis, correlations between problem-solving abilities, self-efficacy and the 18 coping strategies of the ACS were examined for the total sample. As expected, there was a positive correlation between self-efficacy and problem-solving abilities. Concerning the 18 coping strategies measured by the ACS, there were positive correlations between self-efficacy beliefs and *work hard to achieve* and *worry*. Negative correlations were found between problem-solving abilities themselves and *not coping* and *self-blame*. Problem-solving ability correlated positively with *focus on problem-solving, work hard and achieve,* and *worry.*

Intervention effects were then investigated. Results indicated that the intervention did not have a significant effect on self-efficacy beliefs. There was some evidence that the intervention had an impact on problem-solving abilities. Although the difference was not significant over time, there was a meaningful difference between the control and experimental groups after the programme, which was explained by both an improvement, albeit slight, in the intervention group and a decline in the control group. As to coping strategies, there were significant improvements in problem-focused coping over the duration of the programme, but not in Reference to Others coping or Non-Productive coping. Overall, these results provide some support for the effectiveness of the Best of Coping programme (see chapter 12) with adolescents at greater risk for maladjustment. The authors cautioned that results should be interpreted tentatively due to the size of the study, as such small sample sizes can make it difficult to detect differences. Moreover, they suggest that more intensive training programmes may be required for adolescents who exhibit poor problem-solving abilities and self-efficacy.

Decision-making and coping

Adolescents, like all of us, make decisions all the time. There are the everyday decisions such as what to have for breakfast, what to wear to school, when to do homework and what to watch on television. Often these decisions are made rapidly, without stress or concern. From time to time, however, adolescents must also make more difficult decisions, such as what subjects to take at school, whether or not to try cigarette smoking, which parent to live with and what career to pursue. The coping-conflict model proposed by Janis and Mann (1977) draws our attention to the importance of coping when it comes to making decisions. Making decisions can be stressful for numerous reasons; there are concerns about having to make a decision in the first place, about making the *right* decision, and about the negative outcomes that may occur if the wrong decision is made. Moreover, decision-makers are concerned not only about how the decision will affect them but also other people. Social concerns also arise as decision-makers want others to accept and affirm their decision and it can be difficult to identify and implement a decision that satisfies all parties. Because of the stress-provoking elements involved in decision-making, an ability to cope is thus an integral part of the process. In turn, decision-making is an important element in the overall coping process. How an individual makes a decision and the strategies used in the process can be explored for evidence of good versus poor coping.

Decision-making takes on particular importance during the adolescent years, when there are both external pressures to take greater responsibilities for one's choices and internal drives to make one's own lifestyle choices. Concurrently, adolescents also strive for peer acceptance and face social pressures to make decisions that are in accordance with their peer groups and subcultures. Friedman (2000) noted that adolescents are cautious about participating in decision-making, which may be partly attributed to poor decision-making confidence due to a lack of experience, adolescent norms that favour complacency, and the desire to avoid unpleasant choices. While many adolescents (like adults) hesitate to make decisions, adolescence is a period characterized by rapid cognitive development and advances in decision-making abilities to levels that are comparable to adult competencies (Quadrel, Fischhoff and Davis, 1993). For instance, metacognition, which is the ability to think about the cognitive process involved in decision-making, is one form of higher-order thinking that improves during adolescence. Compared to younger adolescents, older adolescents have superior abilities in the decision-making components of creative thinking, evaluating options, identifying a broad array of risks and benefits, and evaluating the credibility of information provided by others (Mann, Harmoni and Power, 1989).

Age differences in decision-making

Quadrel and colleagues (1993) looked at the differences between adults' and adolescents' judgements of the probability of negative outcomes. Assessing the probability of adverse outcomes is an important component in adolescent decision-making, particularly when decisions are about risky behaviours. Specifically, the authors investigated the 'illusion of relative invulnerability', which is a tendency to believe that one is inherently less vulnerable than others to adverse outcomes. This study found that both adults and adolescents have the illusion of invulnerability, but adolescents have this illusion no more than adults.

Difficult decisions

Mann and Friedman (1999, p. 228) use the term 'decision coping' to refer to the 'main patterns or styles used by individuals to deal with or resolve decisional conflict'. What types of decisions adolescents find

Table 11.1 The five decision types emerging from the Fischhoff,
Furby, Quadrel and Richardson (1991) study

Decision type	Description	Example
'Whether to do' decisions	Decisions about actions to take	To lie to parents about going to a party
'To do' decisions	Decisions that involve resolutions	Not to get any detentions this term
Two-option dilemmas	Decisions that have conflicting options	Whether to save money or buy a car
Finite choices	Decision that have a limited number of options	When to complete homework
'What to do about' an issue	Decisions that involve resolving issues	How to rectify a friendship gone wrong

Source: Adapted from Mann and Friedman, 1999.

difficult and how they deal with decision problems are important questions for investigating how adolescents make choices from within a decision-coping framework. In order to identify the types of decisions that adolescents find difficult to make, Fischhoff and colleagues (1991) conducted interviews with adolescents to obtain their descriptions of previous and current decisions. The most common types of difficult decisions expressed were those to do with friendships, followed by parents, health, career plans and school performance. Five decision types emerged from the data analysis and are described in Table 11.1.

The most common decisions reported by adolescents fell within the 'whether to' type, followed by the 'to do' type, the two-option dilemma type, the finite choice type and the 'what to do about an issue' type. Two-option dilemmas are the most classic type, in which an individual must choose between two opposing alternatives. According to the coping-conflict theory, such decisions are the most difficult to make as they represent an internal conflict between one's values or goals. Indeed, during the interviews adolescents explained that such decisions were hard to make because both options had negative aspects.

Mann and Friedman give an example of a boy who decided to live with his father when he was 7 years old because his father lived close to his friends. This represented a concrete decision-making dilemma in the pre-adolescent years. In adolescence he would probably have found the decision much more difficult to make due to a greater awareness of the impact his decision would have on his parents, and of the risks and benefits involved. By seeing both parents now, he meets his need to remain close to both his mother and his father and to please them both.

Adolescents commonly describe decisions to do with study, career and social relationships as the most difficult to make. This finding has been reported in studies of Western adolescents (Mann, Harmoni, Power and Beswick, 1987; Fischhoff *et al.*, 1991) and Israeli adolescents (Friedman, 1991). How adolescents cope with making these decisions has also been explored through interview and questionnaire data. Fischoff and colleagues reported that adolescents commonly coped with their decision concerns by seeking information, seeking social support and trying out various options, all of which are active coping approaches. Other less commonly reported ways of coping included doing nothing and ignoring or putting off the decision, all of which represent passive coping. Friedman further explored the significant others from whom adolescents sought support. He found that adolescents most frequently consulted with friends, followed by parents, no one, other adults (non-parent), teachers, siblings and, last, school counsellors. This agrees with general research on adolescent support-seeking that identifies friends as the main source of support (Frydenberg and Lewis, 1993b; see also Boldero and Fallon on help-seeking in chapter 4). For difficult decisions, however, it may be useful for adolescents to obtain information, advice and support from friends as well as other individuals. It appears that school counsellors or psychologists are underused when it comes to helping adolescents make difficult decisions.

The coping styles used for making difficult decisions

Four coping styles were identified by Janis and Mann (1977) in their development of the coping-conflict model of decision-making: vigilance, hypervigilance, defensive avoidance and complacency. All four styles are available to an individual, with the selection of style seen as partly determined by the time available to make the decision and one's confidence in getting a successful outcome. The vigilance coping style is used when people are confident about reaching a successful outcome and think they have enough time to make the decision. All the options are carefully considered before a final decision is made. The hypervigilance style is used when people believe there is not enough time to make a calculated decision. In their panic, they quickly settle on an option to resolve their stress about having to make the decision. The defensive avoidance style is used when people lack confidence in reaching a successful outcome. They attempt to avoid the conflict by putting the decision off or asking someone else to make the decision for them. The complacency style is used by those who experience no conflict about the alternative options. Regardless of what decision is made, they continue as usual.

Janis and Mann (1977) stated that the vigilance coping style represents adaptive coping, whereas the other three represent maladaptive coping. The extent to which an individual will call upon each coping style depends on time constraints, confidence in reaching a solution, and psychosocial individual differences such as levels of anxiety and previous experiences.

As with coping in general, age-related differences in coping with decision concerns have been reported. One such study investigated this phenomenon in 868 Australian adolescents aged 13–17 years (Mann *et al.*, 1989).

The Flinders Adolescent Decision-Making Questionnaire (Mann, Harmoni and Power, 1988a), a 30-item self-report scale, was used for assessing participants' decision-coping patterns. Overall, results revealed that adolescents of all ages reported using vigilance coping more than avoidance, hypervigilance and complacency when making difficult decisions. More specifically, however, results indicated that compared to younger adolescents, older adolescents reported more vigilance, greater self-confidence in decision-making ability and less avoidance, hypervigilance and complacency. In particular, the greatest reduction in maladaptive coping with increasing age was due to the reduced use of the avoidance and complacency coping styles. Mann and Friedman (1999) explain this reduction first in terms of increasing external pressures from parents, teachers and society to behave responsibly, and second in terms of adolescent development, such as increased confidence, maturity, more experiences and superior thinking abilities.

However, age-related changes in adolescent coping are not always positive. For example, psychological stress that arises from social pressures on adolescent decision-coping patterns may affect adolescent adjustment. A longitudinal study (Nicoll, 1992) investigated the career and study decisions of 166 Australian adolescents who were completing their final year of secondary school. Participants were assessed at the beginning of the year and halfway through the year on the Flinders Adolescent Decision-Making Questionnaire and also on a measure of anxiety. Over the duration of the study 15 per cent of students dropped out of the study, which indicates that they had decided to discontinue their schooling. Results indicated that the adolescents who remained at school reported increases in anxiety and decreases in self-confidence in decision-making over the duration of the study. Moreover, students' decision-coping patterns changed for the worse, with decreases in vigilance and increases in hypervigilance and defensive avoidance coping.

These results were taken as evidence that the stress associated with the final year of schooling can adversely affect adolescents. During this time, adolescents are required to make various career and study decisions, which they perceive as difficult to make. When adolescents are not making effective decisions and lack confidence in their ability to make such decisions, they experience more stress. A negative cycle may occur, with stress increasing poor decision-making and poor decision-making increasing stress. To reduce stress in the final school years and promote effective decision-making it would be beneficial for students to call upon a network of social supports, to have enough time to make the decision and to feel confident in their decision-making abilities. In addition, explicit teaching of the steps involved in effective decision-making and of the disadvantages of making hasty decisions or avoidance could form part of school programmes for preparing students for the final years of school and beyond.

Courses that focus purely on decision-making have also been developed and implemented with adolescents. The GOFER course (Mann *et al.*, 1988a) is one such programme that aims to teach adolescents about the cognitive and emotional factors involved in decision-making. The programme uses a general heuristic framework to help adolescents make effective decisions and informs them about how to deal with social pressures to make particular decisions, to take responsibility for their choices, to maintain commitment to a decision and to obtain appropriate support and information. GOFER is a memory aid used to make it easier for adolescents to remember the steps involved in effective decision-making:

- **G-** goal clarification
- **O-** option generation
- **F-** fact finding
- **E-** consideration of effects
- **R-** review and implementation.

Because of the link between self-esteem and the vigilant coping style, building self-esteem and confidence in decision-making also form important parts of the GOFER course. Evaluations of the course have supported its effectiveness, with adolescents who completed the course showing increases in decision-making confidence and vigilance and decreases in the maladaptive decision-coping styles of hypervigilance, complacency and defensive avoidance (Mann, Harmoni, Power, Beswick and Ormond, 1988b). However, the authors caution that gains are not maintained over an extended period unless there is ongoing reinforcement or there is a provision for booster sessions.

Another decision-making training programme is Pros and Cons (Taal and Sampaio de Carvalho, 1993), developed in the Netherlands. The aim of this nine-week programme was to teach adolescents aged between 11 and 14 years the main principles of decision-making, which included lessons on weighing-up alternatives, planning, interpersonal dilemmas and taking responsibility. An evaluation of the Pros and Cons programme with 87 students and a control group of 99 students (mean age = 12.4) indicated that it increased adolescents' knowledge and understanding of the decision-making process and increased their sense of control over achievements (Taal and Sampaio de Carvalho, 1997). The authors concluded that the programme helped adolescents to make decisions in the direction of their goals and to play a major role in maintaining a commitment to those goals.

Alternatively, adolescents' decision-making abilities can be targeted in coping programmes. The Best of Coping programme is one such programme that aims to equip adolescents with the skills of effective decision-making as part of its general aim of enhancing coping. One entire session of the BOC programme is dedicated to decision-making. Adolescents are asked to recall decisions they have made in the past and to reflect on how they went about making these decisions. They are then taught that in order to make good decisions, they need to consider several things: goals, choices, outcomes and review. Personal goals are important to keep in mind when considering options to ensure a match between significant goals and decisions. The consideration of choices involves brainstorming all the possible options, which should be done without evaluation. Once all options have been identified, each option can be evaluated for its outcome. An evaluation of an option should include identifying the positive and negative outcomes for oneself and for others. Finally, all the information is reviewed and a choice is made. Questions that adolescents should ask themselves are listed in the table below. Adolescents are then provided with sample scenarios to practise decision-making and are asked to use this process with real decisions they have to make. The importance of reviewing decisions is reiterated to point out that even if a poor choice is made, there are always opportunities for change and, at the very least, something to learn.

In summary, there are various ways of teaching adolescents how to make effective decisions, such as through single workshops and longer

Table 11.2 Questions to ask oneself during the decision-making
process

Stage	Questions
Goals	What are my goals? What are my three most important goals?
Choices	What are my options? Without thinking about the outcomes, what are all the choices available? What options would my best friend think of? What options would my mum or dad think of?
Outcomes	What are the benefits/advantages of each option for myself? What are the costs/disadvantages of each option for myself? Who might be affected by the decision I make? What are the benefits/advantages of each option for other people? What are the costs/disadvantages of each option for other people?
Review	Now that I know all the options and the advantages and disadvantages of each, which is the best option? Do I have all the information to make this decision? Who could I talk to about this decision?

courses. The evaluation of the Pros and Cons programme pointed out that younger adolescents aged 11–14 years can be taught the decision-making process. This suggests that targeting students in their earlier years of secondary school may be beneficial so that they should have the skills required to moderate stress in the final years when many difficult career and study decisions must be made.

The deliberation-resolution model of decision-making

Decision-making is a process that has two broad phases, the pre-commitment phase and the post-commitment phase. The pre-commitment phase includes all the steps in making the decision such as identifying and evaluating each option. The post-commitment phase occurs once the decision has been made and involves the actual implementation of the decision. While all pre-commitment and post-commitment tasks are important to the overall process, individuals do not always give equal attention to the two phases. Friedman (1996) developed the deliberation-resolution model for the purposes of breaking down, analysing and explaining adolescent decision-making. Deliberation refers to the pre-commitment phase and resolution refers to commitment and post-commitment tasks. Friedman sees deliberation and resolution as two conceptually discrete phases. Therefore, it is

RESOLUTION

	Low	High
High	vacillation	thoughtful determination
Low	avoidance	undeliberated conclusion

DELIBERATION (row label spanning High/Low on the left)

Figure 11.1 Decision-making coping patterns that involve combinations of low and high activity, according to the deliberation-resolution model

possible for an individual to invest much time and effort in deliberating about the decision and little time in maintaining it. On the other hand, it is possible for an individual to make a hasty decision but then place much effort into ensuring the decision is maintained. Friedman defines three levels of commitment: low, medium and high. These three levels and the two phases above combine to provide a nine-level taxonomy of decision-making processes. For simplicity we will focus on the four patterns that involve combinations of high- and low-activity levels: vacillation, thoughtful determination, avoidance and undeliberated conclusion. These four decision-coping patterns are depicted in Figure 11.1. Avoidance emerges through a combination of low activity during both phases and is similar to the defensive avoidance coping style described previously. In contrast, thoughtful determination emerges through a combination of high activity at both phases and is similar to the vigilant coping style.

To investigate the deliberation-resolution model in adolescent decision-making, Friedman developed the Adolescent Decision Process (ADP) scale. This scale was used to investigate coping with social and personal concerns in a study of 560 Israeli adolescents aged 16–17. Results indicated that, irrespective of whether problems are personal or social, or pressing or not pressing, adolescents most often used thoughtful determination in their decision-making, followed by vacillation, undeliberated conclusion and, last, avoidance. Interestingly, there were no differences between the coping patterns used for social problems and personal problems. Friedman (2000) has also investigated adolescent decision-coping patterns in relation to confidence and experience. Although many adolescents (57 per cent) felt confident in their ability to make decisions, fewer (44 per cent) thought they had enough knowledge and experience to make effective decisions. In addition, a negative correlation was found between vacillation and confidence, which indicates that individuals low on confidence tend to deliberate about making a decision but then do little to implement it. In contrast, a positive correlation was found between thoughtful determination and confidence, which suggests that confident individuals make substantial investments in both deliberating about problems and resolving them.

Career-decisional states in adolescence

Some of the most important and difficult decisions adolescents must make are to do with their careers. 'What do I want to *be*?' 'What do I want to *do*?' Tertiary education or apprenticeship? Travel or university? Move away for university or stay at home? These are just some of the questions facing adolescents which take careful planning, self-reflection and sometimes months or even years of preparation. Adolescents are being asked to consider their professional aspirations in secondary school, especially when it comes to subject selection in the senior years of schooling. They are given opportunities for career exploration through work experience, career counselling and hands-on projects. Nonetheless, making a career decision is complicated and may be stressful for adolescents because of the breadth of possibilities, and the long-term and life-changing effects such decisions may have. For such reasons, researchers and practitioners alike have become interested in the career-decisional states of adolescents.

In particular, researchers are interested in examining differences in personal, social and career-related factors between adolescents who have selected a career path and those who have not. In a review of 15 studies of career decidedness spanning the years 1977–95, Gordon (1998) identified different types of decided and undecided students. Across all studies was the undecided type labelled 'chronically indecisive', which was associated with poorer well-being, anxiety and undesirable personality traits such as neuroticism.

Career indecision was also investigated in a longitudinal Australian study of secondary school students to explore the relationships between career decidedness and career, well-being and personal variables (Creed, Prideaux and Patton, 2005). Two hundred and ninety-two Year 8 students participated in the initial testing and were allocated to either the career-decided or career-undecided group on the basis of how they answered the question 'I have decided on a career and feel comfortable with it. I also know how to go about implementing my choice'. One hundred and seventy-four students (61 per cent) were allocated to the career-decided group and 112 (39 per cent) to the career-undecided group. Students were then reassessed when they were in Year 10, at which time 117 students in the career-decided group and 94 students in the career-undecided group were available. The longitudinal nature of this study provided four groups at time 2:

1   Students who were decided at time 1 and time 2, labelled the decided/decided group (n = 74, 35%)
2   Students who were undecided at time 1 and time 2, coined the undecided/undecided group (n = 44, 21%)
3   Students who were undecided at time 1 and decided at time 2, coined the undecided/decided group (n = 42, 20%)
4   Students who were decided at time 1 and undecided at time 2, coined the decided/undecided group (n = 49, 23%).

Important differences in career development and personal variables were found across the four groups.

The authors postulated that students falling in either the undecided/ decided group or the decided/undecided group were showing developmental indecisiveness. Indeed, some degree of indecision is not pathological and may reflect an active component of the process of career exploration. Engaging in work experience is one way in which adolescents become aware of their skills and attributes and of what profession may best suit them. The current study indicated that students who were no closer to making a career decision at time 2 had had only limited work experience. Thus, career counselling, voluntary work experience and casual employment may be important in helping adolescents gain knowledge of career development.

The relationship between decision-making styles and coping

More recent work has sought to determine the link between decision-making and problem-focused coping, the latter of which refers to the processes involved in solving problems. Although decision-making is indeed a part of problem-solving, they are not identical processes. For example, a person may attempt to solve a problem but still not make a decision. Decision-making involves a commitment to action-implementation. A recent study (Mann, Nota, Soresi, Ferrari and Frydenberg, 2006) investigated the relationship between decision-making style and coping strategies in 566 Italian adolescents (298 females, 268 males) aged 14–17. The authors aimed to show that decision-making and problem-focused coping are overlapping processes but are not identical. Participants completed the Melbourne Decision-Making Questionnaire (Mann, Burnett, Radford and Ford, 1997), and two versions of the ACS. The Melbourne Decision-Making Questionnaire comprises 22 items that measure four decision-making styles. Two styles, hypervigilance and vigilance, are from Janis and Mann's (1977) coping-conflict model of decision patterns. The other two styles are buck-passing, which refers to letting other people make decisions, and procrastination. In this breakdown of decision-making styles, vigilance is considered adaptive and the other three styles maladaptive. Participants completed both the long and the short versions of the ACS (see chapter 3) in order to examine coping in general (long version) and with a nominated concern (short version). To reduce the breadth of analysis, data were analysed at the level of the three coping styles and then at the level of the items best representing each of the three styles. In this study, the Productive coping style was referred to as problem-focused coping. Correlations were the main form of analysis and it was expected that significant but moderate relationships would be found between decision-making and coping.

The vigilance decision-making style was positively associated with problem-focused coping, and hypervigilance and procrastination, which reflect maladaptive decision-making, were associated with Non-Productive coping. Buck-passing was also associated with Non-Productive coping for girls but not for boys. The strongest correlation was between hypervigilance and Non-Productive coping in girls. Further investigation of gender differences revealed that the link between maladaptive decision-making and the representative Non-Productive coping strategy of *quit* (which is about giving up or trying to escape the problem) was stronger for girls than boys. In contrast, the link between vigilance and the representative problem-focused strategy *can do* (which is about working hard on your problem and thinking positively) was stronger in boys than girls. These gender differences support previous findings which indicate that girls have lower self-efficacy beliefs and self-determination than boys (Frydenberg and Lewis, 1993b; Soresi and Nota, 2003). These results revealed a clear association between decision-making and coping, but the correlations were low.

Vigilance and problem-focused coping predicted the *can do* coping response to a problem, with vigilance contributing slightly more to the response than problem-focused coping. Non-Productive coping and procrastination were also found to predict the *quit* coping response, though Non-Productive coping was a much stronger contributor.

These results suggest that unsurprisingly adolescents' choices, and behaviour in how they cope with problems relating to school, friends and family, are explained more by their general coping style than by their decision-making style. It is understandable that one's coping style may influence the adolescents' approach to decisions, especially in the case of Non-Productive coping, which is essentially a failure to face problems and precedes making choices to deal with them.

In summary, Mann and colleagues' (2006) study demonstrated that decision-making styles and problem-focused coping are related processes. Although it is unclear from this study whether decision-making style underpins the coping styles used to deal with a specific problem or vice versa, there was some evidence that coping had more influence on how adolescents chose to deal with problems than did decision-making, particularly when the coping response was to *quit* trying to solve the problem. This suggests that teaching adolescents problem-focused strategies and decision-making skills are both important for managing concerns. They are complementary skills that are likely to have cumulative benefits.

Mann and Friedman (1999) remind us that decision-making is an integral component of coping. They show that decision-making changes over time and so is subject to development, though the exact nature of this development is not known. For example, they point out that when decision-making takes place in a stressful situation, such as the final year of high school, there is an increase in hypervigilance and anxiety. Thus there are indications that there is a need in the senior years for decision-coping skills and coping skills in general. While Mann and Friedman found that both Australian and Israeli teens on the whole are vigilant or 'considered decision makers', this cannot be assumed to hold cross-culturally (as with coping). For example, comparison between Israeli and Australian teens show that the former are more vigilant. The more vigilant the decision-making, the less likely young people are to make risky or unhealthy decisions. Mann and Friedman point out that there is a two-phase decision-training, the pre-decision or deliberation phase and the post-decision resolution or commitment phase. The two phases are conceptually distinct and it is suggested that training be offered in both.

The development of social coping skills

People can be a source of both stress and pleasure. Social coping skills play a major part in determining the quality of interpersonal relationships across a range of contexts. Furthermore, relationships can provide an index of happiness and the support of others is a way of coping with stress. For example, in the Adolescent Coping Scale (1993a) coping strategies such as *seek social support, seek to belong, social action, seek professional help* and *seek relaxing diversions,* either alone or with others, are linked to interpersonal relationships. There are benefits to having good relationships, and the cost of not having them or of being in bad relationships can be high. Thus it is important that adolescents be able to communicate effectively. Not only does their communicative ability influence relationships with family and friends, but also success at school and in the workforce. People need to be able to communicate their thoughts, wants, needs, concerns and ideas. Although the introduction of computers and the Internet has had a significant impact in how we communicate, basic social skills are necessary for building and sustaining relationships in the family, school and community. Basic social skills comprise both verbal and non-verbal communication. It comes as a surprise to many young people that most of our communication occurs by non-verbal means. Argyle (1999) highlighted the importance of non-verbal communication in his writing on the development of social coping skills. He postulated that individuals who are socially incompetent have difficulties with non-verbal communication. For example, they may not make eye contact when greeting people. The development of effective social skills is important not only for adolescents who struggle in this area, but also for those who want social success. Basically, all adolescents can become more effective in how they communicate. The next section gives an overview of pertinent non-verbal and verbal communication described by Argyle (1999), skills that form the foundation of social success, from which more sophisticated abilities can develop.

Non-verbal communication

Non-verbal communication, or body language, is communication without words. People reveal their feelings or convey many messages through their gaze, body posture, facial expression, voice, physical appearance and physical distance.

Gaze

Eye contact is important when conversing with another. It is important when initiating contact or greeting someone to look directly at them as this signals you have noticed their arrival and are comfortable in their presence. When speaking, eye contact helps to maintain the interaction, and also allows the speaker to view any signals coming from the listener. When speaking to more than one person, switching eye contact among the listeners ensures that all feel included. When listening, looking at the speaker conveys interest in what they have to say. Avoiding eye contact negates communication even when this is not the person's intent. For example, a girl may not look at her classmates when she talks to them because she is shy. While no eye contact is detrimental, so too is excessive eye contact. Staring makes others feel uncomfortable. An effective gaze is one that is direct and relaxed.

Body posture

Body posture is a powerful vehicle for getting our message across. Visualize an adolescent boy saying 'I feel very uncomfortable and angry when you laugh at me for getting a question wrong and I would like you to stop' to a classmate. First, visualize him with his shoulders slumped and turned away from the other boy. Now, visualize him saying the same sentence standing tall, hands by his side and directly facing the other boy. It is clear which is more effective? Assertive communication is the result of not only what we say but also how we say it. Body posture also helps maintain the flow of conversation when one is in tune with the other person. Leaning towards someone when they are talking conveys interest. In contrast, rocking or slumping with feet facing away from the person conveys lack of interest or discomfort in being there. When communicating in public, people can convey confidence by standing tall; when in an audience, people can show interest by sitting erect; when having a sensitive conversation, people can build rapport by adopting the other person's postures.

Facial expression

Facial expression is the most important non-verbal form of communication. Humans throughout the globe, and even some other primates such as gorillas and monkeys, convey primary emotions through their facial expressions. The six main facial expressions for emotions are happy, sad, angry, surprised, afraid and disgusted. Children and adolescents who lack social skills may find it difficult to distinguish different facial expressions, which makes it difficult for them to read other people's emotions and to modify their behaviours accordingly. For example, a young boy may fail to detect that his mother is getting angry and continue to bounce a ball inside the house because he cannot read her facial expression. Not only is it important for adolescents to be able to obtain insight into others' feelings via facial expressions, it is also important that they convey their feelings appropriately with their expressions. Smiling when greeting someone indicates that you are happy to see them. Eyes downcast and a frown signals you are sad and may want to talk about your concerns. It is not always socially appropriate to convey emotions and sometimes a poker face (an English expression meaning a straight face) may be required. For example, when a teenager's friend reveals a terrible family secret, she may need to moderate her facial expression of disgust.

Voice

How we say what we say greatly influences the message we send. Consider the following: 'Can you please take your sneakers and school bag into your room?' Now consider: 'Can you *please* take your sneakers and school bag into your room?!!' As can be gathered, a simple change in the expression and tone of the message and a polite request becomes a frustrated appeal. Adolescents can become more effective communicators by using their voice in conjunction with their words. They can exaggerate words or change their tone of voice for impact. They can ensure their messages are heard by speaking in a controlled and clear voice. In addition, one's voice can signal a depressed mood when it is low and slow or happiness when it is more upbeat and expressive.

Physical appearance

The saying 'first impressions count' has a lot of merit. Think about when you meet someone for the very first time. What is it that you see first? On what basis do you form your impressions? Are these impressions lasting? Often, the first things we notice about a person are to do with their physical appearance, such as their gender, clothes and hair. We use this information to piece together an understanding of the person's social class, personality and subculture. Imagine two adolescent boys applying for their first casual job at the local grocery store. The grocery store manager may form a very different impression of the boys if one was wearing ripped jeans and a backward hat and the other his school uniform. Sometimes such impressions are to the detriment of the individual. In the previous example, the first boy may really want the job, may be a hard worker and may actually be the best candidate for the position, but the manager may not employ him because of his first impression of the boy's dishevelled appearance. Adolescents need to be aware of how their appearance can influence how others perceive them. They need to realize that what is acceptable and even 'cool' in their peer group may convey other messages to adults.

Physical distance

Physical distance is the distance between two or more people when they are communicating. Obviously, the space between people is important in verbal communication, as one needs to be able to hear what is being said. More subtle and powerful, however, is the effect physical distance has on comfort levels. Imagine meeting a person for the first time. How do you feel when they stand 3 metres away from you? How do you feel when they stand 30 centimetres away? In both situations it is unlikely that you felt comfortable. While there is no correct formula for all social relationships, a distance of about 3 feet is considered comfortable for most professional or social relationships. This is because of personal space, which refers to the immediate space surrounding a person that they consider their domain. Adolescents need to respect each other's personal space so that they do not feel invaded. Obviously, this may not hold for relationships between family members, close friends and partners. Personal space may become shared places, but it is important that this is by mutual agreement.

Culture

The previous discussion of basic non-verbal communication skills focused broadly on how such skills are expressed and interpreted in Western cultures. With the exception of basic facial expressions, which are largely universal, non-verbal communication tends to be culturally bound. This has important implications for individuals working with adolescents from different cultures. First, there needs to be an awareness of the differences that exist in non-verbal communication; otherwise, messages can be grossly misinterpreted. For example, adolescents from Chinese backgrounds may be uncomfortable with direct eye contact because in their culture it may be a form of intimidation. In many Asian cultures, avoiding eye contact with adults is a sign of respect. The amount of personal space required may also vary across cultures. Even facial expressions, considered universal, may not convey actual feelings. For example, in Japan, individuals are expected to suppress public displays of negative emotions. Because of cross-cultural differences, it is important that teachers and other adults working with adolescents from other cultures are aware that differences in non-verbal communication do exist and they should become informed of these differences. In turn, teachers can help other students to understand cultural differences. Additionally, adolescents who have recently migrated need to be taught about non-verbal communication in their new homeland.

Verbal communication

The ability to speak is innate to humans, but the ability to converse is not. It is something we begin learning through our earliest communications with our caregivers and continue to develop throughout childhood. Argyle (1999) highlighted various aspects of verbal communication that comprise basic social skills, namely speech acts, conversational sequences, accommodation and politeness.

Speech acts

Speech acts are utterances that serve particular functions in communication. Examples of speech acts are making requests, providing information, giving compliments and asking questions. For example, making a request conveys what you need, whereas giving information may enable someone to change their behaviour. Even idle chitchat serves a purpose in that it helps establish a bond between two people. In order for speech acts to be effective, they need to be understood by the receiver. This may be difficult for people who are conversing in a second language.

Conversational sequences

A conversation is the exchange of verbal information and in order for it to be an effective exchange various rules must be followed. The most important rule is that both speakers must be active participants. A common conversation type is the question-and-answer sequence, in which one person's question is followed by an answer. Another conversation sequence is when one person's disclosure of information is followed by a disclosure from the other person. Compliments are also commonly reciprocated and so too are hostile comments.

Conversations should also involve the appropriate amount of information and this should be presented accurately and clearly. Conversation busters occur when adolescents fail to follow conversation rules, such as waiting their turn to speak and answering questions. Interrupting, doing most of the talking, or going off at tangents are also forms of conversation busters.

Accommodation

When in conversation, we tend to modify our tone, rate of speech and volume in order to match the other person's style of speech. This is a reciprocal act which helps ensure two people are on the same wavelength. The degree to which someone will accommodate their style of speech may be influenced by their relationship with the other person. For example, two friends are more likely to adopt a similar style of speech in their conversation than two rival classmates.

Politeness

Politeness is important to social relationships and children are taught from an early age to say 'please' and 'thank you'. Politeness involves the addition of words to add politeness to requests, the expression of gratitude, modifying one's request to protect another's self-esteem, and saying 'no' in an optimistic way. Politeness coveys respect, warmth, appreciation and helps to make social interactions rewarding and pleasant. For example, when asked to help a friend with their schoolwork, rather than a flat 'no', a more polite response would be 'I'm sorry I can't help you because I have my own work to do.'

Gender differences

There are difference in how men and women converse. Males tend to speak more about activities and behaviours and females more about feelings and relationships. Males may dominate conversations more than females, who in turn are more concerned about being polite and maintaining social harmony (Argyle, 1999). There may also be important cross-cultural gender differences. For example, in some cultures, women are not expected to speak to an unrelated male unless he asks her a direct question. Both cultural and gender differences should be considered in adolescent verbal and non-verbal communication.

Ineffective conversational skills

Argyle (1999) identified five common conversational blunders made by adults:

1 Deficiencies in the particular skills required for specific social situations, such as work, meetings, interviews, parties, formal occasions and meeting new people
2 Lack of self-disclosure, which creates a barrier for closeness with others
3 Failure to be polite; rudeness
4 Not contributing to conversations; not initiating conversations
5 Occupying the whole conversation; not considering the other person's point of view; not asking questions of the other.

Teaching adolescents about the importance of verbal communication skills and reflecting on their abilities can draw their attention to conversational blunders that they may be making. From this raised awareness, adolescents are in a position to create change and consequently become more effective in their communications with others.

These conversational skills, along with other skills related to coping, can be applied to the management of all relationships including situations of conflict. It is unrealistic to expect that individuals will get through life without the experience of conflict. A certain amount of conflict is normal and healthy and may even be good for relationships if resolved with positive outcomes. Just as adolescents can be taught how to cope effectively, problem-solve, make decisions, they can also be taught how to resolve conflicts.

Most models for managing conflict take into account both concern for others and concern for the self. Susan Opotow and Morton Deutsch (1999) detail how schools can help young people deal with conflict and violence. These include strategies that relate to co-operative learning in the classroom and conflict-resolution training. Strategies for conflict-resolution training emphasize the importance of identifying one's interests and needs and those of the other so that one can identify common and compatible interests. Added to this is the importance of listening attentively and speaking to make oneself understood.

Thomas and Kilmann (1974) developed a popular conflict-resolution framework based on this two-dimensional model. Their framework consists of five styles for handling conflict:

- Competing – high in concern for the self, characterised by the drive to maximize individual gain at others' expense;

- Collaborating – a drive towards constructing solutions which meet the needs of all involved;
- Avoiding – disengaging from conflict with low concern for the self;
- Accommodating – sacrificing self-interests to satisfy other needs; and
- Compromising – the process of making concessions to arrive at a point of resolution. This style floats somewhere in the middle between co-operativeness and assertiveness whereby the individual is assertive without being dominant and is co-operative without overlooking the needs of the self.

It is easy to see which would be the style that would suit a particular conflict best so that an individual's needs are met. Conflict can also be construed as problems to be solved. Problem-solving is dealt with in the Best of Coping programme in chapter 12.

Summary

This chapter has focused on the learning of coping skills through general instruction, through decision-making, problem-solving and a range of verbal and non-verbal communication skills, all components of coping. Problem-solving is a key resource and it is not just the skills of problem-solving but it is the belief in one's capacities that is also important.

While adolescents have numerous decisions to make, decisions about relationships are most frequently reported. Decisional conflict, putting off decisions, particularly those related to career and study are common. Janis and Mann (1977) identified four decision-making styles, namely vigilance, hypervigilance, defensive avoidance and complacency. The fact that three of these could be aggregated with maladaptive coping demonstrates how stressful making difficult decisions can be. Nevertheless, adolescents generally report using a vigilant approach to decision-making. Vigilance increases with age but girls are more likely to quit or give up. There are indications that it is helpful to provide decision-making training for young people.

Adolescents can benefit from direct teaching of decision-making. The GOFER programme provides a metaphor by which the key steps involved in decision-making can be remembered and implemented. Beneficial outcomes have been shown for both direct decision-making programmes and coping skills training in improving decision-making confidence and understanding of the process. Targeting younger adolescents in preparation for decisions required in later schooling would be considered an effective approach.

Social skills, both verbal and non-verbal, were presented as being important to facilitate relationships with others. Adolescents can benefit from the direct teaching of social coping skills. Their ability to communicate effectively can be influenced by making adolescents more aware of both verbal and non-verbal cues and the differences that exist between genders and across cultures. Teaching adolescents about the importance of verbal communication skills and reflecting on their abilities can draw their attention to conversational mistakes that they may be making.

Since conflict is part of everyday life, skills that help people deal with conflict can also be taught in the context of developing helpful coping skills.

In chapter 12, programmes that address the teaching of coping skills through particular programmes of instruction are presented.

12 Teaching coping skills

Student goals

To finish high school and go to uni. That kind of thing. I am not sure what I want to do yet or anything. Just let it roll, just see what happens.

(Boy, 15)

At the moment I am doing my part time apprenticeship so I am hoping to continue this after school.

(Boy, 17)

I am hoping that this is my last year of school. . . . I am gonna give the trade a shot, to be an electrician.

(Boy, 15)

. . . go into university, study IT and just go on from there. Get a really good job and enjoy it, enjoy working.

(Boy, 16)

I just want to get into uni, become a journalist and earn a lot of money.

(Boy, 16)

. . . I also hope to one day be in the police force.

(Girl, 17)

I hope to get a good score and go to uni and do fashion design.

(Girl, 17)

Broad interest in mental health and well-being has been spurred on by rising rates of psychological disturbance in young people. In order to reduce the number of young people with mental illnesses, and to provide support and services for those already afflicted, the role of schools in enhancing social emotional development has been emphasized in many Western communities. In this chapter the role of schools in teaching coping skills is considered and one programme that has been developed in conjunction with the Adolescent Coping Scale is presented and evaluated. The presentation of the studies highlights the many groups of young people who can benefit in different ways from participation in a coping skills programme.

The role of schools

Schools are now expected to provide students with competencies that go well beyond the academic domain. Moreover, schools play a vital role in identifying and providing assistance to students at risk of mental health problems or who are currently experiencing mental health problems. The World Health Organization has created a model for school mental health initiatives which depicts a filtering of services to match student needs. This model can be differentiated into the three levels of primary prevention, early intervention and intervention (Wyn, Cahill, Holdsworth, Rowling and Carson, 2000). Primary prevention initatives foster psychosocial competencies and well-being in all students. Early intervention initiatives are more targeted and are aimed at students who are at risk of mental health problems. Later intervention initiatives are direct and intensive efforts to assist students who are experiencing mental health problems or who have recently experienced a traumatic event. Education systems may provide general guidelines on the provision of such support, with emphasis on primary prevention and early intervention through the delivery of co-ordinated and comprehensive services for young people, but the particular services and support provided are at each school's discretion, and the specific issues of concern vary across schools. For example, schools may identify different needs depending on whether the setting is primary or secondary, single sex or coeducational, or from the independent or government sector. Nonetheless, some issues are universally accepted as integral to adolescents' well-being, of which one pertinent area is coping.

  Much work has gone into identifying the risk and protective factors that influence adolescent well-being, and various factors have emerged as important. Coping can be a protective factor when Productive strategies are used and a risk factor when Non-Productive strategies are used. Moreover, coping can be influenced by other risk and protective factors in a young person's life. For example, a child who grows up in a high-conflict family may use emotion-focused coping strategies to deal with the fighting, such as *self-blame* or *denial*, which can develop into a maladaptive pattern of coping. In contrast, a child whose parents model appropriate emotional responses to setbacks and efficacy in problem-solving has the benefit of vicariously learning effective coping skills for dealing with challenges. Adolescent coping is influenced not only by family variables, but also by experiences and factors to do with their peers, school and the wider community. There is much that schools can do to enhance young people's capacity to cope with stressors ranging from everyday hassles to unexpected and traumatic events. Moreover, effective coping is not only for those in need, but also for those who desire to succeed. This means that coping is universally important because all young people can benefit from more effective coping.

There are various ways in which schools may work towards the objective of enhanced coping for all. One way is to embed coping into the curriculum by providing preventive programmes that encourage resilience to stress (Sandler, Wolchik, MacKinnon, Ayers and Roosa, 1997). The primary goal of such programmes is to provide young people with adjustment-enhancing skills and circumstances that may buffer them against adverse conditions (Raphael, 1993). In this way it is hoped that the severity of issues arising and the number of young people affected may be reduced. Moreover, such programmes reach all young people, and a secondary effect may be that young people who are not at direct risk of mental health problems also benefit, as they are provided with skills to use should they experience negative events in the future.

Young people who are at risk of mental health problems may become the target of a more direct focus on coping, which can be complemented by specific interventions that target the identified mental health risk, such as depression or anxiety. Schools may identify young people who are at risk of such problems because they are already showing some signs or have been exposed to known risk factors, such as a parent with a mental illness. Students with identified learning difficulties may also benefit from early intervention to help them cope with their academic difficulties.

For young people experiencing mental health problems, lessons in coping are important for two reasons. First, research shows that young people with mental health problems commonly call on less Productive means of coping. For example, adolescents who report more depressive symptoms commonly report using more Non-Productive coping strategies (Seiffge-Krenke and Klessinger, 2000). Therefore, coping intervention can address adolescents' habitual ways of coping with their concerns and promote the use of more Productive coping strategies. Second, young people with mental health problems have an additional and important stressor that affects all aspects of their lives, such as a depressive or anxiety disorder. Coping interventions play a critical role in assisting young people to cope effectively with their mental health concerns.

It can be readily understood that coping is an important element across all three levels of intervention. There is therefore a clear need for schools to have access to programmes that have been empirically evaluated and take factors such as gender differences into account, in order to give adolescents an opportunity to build their skills in the area of socioemotional well-being. However, there are few tested and systematic studies of ways of promoting the mental health of young people. There is a real need to develop preventive programmes, particularly ones that address general coping skills and that are easily offered within a school setting. These may be developed by teachers or counsellors, according to need and to address a particular problem such as relationships, loss of a loved one, or management of conflict, or it may be a structured programme which becomes part of the school curriculum. One such programme, the Best of Coping (Frydenberg and Brandon, 2002a, b, 2007a, b), has been developed as a universal programme to build coping skills for adolescents. It has been evaluated in a number of school settings in and outside Australia. Its capacity to benefit students at the levels of both primary prevention and early intervention has been reported in numerous studies.

Informal instruction

A typical intervention that does not rely on a coping skills programme but uses the conceptual areas of the ACS might be to identify one of the 18 ACS coping strategies, indicating the types of concerns for which it is most effective; the way in which it is manifested in the life of the individual (both when it is effective and when it is not); self-evaluation of additional or alternative strategies, reflecting on times when such a strategy was used to little effect, with a view to identifying ways in which its use could be improved; and the 'brainstorming' of additional strategies which may be construed as effective. Consequently, there would be discussions surrounding the benefits and limitations of each of the coping strategies used.

Each session could also include consideration of an appropriate scenario as a role play to elicit possible strategies to be employed and to provide opportunity for practice. The curriculum would give students a chance to reflect on the effectiveness of their coping actions and the acceptability of additional or alternative coping behaviours. In general such programmes would encourage students to use what are personally the most productive behaviours consistent with each of the 18 strategies of the ACS and to minimize their use of the less productive components, taking into account the particular contexts in which the participants operate.

For example, as part of this reflection, students should be asked to identify the usefulness of strategies such as *tension reduction* (e.g. *make myself feel better by taking alcohol, cigarettes or other drugs)*, *self-blame* (e.g. *accept that I am responsible for the problem*) and *worry* (e.g. *worry about what is happening*) and if necessary to determine how use of these strategies might be minimized. This approach would appear particularly relevant for girls, whose ability to cope decreases significantly during this period. This is accompanied by a greater shift than boys experience in Non-Productive coping during the ages of 12–16, even though they don't differ from boys in their use of Productive coping strategies. Such an approach would also appear consistent with recent literature which argues that it may be more important to well-being to minimize the use of Non-Productive strategies than it is to maximize the use of Productive ones (Chan, 1998; Frydenberg and Lewis, 2002). Additionally, once the coping strategies have been identified young people can relate to the concepts through the use of art, drama or song. That is, whether this is done in an individual or group counselling context, or in the course of a classroom setting within the general curriculum or as part of a structured programme, young people can be encouraged to draw the coping strategies, dramatize them, identify songs or even write lyrics that relate to the strategies. Each of these approaches has been used by practitioners and educators. See also chapter 5, where suggestions are made for groups of young people to discuss their coping so that they can learn from each other. And see chapter 8 for a comprehensive discussion on breaking the cycle of depression and making changes in cognition (pp. 163–169) and chapter 9 in relationship to achieving happiness.

Overall, informal instruction in coping is possible and should be attempted but has not been tested for its efficacy yet.

248   *Adolescent coping*

Table 12.1 An overview of the BOC programme

Module	Aim
1. Map of coping	To explore how each of us deals (or copes) with difficult situations, problems or worries. To look at the different coping strategies.
2. Good thinking	To understand the connection between thoughts and feelings and to learn to evaluate and change thinking.
3. Heading down the wrong track	To look at some Non-Productive coping strategies that people use and to explore some helpful alternatives.
4. Getting along with others	To look at how to get our message across and how to listen to the messages of others.
5. Asking for help	To explore the links that we have with family, friends and the community.
6. Problem-solving	To learn the steps to solving problems and practise using them.
7. Making decisions	To learn to explore and evaluate options to make good decisions.
8. Aiming high – goal setting	To learn about the relationship between goals and achievement. To explore goals for our own futures.
9. Skill building	To discover the elements of effective goal setting and how to write detailed goal plans.
10. Managing time	To evaluate how we spend our time and to learn to manage it in an effective way.

Sources: Frydenberg and Brandon, 2002a, b, 2007a, b.

The Best of Coping programme

The BOC programme (Frydenberg and Brandon, 2002a, b, 2007a, b) is a coping skills programme for adolescents. It is based on the theoretical approach of cognitive behavioural therapy, which asserts that our thoughts control our feelings and our actions. The programme comprises 10 modules and can be delivered to whole classes or small groups of adolescents. Table 12.1 provides an overview of each module's aims. The BOC programme uses a direct instruction approach to teach coping and provides numerous opportunities for

Table 12.2 Best of coping studies

	Study	Year level	Experimental group	Control group
1	Frydenberg et al., 2006 *Melbourne*	15–17 years	n = 113 (M = 57, F = 56) n = 22 'at risk', ↓ Non-Productive ↑ Productive n = 23 'resilient' ↓ Non-Productive ↑ Productive n = 68 'main', ↓ Non-Productive ↑ Productive	n/a
2	Luscombe-Smith et al., 2003 *Melbourne*	Year 10 (16–17 yrs)	n = 83 (M = 39, F = 44) ↑ Reference to Others *(males more than females)*	n/a
3	Cotta, Frydenberg and Poole, 2000 *Melbourne*	Year 7 (11–13 yrs)	n = 43 ↑ Productive (trend) ↓ Non-Productive *(worry)* *wishful thinking, not cope,* *self-blame*	n = 45 ↑ Non-Productive *self-blame* *work hard* *social action*
4	McCarthy, 2001 Unpublished thesis *Melbourne*	Year 7 (11–13 yrs)	n = 179 (M = 100, F = 79) ↓ Non-Productive (trend)	n = 56 (M = 33, F = 23) ↑ Non-Productive (trend)
5	Tollit, 2002 Unpublished thesis *Melbourne*	Year 7 (11–13 yrs)	n = 57 (Female) ↑ Productive (scenarios) ↓ Reference to Others *(also at follow up)*	n = 58 (Female) ↓ Productive

continues overleaf

Table 12.2 (continued)

Study	Year level	Experimental group	Control group
6 Huxley, 2003 Unpublished thesis *Melbourne*	Year 9 (14–16 yrs with a mean age of 14.9 yrs)	n = 24 (n = 15 Female) (n = 11 Male) ↑ *seeking social support* ↑ *social action*	n/a
7 Ferrari *et al.*, 2007 *Northern Italy*	15–17 yrs	n = 13 (M = 2, F = 11) ↑ *focus on positive* ↑ *work hard* ↓ *solve problem* ↓ *wishful thinking* ↓ *tension reduction*	n = 13 (M = 2, F = 11) ↓ *solve problem* ↑ *wishful thinking* ↑ *tension reduction*
8 Frydenberg *et al.*, 2006 *Melbourne*	12–16 yrs	n = 70 (total) ↓ Non-Productive ↑ Productive ↑ *solve the problem (at follow-up)*	(n = 28) ↓ Productive ↑ Non-Productive
9 Frydenberg *et al.*, 2006 *Melbourne*	Year 10 (13–17 yrs)	n = 112 (n = 43 Male) ↑ *invest in close friends* ↓ *wishful thinking* (n = 69 Female) ↑ *tension reduction*	n/a

				n/a
10	Ivens, 2006 *Melbourne*	Year 9 (13–14 yrs)	n = 27 ↑ Productive ↓ Non-Productive ↓ psychological distress	n/a
11	Hawkins *et al.*, 2006 *Melbourne*	Year 9 (14–15 yrs)	n = 27 Main concern ↓ Non-Productive General concerns ↑ Productive ↑ Reference to Others ↓ Non-Productive	n/a
12	Goode, 2006 *Melbourne*	Year 9 (12–15 yrs)	n = 35 ↑ Productive ↑ Reference to Others ↓ Non-Productive ↑ well-being ↑ perceptions of social support	n/a
13	D'Anastasi and and Frydenberg 2005	12–15 yrs	n = 55 ↓ *self-blame* for Australian minority group ↑ *physical recreation* for Anglo-Australian group	n = 48

Key: ↑ increase ↓ decrease; M = male F = female
An earlier version of this table appeared in Frydenberg (2004).

adolescents to practise acquired skills through written activities, role-plays and discussion.

The Adolescent Coping Scale, with its 18 conceptual areas of coping, provides a framework and language with which individuals and groups can obtain their coping profile and make changes in their coping practices. It provides the underpinning of the BOC programme. The programme first introduces adolescents to the language of coping, helps them to identify their own coping profiles, and then encourages them to reduce their use of Non-Productive coping strategies in favour of more Productive ones. Other topics that are addressed include thinking optimistically, effective communication skills, steps to take so as to achieve effective problem-solving, decision-making, goal-setting and time management. The programme also includes a session for the practical building of those coping skills that have been learnt throughout previous sessions.

More specifically, Session 1 provides an introduction to the theoretical framework and language of coping that is first introduced by the Adolescent Coping Scale and which is used in many of the subsequent sessions. Session 2 on Good Thinking helps young people become aware of how they can change the way they think and subsequently how they appraise events (positively or negatively), and how they cope. Session 3 has an emphasis on what not to do. We now have evidence that when it comes to coping it is important to teach young people what not to do as much as what to do. It is the use of the Non-Productive coping strategies such as *worry*, *self-blame* and *tension reduction* that are most readily associated with depression (Cunningham and Walker, 1999). Session 4 emphasizes communication skills, which play an important part in effective interactions. Asking for help depends on the capacity to communicate effectively. The next six sessions, Asking for Help, Problem Solving, Making Decisions, Goal Setting, Goal Getting and Managing Time provide an essential set of skills for high school students. Each of the sessions can focus on a particular topic such as dealing with conflict, both internal and external.

The development of the BOC programme was based on the principle that we can all do what we do better, so it was designed for all adolescents and meets the requirements of a primary prevention initiative. Since its development, numerous studies have evaluated its effectiveness, not only its capacity to enhance the coping skills of adolescents in general, but also its usefulness with adolescents who have particular needs. To follow is an overview of key evaluations of the BOC programme that have been conducted since its development.

These studies are grouped into whether they provide an evaluation of the programme as primary prevention or as early intervention.

The BOC programme as primary prevention

In the first setting (Study 1: Frydenberg, Bugalski, Firth, Kamsner and Poole, 2006) the programme was conducted at a high school in metropolitan Melbourne as part of the Year 10 (16–17 years) curriculum. The sample consisted of 113 students who were divided into the 'at-risk' (22), 'resilient' (23) and 'main' (68) groups based on scores on the Children's Attributional Style Questionnaire (CASQ) (Seligman, 1995) and the Perceived Control of Internal States (PCIS) (Pallant, 2000).

Results in that study showed a significant decrease in Non-Productive coping and an increase in Productive coping for the at-risk group, while the opposite was true for the resilient and main groups.

In the same setting, the second study (Luscombe-Smith, Frydenberg and Poole, 2003) was conducted with 83 students (39 males and 44 females) in Year 10. Results for these showed a significant increase in Reference to Others coping after the programme.

In the second setting (Studies 3 and 4), a total of 323 adolescents in Year 7 (11–13 years) were recruited from a Melbourne high school and divided into treatment and control groups, with the treatment group receiving the programme, through collaboration between school staff and either a school psychologist or a school counsellor. Study 3 (Cotta, Frydenberg and Poole, 2000), with a sample of 88 students, showed significant decreases in Non-Productive coping for the treatment group after the programme (as well as a trend indicating increases in Productive coping). In particular, a decrease was noted in adolescents' use of *worry, wishful thinking, not cope, keep to self* and, probably most importantly, *self-blame*. In contrast, the control group showed a significant increase in *self-blame*, though there were decreases in *working hard*, and also in *social action*. In summary, the programme appeared to be successful in reducing reliance on strategies generally labelled elsewhere as maladaptive, and prevented a decrease in at least one strategy considered helpful.

In contrast, the results of Study 4 (McCarthy, 2001), conducted in the same school two years later with a sample of 235 students, show a trend towards the reduction of Non-Productive coping for the experimental group and an increase for the control group. Although the results failed to reach statistical significance, when examined class by class, there were clearly some classes that benefited and others that did not, indicating the importance of implementation. That is, both the training of instructors and the choice of instructors are likely to affect the outcome.

A fifth study (Tollit, 2002) with 115 Year 7 female participants who were recruited from a single-sex Catholic secondary college located in inner Melbourne, and whose ages ranged from 11 to 13 with a mean age of 12, was conducted using the ACS and three scenarios which described an academic problem, a family relationship problem and a bullying problem. The instrument and scenarios were responded to before the programme and after the treatment group completed the programme. The treatment group also completed these measures at two months following the programme implementation. Results indicated that the treatment group significantly reduced their use of Reference to Others coping from pre-treatment to follow-up and from post-treatment to follow-up. The scenario responses indicated a significant difference post-programme between the proportion of students in the two groups who reported their likelihood of using Productive coping strategies to deal with academic problems and bullying situations, with a greater portion of the treatment group including Productive strategies in their response to the scenarios. Hence the programme appeared to be effective in reducing Reference to Others coping and in promoting the use of Productive coping when confronted with academic stressors and bullying predicaments.

A sixth Australian study was conducted in a Catholic co-educational school in an outer suburb of Melbourne (Huxley, 2003) (N = 24). A member of the school staff, a teacher-librarian who was not the students' regular teacher, ran the study. The first eight sessions of the programme were taught over 12 class periods. The instructor kept detailed self-reflective notes relating to both the process and her own development and there was a six-month follow-up. Changes in the students' attitudes were reflected in the coping skills questionnaire and the responses to the scenarios. Females reduced their reliance on *tension reduction* and males increased their *seeking of social support* and *social action*. Moreover, the teacher reported changes in her own management of teacher stress and life circumstance stress. The students singled out the teacher on many occasions to comment on their own coping and to request further sessions. Thus it would seem that the students and the instructor had developed a common language of coping. However, the responses at six-month follow-up indicated that, since students had lost some of the gains made after the programme, there is a need for ongoing reinforcement of coping language and skills if the benefits are to be maintained.

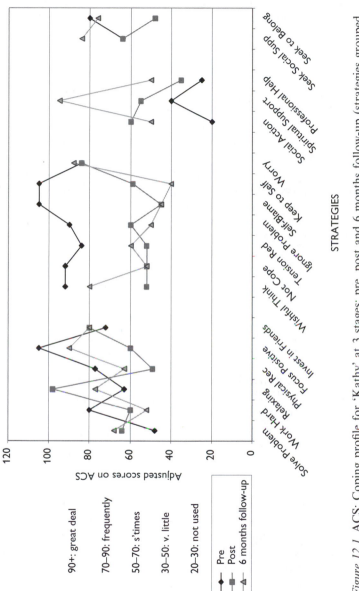

Figure 12.1 ACS: Coping profile for 'Kathy' at 3 stages: pre, post and 6 months follow-up (strategies grouped by style)

Case studies[1]

The profiles below highlight the ways in which participants in the Huxley (2003) study changed following the BOC programme.

'Kathy'

Before participating in the programme Kathy was known to the teacher as a student who had previously experienced social and emotional difficulties. Of all the students involved in the BOC programme Kathy showed the most noticeable change in her coping from before to after the programme.

From Figure 12.1 it can be seen that before the programme the strategies most frequently used were generally Non-Productive: *wishful thinking, not cope, ignore the problem, self-blame, keep to self* and *worry*. The strategies she used the least were those that are classed as referring to others: *social action, seek spiritual support* and *seek professional help*. However, her responses after the programme show an obvious change. Then, *seek relaxing diversions* was shown as the most frequently used strategy and there was a large decrease in her use of the Non-Productive strategies, apart from *worry*, which remained the same. Kathy's post-programme results also indicate an increase in her use of all of the Productive strategies and Reference to Others strategies. Kathy's responses at the six-month follow-up, on the other hand, indicated a trend towards returning to her pre-programme responses with the noticeable exception of *seek spiritual support*, while Kathy made considerable gains following the BOC programme. But the strategies were not sustained beyond six months, suggesting the need for booster sessions.

'Wayne'

As is shown in Figure 12.2, from before to after the programme Wayne increased his use of each of the Productive strategies. His use of *focus on the positive* strategy actually doubled and each of the other Productive strategies showed a considerable increase. Wayne also decreased his use of most of the Non-Productive strategies, and the large decrease in the use of *self-blame* is particularly salient. Wayne's results for the other Reference to Others strategies provides an important contrast. His use of the *social action* and *seek spiritual support* strategies had only a very minor change, but his use of *seek professional help* as a strategy halved from before to after the programme. This is of particular interest as the two sessions for which Wayne was absent focused on Module 5, 'Asking for help'.

Richard and Jodie are examples of students whose ACS responses indicate that there was some change to their coping from before the BOC. However, through reference to additional sources of information, such as their scenario responses and the discussion group, it is clear that the programme affected them in somewhat different ways.

'Richard'

It was well known by the teacher and other staff that Richard was often the target of students' pranks and teasing. He was considered an average student who often lacked confidence. He attended 11 of the 12 BOC sessions and when prompted participated in some of the discussions. Comparisons of Richard's ACS and scenario responses before and after the BOC indicate that his coping did change in a positive direction. After the programme Richard's responses showed that he had increased his use of two of the Productive strategies of *focus on solving the problem* and *focus on the positive*. Richard's use of the other Productive strategies was basically the same, with the exception of his use of the *investing in close friends* strategy, which decreased after the programme. By then he had also decreased his use of five of the Non-Productive strategies: *not cope, ignore the problem, self-blame, keep to self* and *worry*. His use of each of the Reference to Others strategies also increased after the programme.

Before the BOC programme Richard's written response to the bullying scenario, which involved other students spreading rumours, was: 'I'd ask what the rumours were. I'd admit to the nasty rumours.' This is categorized as using the single Non-Productive strategy of *self-blame*. After the programme Richard's response to the same written scenario was very different. He wrote: 'I don't see the problem. Don't care. Rumours don't worry me, but I would prove that the rumours were wrong, which would be easy to do.' This response indicates the use of a range of strategies, particularly the use of the Productive strategies of *focus on solving the problem* and *focus on the positive*. Given the context of the scenario, there is also the possibility that Richard was using the Non-Productive strategy of *wishful thinking*; there is no indication of the overwhelming reliance on *self-blame* as there was before his participation in the BOC programme.

Richard's response to the academic scenario, in which the student had only two days to do an assignment, also reflects a change in his

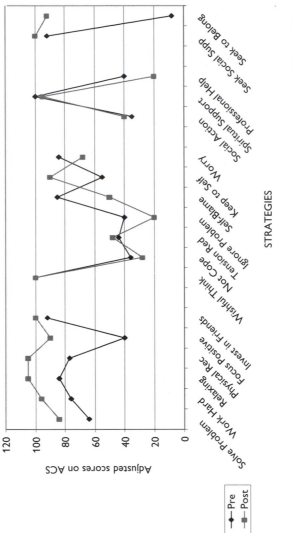

STRATEGIES

Figure 12.2 ACS: Coping profile for 'Wayne' at 2 stages: pre and post (strategies grouped by style)

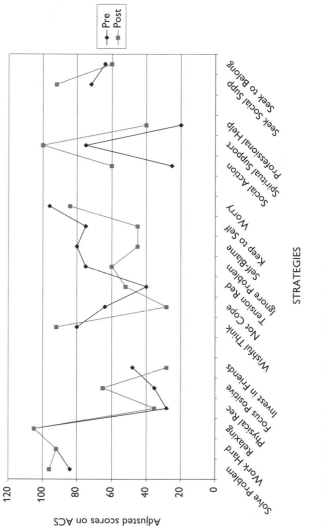

Figure 12.3 ACS: Coping profile for 'Richard' at 2 stages: pre and post (strategies grouped by style)

awareness of coping strategies from pre- to post-programme. Before the BOC programme Richard wrote, 'Do half tonight and half tomorrow', which indicates the use of the Productive strategy of *work hard and achieve*. After the programme Richard's response was similar, though he also emphasized the importance of his response: 'Do it! Just do the work and hope for the best because doing nothing is a negative coping strategy and will get you nowhere. Whereas doing it is a positive coping strategy.'

The response that Richard wrote to the family scenario problem after the BOC programme also indicates his increased use of the *focus on the positive* strategy. This scenario described a situation in which the students needed to tell their parents that a teacher wanted to meet with them to 'discuss your school work'. His pre-BOC response was: 'I'd tell them that just because my teacher wants to talk to you, doesn't mean it's about something bad', while at post-BOC he wrote: 'Tell them that she just wants to congratulate them on such a great son. And that you have been doing the work too well and she wants to put you in the accelerated class.'

It is also interesting that Richard's report before beginning the BOC programme indicated that he was an average student who consistently obtained C or C+ for his academic subjects. His report marks after the programme were mostly A and B+, showing an improvement in academic achievement that was also higher than the class average. The teacher has also observed that he is continuing to conduct himself far more assertively and is often part of lunchtime chess competitions with his peers.

'Jodie'

Jodie also attended 11 of the sessions, but unlike Richard she was generally well liked by both students and staff. During the previous year she had held the position of Middle School prefect and class captain. Jodie's school report preceding the BOC programme showed her as a student whose marks for academic subjects averaged B+. She completed the ACS on three occasions, before beginning the programme, immediately after it and also six months later.

A comparison of Jodie's results from before to after the programme indicate that she increased her use of all but one of the Productive strategies. In particular, her use of the *focus on solving the problem* strategy showed a large increase, though at the six-month follow-up her use of this strategy had a large decrease, while each of the other Productive strategies continued to increase at follow-up. In

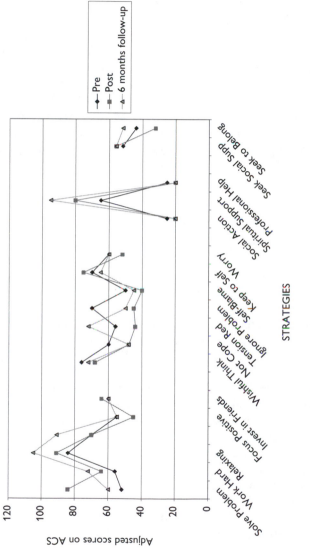

Figure 12.4 ACS: Coping profile for 'Jodie' at 3 stages: pre, post and 6 months follow-up (strategies grouped by style)

regard to the Non-Productive strategies, all but one decreased from before to after the programme. By the six-month follow-up *tension reduction* showed a large increase. Five of the seven Non-Productive strategies generally showed a decrease from before to after the BOC but then an increase from after the BOC to the six-month follow-up. However, the Non-Productive strategy of *keep to self* was the reverse in that it was at her lowest at the six-month follow-up. Each of the Reference to Others strategies had almost the same score each time Jodie completed the ACS, with the exception of *seek spiritual support*, which increased and continued to show an increase at the six-month follow-up.

Jodie's responses to the three scenarios prior to the BOC programme indicated the use of Productive strategies. After the programme her responses were very similar and still showed Productive coping, but she also included a Reference to Others strategy for the academic problem scenario.

The BOC programme as early intervention

In a northern Italian study (Ferrari, Nota, Soresi and Frydenberg, 2007) using an Italian translation of the BOC programme, 26 participants selected from a group of 183 students in a largely rural community, who exhibited low levels of self-efficacy and problem-solving abilities, participated in a 12-session implementation of the programme. The student participants improved their coping and problem-solving abilities as well as demonstrating an increase in their *focus on the positive* and showing a reduction in *wishful thinking* and *tension reduction*.

An adapted version of the BOC programme was used to enable increased opportunity for access by learning-disabled young people in the eighth and ninth studies. The adaptation version of this programme explored the efficacy of taking control, of strategies for optimistic thinking, assertiveness, goal-setting and problem-solving, followed by constructivist learning of these strategies through role-play. Activities included drawing, discussion, direct teaching, modelling and role-play. Emphasis was on situations drawn from students' selected personal goals. Reading and writing were minimized and there was increased opportunity for revision of concepts and skills.

In the eighth study (Frydenberg *et al.*, 2006), 98 students with a specific learning difficulty, aged 12–16, were divided into four groups: the first group received the BOC programme (22 students): the second group received both the BOC programme and a teacher feedback programme (19 students) (the strategy feedback programme involved teachers giving individual feedback to students that focused on finding and using a strategy in response to a particular difficulty); the third group received only the teacher feedback programme (27 students); while the fourth group operated as a control (28 students). Duration of the interventions was 11 weeks: participants in the coping programme received 11 weekly 50-minute sessions. Overall, the BOC programme was associated with increases in Productive coping strategies such as *work hard* and *focus on solving the problem*, and decreases in Non-Productive strategies such as *give up* and *tension reduction*. There were also indications, though not statistically significant, of positive outcomes for students receiving the teacher feedback programme or both programmes, but these were not as definitive as the results for the coping programme group.

In the ninth study (Frydenberg *et al.*, 2006), 112 students aged 13–17 years across four year levels who had been identified as academically low-achieving students completed the modified version of the BOC programme. There were 43 male students and 69 females. Pre-programme results indicated that the female students used more Non-Productive coping strategies, such as *self-blame* and *not cope*, than did the males. Post-programme results indicated that female students were still using Non-Productive strategies more than their male counterparts. Males reported only one significant increase in Productive coping, which was the strategy *invest in close friends*, and one significant reduction in Non-Productive coping, which was *wishful thinking*. Females reported only one change overall, which was an unexpected increased use of *tension reduction*.

In a tenth study (Ivens, 2006), 27 female students aged 13 and 14 years who had all experienced parental separation or divorce participated in the BOC programme (see also chapter 7). The girls received the programme in small groups of five or six. The programme was modified slightly to include a session that focused on anger management and coping with conflict. (See page 166 for the relationship between depression and anger coping and the suggestion that anger management is an important part of learning to cope effectively.) Overall, the BOC programme was associated with increases in Productive coping such as *focus on solving the problem* and *focus on the positive*, and decreases in Non-Productive coping such as *self-blame* and *worry*. Moreover, the girls reported substantial reductions in symptoms of psychological distress after the programme. Interviews with the girls after the programme also revealed that they had more positive feelings about having separated or divorced parents, were having fewer fights with family members and friends, and were more confident in their ability to manage their dual living arrangements.

In an eleventh study (Hawkins, McKenzie and Frydenberg, 2006), 27 self-selected female students aged 14 and 15 years received 11 sessions of the BOC programme in a small-group counselling context. Girls indicated with whom they wanted to form groups and subsequently small groups of two to four students were arranged. The additional session included body-mapping techniques that assist adolescents to develop self-awareness of their emotions. Girls reported reduced Non-Productive coping, and increased Productive coping and Reference to Others for general concerns. In addition, teachers reported reductions in the girls' misbehaviour and increases in their academic engagement.

In a twelfth study (Goode, 2006), 35 female students aged 12–15, who were nominated by school welfare staff and year-level co-ordinators for peer-relatedness difficulties, received the BOC programme in mixed age-groups of approximately four participants. Girls completed the ACS and two other questionnaires before and after the programme. One questionnaire measured general health and well-being and the other measured perceived social support. Overall, the BOC programme was associated with significant increases in Productive coping and Reference to Others and a significant reduction in Non-Productive coping. Additionally, the girls reported significant improvements in well-being and perceived social support over the duration of the programme.

Ethnicity and changes in coping

In another recent study (D'Anastasi and Frydenberg, 2005), the relationship between ethnicity, coping and coping intervention was explored. Fifty-five students aged 12–15 received the BOC as part of their pastoral care programme and an additional 48 students formed the control group. Ethnicity was measured by asking students the language spoken at home. These languages were categorized into the groups of Anglo-Australian (n = 41), European Australian (n = 38), and Australian Minority group (which comprised Asian, African, Middle Eastern and Pacific Islander languages; n = 24). Results indicated a significant difference in the use of the coping strategy *self-blame* (categorized under the Non-Productive coping style) over time as the Australian Minority group significantly decreased the use of this strategy compared to the European Australians and the Anglo-Australians. This suggests that the programme can play an important role in assisting those ethnic groups in the Australian Minority group to decrease their use of some of the negative coping strategies.

In addition, Anglo-Australians showed a significant increase in the use of physical recreation (categorized under the Productive coping style) compared to other ethnic groups involved in the programme. This finding is consistent with past research by Frydenberg and colleagues (2003) which suggests that Anglo-Australians have a keen interest in and pursuit of sports, reflected in their enthusiastic involvement in community leisure activities and in international events such as the Olympics. Increases in the use of physical recreation by Anglo-Australians also reflect past research findings that indicate that using physical recreation may be more applicable to address the type of concerns that Anglo-Australians experience compared to other ethnic groups, who may have different concerns requiring different types of coping strategies (Frydenberg and Lewis, 1993b).

Summary of BOC research

Collectively, with some reservations, the studies demonstrate the general efficacy of the BOC programme for young people aged 11–17 when well-trained facilitators or school psychologists implement the programme. Sometimes, however, the changes are modest and not maintained over a six-month period. This would suggest the need to provide instruction over a longer period; alternatively, there are indications that booster sessions are warranted. The studies covered a variety of year levels, school settings, targeted concerns, and one study reported on the translation of the programme into Italian. These studies demonstrated the BOC programme's inherent flexibility to address various types of student groups from whole classes (universal) to small groups of targeted students (early intervention). Specifically, three studies were evaluations of modified versions of the BOC programme to match the needs of the particular adolescent sample.

There was some evidence in these studies that programme outcomes may be enhanced when the programme is facilitated by psychologists or teachers with adequate training, rather than by teachers with minimal preparation. An additional benefit for teachers was highlighted in the Huxley (2003) study, which revealed that the teacher personally benefited from facilitating the programme. This suggests that the more involved the facilitators are with the programme, the better the programme outcomes for both instructors and students. There is also support for a whole-school approach to the development of effective coping skills.

Evaluation of this programme also highlights the fact that the participants' self-efficacy increased significantly when compared to that of non-participants. This finding suggests that the programme is useful in developing a sense of psychological control for participants. A belief in one's sense of psychological control will direct whether one will attempt to cope with a situation or not. Once individuals have a sense of their own capabilities, it is more likely that they will approach their problems with the aim of solving them rather than avoiding them. In addition, self-efficacy has also been associated with a reduction in depressive symptoms and improvements in academic performance and health (Burger, 1985). As a result, programme participants with higher levels of self-efficacy would be expected to use more Productive coping strategies and fewer avoidant strategies. When the programme was introduced in a girls' school (Tollit, 2002), the students reduced their resorting to the assistance of others and this was maintained over a follow-up period. When students were asked to indicate how they would cope with hypothetical situations relating to academic problems and to bullying, there was an increased use of Productive strategies after the programme.

In the Italian study there was a most interesting finding in relation to problem-solving skills in that, if conflicts are construed as problems to be solved, the increase in problem-solving skills is useful for managing conflict, and thus a highly desirable outcome.

The three studies that evaluated the BOC programme in a small-group counselling context (Goode, 2006; Hawkins *et al.*, 2006; Ivens, 2006) reported the greatest changes in coping over all the studies. This indicates that the programme's content and context both contribute to programme outcomes. Running the BOC programme in a counselling context with girls of parental separation or divorce also contributed to the success of the intervention in the Ivens study. It appears that, while there may be ample reasons to provide preventive programmes that cater for all adolescents, there are specific benefits from providing coping programmes to small groups of students, particularly those who have additional needs or stressors.

Overall, the BOC programme has benefits for students at risk or who have experienced negative life events such as family breakdown. Such groups of young people are often the ones who manage conflict least satisfactorily. The studies clearly indicate that where teachers, together with psychologists or counsellors, are involved in the delivery of the programme, the programme was more successful, as it was where the instructors received more substantial training. Teachers can play an important role in prevention and early intervention programmes and activities that strengthen the resilience of students as they learn and develop. Good training of instructors and ongoing support are likely to maximize the benefits for participants.

In general, the studies highlight the value of teaching adolescents cognitive-based skills in coping in order to facilitate the use of interpersonal resources. However, factors that contribute to resilience over and above coping skills need to be acknowledged. For example, some exposure to stress and conflict, rather than the avoidance of these, is likely to promote healthy development. Family, peer and school supports also play an important part. Additionally, the building of resources that are perceived to be of value to young people in the management of their everyday lives, and which include coping skills, is beneficial.

Other coping programmes

There are few coping programmes available which have a universal focus, and most have been developed to address specific problems rather than for flexibility in delivery. For example, the Anger Coping Program was specifically designed for adolescents who have been identified by their teachers as being aggressive and disruptive (Lochman, Dunn and Klimes-Dougan, 1993). Another programme, the Adolescent Coping with Emotions programme, was specifically designed as early intervention for depression but has been further developed into a universal depression-prevention programme (Kowalenko, Wignall, Rapee, Simmons, Whitefield and Stonehouse, 2002). Therefore, the broad applicability of the BOC programme is unique. A further strength of the programme is its inbuilt mechanism for engaging students and also for monitoring changes in coping over the duration of the programme. We are not aware of any other programme which has an inbuilt measure such as the Adolescent Coping Scale. Some of these coping programmes are presented in Table 12.3.

Future directions: Computer-based coping programmes

In order for coping programmes to be effective they must be engaging. Adolescents today live in a technological world and have access to an infinite number of resources and an endless supply of information via the Internet. Internet resources that address mental health issues are common and provide for anonymous access of important and often very sensitive information. Despite the expanse of computer-based resources, there are few computer-based psycho-educational

Table 12.3 Adolescent coping intervention programmes

Author(s)	Programme name	Programme goals	Overview of programme	Level of intervention	Who the programme is for?	Who implements the programme?
Frydenberg and Brandon (2002a, b, 2007a, b)	The Best of Coping	To teach adolescents coping skills in order to reduce their use of Non-Productive coping strategies and increase their use of Productive strategies	School-based A coping skills programme 10 50-min. sessions	Various Whole class (universal) Small group (intervention and early intervention)	All adolescents Can be run with small groups of adolescents with additional needs or risk factors	Trained facilitator (e.g., teacher) School psychologist
Good Grief (1996)	Seasons for Growth	To provide young people with the opportunity to understand and cope with grief and loss	Multi-settings A grief education programme 8 formal 40–60 min. sessions, celebration and 2 booster sessions	Small group Early intervention to post-incident intervention	Adolescents who have experienced grief or loss, such as the death of a loved one or following parental separation or divorce	Trained facilitator, 'companion' (e.g., teacher, youth worker) School psychologist

Hayes and Morgan (2005)	Helping Adolescents Cope psycho-educational programme	Adapted from the Coping with Stress programme			Adolescents aged 12–16 years
Shochet, Holland and Whitefield (1997)	Resourceful Adolescent Program (RAP)	The prevention of depression	School-based 11 45–60 min. sessions	Universal groups of maximum 15 adolescents	Adolescents aged 12–16 years
Kowalenko, Wignall, Rapee, Simmons, Whitefield and Stonehouse (2002)	The Adolescent Coping with Emotions (ACE)	To prevent depression in young people and improve their mood state, school functioning and coping skills	School-based	Universal: ACE-U Early intervention: ACE-1 (for at-risk students identified by current depressive symptoms)	*All students:* ACE-U: groups of 12–15 adolescents *Students at risk for depression:* ACE-1: groups of 8–10 adolescents Adolescents aged 12–15 years · ACE-U: trained teacher, school counsellor or school psychologist ACE-1: Two leaders who are trained teachers and/or school psychologists

programmes for adolescents. Given the increase in computer-based learning in schools, it is interesting that this mode of learning has not been more readily applied to the teaching of socioemotional competencies.

One computer-based coping skills programme, developed over three years, is Coping for Success (Frydenberg, 2007). It is an extension of the pencil-and-paper version of the BOC programme, is underpinned by the same theoretical constructs and follows a parallel sequence of modules. Coping for Success makes use of the interactive element offered by the computer, and includes video inserts of adolescents talking about issues relevant to the programme's content. In addition, photos replace the cartoons used in the BOC programme and there are quizzes at the end of each module to evaluate one's learning. Each module has a set of activities to complete. The user can either print out a workbook of activities and complete these in writing throughout the programme, or type their answers in the Word documents provided.

Coping for Success has been designed to be flexible in use. Within the school, the programme can be delivered to whole classes of students in computer laboratories or downloaded onto students' personal laptops. Students can complete the modules independently, but can regroup to talk about their answers to the activities and to share their learning. Although the role of facilitators is reduced in Coping for Success, ideally facilitators need to ensure that students are completing the programme and also guide students in group discussions. Coping for Success can also be delivered to small groups of students similar to the whole-class approach, yet with more opportunities for discussion and for tailoring the programme to specific concerns.

Because Coping for Success was designed for independent and self-paced learning, it does not need to be delivered in a group format. Individual students can complete it independently. Schools may choose to provide the programme as a resource for individual students to complete outside class hours. Students who may be interested in the programme include those with mental health problems, academic concerns or relationship worries. Additionally, students without identified problems, but who want to boost their ability to succeed in life, may also choose to complete the programme. For instance, at the pivotal times of entering the senior years of secondary school, or when moving from secondary school to university, the programme may help to smooth transitions.

There is also scope for Coping for Success to be linked with the clinical work of psychologists. Because the programme is based on cognitive behavioural principles, adolescents receiving psychotherapy could be assigned one module at a time to complete as homework. Further evaluations of the programme are needed to determine its effectiveness. However, given that computer-based learning engages adolescents, Coping for Success holds promise.

An evaluation of an earlier version of Coping for Success was conducted (Panizza and Frydenberg, 2006) with 192 14–15-year-old students who participated in a study that compared three delivery modes (facilitated by a teacher alone, facilitated by a teacher and supported by a psychologist, and delivered by the psychologist only) and two formats (the pencil-and-paper format was the BOC programme and the computer format was Coping for Success). This study used an earlier version of Coping for Success, which has since been extensively modified. Thus the results of this study would probably be augmented had the final version of Coping for Success been used. Results indicated that the computer-based group was the only group to increase its use of Reference to Others, obtain a trend towards decreases in Non-Productive coping and obtain a trend towards increases for Productive coping. This indicates that programme outcomes were greater for students who completed Coping for Success than for the BOC programme. However, there were additional factors which may have contributed to the enhanced outcomes for the computer-based group such as the support of the school psychologist and the small-group delivery (teachers independently facilitated the BOC programme with whole classes of students). Nonetheless, this study provides preliminary evidence of the efficacy of the Coping for Success programme for adolescents. The programme is recommended for use in clinical contexts, with adolescents at risk for mental health problems, and with individual adolescents who complete the programme outside school or as a self-paced programme to augment for the pencil-and-paper BOC.

Coping programmes in other settings

Generally, coping programmes for adolescents are run in schools. But there is great potential for such programmes to be offered to adolescents in other settings. This is particularly important for accessing adolescents who do not attend formal schooling. One way in which older adolescents have been provided with an intervention that targets coping is via training courses for long-term unemployed youth. Creed, Machin and Hicks (1999) evaluated a three-day programme for 43 long-term unemployed adolescents (mean age 19 years). The training programme, which was facilitated by trained psychologists, was also based on cognitive behavioural principles and was aimed at improving the general well-being of participants via coping skills training. Participants were assessed for well-being, self-esteem and positive and negative affect before and after the programme. Results showed significant improvements in participants' coping from before to after, which was measured in terms of recreational use, stress-reducing personal activities, social support and cognitive coping strategies. In addition, there were significant reductions in psychological distress and in negative affect and significant increases in self-esteem and in positive affect. What this study found, which is similar to previous evaluations of the BOC programme (Frydenberg *et al.*, 2006), is that participants with greater levels of psychological distress benefited the most. Overall, the study demonstrated that coping programmes can improve the well-being and management of stress of long-term unemployed adolescents. But it did fail to show a link between the programme and successful employment, which suggests that coping should be just one part of an intervention that tackles entrenched situations or behaviours.

Summary

There is merit in fostering coping skills development, particularly in the educational context since that is an accessible locale for intervention. Additionally, it is generally recognized that schools have a growing responsibility to provide social-emotional learning opportunities for students. Although there is inevitable competition as to what to include in an already crowded curriculum, the benefits of social-emotional skills-based instruction are emerging. Informal teaching as well as programmes designed for universal intervention, or those focusing on targeted intervention with particular populations, are recommended. The BOC programme has been evaluated both as a universal skill building and as a targeted programme for young people with special needs, such as those with learning difficulties, mental health problems including depression and anxiety, separation or grief or socialization problems. While the evaluations demonstrated gains, particularly for students who had been targeted as being 'at risk', there is a general consensus that to maximize the benefits to be achieved through the programme, and for gains to be retained, there need to be extended sessions. These booster sessions can be provided within the school community. Additionally, parents need to be brought on board.

The training and support that is provided to instructors is also important. Several programmes other than the BOC were noted. These often target particular groups such as those requiring anger management to deal with their anger. Finally, a computer-aided programme, Coping for Success, was presented as an indication and a signal of the likelihood of increased use of multimedia in the social-emotional training of young people.

13 What we have learned and what might follow

Since the turn of the twenty-first century marked the arrival of the positive psychology movement there has been an explosion of interest in resilience, optimism, hope and well-being. So much so that there is often a convergence between faith and health-related phenomena that are not always associated with empirical evidence. The interest in coping has preceded the positive psychology movement in historical terms but fits comfortably within that framework. Additionally it is well grounded in scientific research.

Coping in the broadest terms is about adaptation. That is how we deal with the circumstances that confront us during the course of everyday life. But coping is more than adaptation. It is about achieving good outcomes. The principle of this volume is that we can all do what we do better. Coping theory and its applications provides opportunities to understand more about our capacity for growth. By operationalizing coping into its component parts we have a language with related concepts and constructs to help us to make conscious efforts to make what we do more productive and also to reduce our reliance on non-productive ways of dealing with circumstances. While much of the theorizing has relied on adult research, there are clear advances that relate to the world of adolescents. These include the resource theories of coping, proactive coping, happiness, optimism and well-being. Each of these allows us to consider educational tools and opportunities.

For more than three decades there has been extensive research in the area of coping in the social sciences including medicine, psychology, nursing and education. The proliferation of research has been motivated by our efforts to understand what makes some people deal with life circumstances better than others: what are the factors that contribute to our well-being and what factors help us to thrive and achieve success. We now know that some of these questions can only be understood if we construe coping as a complex phenomenon that is part of the person–environment interaction. It is not coping alone that explains adaptation but also environmental and personality factors. What helps to make coping so important in our understanding of human endeavour is that it readily lends itself to cognitive-behavioural intervention and provides a gateway for prevention, intervention and growth.

Responses to stress

Since coping is predicated on our understandings of what is stress, it is important to acknowledge the multiple understandings of stress that have emerged in recent years. The original conceptualizations that relate to 'flight and fight' proposed by Cannon (1932) and extended by Selye (1976) have been challenged by Taylor and her colleagues (Taylor, Klein, Lewis, Gruenwald Gurung and Updegraff, 2000), who have made a clear-cut distinction between how males and females generally respond to stress. The female model is more about 'tending and befriending', that is, nurturing and relating. Thus an understanding of the stress response is closely related to our conceptualization of coping.

Since the seminal research of Richard Lazarus in the coping field in the 1960s, researchers working with adults have led the field in providing new insights and developments in conceptualization and measurement. This is understandable given that there is such diversity in adult situations. A number of key areas have emerged in recent years. They include the resource theories of coping, communal and proactive coping, and dual process coping.

Hobfoll's (1998) Conservation of Resources theory emphasizes the accumulation and maintenance of resources as a buffer against stress. This highly sociocultural theory that recognizes what is important, necessary and valued in a particular culture cautions us not to make assumptions about the world of others without examining the context closely. Hobfoll's resource theory is becoming increasingly recognized and translated into the world of adolescents. We do know that adolescents also accumulate resources, albeit different ones from those valued by adults. These include resources such as having a friend, having support from parents and having adequate food and a home. Hobfoll's conceptualizing of communal coping highlights the importance of belonging to a group, both family and friends. These groups are embedded in a community or cultural context. The proactive conceptualization of coping emphasizes the value of being goal-directed and planning for events which are likely to contribute to successful outcomes. While these modes of coping are well established in the adult domains, there is emerging evidence that they hold true for adolescents.

Measurement

Much of our research on coping is gleaned from responses to questionnaires, usually by asking respondents to indicate how they cope after the event. This is sound in that it provides the basis from which we can get empirical data and make valid and reliable judgements about populations. However, there are inherent weaknesses in this approach in that questionnaires are either unduly long and do not retain the interest of the subjects or are too short to be helpful in explaining a phenomenon. Additionally, there are issues that relate to the reliability of recall. Narrative approaches provide an alternative to questionnaire approaches but have been found to have a strong convergence (Moskowitz and Wrubel, 2000). Another approach is the responses to hypothetical scenarios, which indicate how a person might deal with a situation in a future sense. A multi-method approach is most likely to yield the most reliable results.

The broad groupings of coping that have been found to be helpful include problem-focused and emotion-focused ones (Folkman and Lazarus, 1988a). Others, like Billings and Moos (1981), have three categories that include Active Cognitive (see the positive side of things) and Active Behavioural and Avoidant coping. Others, like Pearlin and Schooler (1978), proposed more metacognitive strategies such as finding meaning in the situation. This approach may have applications in the school context, where meaning and value are ascribed to content, thus giving purpose for effort. The fact that there is a lack of consensus on the core categories involved makes comparisons between studies difficult. However, as Skinner, Edge, Altman and Sherwood (2003) point out in their comprehensive review and critique of the structure of coping, there is value in organizing 'families' according to the adaptive processes. The importance of identifying what are adaptive and maladaptive coping strategies has proven to be important for understanding applications.

In the adolescent arena similar nomenclature or categories have been readily adopted, but what makes most sense is the Productive and Non-Productive categorization and a third category that focuses on how one relates to others. These categories remain broad and do not readily lead to behavioural change, so the more narrow categories such as those identified by the Adolescent Coping Scale are more likely to be useful in that they can lead to self-directed change.

The validation of instruments like the Adolescent Coping Scale also tells us that there is a clear relationship between a host of variables such as depression and coping and achievement and productive ways of coping.

Coping effectiveness

There has been considerable debate and research on coping effectiveness. A coping strategy is not inherently good or bad. It depends on the situation (Lazarus and Folkman, 1984); what is helpful in one situation may not be helpful in another. For example, before an exam, dealing with the problem in the form of preparation is helpful and after the exam relaxation or distancing may be appropriate. Sometimes the problem is not solvable, for example in the situation of a chronic illness, and therefore an effective outcome is about being able to manage the situation so that the individual retains equilibrium or a sense of hope.

There have been advances in our understanding of age-related factors in coping. The few longitudinal studies have confirmed and amplified what we have known from cross-sectional data. There is a growing vulnerability with age, particularly for girls who use *self-blame, tension reduction* and resort to professing their inability to cope. We also know that childhood experience has an impact on adolescence in a general sense. However, there is now convincing evidence that an accumulation of adverse childhood experiences such as a history of sexual abuse, parental abuse, parental rejection or familial conflict lead to the likelihood of the adolescence being susceptible to using a range of Non-Productive coping strategies such as those associated with substance abuse or self-harming behaviours.

Depression

There are pleasing signs on the horizon. We know that resilience is associated with self-esteem, optimism, perceived mastery, the use of social support, and approach-oriented coping such as problem-solving. We also know that those who are high in hope and subsequently likely to be optimistic are likely to see themselves as efficacious problem-solvers. Components of hope are established early. But there is promise in teaching young people not only good problem-solving skills but to see themselves as efficacious problem-solvers.

Those individuals who lack confidence in their ability to solve problems are going to be less successful in coping effectively. Furthermore, developing an individual's problem-solving efficacy needs to be part of coping skills training.

Depression exists as part of our culture. What is helpful is that we know that a high usage of Non-Productive coping is associated with depression while the restricted use of Non-Productive and high usage of Productive coping strategies is likely to be associated with achievement and well-being. There is an increase in the prevalence of adolescents who experience a depressive episode. This is particularly concerning given research highlighting the connection between depression, coping, stress and suicide. We also know that we can teach adolescents to develop helpful coping skills. This is the greatest advance to date and a cause for optimism.

Anxiety is a component of depression and often a precursor to depression. Anxiety sensitivity, the fear of anxiety-related body sensations is a recently identified construct. This also has clear implications for how we can teach young people to cope with these sensations to minimize the impact and likelihood of depressive episodes occurring.

Emotions

Emotions play an important part in the coping process. They can facilitate coping, for example when there are positive emotions like optimism; or they can obstruct the coping process when there are emotions such as anger or despair. In the adult arena it has been demonstrated that emotions play a part but there are elements of emotions that are positive – for example, I take time to figure out what I am feeling, or I feel free to express emotions. In the adolescent arena what is more important is the regulation of emotions. There is a co-occurrence of both positive and negative emotions and the use of both Productive and Non-Productive coping strategies generally occurs in each encounter. With adolescents, in addition to the emphasis on emotion regulation, the fostering of positive emotions is important.

Emotional regulation is both the influence of emotions experienced by the individual and control of these emotions (conscious or unconscious). Eisenberg and colleagues (1997) identify two types of emotion regulation, one that controls the internal feeling state and the associated physiological processes, and another that concerns the regulation of the behavioural concomitants.

In addition to the importance of the regulation of emotions, notions of emotional competence are important for getting on in the world and the use of positive emotions such as joy, hope and satisfaction, to improve adaptation and performance. The concept of emotional intelligence and the related concepts of emotional competence are impacted by social evaluative concerns and the importance placed on relationships, particularly how the individual is perceived by others. These are aspects of adaptation that can be assisted through the teaching of coping skills.

Recent learning

We know unequivocally that culture makes a difference. Whether we take culture as ethnicity, a community of individuals within a locale, or a group with common values or interests, differences are likely to occur and are likely to be relevant when we are considering interventions. What the needs are in one setting may not be relevant in another. Similarly, what works in one setting may not work in another. New insights in coping research are assured if one takes settings into account.

A culturally embedded phenomenon is the increase in the rate of separation and divorce in Western communities, which is creating a generation of children who may have experienced trauma or loss. Children with separated parents are no longer the minority. The need to support and assist these children with strategies to deal with their changing family circumstances is important, and coping skills can contribute to that end.

Bullying is a phenomenon of which we have become increasingly aware. The advent of the e-generation has led to the phenomenon of cyber-bullying, a significant stressor that touches the lives of most, if not all, adolescents. Developing research in the prevalence of cyber-bullying and associated outcomes needs to be on the agenda. Such an indirect method of harassment requires a direct approach to up-skilling both adolescents and parents on how to deal with this pervasive problem.

The positive psychology movement continues to make advances with its focus on potential rather than deficits. The concept of chronic happiness has entered the vernacular as a term used to describe someone who is genuinely happy for a significant period. Controversy lies in the term 'chronic', typically used to describe negative emotional, psychological and physical states. Mindfulness is another new concept. It is about being completely aware and fully engaged in whatever you are doing in present time. This is somewhat different from Csikszentmihaly's (1990) concept of 'flow', where one is so engaged in an activity that times stands still. There is a greater awareness and knowledge of mindfulness therapies and an increase in mindfulness practitioners.

Given recent advances in children's social and emotional learning research and practice, social and emotional development programmes are now being implemented in more than 50 per cent of schools in the United States (Foster, Rollefson, Doksum, Noonan, Robinson and Teich, 2005): emotional learning programmes, as well as skills with which to evaluate such programmes.

Social and emotional learning programmes are based on the premise that social and emotional competence can be learned. Social and emotional competence includes key qualities which, when put into practice, produce socially and emotionally healthy and productive individuals, as well as safe and responsive communities. Qualities include reflection and empathy, flexible and creative problem-solving and decision-making, control of impulses, clear and direct communication, and self-motivation. There is a growing body of research showing that social and emotional factors influence children's health, citizenship, achievement motivation, school connection and academic learning (Greenberg *et al.*, 2003; Zins, Weissberg, Wang and Walberg, 2004). The teaching of coping skills fits within such a framework.

In keeping with the positive psychology movement, much of the coping research reported in this volume is underscored by the premise that we have the potential to improve our performance in our endeavours. There are programmes of direct instruction which can be applied universally or to individuals or groups with a particular concern that they wish to deal with. The strategies taught include communication skills, which can be readily developed from what is known about how to get along with others, or decision-making or problem-solving as key elements. Indirect instruction can use key coping concepts such as those identified by the ACS.

It is possible to develop generic coping skills or anticipatory and proactive ones. The goal is essentially about building up coping resources and guarding against resource loss. It is also important to consider the collective and co-operative aspects of coping, whether it be in the family or school setting such as in the classroom, which foster a climate of positive emotions, goal attainment and effective learning in a co-operative communal context. While an increase in use of Productive coping strategies and a decrease in use of Non-Productive strategies is generally an ideal to strive for, it is the use of *self-blame* that is most strongly to be discouraged.

There have been considerable advances in the development of coping skills. Advances have been made in our understanding of the relationship between problem-solving (particularly the belief in an individual's capacity to solve problems) and the relationship between decision-making and coping.

Coping skills programmes need to be developed or adapted for particular contexts. They may be generic or focus on a particular situation of need such as when there is grief or loss or impending challenge such as transition from one school to another. These programmes need to be evaluated. We also know that the training of instructors and the provision of ongoing instruction or booster sessions for students are all-important in retaining gains over an extended period. Such programmes need to be incorporated into the social and emotional programming throughout the school years. The gains reported by individuals, while promising, need to be calibrated through the reporting of real changes in behaviour that have been observed by others.

Engaging young people in schools is a challenging task. Increasing young people's coping resources contributes to the task, as do programmes that meet students' needs, along with the provision of mentors and supports. This is likely to make a difference to how young people cope in school. At the other end of the adolescent spectrum, where young people are gifted and talented, the nurturing of talents, the recognition that those young people are good problem-solvers but are likely to do it alone, highlights the need for us to think of ways in which these young people can be connected better to their peers.

In sum, we have learned that coping is a multidimensional construct that represents the way we respond to environmental demands and the changing circumstances across the lifespan. The resources available to the individual in a given situation are all-important. Coping is strongly related to the regulation of emotions and certain types of avoidant or negative coping strategies are associated with poor mental health outcomes. In contrast, instrumental problem-oriented coping including the seeking of social support are generally associated with positive outcomes.

The good news is that coping has become part of our everyday vernacular. We know a great deal about the phenomenon and we also know that coping strategies can be taught. Teaching can be embedded in a school curriculum or as a stand-alone programme of instruction, or during the course of clinical intervention. Both pencil-and-paper programmes and computer-delivery programmes are available for universal or targeted delivery. What remains to be done is a comprehensive evaluation to be undertaken. Where school communities are

282 Adolescent coping

involved and committed both adults and adolescents learn to speak the same language of coping. Furthermore, there needs to be training and support for instructors.

What the future holds for coping research?

There are an infinite number of questions that remain unanswered in the world of coping. For example, how much can we learn from the world of athletes or those who have experienced trauma and have recovered well? There is little research in the coping literature that looks at those who traversed adolescence well and achieved success or those who have recovered from trauma and loss so that we can learn from their experience. Additionally, despite our recognition of the importance of both dispositional and contextual factors in the coping process, the inevitable difficulty in resolving the nature/nurture debate means that we are unlikely to be able to unravel the relative contribution of heredity and environment, as well as the interplay between contextual and dispositional factors. But given that it is the environment which we can best impact, it is important to continue to identify the factors within the environment which make all the difference.

We have an understanding of the mechanism of self-blame but know less about denial – the way in which denial works as both a helpful and unhelpful coping strategy. And what the long-term consequences of the use of denial and some of the other coping strategies are is important. For example, if one uses these strategies over an extended period, what are the implications for adult coping? We know, for example, that secure young people develop their active and internal coping styles much more quickly between 14 and 21 years than insecure adolescents. And this is not the case for the withdrawal coping style (Seiffge-Krenke and Beyers, 2005).

Metacognitive strategies that help individuals ascribe meaning to a situation need to be understood better in the adolescent context, in particular since they hold promise for educational settings. The use of reflective journals has been under-utilized in coping research. Diary studies are infrequent, as are studies that monitor behaviours at critical points in one's life. DeLongis and Holtzman (2005) point out that we now have statistical tools such as multilevel modelling that enable the analysis of daily data to the point where important questions can be addressed such as how the same individual responds to situations at multiple time points. Overall, there is a reduced reliance on recall or response to hypothetical situations. It is possible to consider context as well how coping unfolds over time.

In this ever-changing world it is difficult to predict what is the next challenge that young people will be required to deal with. In the multimedia-infused world which young people are a part of we already know the rise of intrusion into personal space, the advent of cyber-bullying, the redefinition of relationships that are based on virtual worlds and electronic communications. What does all this mean for relationships and the skills that are needed to develop and sustain healthy interpersonal relationships?

While there is always more that we can learn about the management of stress, the development of resilience and how to achieve the best outcomes in our endeavours, we have made many advances in our understanding of the world of adolescent coping. Just as there are differences between how girls and boys cope, how the same people cope in different situations and how age, culture and context make all the difference, what needs to be remembered is that what we learn in one community cannot be transposed into another. The context is all-important. It is good to understand key principles but then we need to look at context – culture in particular – so that there is no mass extrapolation from one culture to another but rather a considered situational or contextual approach. We can never be too complacent in our efforts to understand how young people are coping in their changing worlds.

Notes

3 The measurement of coping

1 Many of the studies presented in this sequence were previously reported by Frydenberg and Lewis (1999a) in the *Australian Journal of Guidance Counselling*, *9*, 19–36 in a paper titled Academic and general well-being: The relationship with coping.
2 Discriminant function analysis is a statistical procedure to predict group membership.

4 The correlates of coping

1 This study is discussed in greater detail in chapter 5 pp. 91–99.

5 Gender and coping

1 This study was reported in full by Frydenberg, E. and Lewis, R. in the *British Journal of Educational Psychology* (1999). Things don't get better just because you're older: A case for facilitating reflection, *69*, 83–96.
2 This study was reported in full in the *American Educational Research Journal* as Frydenberg, E. and Lewis, R. (2000). Coping with stresses and concerns during adolescence: A longitudinal study, *37*, 727–745.

9 Resilience and happiness

1 The term 'chronic happiness' was used by Lyubomirsky and colleagues to illustrate a quantity more substantial than momentary happiness, but also transitory over time. Although meaningful endeavours have the potential to alter one's level of chronic happiness, this is not as simple as alterations to momentary happiness. Chronic happiness levels, in operational terms, are based on an individual's retrospective judgement of their mood over a specified period and thus are less amenable to change.

10 Coping and achievement

1 An ironman or woman competition is a combination of three water events. There is a swim leg which is about 400 metres, followed by a Malibu board leg and finally a ski leg. The Malibu and the ski leg are about 800m of paddling and in between you have to run along the beach and pick up your next piece of apparatus. So it takes probably about 15–20 minutes to complete the event. It is quite a gruelling event which is in the upper echelon of competition in surf lifesaving.
2 Australian term for school lunch kiosk.

12 Teaching coping skills

1 Appreciation to Linda Huxley for permission to use the case studies.

References

Abdelnoor, A. and Hollins, S. (2004). How children cope at school after family bereavement. *Educational and Child Psychology, 21*(3), 85–94.

Achenbach, T.M. (1988). Integrating assessment and taxonomy. In M. Rutter, H. Tuma and I.S. Lann (eds), *Assessment and diagnosis in child psychopathology* (pp. 300–343). New York: Guilford Press.

Adams, S., Kuebli, J., Boyle, P.A. and Fivush, R. (1995). Gender differences in parent–child conversations about past emotions: A longitudinal investigation. *Sex Roles, 33*, 309–323.

Affleck, G. and Tennen, H. (1996). Construing benefits from adversity: Adaptational significance and dispositional underpinnings. *Journal of Personality, 64*, 899–922.

Agaibi, C.E. and Wilson, J.P. (2005). Trauma, PSTD, and resilience. *Trauma, Violence and Abuse, 6*(3), 195–216.

Aldwin, C.M. (2007). *Stress, coping, and development: An integrative perspective*, (2nd edition). New York: Guilford Press.

Alsaker, F.D. and Flammer, A. (1999). Cross-national research in adolescent psychology: The Euronet Project. In F.D. Alsaker and A. Flammer (eds), *The adolescent experience: European and American adolescents in the 1990's (Euronet)* (pp. 1–14). Mahwah, NJ: Lawrence Erlbaum Associates.

Amato, P.R. (2001). Children of divorce in the 1990s: An update of the Amato and Keith (1981) meta-analysis. *Journal of Family Psychology, 15*(3), 355–370.

Amato, P.R. and Keith, B. (1991). Parental divorce and the well-being of children: A meta-analysis. *Psychological Bulletin, 110*, 26–46.

American Psychiatric Association (APA) (2000). *Diagnostic and statistical manual of mental disorders*, (4th edition) – Text revision (DSM-IV-TR). Washington, DC: American Psychiatric Association.

Anderson, J.C. (1994). Epidemiological issues. In T.H. Ollendick, N.J. King and W. Yule (eds), *International handbook of phobic and anxiety disorders in children and adolescents* (pp. 43–66). New York: Plenum Press.

Argyle, M. (1994). *The psychology of interpersonal behaviour*, (5th edition). London: Penguin.

Argyle, M. (1999). The development of social skills. In E. Frydenberg (ed.), *Learning to cope: Developing as a person in complex societies* (pp. 81–106). Oxford: Oxford University Press.

Asarnow, J.R., Carlson, G.A. and Guthrie, D. (1987). Coping strategies, self-perceptions, hopelessness, and perceived family environments in depressed and suicidal children. *Journal of Consulting and Clinical Psychology*, *55*(3), 361–366.

Aseltine, R.H. (1996). Pathways linking parental divorce with adolescent depression. *Journal of Health and Social Behavior*, *37*(2), 133–148.

Aspinwall, L.G. and Taylor, S.E. (1997). A stitch in time: Self-regulation and proactive coping. *Psychological Bulletin*, *121*, 417–436.

Australian Bureau of Statistics (2004). *Divorces, Australia* (cat. no. 3307.0.55. 001). Retrieved 21 April 2006, from http://www.abs.gov.au/AUSSTATS/abs@nsf/Lookup/3307.0.55.001Main+Features1205?OpenDocument

Australian Bureau of Statistics (2005, 24 February). *ABS 4221.0 Schools, Australia.* Media release. Retrieved 29 March, 2005, from http://www.abs.gov.au/Ausstats/abs@nsf/0/1e44bcdef87bca2fa2568a9000139e7?Opendownload

Australian Catholic University (1996). *The perceived stress scale.* Melbourne: Australian Catholic University.

Australian Institute of Health and Welfare (AIHW) (2003). *Australia's young people: Their health and wellbeing 2003.* AIHW Cat. No. PHE 50. Canberra: AIHW.

Averill, J.R. (1994). Emotions are many splendored things. In P. Ekman and R.J. Davidson (eds), *The nature of emotion: Fundamental questions* (pp. 99–102). New York: Oxford University Press.

Averill, J.R. and Thomas-Knowles, C. (1991). Emotional creativity. In K.T. Strongman (ed.), *International Review of Studies on Emotion* (vol. 1, pp. 269–299). New York: Wiley.

Ayers, T.S., Sandler, I.N., West, S.G. and Roosa, M.W. (1996). A dispositional and situational assessment of children's coping: Testing alternative models of coping. *Journal of Personality*, *64*, 923–958.

Band, E.B. and Weisz, J.R. (1988). How to feel better when it feels bad: Children's perspectives on coping with everyday stress. *Developmental Psychology*, *24*, 247–253.

Beck, A. (1987). Cognitive therapy. In J. Zeig (ed.), *Evolution of psychotherapy* (pp. 55–68). New York: Bruner/Mazel.

Belzer, K.D., D'Zurilla, T.J. and Maydeu-Olivares, A. (2002). Social problem solving and trait anxieties predictor of worry in a college student population. *Personality and Individual Differences*, *33*, 573–585.

Berkman, L.F. and Syme, S.L. (1979). Social networks, host resistance, and mortality: A nine year follow-up study of Alameda county residents. *American Journal of Epidemiology*, *109*, 186–204.

Best, R. (2006). Deliberate self-harm in adolescence: A challenge for schools. *British Journal of Guidance and Counselling*, *34*, 161–174.

Billings, A.G. and Moos, R.H. (1981). The role of coping responses and social resources in attenuating stress of life events. *Journal of Behavioral Medicine*, *4*, 157–189.

Birmaher, B., Ryan, N.D., Williamson, D.E., Brent, D.A., Kaufman, J., Dahl, R.E., Perel, J. and Nelson, B. (1996). Childhood and adolescent depression: A review of the past 10 years. Part I. *Journal of the American Academy of Child and Adolescent Psychiatry*, *35*, 1427–1439.

Blinder, B.J., Cumella, E.J. and Sanathara, V.A. (2006). Psychiatric comorbidities of female inpatients with eating disorders. *Psychosomatic Medicine*, *68*(3), 454–462.

Bloom, L., Margulis, C., Tinker, E. and Fujita, N. (1996). Early conversations and word learning: Contributions from child and adult. *Child Development*, *67*, 3154–3175.

Boehm, K.E., Schondel, C.K., Ivoska, W.J., Marlowe, A.L. and Manke-Mitchell, L. (1998). Calls to teen line: Representative concerns of adolescents. *Adolescence*, *33*, 797– 803.

Boekaerts, M. (1999). Coping in context: Goal frustration and goal ambivalence in relation to academic and interpersonal goals. In E. Frydenberg (ed.), *Learning to cope: Developing as a person in complex societies* (pp. 175–197). Oxford: Oxford University Press.

Boekaerts, M. (2002a). Intensity of emotions, emotional regulation, and goal framing: How are they related to adolescents' choice of coping strategies? *Anxiety, Stress and Coping*, *15*(4), 401–412.

Boekaerts, M. (2002b). Meeting challenges in a classroom context. In E. Frydenberg (ed.), *Beyond coping: Meeting goals, challenges and visions* (pp. 129–148). Oxford: Oxford University Press.

Boice, M. (1998). Chronic illness in adolescence. *Adolescence*, *33*(132), 927–939.

Boldero, J. and Fallon, B. (1995). Adolescent help-seeking: What do they get help for, and from whom? *Journal of Adolescence*, *18*(2), 193–209.

Boldero, J., Frydenberg, E. and Fallon, B. (1993). Self concept and coping in adolescence. Paper presented at the 28th Annual Conference of the Australian Psychological Society, Gold Coast, Queensland, Australia.

Bolger, N. (1990). Coping as a personality process: A prospective study. *Journal of Personality and Social Psychology*, *59*, 525–537.

Bolger, N. and Eckenrode, J. (1991). Social relationships, personality and anxiety during a major stressful event. *Journal of Personality and Social Psychology*, *61*, 440–449.

Bourke, L. (2002). 'How can you deal with that?' Coping strategies among young residents of a rural community in New South Wales. *Journal of Family Studies*, *8*(2), 197–212.

Bourke, S. and Smith, M. (December, 1989). Quality of life and intentions for further education. Paper presented at the Annual Conference of the Australian Association for Research in Education, Adelaide, SA, Australia.

Boyd, C.P. Kostanski, M., Gullone, E., Ollendick, T.H. and Shek, D.T. (2000). Prevalence of anxiety and depression in Australian adolescents:

Comparisons with worldwide data. *The Journal of Genetic Psychology*, *161*(4), 479–492.

Braswell, L. and Bloomquist, M.L. (1991). *Cognitive-behavioural therapy for children with attention deficits and hyperactivity: A child, family and school model*. New York: Guilford Press.

Brickman, P. and Campbell, D.T. (1971). Hedonic relativism and planning the good society. In M.H. Appley (ed.), *Adaptation-level theory* (pp. 287–302). New York: Academic Press.

Brodzinsky, D.M., Elias, M.J., Steiger, C., Simon, J., Gill, M. and Hitt, J.C. (1992). Coping scale for children and youth: Scale development and validation. *Journal of Applied Developmental Psychology*, *13*, 195–214.

Browne, D. (2002). Coping alone: Examining the prospects of adolescent victims of child abuse placed in foster care. *Journal of Youth and Adolescence*, *31*(1), 57–66.

Buchanan, C.M., Maccoby, E.E. and Dornbusch, S.M. (1996). *Adolescents after divorce*. Cambridge, MA: Harvard University Press.

Bugalski, K. and Frydenberg, E. (2000). Promoting effective coping in adolescents 'at-risk' for depression. *Australian Journal of Guidance and Counselling*, *10*(1), 111–132.

Burger, J.M. (1985). Desire for control and achievement-related behaviours. *Journal of Personality and Social Psychology*, *48*, 1520–1533.

Burnett, P.C. and Fanshawe, J.P. (1996) Measuring school-related stressors in adolescence. *Journal of Youth and Adolescence*, *24*(4), 415–428.

Buss, A. and Plomin, R. (1984). *Temperament: Early developing personality traits*. Hillsdale, NJ: Erlbaum.

Byrne, B. (2000). Relationship between anxiety, fear, self-esteem, and coping strategies in adolescence. *Adolescence*, *35*(137), 201–215.

Caldwell, L.L., Darling, N., Payne, L.L. and Dowdy, B. (1999). 'Why are you bored?': An examination of psychological and social control causes of boredom among adolescents. *Journal of Leisure Research*, *31*(2), 103–121.

Calsbeek, H., Rijken, M., Bekkers, M.J.T.M., van Berge Henegouwen, G.P. and Dekker, J. (2006). School and leisure activities in adolescents and young adults with chronic digestive disorders: Impact of burden of disease. *International Journal of Behavioral Medicine*, *13*, 121–130.

Cannon, W.B. (1932). *The wisdom of the body*. New York: Norton.

Cantril, H. (1964). The human design. *Journal of Individual Psychology*, *20*, 129–136.

Carr, A. (2001). *What works with children and adolescents?* London: Routledge.

Carver, C.S., Scheier, M.F. and Weintraub, J.K. (1989). Assessing coping strategies: A theoretically based approach. *Journal of Personality and Social Psychology*, *56*, 267–283.

Causey, D.L. and Dubow, E.F. (1992). Development of a self-report coping measure for elementary school children. *Journal of Clinical Child Psychology*, *21*, 47–59.

Chambers, S.M. (1999). The effect of family talk on young children's development and coping. In E. Frydenberg (ed.), *Learning to cope: Developing as a person in complex societies* (pp. 130–149). Oxford: Oxford University Press.

Chan, D. (1998). Stress, coping strategies, and psychological distress among secondary school teachers in Hong Kong. *American Educational Research Journal*, *35*(1), 145–163.

Chang, E.C. (2002). Predicting suicide ideation in an adolescent population: Examining the role of social problem solving as a moderator and a mediator. *Personality and Differences*, *32*, 1279–1291.

Chaplin, T.M., Gillham, J.E., Reivich, K., Elkon, A.G.L., Feres, D.R., Wilder, B. *et al.* (2006). Depression prevention for early adolescent girls: A pilot study of all girls versus co-ed groups. *Journal of Early Adolescence*, *26*(1), 110–126.

Chapman, P.L. and Mullis, R.L. (1999). Adolescent coping strategies and self-esteem. *Child Study Journal*, *29*(1), 69–77.

Chase-Lansdale, P.L. (1995). The long-term effects of parental divorce on the mental health of young adults: A developmental perspective. *Child Development*, *66*(6), 1614–1634.

Cheng, S.T. and Chan, A.C.M. (2003). The development of a brief measure of school attitude. *Educational and Psychological Measurement*, *63*, 1060–1070.

Cherlin, A.J., Kiernan, K.E. and Chase-Lansdale, P.L. (1995). Parental divorce in childhood and demographic outcomes in young adulthood. *Demography*, *32*, 299–316.

Cheshire, G. and Campbell, M. (1997). Adolescent coping: Differences in the styles and strategies used by learning disabled students compared to non-learning disabled students. *Australian Journal of Guidance and Counselling*, *7*(1), 65–73.

Christ, G.H., Siegel, K. and Christ, A.E. (2002). Adolescent grief. *Journal of the American Medical Association*, *288*, 1269–1278.

Christenson, S.L. and Carroll, E.B. (1999). Strengthening the family–school partnership through 'Check & Connect'. In E. Frydenberg (ed.), *Learning to cope: Developing as a person in complex societies* (pp. 248–276). Oxford: Oxford University Press.

Christenson, S.L., Sinclair, M.F., Thurlow, M.L. and Evelo, D. (1999). Promoting student engagement with school using the Check and Connect model. *Australian Journal of Guidance and Counseling*, *9*(1), 169–184.

Cogan, N., Riddell, S. and Mayes, G. (2004). Children living with parental mental health problems: Do young people adopt their parents' coping style? In E. Frydenberg (ed.), *Thriving, surviving or going under: Coping with everyday lives* (pp. 45–78). Greenwich: Information Age Publishing.

Coggan, C., Bennett, S., Hooper, R. and Dickinson, P. (2003). Association between bullying and mental health status in New Zealand adolescents. *International Journal of Mental Health Promotion*, *5*(1), 116–22.

Cohen, L. and Frydenberg, E. (1996). *Coping for capable kids*. Waco: Prufrock Press.

Coleman, J.C. and Hendry, L.B. (1999). *The nature of adolescence*, (3rd edition). London: Routledge.

Coleman, J.S. (1987). Families and schools. *Educational Researcher*, *16*(6), 32–38.

Collins, J.K. and Harper, J.F. (1974). Problems of adolescents in Sydney, Australia. *Journal of Genetic Psychology*, *125*, 189–194.

Collins, N. and Harvey, D. (2001). A pilot study of mood, gender role and identity in Anglo and non-Anglo adolescent girls. *Journal of Intercultural Studies*, *22*(1), 69–77.

Compas, B.E. (1987). Coping with stress during childhood and adolescence. *Psychological Bulletin*, *101*, 393–403.

Compas, B.E. (1995). Promoting successful coping during adolescence. In M. Rutter (ed.), *Psychosocial disturbances in young people*. Cambridge: Cambridge University Press.

Compas, B.E., Connor-Smith, J.K., Saltzman, H., Thomsen, A.H. and Wadsworth, M.E. (2001). Coping with stress during childhood and adolescence: Problems, progress, and potential theory and research. *Psychological Bulletin*, *127*, 87–127.

Compas, B.E., Malcarne, V.L. and Fondacaro, K.M. (1988). Coping with stressful events in older children and adolescents. *Journal of Consulting and Clinical Psychology*, *56*, 405–411.

Compas, B.E., Phares, V. and Ledoux, N. (1989). Stress and coping preventive interventions for children and adolescents. In L.A. Bond and B.E. Compas (eds), *Primary prevention and promotion in the schools* (pp. 319–340). Newbury Park, CA: Sage.

Connor-Smith, J.K., Compas, B.E., Wadsworth, M.E., Thomsen, A.H. and Saltzman, H. (2000). Responses to stress in adolescence: Measurement of coping and involuntary stress responses. *Journal of Consulting and Clinical Psychology*, *68*, 974–992.

Coopersmith, S. (1967). *The antecedents of self-esteem*. Palo Alto, CA: Consulting Psychologists Press.

Copeland, E.P. and Hess, R.S. (1995). Differences in young adolescents' coping strategies based on gender and ethnicity. *Journal of Early Adolescence*, *15*, 203–219.

Costa, P.T. Jr., Somerfield, M.R. and McCrae, R.R. (1996). Personality and coping: A reconceptualisation. In M. Zeidner and N.M. Endler (eds). *Handbook of coping* (pp. 44–61). New York: Wiley.

Cotta, A., Frydenberg, E. and Poole, C. (2000). Coping skills training for adolescents at school. *The Australian Educational and Developmental Psychologist*, *17*, 103–116.

Cotton, S., Zebracki, K., Rosenthal, S.L., Tsevat, J. and Drotar, D. (2006). Religion/spirituality and adolescent health outcomes: A review. *Journal of Adolescent Health*, *38*, 472–480.

Cousins, N. (1976). Anatomy of an illness (as perceived by the patient). *New England Journal of Medicine, 295*, 1458–1463.

Cox, T., Gotts., G., Boot, N. and Kerr, J. (1985). Physical exercise, employee fitness and the management of health at work. *Work and Stress, 2*(1), 71–77.

Craig, W.M. (1998). The relationship among bullying, victimization, depression, anxiety, and aggression in elementary school children. *Personality and Individual Differences, 24*(1), 123–130.

Creed, P.A., Machin, M.A. and Hicks, R.E. (1999). Improving mental health status and coping abilities for long-term unemployed youth using cognitive-behaviour therapy based training interventions. *Journal of Organizational Behaviour, 20*(6), 963–978.

Creed, P., Prideaux, L. and Patton, W. (2005). Antecedents and consequences of career decisional states in adolescence. *Journal of Vocational Behavior, 67*, 397–412.

Cross, S.E. and Madson, L. (1997). Models of the self: Self-construals and gender. *Psychological Bulletin, 122*, 5–37.

Csikszentmihalyi, M. (1990). *Flow: The psychology of optimal experience.* New York: Harper & Row.

Csikszentmihalyi, M. and Larson, R. (1984). *Being adolescent.* New York: Basic Books.

Csikszentmihalyi, M., Rathunde, K. and Whalen, S. (1993). *Talented teenagers: The roots of success and failure.* New York: Cambridge University Press.

Cummings, E.M., Davies, P.T. and Simpson, K.S. (1994). Marital conflict, gender, and children's appraisals and coping efficacy as mediators of child adjustment. *Journal of Family Psychology, 8*(2), 141–149.

Cunningham, E. (1997). A model of predicting adolescent depressive syndromes using teacher and self-evaluations. Unpublished Bachelor of Science (Honours), Department of Psychology, Monash University, Melbourne.

Cunningham, E. and Walker, G. (1999). Screening for at risk youth: Predicting adolescent depression from coping styles. *Australian Journal of Guidance and Counselling, 9*(1), 37–46.

Curry, L.A., Snyder, C.R., Cook, D.L., Ruby, B.C. and Rehm, M. (1997). The role of hope in academic and sport achievement. *Journal of Personality and Social Psychology, 73*, 1257–1267.

D'Anastasi, T. and Frydenberg, E. (2005). Ethnicity and coping: What young people do and what young people learn. *Australian Journal of Guidance and Counselling, 15*(1), 43–59.

D'Zurilla, T.J. and Nezu, A. (1982). Social problem solving in adults. In P.C. Kendall (ed.), *Advances in cognitive-behavioral research and therapy* (vol. 1). New York: Academic Press.

D'Zurilla, T.J. and Nezu, A. (1990). Development and preliminary evaluation of the Social Problem-Solving Inventory (SPSI). *Psychological Assessment,* 2, 156–163.

D'Zurilla, T.J. and Sheedy, C.F. (1991). Relations between social problem solving ability and subsequent level of psychological stress in college students. *Journal of Personality and Social Psychology, 61*, 841–846.

D'Zurilla, T.J. and Sheedy, C.F. (1992). The relation between social problem solving ability and subsequent level of academic competence in college students. *Cognitive Therapy and Research, 16*, 589–599.

Dacey, J.S. and Fiore, L.B. (2000). *Your anxious child: How parents and teachers can relieve anxiety in children.* San Francisco, CA: Jossey-Bass Inc.

Davies, S. (1995). The relationship between beliefs held by gifted students and the strategies they use. Unpublished Master of Educational Psychology project, University of Melbourne, Melbourne.

Davison, G.C., Neale, J.M. and Kring, A.M. (2004). *Abnormal psychology,* (9th edition). Hoboken, NJ: John Wiley and Sons.

De Anda, D., Baroni, S., Boskin, L., Buchwald, L., Morgan, J., Ow, J., Gold, J.S. and Weiss, R. (2000). Stress, stressors and coping among high school students. *Children and Youth Services Review, 22*(6), 441–463.

De Corte, E., Verschaffel, L. and Op't Eynde, P. (2000). Self-regulation: A characteristic and a goal of mathematics education. In M. Boekaerts, P.R. Pintrich and M. Zeidner (eds), *Handbook of self-regulation* (pp. 687–726). San Diego, CA: Academic Press.

DeLongis, A. and Holtzman, S. (2005). Coping in context: The role of stress, social support, and personality in coping. *Journal of Personality, 73*, 1633–1656.

De Vaus, D.A. and Gray, M. (2004). The changing living arrangements of children: 1946–2001. *Journal of Family Studies, 10*(1), 9–19.

Diener, E. and Lucas, R.E. (1999). Personality and subjective well-being. In D. Kahneman, E. Diener and N. Schwartz (eds), *Well-being: The foundations of hedonic psychology* (pp. 213–229). New York: Russell Sage Foundation.

Dise-Lewis, J.E. (1988). The Life Events and Coping Inventory: An assessment of stress in children. *Psychosomatic Medicine, 50*, 484–499.

Dohnt, H.K. and Tiggemann, M. (2006). Body image concerns in young girls: The role of peers and media prior to adolescence. *Journal of Youth and Adolescence, 35*(2), 141–151.

Donohue, K.C. and Gullotta, T.P. (1983). The coping behaviour of adolescents following a move. *Adolescence, 18*(70), 391–401.

Dornbusch, S.M., Laird, J. and Crosnoe, R. (1999). Parental and school resources that assist adolescents in coping with negative peer influences. In E. Frydenberg (ed.), *Learning to cope: Developing as a person in complex societies* (pp. 277–298). Oxford: Oxford University Press.

Dreman, S. (1999). The experience of divorce and separation in the family: A dynamic systems perspective. In E. Frydenberg (ed.), *Learning to cope:*

Developing as a person in complex societies (pp. 150–174). Oxford: Oxford University Press.

Dryfoos, J.G. (1990). *Adolescents at risk: Prevalence and prevention*. New York: Oxford University Press.

Dumont, M. and Provost, M.A. (1999). Resilience in adolescents: Protective role of social support, coping strategies, self-esteem, and social activities on experience of stress and depression. *Journal of Youth and Adolescence*, *28*(3), 343–364.

Dweck, C.S. (1998). The development of early self-conceptions: Their relevance to motivational processes. In J. Heckhausen and C.S. Dweck (eds), *Motivation and self-regulation across the life-span* (pp. 257–280). New York: Cambridge University Press.

Ebata, A. and Moos, R. (1991). Coping and adjustment in distressed and healthy adolescents. *Journal of Applied Developmental Psychology*, *12*, 33–54.

Ebata, A.T. and Moos, R.H. (1994). Personal, situational, and contextual correlates of coping in adolescence. *Journal of Research on Adolescence*, *4*(1), 99–125.

Edgar, D. (1999). Families as the crucible of competence in a changing social ecology. In E. Frydenberg (ed.), *Learning to cope: Developing as a person in complex societies* (pp. 109–129). Oxford: Oxford University Press.

Eisenberg, N., Fabes, R.A. and Guthrie, I.K. (1997). Coping with stress: The roles of regulation and development. In S.A. Wolchik and I.N. Sandler (eds), *Handbook of children's coping: Linking theory and intervention* (pp. 41–70). New York: Plenum.

Elgar, F.J., Arlett, C. and Groves, R. (2003). Stress, coping, and behavioural problems among rural and urban adolescents. *Journal of Adolescence*, *26*, 574–585.

Elkind, D. (1988). *The hurried child: Growing up too fast too soon* (rev. edn). Reading: Addison-Wesley.

Elias, M.J. and Tobias, S.E. (1996). *Social problem solving*. New York: Guilford Press.

Emery, R.E. (1988). Marriage, divorce, and children's adjustment. *Developmental Clinical Psychology and Psychiatry Services* (vol. 14). California: Sage Publications.

Epstein, S. (1990). Cognitive-experiential self theory. In L.A. Pervin (ed.), *Handbook of personality: Theory and research* (pp. 165–192). New York: Guilford Press.

Epstein, S. (1994). Integration of the cognitive and the psychodynamic unconscious. *American Psychologist*, *49*, 709–724.

Evans, E., Hawton, K. and Rodham, K. (2005). In what ways are adolescents who engage in self-harm or experience thoughts of self-harm different in terms of help-seeking, communication and coping strategies? *Journal of Adolescence*, *28*(4), 573–587.

Evans, E., Hawton, K., Rodham, K. and Deeks, J. (2005). The prevalence of suicidal phenomena in adolescents: A systematic review of population-based studies. *Suicide and Life-Threatening Behavior*, *35*(3), 239–250.

Fahs, M.E. (1986, April). Coping in school: Correlations among perceptions of stress, coping styles, personal attributes and academic achievement in inner-city junior high school students. Paper delivered to the Annual Meeting of the American Educational Research Association, San Francisco.

Fallon, B., Frydenberg, E. and Boldero, J. (1993). Perceptions of family climate and adolescent coping. Paper presented at the 28th annual conference of the Australian Psychological Society, Gold Coast (Sept.).

Fanshawe, J.P. and Burnett, P.C. (1991). Assessing school-related stressors and coping mechanisms in adolescents. *British Journal of Educational Psychology*, *61*, 92–98.

Farber, M.L. (1968). *Theory of suicide*. New York: Funk and Wagnall's.

Farber, S.S., Primavera, J. and Felner, R.D. (1983). Older adolescents and parental divorce: Adjustment problems and mediators of coping. *Journal of Divorce*, *7*, 59–75.

Feldman, S.S., Fisher, L., Ransom, D.C. and Dimiceli, S. (1995). Is 'what is good for the goose good for the gander?': Gender differences in relationships between adolescent and adult adaptation. *Journal of Research on Adolescence*, *5*, 333–336.

Fergusson, D.M. and Lynskey, M.T. (1996). Adolescent resiliency to family adversity. *Journal of Child Psychology and Psychiatry*, *37*, 281–292.

Ferrari, L., Nota, L., Soresi, S. and Frydenberg, E. (2007). The Best of Coping: A training to improve coping strategies. In *Emerging thought and research on student, teacher and administrator stress and coping* (pp. 49–75). Volume in Series on Stress and Coping in Education, Greenwich: Information Age Publishing.

Fields, L. and Prinz, R.J. (1997). Coping and adjustment during childhood and adolescence. *Clinical Psychology Review*, *17*(8), 937–976.

Filipas, H.H. and Ullman, S.E. (2006). Child sexual abuse, coping responses, self-blame, posttraumatic stress disorder, and adult sexual revictimization. *Journal of Interpersonal Violence*, *21*(5), 652–672.

Finkelstein, D.M., Kubzansky, L.D., Capitman, J. and Goodman, E. (2007). Socioeconomic differences in adolescent stress: The role of psychological resources. *Journal of Adolescent Health*, *40*, 127–134.

Fischhoff, B., Furby, L., Quadrel, M.J. and Richardson, E. (1991). Adolescents' construal of choices: Are their decisions our 'decisions'? Unpublished manuscript, Carnegie Mellon University, Pittsburgh, PA.

Fisher, S. (1989). *Homesickness, cognition and health*. London: Lawrence Erlbaum Associates.

Fivush, R. and Fromhoff, F.A. (1988). Styles and structure in mother–child conversations about the past. *Discourse Processes*, *11*, 337–355.

Folkman, S. (1982). An approach to the measurement of coping. *Journal of Occupational Behaviour*, *3*, 95–107.

Folkman, S. (1997). Positive psychological states and coping with severe stress. *Social Psychology Medicine, 45*, 1207–1221.

Folkman, S. and Lazarus, R.S. (1980). An analysis of coping in a middle-aged community sample. *Journal of Health and Social Behavior, 21*, 219–239.

Folkman, S. and Lazarus, R. (1988a). The relationship between coping and emotion: Implications for theory and research. *Social Science Medicine, 26*(3), 309–317.

Folkman, S. and Lazarus, R. (1988b). *Ways of Coping Questionnaire Test Booklet*. Palo Alto, CA: Consulting Psychologists Press.

Folkman, S., Lazarus, R.S., Gruen, R.J. and DeLongis, A. (1986). Appraisal, coping, health status, and psychological symptoms. *Journal of Personality and Social Psychology, 50*, 571–579.

Folkman, S., Lazarus, R.S., Pimley, S. and Novacek, J. (1987). Age differences in stress and coping processes. *Psychology and Aging, 2*, 171–184.

Folkman, S. and Moskowitz, J.T. (2000). Positive affect and the other side of coping. *American Psychologist, 55*, 647–654.

Folkman, S. and Moskowitz, J.T. (2004). Coping: Pitfalls and promise. *Annual Review of Psychology, 55*, 735–774.

Fonagy, P., Steele, M., Steele, H., Higgitt, A. and Target, M. (1994). The Emanuel Miller Memorial Lecture 1992. The theory and practice of resilience. *Journal of Child Psychology and Psychiatry and Allied Disciplines, 20*, 459–466.

Foster, S., Rollefson, M., Doksum, T., Noonan, D., Robinson, G. and Teich, J. (2005). *School mental health services in the United States, 2002–2003*. DHHS Pub. No. (SMA) 05–4068. Rockville, MD: Center for Mental Health Services, Substance Abuse and Mental Health Services Administration.

Frank, J.D. (1968). The role of hope in psychotherapy. *International Journal of Psychiatry, 5*, 383–395.

Frank, J.D. (1975). The faith that heals. *The John Hopkins Medical Journal, 137*, 127–131.

Frankl, V.E. (1992). *Man's search for meaning: An introduction to logotherapy* (4th edn). Boston, MA: Beacon.

Fredrickson, B.L. (1998). What good are positive emotions? Review of *General Psychology: Special Issue: New Directions in Research on Emotion, 2*, 300–319.

Fredrickson, B.L. (2001). The role of positive emotions in positive psychology: The broaden-and-build theory of positive emotions. *American Psychologist: Special Issue, 56*, 218–226.

Freud, S. (1964). The neuro-psychoses of defense. In J. Strachey (ed. and translator), *The standard edition of the complete psychological works of Sigmund Freud* (pp. 45–61). London: Hogarth. (Originally published in 1894.)

Friedman, I.A. (1991). Areas of concern and sources of advice for Israeli adolescents. *Adolescence, 26*(104), 967–976.

Friedman, I.A. (1996). Deliberation and resolution in decision making processes: A self-report scale for adolescents. *Educational and Psychological Measurement, 56,* 881–890.

Friedman, I.A. (2000). Coping patterns in adolescent decision-making: The deliberation-resolution model. Paper presented at the American Education Research Association annual meeting, April 2000, New Orleans.

Frijda, N.H. (1993). Moods, emotions, episodes and emotions. In M. Lewis and J.M. Haviland (eds), *Handbook of emotions* (pp. 381–403). New York: Guilford.

Frydenberg, E. (1993). The coping strategies used by capable adolescents. *Australian Journal of Guidance and Counselling, 3*(1), 1–9.

Frydenberg, E. (1997). *Adolescent coping: Research and theoretical perspectives.* London: Routledge.

Frydenberg, E. (ed.) (2002). *Beyond coping: Meeting visions, goals and challenges.* Oxford: Oxford University Press

Frydenberg, E. (2004). Teaching young people to cope. In E. Frydenberg (ed.), *Thriving, surviving, or going under: Coping with everyday lives* (pp. 180–206). Greenwich: Information Age Publishing.

Frydenberg, E. (2007). *Coping for success.* ISBN 978-0-7340-2741-2 University of Melbourne's eShowcase web site – http://eshowcase.unimelb.edu.au/eshowcase/FMPro

Frydenberg, E. and Brandon, C. (2002a). *The Best of Coping: Instructors' manual.* Melbourne: Oz Child.

Frydenberg, E. and Brandon, C. (2002b). *The Best of Coping: Student workbook.* Melbourne: Oz Child.

Frydenberg, E. and Brandon, C. (2007a). *The Best of Coping: Instructors' manual.* Melbourne: Oz Child.

Frydenberg, E. and Brandon, C. (2007b). *The Best of Coping: Student workbook.* Melbourne: Oz Child.

Frydenberg, E., Bugalski, K., Firth, N., Kamsner, S. and Poole, C. (2006). Teaching young people to cope: Benefits and gains for at risk students. *The Australian and Developmental Psychologist, 23*(1), 91–110.

Frydenberg, E. and Lewis, R. (1991a) Adolescent coping: The different ways in which boys and girls cope. *Journal of Adolescence, 14,* 119–133.

Frydenberg, E. and Lewis, R. (1991b). Adolescent coping styles and strategies: Is there functional and dysfunctional coping? *Australian Journal of Guidance and Counselling, 1*(1), 1–8.

Frydenberg, E. and Lewis, R. (1993a). *Manual: The Adolescent Coping Scale.* Melbourne: Australian Council for Educational Research.

Frydenberg, E. and Lewis, R. (1993b). Boys play sport and girls turn to others: Age, gender and ethnicity as determinants of coping. *Journal of Adolescence, 16,* 252–266.

Frydenberg, E. and Lewis, R. (1993c). Stress in the family: How adolescents cope. Paper presented at the 28th Annual Conference of the Australian Psychological Society, Gold Coast (Sept.).

Frydenberg, E. and Lewis, R. (1994). Coping with different concerns: Consistency and variation in coping strategies used by adolescents. *Australian Psychologist*, *29*, 45–48.

Frydenberg, E. and Lewis, R. (1996a). The Adolescent Coping Scale: Multiple forms and applications of a self report inventory in a counselling and research context. *European Journal of Psychological Assessment*, *12*(3), 216–227.

Frydenberg, E. and Lewis, R. (1996b). Measuring the concerns of Australian adolescents: Developing a concise classificatory system. *Australian Educational Research*, *23*, 47–64.

Frydenberg, E. and Lewis, R. (1999a). Academic and general wellbeing: The relationship with coping. *Australian Journal of Guidance and Counselling*, *9*(1), 19–36.

Frydenberg, E. and Lewis, R. (1999b). Things don't get better just because you're older: A case for facilitating reflection. *British Journal of Educational Psychology*, *69*, 81–94.

Frydenberg, E. and Lewis, R. (2000). Teaching coping to adolescents: When and to whom. *American Educational Research Journal*, *37*, 727–745.

Frydenberg, E. and Lewis, R. (2002). Adolescent well-being: Building young people's resources. In E. Frydenberg (ed.), *Beyond coping: Meeting goals, visions and challenges* (pp. 175–194). Oxford: Oxford University Press.

Frydenberg, E., Lewis, R., Ardila, R., Cairns, E. and Kennedy, G. (2000). Adolescent concern with social issues: An exploratory comparison between Australian, Colombian, and Northern Irish students. *Peace and Conflict: Journal of Peace Psychology*, *7*(1), 59–76.

Frydenberg, E., Lewis, R., Kennedy, G., Ardila, R., Frindte, W. and Hannoun, R. (2003). Coping with concerns: An exploratory comparison of Australian, Colombian, German and Palestinian adolescents. *Journal of Youth and Adolescence*, *32*(1), 59–66.

Frydenberg, E., Muller, D. and Ivens, C. (2006). The experience of loss: Coping and the Seasons for Growth Program. *The Australian Educational and Development Psychologist*, *23*(1), 45–68.

Frye, A.A. and Goodman, S.H. (2000). Which social problem-solving components buffer depression in adolescent girls? *Cognitive Therapy and Research*, *24*, 637–650.

Galaif, E.R., Sussman, S., Chou, C. and Wills, T.A. (2003). Longitudinal relations among depression, stress, and coping in high risk youth. *Journal of Youth and Adolescence*, *32*(4), 243–258.

Ganim, Z. and Frydenberg, E. (2006). Attitudes to school, coping, wellbeing and stress: An examination of VCAL students. *The Australian Educational and Developmental Psychologist*, *23*(1), 7–26.

Gardner, H. (1983). *Frames of mind*. New York: Basic Books.

Garmezy, N. (1985). Stress-resistant children: The search for protective factors. *Journal of Child Psychology and Psychiatry: Recent Research in*

Developmental Psychopathology (book supplement no. 4, pp. 213–233). Oxford: Pergamon Press.

Garmezy, N. (1988). Stressors of childhood. In N. Garmezy and M. Rutter (eds), *Stress, coping and development in children* (pp. 43–84). New York: McGraw Hill.

Gibson-Kline, J. (1996). *Adolescence: From crisis to coping. A thirteen nation study*. Oxford: Butterworth-Heinemann.

Gladwell, M. (2000). *The tipping point: How little things can make a big difference*. Boston, MA: Little, Brown and Company.

Goleman, D. (1998). *Working with emotional intelligence*. London: Bloomsbury.

Good Grief (1996). *Seasons for growth*. Sydney, Australia: MacKillop Foundation.

Goode, L. (2006). An evaluation of the Best of Coping: How does the program affect the social support and wellbeing of adolescent females? Unpublished Master's thesis, University of Melbourne, Australia.

Goodyer, I.M. (1990). *Life experience, developmental and childhood psychopathology*. Chichester: John Wiley.

Gordon, V.N. (1998). Career decidedness types: A literature review. *The Career Development Quarterly*, *46*, 386–403.

Graham, A.P. (2004). Life is like the seasons: Responding to change, loss and grief through a peer based education program. *Childhood Education*, *80*(6), 317–321.

Grant, K.E. and Compas, B.E. (1995). Stress and anxious-depressed symptoms among adolescents: Searching for mechanisms of risk. *Journal of Consulting and Clinical Psychology*, *63*, 1015–1021.

Greenberg, M.T., Weissberg, R.P., O'Brien, M.U., Zins, J.E., Fredericks, L., Resnik, H. and Elias, M.J. (2003). Enhancing school-based prevention and youth development through coordinated social, emotional, and academic learning. *American Psychologist*, *58*, 466–474.

Greenglass, E.R. (2002). Proactive coping and quality of life management. In E. Frydenberg (ed.), *Beyond coping: Meeting goals, visions, and challenges* (pp. 37–62). New York: Oxford University Press.

Griffith, M.A., Dubow, E.F. and Ippolito, M.F. (1999). Developmental and cross-situational differences in adolescents' coping strategies. *Journal of Youth and Adolescence*, *29*(2), 183–204.

Grogan, S. (1999). *Body image. Understanding body dissatisfaction in men, women and children*. New York: Routledge.

Gumbiner, J. (2003). *Adolescent assessment*. Hoboken, NJ: John Wiley and Sons.

Haines, J. and Williams, C.L. (2003). Coping and problem solving of self-mutilators. *Journal of Clinical Psychology*, *59*(10), 1097–1106.

Halstead, M., Johnson, S.B. and Cunningham, W. (1993). Measuring coping in adolescents: An application of the Ways of Coping Checklist. *Journal of Clinical Child Psychology*, *22*(3), 337–344.

Halvarsson, K., Lunner, K. and Sjödén, P. (2001). Development of a Swedish version of the Adolescent Coping Orientation for Problem Experiences (A-Cope). *Scandinavian Journal of Psychology, 42*(5), 383–388.

Hampel, P. and Petermann, F. (2005). Age and gender effects on coping in children and adolescents. *Journal of Youth and Adolescence, 34*(2), 73–83.

Hampel, P. and Petermann, F. (2006). Perceived stress, coping and adjustment in adolescents. *Journal of Adolescent Health, 38*, 409–415.

Hampel, P., Petermann, F. and Dickow, B. (2001). *The German Coping Questionnaire by Janke and Erdmann adapted for children and adolescents* (German). Göttingen: Hogrefe.

Hampel, P., Rudolph, H., Stachow, R., Lass-Lentzsch, A. and Petermann, F. (2005). Coping in children and adolescents with chronic diseases. *Anxiety, Stress, and Coping, 18*, 145–155.

Harrington, R. (1993). *Depressive disorder in childhood and adolescence.* Chichester: John Wiley & Sons.

Harrison, L. and Harrington, R. (2001). Adolescents' bereavement experiences. Prevalence, association with depressive symptoms, and use of services. *Journal of Adolescence, 24*, 159–169.

Hauser, S.T. and Bowlds, M.K. (1990). Stress, coping and adaptation. In S.S. Feldman and G.R. Elliott (eds), *At the threshold: The developing adolescent* (pp. 388–413). Cambridge, MA: Harvard University Press.

Hawkins, S., McKenzie, V. and Frydenberg, E. (2006). The process of change: Coping skills training to adolescent girls in a small group counselling context. *The Australian Educational and Developmental Psychologist, 23*(1), 69–90.

Hay, P. and Bacaltchuk, J. (2001). Clinical review. Extracts from 'Clinical Evidence': Bulimia nervosa. *British Medical Journal, 23*, 33–37.

Hayes, C. and Morgan, M. (2005). Evaluation of a psychoeducational program to help adolescents cope. *Journal of Youth and Adolescence, 34*(2), 111–121.

Heaven, P. (1997). *Contemporary adolescence.* Melbourne: MacMillan Educational Services.

Heinicke, B., Paxton, S., McLean, S. and Wertheim, E. (2007). Internet delivered targeted group intervention for body dissatisfaction and disordered eating in adolescent girls: A randomised controlled trial. *Journal Abnormal Child Psychology, 35*, 379–391.

Heinrich, L.M. and Gullone, E. (2006). The clinical significance of loneliness: A literature review. *Clinical Psychology Review, 26*, 695–718.

Henry, J., Dalton, J., Wilde, R., Walsh, J. and Wilde, C. (2002, July). *Evaluation of VCAL trial: Interim report.* Melbourne, Victoria: Ripvet.

Heppner, P.P., Baumgardner, A.B. and Jackson, J. (1985). Problem solving self appraisal, depression, and attributional styles: Are they related? *Cognitive Therapy and Research, 9*, 105–113.

Heppner, P.P., Kampa, M. and Bruining, L. (1987). The relationship between problem solving self appraisal and indices of physical and psychological health. *Cognitive Therapy and Research, 11*, 155–168.

Heppner, P.P. and Petersen, C.H. (1982). The development and implications of a personal problem solving inventory. *Journal of Counseling Psychology, 29*, 66–75.

Heppner, P.P., Reeder, B.L. and Larson, L.M. (1983). Cognitive variables associated with personal problem solving appraisal: Implication for counseling. *Journal of Counseling Psychology, 30*, 537–545.

Heppner, P.P., Wei, M., Lee, D.G., Wang, Y.W. and Pretorius, T.B. (2002). Examining the generalizability of problem solving appraisal in Black South Africans. *Journal of Counseling Psychology, 49*, 484–498.

Herman-Stahl, M. and Petersen, A.C. (1996). The protective role of coping and social resources for depressive symptoms among young adolescents. *Journal of Youth and Adolescence, 25*(6), 733–754.

Herman-Stahl, M., Stemmler, M. and Petersen, A.C. (1995). Approach and avoidant coping: Implications for adolescent health. *Journal of Youth and Adolescence, 24*, 649–665.

Hess, R.S. and Copeland, E.P. (2001). Students' stress, coping strategies, and school completion: A longitudinal perspective. *School Quarterly Journal, 16*, 389–405.

Hetherington, E.M. (1989). The role of individual differences and family relationships in children's coping with divorce and remarriage. In P. Cowan and E.M. Hetherington (eds), *Family transitions* (pp. 165–194). Hillsdale, NJ: Lawrence Erlbaum Associates.

Hetherington, E.M., Stanley-Hagan, M. and Anderson, E.R. (1989). Marital transitions: A child's perspective. Special issue: Children and their development: Knowledge base, research agenda, and social policy application. *American Psychologist, 44*(2), 303–312.

Hines, A.M. (1997). Divorce related transitions, adolescent development, and the role of the parent–child relationship: A review of the literature. *Journal of Marriage and the Family, 59*, 375–388.

Hobfoll, S.E. (1988). *The ecology of stress.* Washington, DC: Hemisphere.

Hobfoll, S.E. (1998). *Culture and community.* New York: Plenum.

Hobfoll, S.E. (2001). The influence of culture, community, and the nested-self in the stress process: Advancing conservation of resources theory. *Applied Psychology: An International Review, 50*(3), 337–421.

Hobfoll, S.E. (2002). Alone together: Comparing communal versus individualistic resiliency. In E. Frydenberg (ed.), *Beyond coping: Meeting goals, visions, and challenges* (pp. 63–82). New York: Oxford University Press.

Hock, R.R. (1999). *Forty studies that changed psychology: Explorations into the history of psychological research.* Englewood Cliffs, NJ: Prentice Hall.

Holmes, T.H. and Rahe, R.H. (1967). The social readjustment rating scale. *Journal of Psychosomatic Research, 11*(2), 213–218.

Hui, E.K.P. (2000). Personal concerns and their causes: Perceptions of Hong Kong Chinese adolescent students. *Journal of Adolescence, 23*, 189–203.

Hutchinson, M.J. (2005). How does childhood and adolescent grief impact academic performance and behaviour? *Dissertation Abstracts International: Section B: The Sciences and Engineering, 65*(9-B).

Huxley, L. (2003). [Teacher and student coping]. Unpublished raw data. University of Melbourne, Australia.

Ivens, C. (2006). The Best of Coping program: Small group counseling for adolescent girls who have experienced parental separation or divorce. Unpublished Master's Thesis, The University of Melbourne, Australia.

Izard, C.E. (1993). Organizational and motivational functions of discrete emotions. In M. Lewis and J. Haviland (eds), *Handbook of emotions* (pp. 631–641). New York: Guilford.

Janis, I.L. and Mann, L. (1977). *Decision making: A psychological analysis of conflict, choice and commitment.* New York: Free Press.

Janosz, M., Leblanc, M., Boulerice, B. and Tremblay, R.E. (1997). Disentangling the weight of school dropout predictors: A test of two longitudinal samples. *Journal of Youth and Adolescence, 26*, 733–762.

Jenkin, C. (1997). The relationship between self-efficacy and coping: Changes following an Outward Bound program. Unpublished Master of Educational Psychology project, University of Melbourne, Melbourne.

Jenkins, P.H. (1997). School delinquency and the social bond. *Journal of Research in Crime and Delinquency, 34*, 337–367.

Jerusalem, M. and Schwarzer, R. (1988). Anxiety and self-concept as antecedents of stress and coping: A longitudinal study with German and Turkish adolescents. *Personality and Individual Differences, 10*(7), 785–792.

Johnson, D.W. and Johnson, R.T. (2002). Teaching students how to cope with adversity: The three Cs. In E. Frydenberg (ed.), *Beyond coping: Meeting goals, visions, and challenges* (pp. 195–218). New York: Oxford University Press.

Johnson, S. (1979). Children's fears in the classroom setting. *School Psychology Digest, 8*, 382–396.

Jones, B. and Frydenberg, E. (2003). Anxiety in children: The importance of the anxiety sensitivity factor. *Australian Journal of Guidance and Counselling, 13*(2), 145–158.

Jones, E.E. and Berglas, S. (1978). Control of attributions about the self through self-handicapping: The appeal of alcohol and the role of underachievement. *Journal of Personality and Social Psychology, 61*, 981–991.

Jose, P.E., D'Anna, C.A., Cafasso, L.L., Bryant, F.B., Chiker, V., Gein, N. and Zhezmer, N. (1998). Stress and coping among Russian and American early adolescents. *Developmental Psychology, 34*(4), 757–769.

Kagan, J. (1983). Stress and coping in early development. In N. Garmezy and M. Rutter (eds), *Stress, coping and development in children* (pp. 191–216). New York: McGraw-Hill.

Kanner, A.D., Feldman, S.S., Weinberger, D.A. and Ford, M.E. (1987). Uplifts, hassles, and adaptational outcomes in early adolescents. *Journal of Early Adolescence, 7*(4), 371–394.

Kaplan, D.S., Damphouse, K.R. and Kaplan, H.B. (1994). Mental health implications of not graduating from school. *Journal of Experimental Education, 62*, 105–123.

Kaslow, N.J., Tanenbaum, R.L. and Seligman, M.E.P. (1978). The KASTAN-R: A children's attributional style questionnaire (KASTAN-R-CASQ). University of Pennsylvania (unpublished manuscript).

Kassinove, H., Crisci, R. and Teigerman, S. (1977). Developmental trends in rational thinking: Implications for rational-emotive school mental health programs. *Journal of Community Psychology, 5*, 266–274.

Kellmann, M. (2003). Underrecovery and overtraining: Different concepts – similar impact. *Olympic Coach, 15*(3), 3–4.

Kellmann, M. and Kallus, K.W. (1999). Mood, recovery-stress state, and regeneration. In M. Lehmann, C. Foster, U. Gastmann, H. Keizer and J.M. Steinacker (eds), *Overload, fatigue, performance incompetence, and regeneration in sport* (pp. 101–117). New York: Plenum.

Kelly, H. (2002, April 17). New paths lead back to school. *The Age*, Education section, 3.

Kids Help Line (2006). Kids Help Line 2006: Infosheet. Retrieved 25 August 2007 from http://www.kidshelp.com.au/upload/18423.pdf.

Kiesler, S. and Sproull, L. (1992). Group decision making and communication technology. *Organizational Behavior and Human Decision Processes, 52*, 96–123.

King, N.J., Gullone, E., Tonge, B.J. and Ollendick, T.H. (1993). Self-reports of panic attacks and manifest anxiety in adolescents. *Behaviour Research and Therapy, 31*(1), 111–116.

Kokkinos, C.M. and Panayiotou, G. (2004). Predicting bullying and victimization among early adolescents: Associations with disruptive behavior disorders. *Aggressive Behavior, 30*(6), 520–533.

Konu, A.I., Lintonen, T.P. and Rimpela, M.K. (2002). Factors associated with schoolchildren's general subjective well-being. *Health Education Research, 17*, 155–165.

Kot, L. and Shoemaker, H.M. (1999). Children of divorce: An investigation of the developmental effects from infancy through adulthood. *Journal of Divorce and Remarriage, 31*(1/2), 161–178.

Kouzma, N.M. and Kennedy, G.A. (2004). Self-reported sources of stress in senior high school students. *Psychological Reports, 94*, 314–317.

Kovacs, M. (1992). *Children's Depression Inventory Manual*. Toronto: Multi-Health Systems.

Kowalenko, N., Wignall, A.W., Rapee, R., Simmons, J., Whitefield, K. and Stonehouse, R. (2002). The ACE Program: Working with schools to promote emotional health and prevent depression. *Youth Studies Australia, 21*(2), 23–30.

Kraaij, V., Garnefski, N., Jan de Wilde, E., Dijkstra, A., Gebhardt, W., Maes, S. and ter Doest, L. (2003). Negative life events and depressive symptoms in late adolescence: Bonding and cognitive coping as vulnerability factors? *Journal of Youth and Adolescence, 32*(3), 185–193.

Kumpulainen, K., Rasanen, E. and Puura, K. (2001). Psychiatric disorders and the use of mental health services among children involved in bullying. *Aggressive Behavior, 27*(2), 102–110.

Kuo, B.C.H., Roysircar, G. and Newby-Clark, I.R. (2006). Development of the Cross-Cultural Coping Scale: Collective, avoidance and engagement coping. *Measurement and Evaluation in Counseling and Development, 39*, 161–181.

Kurdek, L.A. and Sinclair, R.J. (1988). Adjustment of young adolescents in two-parent nuclear, stepfather, and mother-custody families. *Journal of Consulting and Clinical Psychology, 56(1)*, 91–96.

Lade, L., Frydenberg, E. and Poole, C. (1998). Daughters don't merely imitate their mothers' coping styles: A comparison of coping strategies used by mothers and daughters. *The Australian Educational and Developmental Psychologist, 15*(1), 62–69.

Lang, M. and Tisher, M. (2004). *Children's Depression Scale* (3rd edition). Melbourne: ACER Press.

Lang, P.J. (1984). Cognition in emotion: Concept and action. In C. Izard, J. Kagan and R. Zajonc (eds), *Emotions, cognition and behaviour* (pp. 192–226). Cambridge: Cambridge University Press.

Largo-Wright, E., Petersen, P.M. and Chen, W.W. (2005). Perceived problem solving, stress, and health among college students. *American Journal of Health Behavior, 29*(4), 360–370.

Larson, L.M. and Heppner, P.P. (1985). The relationship of problem solving appraisal to career decision and indecision. *Journal of Vocational Behavior, 26*, 55–65.

Larson, L.M., Piersel, W.C., Imao, R.A. and Allen, S.J. (1990). Significant predictors of problem solving appraisal. *Journal of Counseling Psychology, 37*, 482–490.

Larson, R.W. (1990). The solitary side of life: An examination of the time people spend alone from childhood to old age. *Developmental Review, 10*, 155–183.

Larson, R.W. and Verma, S. (1999). How children and adolescents spend time across the world: Work, play and developmental opportunities. *Psychological Bulletin, 125*(6), 701–736.

Lazarus, R.S. (1991). *Emotion and adaptation.* New York: Oxford University Press.

Lazarus, R.S. (1993). Coping theory and research: Past, present and future. *Psychosomatic Medicine, 55*, 234–247.

Lazarus, R.S. (2003). Does the positive psychology movement have legs? *Psychological Inquiry, 14*(2), 93–109.

Lazarus, R.S. and Folkman, S. (1984). *Stress, appraisal and coping.* New York: Springer.

Lazarus, R.S. and Launier, R. (1978). Stress-related transactions between person and environment. In A. Pervin and M. Lewis (eds), *Perspectives in international psychology* (pp. 189–217). New York: Plenum.

Lee, V.E., Burkam, D.T., Zimiles, H. and Ladewski, B. (1994). Family structure and its effect on behavioural and emotional problems in young adolescents. *Journal of Research on Adolescence, 4*(3), 405–437.

Leeper, R.W. (1948). A motivational theory of emotions to replace 'emotions as disorganised response'. *Psychological Bulletin, 55,* 5–21.

Leitenberg, H., Gibson, L.E. and Novy, P. (2004). Individual differences among undergraduate women in methods of coping with stressful events: The impact of cumulative childhood stressors and abuse. *Child Abuse and Neglect, 28,* 181–192.

Lewin, K. (1936) *Principles of topological psychology.* New York: McGraw-Hill.

Lewinsohn, P.M., Petit, J.W., Joiner, T.E. and Seeley, J.R. (2003). The symptomatic expression of depressive disorder in adolescents and young adults. *Journal of Abnormal Psychology, 112,* 244–252.

Lewis, R. (1999). Teachers coping with the stress of classroom. *Social Psychology of Education, 3,* 1–17.

Lewis, R. and Frydenberg, E. (2004a). Students' self-evaluations of their coping: How well do they do it? In E. Frydenberg (ed.), *Thriving, surviving, or going under: Coping with everyday lives* (pp. 25–43). Greenwich: Information Age Publishing.

Lewis, R. and Frydenberg, E. (2004b). Thriving, surviving or going under: which coping strategy relates to which outcomes? In E. Frydenberg (ed.), *Thriving, surviving or going under: Coping with everyday lives* (pp. 3–24). Greenwich: Information Age.

Lewis, R. and Frydenberg, E. (2005). Concomitants of failure to cope: What we should teach adolescents. *British Journal of Educational Psychology, 72*(3), 419–431.

Lewis, R. and Frydenberg, E. (2007). When problem-solving is not perceived as effective: How do young people cope? In *Emerging thought and research on student, teacher and administrator stress and coping* (pp. 35–48). Greenwich: Information Age Publishing.

Li, C.E., DiGiuseppe, R. and Froh, J. (2006). The roles of sex, gender, and coping in adolescent depression. *Adolescence, 41*(163), 409–415.

Li, H., Lin, C., Bray, M.A. and Kehle, T.J. (2005). The measurement of stressful events in Chinese college students. *Psychology in the Schools, 42*(3), 315–323.

Lochman, J.E., Dunn, S.E. and Klimes-Dougan, B. (1993). An intervention and consultation model from a social cognitive perspective: A description of the Anger Coping program. *School Psychology Review, 22*(3), 458–471.

Lodge, J. and Frydenberg, E. (2006). Verbal insults: Experiences, responses, and factors associated with victimisation in the school setting. In P. Buchwald (ed.), *Stress and anxiety – application to health, community, work place, and education* (pp. 347–366). Cambridge: Scholar Press Ltd.

Lodge, J. and Frydenberg, E (2007). Profiles of adolescent coping and cyber-bullying: Insights for school practitioners. *The Australian Educational and Developmental Psychologist*, *24*, 45–58.

Lodge, J., Frydenberg, E., Care, E., Tobin, M. and Begg, B. (2007). Enhancing Wellbeing and Learning in Middle Years Classrooms: ARC Linkage Project (06/07).

Logan, G.D. (1988). Toward an instance theory of automatization. *Psychological Review*, *95*, 429–527.

Logan, G.D. (1989). Automatization and cognitive control. In J.A. Bargh and J.S. Uleman (eds), *Unintended thought* (pp. 52–74). New York: Guilford.

Lohman, B.J. and Jarvis, P.A. (2000). Adolescent stressors, coping strategies, and psychological health studied in the family context. *Journal of Youth and Adolescence*, *29*(1), 15–43.

Luscombe-Smith, N., Frydenberg, E. and Poole, C. (2003). Broadening social networks: Outcomes of a coping skills program. *Australian Journal of Guidance and Counselling* (Special issue), *13*(1), 22–35.

Luthar, S.S. (1993). Annotation: Methodological and conceptual issues in research on childhood resilience. *Journal of Child Psychology and Psychiatry*, *34*, 441–453.

Lyubomirsky, S., King, L. and Diener, E. (2005). The benefits of frequent positive affect: Does happiness lead to success? *Psychological Bulletin*, *131*(6), 803–855.

Lyubomirsky, S., Sheldon, K.M. and Schkade, D. (2005). Pursuing happiness: The architecture of sustainable change. *Review of General Psychology*, *9*(2), 111–131.

Lyubomirsky, S., Tucker, K.L., Caldwell, N.D. and Berg, K. (1999). Why ruminators are poor problem solvers: Clues from the phenomenology of dysphoric rumination. *Journal of Personality and Social Psychology*, *77*, 1041–1060.

McCarthy, K. (2001). Assessing the effectiveness of Bright Lives – Best of Coping program in adolescents across three secondary schools in Melbourne. Unpublished thesis, Master of Educational Psychology, University of Melbourne.

McKenzie, V. and Frydenberg, E. (2004). Young people and their resources. In E. Frydenberg (ed.), *Thriving, surviving, or going under: Coping with everyday lives* (pp. 79–108). Greenwich: Information Age Publishing.

McKenzie, V., Frydenberg, E. and Poole, C. (2004). What resources matter to young people: The relationship between resources and coping style. *The Australian Educational and Developmental Psychologist*, *19*(1), 78–96.

McTaggart, H. (1996). Students at risk of school exclusion: How they cope. Unpublished Master of Educational Psychology project, University of Melbourne, Melbourne.

Maddi, S.R. and Kobassa, S.C. (1984). *The hardy executive: Health under stress*. Homewood, IL: Dow Jones-Irwin.

Magen, Z. (1998). *Exploring adolescent happiness*. New York: Sage.

Magen, Z. and Aharoni, R. (1991). Adolescents contributing towards others: Relationship to positive experiences and transpersonal commitment. *Journal of Humanistic Psychology*, *31*, 126–143.

Mahon, N.E. and Yarcheski, A. (2002). Alternate theories of happiness in early adolescence. *Clinical Nursing Research*, *11*, 306–323.

Mann, L., Burnett, P., Radford, M. and Ford, S. (1997). The Melbourne Decision Making Questionnaire: An instrument for measuring patterns for coping with decisional conflict. *Journal of Behavioural Decision Making*, *10*, 1–19.

Mann, L. and Friedman, I. (1999). Decision making and coping in adolescence. In E. Frydenberg (ed.), *Learning to cope: Developing as a person in complex societies* (pp. 225–247). Oxford: Oxford University Press.

Mann, L., Harmoni, R. and Power, C. (1988a). *GOFER: Basic principles of decision making*. Woden, ACT: Curriculum Development Centre.

Mann, L., Harmoni, R. and Power, C. (1989). Adolescent decision making: The development of competence. *Journal of Adolescence*, *12*, 265–278.

Mann, L., Harmoni, R., Power, C. and Beswick, G. (1987). Understanding and improving decision making in adolescents. Unpublished manuscript, Flinders University, South Australia.

Mann, L., Harmoni, R., Power, C., Beswick, G. and Ormond, C. (1988b). Effectiveness of the GOFER course in decision making for high school students. *Journal of Behavioural Decision Making*, *1*, 159–168.

Mann, L., Nota, L., Soresi, S., Ferrari, L. and Frydenberg, E. (2006). The relationship between decision-making and coping strategies in adolescence. Unpublished manuscript, University of Padua.

Manzi, P.A. (1986). Cognitive appraisal: Stress and coping in teenage employment. *The Vocational Guidance Quarterly*, *34*, 161–170.

March, J.S. (ed.) (1995). *Anxiety disorders in children and adolescents*. New York: Guilford Press.

Marland, S.P. (1972). *Education of the gifted and talented, Volume 1: A report of the Congress of the United States by the U.S. Commissioner of Education.* Washington, DC: US Government Printing Office.

Marsh, H.W. (1989). Age and sex effects in multiple dimensions of self-concept: Preadolescence to early adulthood. *Journal of Educational Psychology*, *81*, 417–430.

Marsh, H.W. (1994). Using the national longitudinal study of 1988 to evaluate theoretical model of self-concept: The self-description questionnaire. *Journal of Educational Psychology*, *86*(3), 439–456.

Mason, R.C., Clark, G., Reeves, R.B. and Wagner, B. (1969). Acceptance and healing. *Journal of Religion and Health*, *8*, 123–142.

Matheny, K.B., Curlette, W.L., Aysan, F., Herrington, A., Gfroerer, C.A., Thompson, D. *et al.* (2002). Coping resources, perceived stress, and life satisfaction among Turkish and American university students. *International Journal of Stress Management*, *9*, 81–97.

Mattison, R.E. (1992). Anxiety disorders. In S.R. Hooper, G.W. Jynd and

R.E. Mattison (eds), *Child psychopathology: Diagnostic criteria and clinical assessment* (pp. 179–202). Hillsdale, NJ: Lawrence Erlbaum Associates.

Meijer, S.A., Sinnema, G., Bijstra, J.O., Mellenbergh, G.J. and Wolters, W.H.G. (2002). Coping style and locus of control as predictors for psychological adjustment of adolescents with chronic illness. *Social Science and Medicine, 54*, 1453–1461.

Melges, R. and Bowlby, J. (1969). Types of hopelessness in psychopathological processes. *Archives of General Psychiatry, 20*, 690–699.

Meltzer, H., Harrington, R., Goodman, R. and Jenkins, R. (2001). *Children and adolescents who try to harm, hurt or kill themselves.* London: National Statistics Office/HMSO.

Menaker Tomchin, E., Callahan, C.M., Sowa, C. and May, K. (1996). Coping and self-concept: Adjustment patterns of gifted adolescents. *The Journal for Secondary, Gifted Education, 8*(1), 16–27

Menninger, K. (1959). The academic lecture on hope. *The American Journal of Psychiatry, 116*, 481–491.

Mental health: A report of the Surgeon General (1999). Rockville, MD: US Department of Health and Human Services, Office of the Surgeon General, SAMHSA. [Online] Retrieved 23 April 2007, from http://mentalhealth. samhsa.gov/cmhs/surgeongeneral/surgeongeneralrpt.asp

Millstein, S.G. and Halper-Felsher, B.L. (2002). Judgements about risk and perceived invulnerability in adolescents and young adults. *Journal of Research on Adolescence, 12*(4), 399–422.

Mnet (2001). Young Canadians in a Wired World-Mnet Survey. [Online] Retrieved 16 September 2006, from http://www.mediaawareness.ca/english/special_initiatives/surveys/index.cfm.

Montemayor, R. (1984). Picking up the pieces: The effects of parental divorce on adolescents with some suggestions for school-based intervention programs. *Journal of Early Adolescence, 4*, 289–314.

Moore, D. and Schultz, N.R. (1983). Loneliness at adolescence: Correlates, attributions, and coping. *Journal of Youth and Adolescence, 12*, 95–100.

Moore, S. (1999). Sexuality in adolescence: a suitable case for coping? In E. Frydenberg (ed.), *Learning to cope: Developing as a person in complex societies* (pp. 64–80). Oxford: Oxford University Press.

Moos, R.H. (1990). *Coping Response Inventory – Youth Form, Preliminary Manual.* Palo Alto, CA: Stanford University Medical Clinic.

Moos, R.H. and Billings, A.G. (1982). Conceptualising and measuring coping resources and processes. In L. Goldberger and S. Brenitz (eds), *Handbook of stress: Theoretical and clinical aspects* (pp. 212–230). New York: Free Press.

Moos, R.H. and Holahan, C.J. (2003). Dispositional and contextual perspectives on coping: Towards an integrative framework. *Journal of Clinical Psychology, 59*, 1387–1403.

Moos, R.H. and Moos, B.S. (1986). *Family environment scale manual* (2nd edition). Palo Alto, CA: Consulting Psychologists Press.

Moskowitz, J.T. and Wrubel, J. (2000). Apples and oranges: Using qualitative and quantitative approaches to coping assessment. Paper presented at the American Psychological Society, Miami, Florida.

Mott, F.L., Kowaleskijones, L. and Menaghan, E.G. (1997). Paternal absence and child behavior: Does a child's gender make a difference? *Journal of Marriage and the Family*, *59*, 103–118.

Moulds, J.D. (2003). Stress manifestation in high school students: An Australian sample. *Psychology in the Schools*, *40*(4), 391–402.

Mowrer, O.H. (1960). *The psychology of hope*. San Francisco: Jossey-Bass.

Muldoon, O.T. (1996). Stress, appraisal and coping: A psychosocial approach. Unpublished PhD thesis, Queens University, Belfast.

Muldoon, O. and Cairns, E. (1999). Children, young people, and war: Learning to cope. In E. Frydenberg (ed.), *Learning to cope: Developing as a person in complex societies* (pp. 322–340). Oxford: Oxford University Press.

Muller, D. and Saulwick, I. (1999). *An evaluation of the Seasons for Growth program: Consolidated report*. Canberra, ACT: Commonwealth of Australia.

Murberg, T.A. and Bru, E. (2004). School-related stress and psychosomatic symptoms among Norwegian adolescents. *School Psychology International*, *25*, 317–332.

Murberg, T.A. and Bru, E. (2005). The role of coping styles as predictors of depressive symptoms among adolescents: A prospective study. *Scandinavian Journal of Psychology*, *46*, 385–393.

Myers, D.G. (2000). The funds, friends and faith of happy people. *American Psychologist*, *55*, 56–67.

Nansel, T.R., Overpeck, M., Pilla, R.S., Ruan, W.J., Simons-Morton, B. and Scheidt, T. (2001). Bullying behaviours among US youth: Prevalence and association with psychosocial adjustment. *Journal of the American Medical Association*, *285*(16), 2094–2100.

National Children's Home (2005). Putting U in the picture. Mobile Bullying Survey 2005. [Online]. Retrieved 16 September 2006, from http://www.nch.org.uk/information/index.php?i=237

Natvig, G.K., Albrektsen G. and Qvarnstrom, U. (2003). Associations between psychosocial factors and happiness among school adolescents. *International Journal of Nursing Practice*, *9*(33), 166–175.

Neill, L. (1996). Ethnicity, gender, self-esteem and coping styles: A comparison of Australian and South-East Asian adolescents. Unpublished graduate Diploma of Counselling Psychology project, Royal Melbourne Institute of Technology.

Neill, L.M. and Proeve, M.J. (2000). Ethnicity, gender, self-esteem, and coping styles: A comparison of Australian and South-East Asian secondary students. *Australian Psychologist*, *35*, 216–220.

Nelson, M. (2003). School Bullies Going High Tech. [Online] Retrieved 14 July 2004, from http://www.canoe.ca/NewsStand/LondonFreePress/News/2003/09/02/174030.html

Newby, W.N., Brown, R.T., Pawletko, T.M., Gold, S.H. and Whitt, J.K. (2000). Social skills and psychological adjustment of child and adolescent cancer survivors. *Psycho-Oncology*, *9*(2), 112–126.

Nezu, A.M. and Ronan, G.F. (1988). Stressful life events, problem solving and depressive symptoms: A prospective analysis. *Journal of Counseling Psychology*, *35*, 134–138.

Nicholson, S.I. and Antill, K.K. (1981). Personal problems of adolescents and their relationship to peer acceptance and sex role identity. *Journal of Youth and Adolescence*, *10*, 309–325.

Nicoll, J. (1992). A longitudinal study of psychological stress and decision making in final year high school students. Unpublished fourth-year thesis, Department of Psychology, University of Melbourne.

Nolen-Hoeksema, S. and Girgus, J.S. (1994). The emergence of gender differences in depression during adolescence. *Psychological Bulletin*, *115*, 424–443.

Noppe, I.C. and Noppe, L.D. (2004). Adolescent experiences with death: Letting go of immortality. *Journal of Mental Health Counselling*, *26*(2), 146–167.

Norman, J. and Harris, M. (1981). *The private life of the American teenager*. New York: Rawson, Wade.

Nota, L. and Soresi, S. (1998). Studenti indecisi e scelta della facoltà universitaria [Undecided students and choice of a university faculty]. *Supplemento a Psicologia e Scuola*, *90*, 127–136.

Noto, S.S. (1995). The relationship between coping and achievement: A comparison between adolescent males and females. Unpublished Master of Educational Psychology project, University of Melbourne, Melbourne.

Nounopoulos, A., Ashby, J.S. and Gilman, R. (2006). Coping resources, perfectionism, and academic performance among adolescents. *Psychology in the Schools*, *43*(5), 613–622.

Nurmi, J., Poole, M.E. and Kalakoski, V. (1994). Age differences in adolescent future-oriented goals, concerns and related temporal extension in different sociocultural contexts. *Journal of Youth and Adolescence*, *23*(4), 471–487.

O'Halloran, M. and Carr, A. (2000). Adjustment to parental separation or divorce. In A. Carr (ed.), *What works with children and adolescents?* (pp. 280–299). London: Routledge.

Offer, D. and Offer, J.B. (1975). *From teenage to young manhood: A psychological study*. New York: Basic Books.

Ollendick, T.H. (1995). Cognitive behavioural treatment of panic disorder with agoraphobia in adolescents: A multiple baseline design analysis. *Behaviour Therapy*, *26*, 517–531.

Olsson, C.A., Bond, L., Burns, J.M., Vella-Brodrick, D. and Sawyer, S.M. (2003). Adolescent resilience: a concept analysis. *Journal of Adolescence*, *26*, 1–11.

Olszewski, P., Kulieke, M.J. and Buescher, T. (1987). The influence of the family environment on the development of talent: A literature review. *Journal for the Education of the Gifted, 11*, 6–28.

Olweus, D. (1993). *Bullying at school: What we know and what we can do. Understanding children's worlds.* Malden, MA: Blackwell Publishers.

Opotow, S. and Deutsch, M. (1999). Learning to cope with conflict and violence: How schools can help youth. In E. Frydenberg (ed.), *Learning to Cope* (pp. 198–224). Oxford: Oxford University Press.

Owens, J.S. and Murphy, C.E. (2004). Effectiveness research in the context of school-based mental health. *Clinical Child and Family Psychology Review, 7*(4), 195–209.

Pallant, J.F. (2000). Development and validation of a scale to measure perceived control of internal states. *Journal of Personality Assessment, 75*, 308–337.

Panizza, T. and Frydenberg, E. (2006). Evaluating the Best of Coping: How do content and mode of delivery influence program outcomes? *Special Issue, The Australian Educational and Developmental Psychologist*, 110–130.

Parsons, A., Frydenberg, E. and Poole, C. (1996). Overachievement and coping strategies in adolescent males. *British Journal of Educational Psychology, 66*, 109–114.

Patterson, J.M. and McCubbin, H.I. (1987). Adolescent coping style and behaviors: Conceptualization and measurement. *Journal of Adolescence, 10*(2), 163–186.

Pearlin, L. and Schooler, C. (1978). The structure of coping. *Journal of Health and Social Behavior, 19*, 2–21.

Pedro-Carroll, J.L. and Cowen, E.L. (1985). The Children of Divorce Intervention Program: An investigation of the efficacy of a school-based prevention program. *Journal of Consulting and Clinical Psychology, 53*, 603–611.

Pekrun, R., Goetz, T., Titz, W. and Perry, R.P. (2002). Positive emotions in education. In E. Frydenberg (ed.), *Beyond coping: Meeting goals, visions, and challenges* (pp. 149–173). New York: Oxford University Press.

Peplau, L.A. and Perlman, D. (eds) (1982). *Loneliness.* New York: Wiley.

Phelps, S.B. and Jarvis, P.A. (1994). Coping in adolescence: Empirical evidence for a theoretically based approach to assessing coping. *Journal of Youth and Adolescence, 23*(3), 359–371.

Piko, B. (2001). Gender differences and similarities in adolescents' ways of coping. *Psychological Record, 51*, 223–235.

Pipher, M. (1995). *Reviving Ophelia.* Sydney: Doubleday.

Plunkett, S.W., Radmacher, K.A. and Moll-Phanara, D. (2000). Adolescent life events, stress and coping: A comparison of communities and genders. *Professional School Counselling, 3*(5), 356–366.

Polivy, J. and Herman, C. (2002). Causes of eating disorders. *Annual Review of Psychology, 53*, 187–213.

Poot, A.C. (1997). Client factors which moderate outcome in an adolescent psychotherapy treatment program. Unpublished Master of Counselling, School of Education, La Trobe University, Melbourne.

Prelow, H.M., Weaver, S.R. and Swenson, R.R. (2006). Competence, self-esteem, and coping efficacy as mediators of ecological risk and depressive symptoms in urban African American and European American Youth. *Journal of Youth and Adolescence, 35*, 507–517.

Preuss, L.J. and Dubow, E.F. (2004). A comparison between intellectually gifted and typical children in their coping responses to a school and peer stressor. *Roeper Review, 26*(2), 105–111.

Printz, B.L., Shermis, M.D. and Webb, P.M. (1999). Stress-buffering factors related to adolescent coping: A path analysis. *Adolescence, 34*(136), 715–735.

Prior, M. (1999). Resilience and coping: The role of individual temperament. In E. Frydenberg (ed.), *Learning to cope: Developing as a person in complex societies* (pp. 33–52). Oxford: Oxford University Press.

Prior, M., Sanson, A., Smart, D. and Oberklaid, F. (2000). *Pathways from infancy to adolescence: Australian temperament project 1983–2000*. Melbourne, Australia: Australian Institute of Family Studies.

Quadrel, M.J., Fischhoff, B. and Davis, W. (1993). Adolescent (in)vulnerability. *American Psychologist, 48*, 102–116.

Quince, S., Bernard, D., Booth, M., Kang, M., Usherwood, T., Alperstein, G. and Bennett, D. (2003). Health and access issues among Australian adolescents: A rural–urban comparison. *Rural and Remote Health, 3*(245), online: 1–11.

Rachman, S. (1998). *Anxiety*. Hove, East Sussex: Psychology Press Ltd.

Rapee, R. and Barlow, D.H. (1993). Generalized anxiety disorder, panic disorder and the phobias. In P.B. Sutker and H.E. Adams (eds), *Comprehensive handbook of psychopathology* (2nd edn, pp. 109–127). New York: Plenum Press.

Raphael, B. (1993). Adolescent resilience: The potential impact of personal development in schools. *Journal of Paediatric Child Health, 29*, 31–36.

Rauste-von-Wright, M. and Rauste-von-Wright, J. (1981). A longitudinal study of psychosomatic symptoms in healthy 11–18 year old girls and boys. *Journal of Psychosomatic Research, 25*(6), 525–534.

Raymo, J.M., Iwasawa, M. and Bumpass, L. (2004). Marital dissolution in Japan: Recent trends and patterns. *Demographic Research, 11*, 395–420.

Reid, G.J., Gilbert, C.A. and McGrath, P.J. (1998). The Pain Coping Questionnaire: Preliminary validation. *Pain, 76*, 83–96.

Reiss, S.D. and Heppner, P. (1993). Examination of coping resources and family adaptation in mothers and daughters of incestuous versus nonclinical families. *Journal of Counseling Psychology, 40*, 100–108.

Reiss, S. and McNally, R.J. (1985). The expectancy model of fear. In S. Reiss and R.R. Botzin (eds), *Theoretical issues in behavior therapy* (pp. 101–121). New York: Academic Press.

Renzulli, J.S. (1986). The three-ring conception of giftedness: A developmental model for creative productivity. In R.J. Sternberg and J.E. Davidson (eds), *Conceptions of giftedness*. New York: Cambridge University Press.

Resnick, M.D., Bearman, P.S., Blum, R.W., Bauman, K.E., Harris, K.M., Jones, J., Tabor, J., Beuhring, T., Sieving, R.E., Shew, M., Ireland, M., Bearinger, L.H. and Udry, J.R. (1997). Protecting adolescents from harm: Findings from the national longitudinal study on adolescent health. *The Journal of the American Medical Association, 278*(10), 795–878.

Reynolds, W.M. (2001). Reynolds Adolescent Adjustment Screening Inventory. Odessa, FL: PAR (Psychological Assessment Resources, Inc.).

Richardson, C.D. and Rosen, L.A. (1999). School-based interventions for children of divorce. *Professional School Counseling, 3*(1), 21–27.

Richardson, G.E. (2002). The metatheory of resilience and resiliency. *Journal of Clinical Psychology, 58*(3), 307–321.

Rigby, K. and Slee, P.T. (1991). Bullying among Australian school children: Reported behaviour and attitudes toward victims. *Journal of Social Psychology, 131*, 615–627.

Roberts, C. (1999). The prevention of depression in children and adolescents. *Australian Psychologist, 34*(1), 49–57.

Roberts, J.A., Tanner, J.F. and Manolis, C. (2005). Materialism and the family structure–stress relation. *Journal of Consumer Psychology, 15*, 183–190.

Rogers, P., Qualter, P., Phelps, G. and Gardner, K. (2006). Belief in the paranormal, coping and emotional intelligence. *Personality and Individual Differences, 41*(6), 1089–1105.

Roker, D., Player, K. and Coleman, J. (1999). Young people's voluntary and campaigning activities as sources of political education. *Oxford Review of Education, 25*(1 and 2), 185–198.

Rollin, S.A., Anderson, C.W. and Buncher, R.M. (1999). Coping in children and adolescents: A prevention model for helping kids avoid or reduce at-risk behaviour. In E. Frydenberg (ed.), *Learning to cope: Developing as a person in complex societies* (pp. 299–321). Oxford: Oxford University Press.

Rook, R.S. (1984). Research on social support, loneliness, and social isolation: Toward an integration. *Review of Personality and Social Psychology, 5*, 239–264.

Rose, A.J. (2002). Co-rumination in the friendships of girls and boys. *Child Development, 73*(6), 1830–1843.

Rose, R.J., Koskenvuo, M., Kaprio, J., Sarna, S. and Langinvainio, H. (1988). Shared genes, shared experiences, and similarity of personality: Data from 14,288 adult Finnish co-twins. *Journal of Personality and Social Psychology, 54*(1), 161–171.

Rosenberg, M. (1989). *Society and the adolescent self-image*. Middletown, CT: Wesleyan University Press.

Rosenthal, D. and Hansen, J. (1980). Comparison of adolescents' perceptions and behaviours in two parent families. *Journal of Youth and Adolescence, 9*, 407–417.

Rothbaum, F. and Weisz, J.R. (1994). Parental caregiving and child externalising behaviour in nonclinical samples: a meta-analysis. *Psychological Bulletin, 116*, 55–74.

Roussi, P., Rapti, F. and Kiosseoglou, G. (2006). Coping and psychological sense of community: An exploratory study of urban and rural areas in Greece. *Anxiety, Stress and Coping, 19*(2), 161–173.

Rudolph, K.D. and Conley, C.S. (2005). The socioemotional costs and benefits of social-evaluative concerns: Do girls care too much? *Journal of Personality, 73*(1), 115–137.

Rudolph, K., Dennig, M. and Weisz, J. (1995). Determinants and consequences of children coping in a medical setting: Conceptualisation, review and critique. *Psychological Bulletin, 118*(3), 328–357.

Rumberger, R.W. (1987). High school dropouts: A review of the issues and evidence. *Review of Educational Research, 57*, 101–121.

Ruschena, E., Prior, M., Sanson, A. and Smart, D. (2005). A longitudinal study of adolescent adjustment following family transitions. *Journal of Child Psychology and Psychiatry, 46*(4), 353–363.

Rutter, M. (1980). *Changing youth in a changing society*. Cambridge, MA: Harvard University Press.

Rutter, M. (1981). Stress, coping and development: Some issues and some questions. *Journal of Child Psychology and Psychiatry, 22*(4), 323–356.

Rutter, M. (1985). Resilience in the face of adversity: Protective factors and resistance to psychiatric disorders. *British Journal of Psychiatry, 147*, 589–611.

Rutter, M., Maughan B., Mortimore, P., Ouston, J. and Smith, A. (1979). *Fifteen thousand hours: Secondary school and its effects on children.* London: Open Books.

Rutter, M. and Rutter, M. (1992). *Developing minds: Challenge and continuity across the life-span*. London: Penguin.

Ryckman, R.M., Robins, M.A., Thornton, B. and Cantrell, P. (1982). Development and validation of a self-efficacy scale. *Journal of Personality and Social Psychology, 42*, 891–900.

Saarni, C. (1990). Emotional competence: How emotions and relationships become integrated. In R. Thompson (ed.), *Nebraska symposium on motivation: Socio-emotional development* (vol. 36, pp. 115–182). Lincoln: University of Nebraska Press.

Saarni, C. (1997). Emotional competence and self-regulation in childhood. In P. Salovey and D. Sluyter (eds), *Emotional development and emotional intelligence: Educational implications* (pp. 35–66). New York: Basic Books.

Sadowski, C. and Kelly, M.L. (1993). Social problem solving in suicidal adolescents. *Journal of Consulting and Clinical Psychology, 61*(1), 121–127.

Salovey, P. and Mayer, J.D. (1989–1990). Emotional intelligence. *Imagination, Cognition and Personality, 9*, 185–211.

Sandler, I.N., Ayers, T.S., Wolchik, S.A., Tein, J., Kwok, O., Haine, R.A. *et al.* (2003). The Family Bereavement Program: Efficacy evaluation of a theory-based prevention program for parentally bereaved children and adolescents. *Journal of Counseling and Clinical Psychology, 71*(3), 587–600.

Sandler, I.N., Wolchik, S.A., MacKinnon, D., Ayers, T.S. and Roosa, M.W. (1997a). Developing linkages between theory and intervention in stress and coping processes. In S.A. Wolchik and I.N. Sandler, *Handbook of children's coping: Linking theory and intervention* (pp. 3–40). New York: Plenum Press.

Sandler, I.N., Wolchik, S.A., MacKinnon, D., Ayers, T.S. and Roosa, M.W. (1997b). *Handbook of children's coping: Linking theory and intervention.* New York: Plenum Press.

Satir, V. (1988). *The new people making.* Mountain View, CA: Science and Behavior Books.

Sawyer, M.G., Kosky, R.J., Graetz, B.W., Arney, F. and Zubrick, P.B. (2000). The National Survey of Mental Health and Wellbeing: The child and adolescent component. *Australian and New Zealand Journal of Psychiatry, 34*, 214–220.

Schachtel, E. (1959). *Metamorphosis.* New York: Basic Books.

Schmale, A.H. and Iker, H.P. (1966). The affect of hopelessness and the development of cancer. *Psychosomatic Medicine, 28*, 714–721.

Schmeelk-Cone, K.H. and Zimmerman, M.A. (2003). A longitudinal analysis of stress in African American youth: Predictors and outcomes of stress trajectories. *Journal of Youth and Adolescence, 32*, 419–430.

Schmidt, S., Petersen, C. and Bullinger, M. (2003). Coping with chronic disease from the perspective of children and adolescents: A conceptual framework and its implications for participation. *Child Care, Health and Development, 29*(1), 63–75.

Schönpflug, U. and Jansen, X. (1995). Self concept and coping with developmental demands in German and Polish adolescents. *International Journal of Behavioural Development, 8*, 385–404.

Schotte, D.E. and Clum, G.A. (1987). Problem-solving skills in suicidal psychiatric patients. *Journal of Consulting and Clinical Psychology, 55*(1), 49–54.

Schwarzer, R. and Taubert, S. (2002). Tenacious goal pursuits and striving toward personal growth: Proactive coping. In E. Frydenberg (ed.), *Beyond coping: Meeting goals, visions, and challenges* (pp. 19–36). New York: Oxford University Press.

Seiffge-Krenke, I. (1992). Coping behaviour of Finnish adolescents: Remarks on a cross-cultural comparison. *Scandinavian Journal of Psychology, 33*, 301–314.

Seiffge-Krenke, I. (1995). *Stress, coping, and relationships in adolescence.* Mahwah, NJ: Lawrence Erlbaum.

Seiffge-Krenke, I. (1998). *Adolescents' health: A developmental perspective.* Mahwah, NJ: Lawrence Erlbaum.

Seiffge-Krenke, I. (2000a). Causal links between stressful events, coping style, and adolescent symptomatology. *Journal of Adolescence, 23,* 675–691.

Seiffge-Krenke, I. (2000b). Early and mid adolescents' precursors of depressive symptoms in late adolescence: What is distinctive for females as compared to males? *Adolescence, 23,* 1–17.

Seiffge-Krenke, I. (2001). Coping with illness in adolescence: An overview of research from the past 25 years. In I. Seiffge-Krenke, *Diabetic adolescents and their families* (pp. 9–24). New York: Cambridge University Press.

Seiffge-Krenke, I. (2004). Adaptive and maladaptive coping styles: Does intervention change anything? *European Journal of Developmental Psychology, 1*(4), 367–382.

Seiffge-Krenke, I. and Beyers, W. (2005). Coping trajectories from adolescence to young adulthood: Links to attachment state of mind. *Journal of Research on Adolescence, 15,* 561–582.

Seifgge-Krenke, I. and Klessinger, N. (2000). Long-term effects of avoidant coping on adolescents' depressive symptoms. *Journal of Youth and Adolescence, 29,* 617–630.

Seiffge-Krenke, I. and Shulman, S. (1990). Coping style in adolescence. A cross-cultural study. *Journal of Cross-Cultural Psychology, 21,* 351–377.

Seiffge-Krenke, I. and Stemmler, M. (2002). Factors contributing to gender differences in depressive symptoms: A test of three developmental models. *Journal of Youth and Adolescence, 31,* 405–418.

Seligman, M.E. (1992). *Learned optimism.* Australia: Random House.

Seligman, M.E. (1995). *The optimistic child.* North Sydney, NSW: Random House Australia.

Seligman, M.E.P. and Csikszentmihalyi, M. (2000). Positive psychology: An introduction. *American Psychologist, 55*(1), 5–14.

Selye, H. (1950). *The physiology and pathology of exposure to stress.* Montreal: Acta.

Selye, H. (1976). *Stress in health and disease.* Reading, MA: Butterworth.

Shapiro, J.P., Friedberg, R.D. and Bardenstein, K.K. (2006). *Child and adolescent therapy: Science and art.* New York: John Wiley & Sons.

Sheffield, J.K., Spence, S.H., Rapee, R.M., Kowalenko, N., Wignall, A., Davis, A. and McLoone, J. (2006). Evaluation of universal, indicated, and combined cognitive-behavioral approaches to the prevention of depression among adolescents. *Journal of Consulting and Clinical Psychology, 74*(1), 66–79.

Shever, M., Maddux, J.E., Mercadante, B., Prentice-Dunne, S., Jacobs, B. and Rogers, R.W. (1982). The self-efficacy scale: Construction and validation. *Psychological Reports, 51,* 663–671.

Shoal, G.D., Castaneda, J.O. and Giancola, P.R. (2005). Worry moderates the relation between negative affectivity and affect-related substance use in adolescent males: A prospective study of maladaptive emotional self-regulation. *Personality and Individual Differences, 38*(2), 475–485.

References 317

Shochet, I., Holland, D. and Whitefield, K. (1997). *Resourceful adolescent program: Group leader's manual*. Brisbane, Queensland: Griffith University.

Shulman, S. (1993). Close relationships and coping behaviour in adolescence. *Journal of Adolescence*, *16*, 267–283.

Simonton, O.C., Matthews-Simonton, S. and Creighton, J.L. (1978). *Getting well again*. New York: Bantam Books.

Sinha, B.K., Willson, L.R. and Watson, D.C. (2000). Stress and coping among students in India and Canada. *Canadian Journal of Behavioural Science*, *32*(4), 218–225.

Skaalvik, S. (2004). Reading problems in school children and adults: Experiences, self-perceptions and strategies. *Social Psychology of Education*, *7*, 105–125.

Skinner, E.A., Edge, K., Altman, J. and Sherwood, H. (2003). Searching for the structure of coping: A review and critique of category systems for classifying ways of coping. *Psychological Bulletin*, *129*, 216–269.

Skinner, E.A. and Wellborn, J.G. (1997). Children's coping in the academic domain. In A. Wolchik and S.A. Sandler (eds), *Handbook of children's coping* (pp. 387–422). New York: Plenum Press.

Skinner, E.A. and Zimmer-Gembeck, J. (2007). The development of coping. *Annual Review of Psychology*, *58*, 119–144.

Smiley, P. and Dweck, C.S. (1994). Individual differences in achievement goals among young children. *Child Development*, *65*, 1723–1743.

Smith, C.A. (1991). The self, appraisal, and coping. In C.R. Snyder and D.R. Forsyth (eds), *Handbook for social and clinical psychology: The health perspective* (pp. 116–137). Elmsford, NY: Pergamon.

Smith, L. and Sinclair, K.E. (1998). Stress and learning in the higher school certificate. Unpublished master's thesis, University of Sydney, Sydney, Australia.

Smith, M.B. (1983). Hope and despair: Keys to the socio-psychodynamics of youth. *American Journal of Orthopsychiatry*, *53*(3), 388–399.

Snyder, C.R. (1989). Reality negotiation: From excuses to hope and beyond. *Journal of Social and Clinical Psychology*, *8*, 130–157.

Snyder, C.R. (1994). *The psychology of hope: You can get there from here*. New York: Free Press.

Snyder, C.R. (1998). A case for hope in pain, loss and suffering. In J.H. Harvey, J. Omarzu and E. Miller (eds), *Perspectives on loss: A sourcebook* (pp. 63–79). Washington, DC: Taylor & Francis.

Snyder, C.R. (1999). Coping: Where are you going? In C.R. Snyder (ed.), *Coping: The psychology of what works* (pp. 324–333). New York: Oxford University Press.

Snyder, C.R., Cheavens, J. and Micheal, S.T. (1999). Hoping. In C.R. Snyder (ed.), *Coping: The psychology of what works* (pp. 205–227). New York: Oxford University Press.

Snyder, C.R., Harris, C., Anderson, J.R., Holleran, S.A., Irving, L.M., Sigmon Yoshinobu, L., Gibb, J., Langell, C. and Harney, P. (1991). The will and the ways: Development and validation of an individual difference measure of hope. *Journal of Personality and Social Psychology*, *60*, 570–585.

Snyder, C.R., Hoza, B., Pelham, W.E., Rapoff, M., Ware, L. Danovsky, M. *et al.* (1997). The development of and validation of the Children's Hope Scale. *Journal of Paediatric Psychology*, *22*, 399–421.

Snyder, C.R. and Lopez, S.J. (eds) (2002). *Handbook of positive psychology*. New York: Oxford University Press.

Snyder, C.R., Sympson, S.C., Ybasco, F.C., Borders, T.F., Babyak, M.A. and Higgins, R.L. (1996). Development and validation of the State Hope Scale. *Journal of Personality and Social Psychology*, *70*, 321–335.

Sonderegger, R., Barrett, P.M. and Creed, P.A. (2004). Models of cultural adjustment for child and adolescent migrants to Australia: Internal process and situational factors. *Journal of Child and Family Studies*, *13*(3), 357–371.

Soresi, S. and Nota, L. (2003). *Clipper: Portfolio per l'orientamento di studenti di scuola superiore* [*Clipper: Instrument for vocational guidance of high school students*]. Firenz, Italy: ITER-Organizzazioni Speciali.

Spangler, G., Pekrun, R., Kramer, K. and Hofmann, H. (2002). Students' emotions, physiological reactions, and coping in academic exams. *Anxiety, Stress and Coping*, *15*(4), 413–432.

Spence, S. (1996). The prevention of anxiety disorders in childhood. In P. Cotton and H. Jackson (eds), *Early intervention and prevention in mental health* (pp. 87–107). Melbourne, Victoria: The Australian Psychological Society.

Spence, S.H., Sheffield, J.K. and Donovan, C.L. (2003). Preventing adolescent depression: An evaluation of the Problem Solving for Life program. *Journal of Counseling and Clinical Psychology*, *71*(1), 3–13.

Spielberger, C.C. (ed.) (1966). *Anxiety and behavior*. New York: Academic Press.

Spirito, A., Francis, G., Overholser, J. and Frank, N. (1996). Coping, depression, and adolescent suicide attempts. *Journal of Clinical Child Psychology*, *25*(2), 147–155.

Spirito, A., Stark, L., Gill, K.M. and Tyc, V.L. (1995). Coping with everyday and disease-related stressors by chronically ill children and adolescents. *Journal of the American Academy of Child and Adolescent Psychiatry*, *34*(3), 283–290.

Spirito, A., Stark, L. and Williams, C. (1988). Development of a brief coping checklist for use with paediatric populations. *Journal of Paediatric Psychology*, *13*, 555–574.

Spitzer, R.L., Yanovski, S., Wadden, T., Wing, R., Marcus, M.D., Stunkard, A. *et al.* (1993). Binge eating disorder: Its further validation in a multisite study. *International Journal of Eating Disorders*, *13*, 137–154.

Stallard, P., Velleman, R., Langford, J. and Baldwin, S. (2001). Coping with psychological distress in children involved in road traffic accidents. *British Journal of Clinical Psychology*, *40*, 197–208.

Stanton, A.L., Danoff-Burg, S., Cameron, C.L. and Ellis, A.P. (1994). Coping through emotional approach: Problems of conceptualisation and confounding. *Journal of Personality and Social Psychology*, *66*, 350–362.

Stark, L.J., Spirito, A., Williams, C.A. and Guevremont, D.C. (1989). Common problems and coping strategies, I: Findings with normal adolescents. *Journal of Abnormal Child Psychology*, *17*(2), 203–212.

Start, K.B. (1990). Is high intelligence a valid reason for depriving the deprived? In C.W. Taylor (ed.), *Expanding awareness of creative potentials world wide*. Salt Lake City, UT: Trillium Press.

Stern, M. and Zevon, M.A. (1990). Stress, coping, and family environment: The adolescent's response to naturally occurring stressors. *Journal of Adolescent Research*, *5*(3), 209–305.

Stevenson, R. (1996). Academic self-concept, perceived stress and adolescents' coping styles in the VCE. Unpublished Bachelor of Social Science (Family Studies), Australian Catholic University.

Stone, A.A., Kennedy-Moore, E. and Neale, J.M. (1995). Association between daily coping and end-of-day mood. *Health Psychology*, *14*, 341–349.

Stone, A.A. and Neale, J.M. (1984). New measure of daily coping: Development and preliminary results. *Journal of Personality and Social Psychology*, *46*, 892–906.

Stotland, E. (1969). *The psychology of hope*. San Francisco, CA: Jossey-Bass.

Straker, G., Mendelsohn, M. and Tudin, P. (1995). The effects of diverse forms of political violence on the emotional and moral concerns of youth. In H. Adam, P. Reidesser, H. Riquelme, A. Verderber and J. Walter (eds), *Children: war and persecution*. (Proceedings of the Congress) (pp. 115–123). Hamburg: Secolo.

Suldo, S.M. and Huebner, E.S. (2004). Does life satisfaction moderate the effects of stressful life events on psychopathological behavior during adolescence? *School Psychology Quarterly*, *19*(2), 93–105.

Sullivan, P.F. (1995). Mortality in anorexia nervosa. *American Journal of Psychiatry*, *152*(7), 1073–1074.

Suls, J., David, J.P. and Harvey, J.H. (1996). Personality and coping: Three generations of research. *Journal of Personality*, *64*, 711–735.

Sun, Y. (2001). Family environment and adolescents' well-being before and after parents' marital disruption. A longitudinal analysis. *Journal of Marriage and Family*, *63*, 697–713.

Swiatek, M.A. (2001). Social coping among gifted high school students and its relationship to self-concept. *Journal of Youth and Adolescence*, *30*(1), 19–32.

Swanson, S. and Howell, C. (1996). Test anxiety in adolescents with learning disabilities and behaviour disorders. *Exceptional Children*, *62*(5), 389–398.

Szczepanski, H. (1995). A study of homesickness phenomenon among female boarding high school students. Unpublished Master of Educational Psychology project, University of Melbourne, Melbourne.

Taal, M. and Sampaio de Carvalho, F. (1993). *Pros and cons. Lessons in choosing* (in Dutch). Nijmegen, The Netherlands: Berkhout.

Taal, M. and Sampaio de Carvalho, F. (1997). Stimulating adolescents' decision-making. *Journal of Adolescence, 20,* 223–226.

Tabachnick, B.G. and Fidell, L.S. (2001). *Using multivariate statistics* (4th edition). Needham Heights, MA: Allyn & Bacon.

Tam, V.C. and Lam, R.S. (2005). Stress and coping among migrant and local-born adolescents in Hong Kong. *Youth and Society, 36*(3), 312–332.

Tannenbaum, A. (1991). The social psychology of giftedness. In N. Colangelo and G.A. Davis (eds), *Handbook of gifted education,* (pp. 27–44). Boston: Allyn and Bacon.

Tat, F.E. (1993). The use of coping strategies and styles in 2,264 Australian adolescent twins. Unpublished Master's thesis, University of Melbourne, Melbourne.

Tausig, M. and Michello, J. (1988). Seeking social support. *Basic and Applied Social Psychology, 9,* 1–12.

Taylor, S. (1993). The structure of fundamental fears. *Journal of Behaviour Therapy and Experimental Psychiatry, 24,* 289–299.

Taylor, S.E. (1989). *Positive illusions: Creative self-deception and the healthy mind.* New York: Basic Books.

Taylor, S.E. and Brown, J.D. (1988). Illusion and well-being: A social psychological perspective on mental health. *Psychological Bulletin, 103,* 193–210.

Taylor, S.E. and Brown, J.D. (1994). Positive illusions and well-being: Separating fact from fiction. *Psychological Bulletin, 116,* 21–26.

Taylor, S., Klein.L., Lewis, B.P., Gruenwald, T.L., Gurung, R.A. and Updegraff, J.A. (2000). Biobehavioural responses to stress in females: Tend-and-befriend, not fight-or-flight. *Psychological Review, 107,* 411–429.

Thomas, K.W. and Kilmann, R.H. (1974). *Thomas-Kilmann Conflict Mode Instrument.* Palo Alto, CA: Consulting Psychologists Press.

Thompson, R.A. (1994). Emotion regulation: A theme in search of definition. *Monographs of the Society for Research in Child Development, 59,* 25–52.

Thuen, E. and Bru, E. (2004). Coping styles and emotional behavioural problems among Norwegian Grade 9 students. *Scandinavian Journal of Educational Research, 48*(5), 493–510.

Tollit, M. (2002). Assessing the effectiveness of the Best of Coping program with female adolescent students. Unpublished Master's thesis, University of Melbourne, Melbourne.

Tugade, M.M. and Fredrickson, B.L. (2004). Resilient individuals use positive emotions to bounce back from negative emotional experiences. *Journal of Personality and Social Psychology, 86*(2), 320–333.

United Nations (2004). *World Fertility Report 2003.* ESA/P/WP.189. Retrieved 21 November 2006 from http://www.un.org/esa/population/publications/worldfertility/World_Fertility_Report.htm

United Nations Population Fund (n.d.). State of population 2003. Retrieved 27 October 2005, from http://www.unfpa.org/swp/2003/english/ch1/

Van Tassel-Baska, J.L. and Olszewski-Kubilius, P. (eds) (1989). *Patterns of influence on gifted learners: The home, the self and the school.* New York: Teachers College Press.

Varni, J.W., Katz, E.R., Colegrove, R. and Dolgin, M. (1996). Family functioning predictors of adjustment in children with newly diagnosed cancer: A prospective analysis. *Journal of Child Psychology and Psychiatry*, *37*, 321–328.

Verhulst, F. (2001). Community and epidemiological aspects of anxiety disorders in children. In W.K. Silverman and P.D.A. Treffers (eds), *Anxiety disorders in children and adolescents: Research, assessment and intervention* (pp. 273–292). Cambridge: Cambridge University Press.

Verhulst, F.C., Achenbach, T.M., van der Ende, J., Erol, N., Lanbert, M.C., Leung, P.W., Silva, M.A., Zilber, N. and Zubrick, S.R. (2003). Comparisons of problems reported by youths from seven countries. *American Journal of Psychiatry*, *160*, 1479–1485.

Victorian Curriculum and Assessment Authority (VCAA) (2005). *Where to now? Guide to the VCE, VCAL and Apprenticeships and Traineeships for 2006.* East Melbourne, Victoria: VCCA.

Violato, C. and Holden, W.B. (1988). A confirmatory factor analysis of a four-factor model of adolescent concerns. *Journal of Youth and Adolescence*, *17*(1), 101–113.

Walberg, H.J., Tsai.T., Weinstein, T., Gabriel, C.L., Rasher, S.P., Rosecrans, T., Rovai, E., Ide, J., Trujillo, M. and Vukosavich, P. (1981). Childhood traits and environmental conditions of highly eminent adults. *Gifted Child Quarterly*, *25*(3), 103–107.

Warner, S. and Moore, S. (2004). Excuses, excuses: Self-handicapping in an Australian adolescent sample. *Journal of Youth and Adolescence*, *33*(4), 271–282.

Washburn-Ormachea, J.M., Hillman, S.B. and Sawilowsky, S.S. (2004). Gender and gender-role orientation differences in adolescent coping with peer stressors. *Journal of Youth and Adolescence*, *33*, 31–40.

Wassef, A., Ingham, D., Collins, M.L. and Mason, G. (1995). In search of effective programs to address students' emotional distress and behavioural problems. *Adolescence*, *30*, 523–239.

Watson, D., David, J.P. and Suls, J. (1999). Personality, affectivity, and coping. In C.R. Snyder (ed.), *Coping: The psychology of what works* (pp. 119–140). New York: Oxford University Press.

Watson, D. and Hubbard, B. (1996). Adaptational style and dispositional structure: Coping in the context of the five-factor model. *Journal of Personality*, *64*, 734–774.

Weisberg, P.S. and Springer, K.J. (1961). Environmental factors in creative function: A study of gifted children. *Archives of General Psychiatry*, *5*, 64–74.

Weiss, R.S. (1974). *Loneliness: The experience of emotional and social isolation.* Cambridge, MA: MIT Press.

Weissman, M.M., Wolk, S., Goldstein, R.B., Moreau, D., Adams, P., Greenwald, S. *et al.* (1999). Depressed adolescents grown up. *Journal of the American Medical Association, 281*(18), 1707–1713.

Weisz, J.R., McCabe, M.A. and Dennig, M.D. (1994). Primary and secondary control among children undergoing medical procedures: Adjustment as a function of coping style. *Journal of Consulting and Clinical Psychology, 62*(2), 324–332.

Werner, E.E. (2004). Resilience in development. In C. Morf and O. Aydak (eds), *Directions in personality psychology* (pp. 168–173). Englewood Cliffs, NJ: Prentice Hall.

Werner, E.E. and Smith, R.S. (1982). *Vulnerable but invincible.* New York: McGraw-Hill.

Werner, E.E. and Smith, R.S. (1989). *A longitudinal study of resilient children and youth.* New York: Adams-Bannister-Cox.

Werner, E.E. and Smith, R.S. (1992). *Overcoming the odds: High risk children from birth to adulthood.* New York: Cornell University Press.

West, P. and Sweeting, H. (2003). Fifteen, female and stressed: Changing patterns of psychological distress over time. *Journal of Child Psychology and Psychiatry, 44*(3), 399–411.

White, V., Hill, D., Hopper, J. and Frydenberg, E. (1995). Personality and coping: A longitudinal study of the association between personality and coping among a sample of Australian adolescent twins. Paper presented at the Australian Psychological Society Conference, Perth, Australia.

Whitney, I. and Smith, P.K. (1993). A survey of the nature and extent of bullying in junior/middle and secondary schools. *Educational Research, 35*(1), 3–25.

Wills, T.A. (1986). Stress and coping in early adolescence: Relationships to substance use in urban school samples. *Health Psychology, 5*(3), 503–529.

Wills, T.A., Sandy, J.M., Yaeger, A.M., Cleary, S.D. and Shinar, O. (2001). Coping dimensions, life stress, and adolescent substance use: A latent growth analysis. *Journal of Abnormal Psychology, 110*, 309–323.

Wilson, J.P. and Agaibi, C. (2005). The resilient trauma survivor. In J.P. Wilson (ed.), *The posttraumatic self: Restoring meaning and wholeness to personality* (pp. 195–216). New York: Routledge.

Wolfradt, U., Hempel, S. and Miles, J.N.V. (2003). Perceived parenting styles, depersonalisation, anxiety and coping behaviour in adolescents. *Personality and Individual Differences, 34*(3), 521–532.

Wolke, D., Woods, S., Stanford, K. and Schulz, H. (2001). Bullying and victimization of primary school children in England and Germany: Prevalence and school factors. *British Journal of Psychology, 92*(4), 673–696.

Woodward, J.C. and Kalyan-Masih, V. (1990). Loneliness, coping strategies and cognitive styles of the gifted rural adolescent. *Adolescence, 25*, 977–988.

Worden, J.W. (1991). *Grief counselling and grief therapy: A handbook for the mental health practitioner* (2nd edn). London: Springer.

Worden, J.W. (2001). Children who lose a parent to divorce and children who lose a parent to death. *Grief Matters*, *4*(1), 3–5.

Worden, J.W. and Silverman, P.S. (1996). Parental death and the adjustment of school-aged children. *Omega*, *33*(2), 91–102.

World Health Organization (WHO) (1992). *The ICD-10 Classification of Mental and Behavioural Disorders*. Geneva: WHO.

World Health Organization (WHO) (1997). *Child-friendly schools checklist*. Geneva: WHO.

World Health Organization (WHO) (2001). *The World Health Report 2001: New understanding, new hope*. Geneva: WHO.

World Health Organization (WHO) (2002). *Prevention of suicidal behaviours: A task for all*. Geneva: WHO.

World Health Organization (WHO) (2006). *Preventing suicide: A resource for counsellors*. Geneva: WHO.

Wyn, J., Cahill, H., Holdsworth, R., Rowling, L. and Carson, S. (2000). MindMatters: A whole-school approach promoting mental health and wellbeing. *Australian and New Zealand Journal of Psychiatry*, *34*, 594–601.

Zimmer-Gembeck, M.J. and Locke, E.M. (2007). The socialization of adolescent coping behaviours: Relationships with families and teachers. *Journal of Adolescence*, *30*, 1–16.

Zimmerman, B. and Cleary, T. (2006). Adolescents' development of personal agency: The role of self-efficacy beliefs and self-regulatory skill. In F. Pajares and T. Urdan (eds), *Self-efficacy beliefs of adolescents* (pp. 45–69). Greenwich, CT: Information Age Publishing.

Zins, J.E., Weissberg, R.P., Wang, M.C. and Walberg, H.J. (eds) (2004). *Building academic success on social and emotional learning: What does the research say?* New York: Teachers College Press.

Zulig, K.J., Valois, R.F., Huebner, E.S. and Drane, J.W. (2005). Adolescent health-related quality of life and perceived satisfaction with life. *Quality of Life Research*, *14*, 1573–1584.

Index

Note: *italic* page numbers denote references to Figures/Tables.